JOHN BARBIROLLI

Portrait study, 1968.

JOHN
BARBIROLLI

A BIOGRAPHY

BY

CHARLES REID

ILLUSTRATED

TAPLINGER PUBLISHING COMPANY
NEW YORK

*First published in the United States in 1971
by Taplinger Publishing Co., Inc.
New York, New York*

Copyright © 1971 by Charles Reid

International Standard Book Number 0–8008–4408–4

Library of Congress Catalog Card Number 72–163476

PRINTED IN GREAT BRITAIN

FOR LOUISE

CONTENTS

LIST OF ILLUSTRATIONS

FOREWORD

IN this account the reader will come upon many utterances
by Sir John Barbirolli either within quotation marks or in
third-person paraphrase. The greater number of these are
things he said to me and were noted, usually in his presence
and at the time, or (in the case of certain important dialogues)
put on to recording tape. To acknowledge and date each of
these 'quotes' would have cluttered the text unduly or weighted
too many pages with footnotes. Where Barbirolli speaks in
this narrative without documentation to the contrary, it may
in general be concluded that the source is my own archive of
transcripts. These transcripts comprise scores of thousands of
words that were spoken specifically for me: although not
necessarily to me alone, for, in telling of his origins and
struggles and their afterglow of achievement, Barbirolli used
much the same phraseology to several sympathetic ears to the
end of his days. 'Sympathetic' is used here, of course, in the
French sense. *Sympathie* is a liking based on affinity (perhaps
on differences too, provided these are right in degree and
kind) and, above all, on admiration. If the admiration is
mutual, so much the better.

I saw Barbirolli conduct for the first time (a *Mastersingers*
occasion) when he was twenty-nine and musical director of a
touring opera company run by and from Covent Garden. My
first talks with him were in 1943, when he was newly back
from New York and re-launching the Hallé Orchestra; and,
a little over a year later, at his mother's place in Streatham,
on his return from symphony concerts for the Forces in liberated Italy. Apart from informal and casual talks, I had 'set'
interviews with him down the years that followed as a staff

profile writer of the *Observer* and as a feature writer for various
other publications or channels, among them the *Evening Standard*,
the late *News Chronicle*, the *Daily Mail*, the American monthly
High Fidelity, a special biographical archive of Electric and
Musical Industries Ltd., and the B.B.C.'s Monitor programme,
which put out 'Sir John Barbirolli: a Portrait', myself being
the researcher and interviewer, in March 1965. Although all
my formal interviews with him were for commissioned articles
or script, much of what he told me neither saw print nor
reached the listener's ear because of limits on space or time.
Most of what didn't transpire then forms part of the narrative
now.

As shown by detailed acknowledgments below, this book's
provenance takes in much other testimony than his own. I
have drawn on the memories of Lady Barbirolli; of friends from
his student days; of singers who went out on his early operatic
tours and some who sang for him nearly forty years later; of
fellow players in chamber concerts and on orchestral platforms during the 1920s or earlier; and of some who played for
him during those last macabre months of 1970, when, as he
knew full well, Death stalked him to every rostrum and spied
upon his sleep, the little sleep that came his way. Much data
came from those who served him when he was remodelling
great British orchestras and directing (almost single-handed a
good deal of the time) one of the world's greatest, the New
York Philharmonic. As musical director or guest conductor, he
was with the Philharmonic for seven and a half years, successor to Arturo Toscanini, who was incomparable and with
whom, nevertheless, he was ruthlessly compared. The second
half of his term in New York was overcast by war. War conditions are not conducive to the exchange of international
concert news. How was Barbirolli faring at Carnegie Hall?
What sort and size of audiences was he getting? What incidence
and volume of ovation? The little that reached us then and
much that saw print later gave the impression that he was
doing or had done famously; that Carnegie Hall was one big
bed of roses, with crumpled petals a rarity and thorns un-
thinkable.

As will be seen from my New York chapters, the story was
hardly as roseate or as simple—or as insipid—as that. An

artist whose path is without declivities and shadow is probably
not much of an artist. A biographer who pretends that the
shadow and the declivities are not there is hardly a biographer
at all.

Reverting to the matter of *sympathie*. From our first encounter
I 'took' to Barbirolli on several counts. The most important
count of the lot was love of music. Many conductors have
been so much in love with themselves that music ranked in
their eyes more as washpot than as Holy Grail. Barbirolli's
love of music was absolute and consuming. It wrung him,
racked his nerves, charged him with joy and ebullience,
counterbalancing these latter gifts with an awe that sometimes
smacked almost of dread. Before any performance, whether as
executant or conductor, he quivered with anxiety (as do many),
even with anguish. Before going on to play 'cello in the
string quartet and string quintet of Edward Elgar at the
centenary concerts in Manchester, he said to a friend in the
wings: 'If you know any prayers, my boy, say them all for
me—*now*.' Some minutes later he was on the platform and
making his bow, the very picture of tranquil confidence. Lady
Barbirolli, who had heard his genuinely desperate plea for
prayers, whispered to her companion: 'Look at him! He's not
even nervous!' And so it was. When music was imminent,
when he was on the point of settling down to it and making
it, he seemed to feel the touch as of a therapeutic wand a few
bars ahead of the opening beat, so to say.

Nor could he—who might be supposed to have too much—
ever have enough. Something is said later in this book about
string quartets, himself as 'cello, which he recruited for
'recreational', sparetime playing from every orchestra with
which he had much to do. Two anecdotes are more apposite
here than they would be in the main narrative. Both concern
concerto pianists and date from years when seven concerts a
week and eight rehearsals on top from one extreme of England
to the other were, as he saw the case, nothing to complain
about.

In Harrogate one day he rehearsed the Hallé from 10 a.m.
After an hour and a half he dismissed the players for their
statutory 'breather'. Business of the day included a Mozart

piano concerto. He and the pianist stayed on the platform chatting. Barbirolli picked up a 'cello and started on the E minor Sonata, Op. 38, of Brahms. The pianist joined him. Both played from memory. There wasn't time to get through the whole sonata. For them it was breather enough, however. And a delight.

The pianist in the second anecdote chanced to have non-musical business in Blackpool, where Barbirolli and the Hallé were down for a morning rehearsal and an evening programme which, as it happened, included no concerto. The afternoon was to have been free. On the strength of his pianist friend's presence in the town Barbirolli had a piano brought at short notice into the theatre they were playing and invited him to an afternoon of chamber music. Brahms again. With three leading strings from the Hallé, he and his friend did the F minor Quintet Op. 34. After that the pianist withdrew to the stalls and listened while the others did the Debussy String Quartet in G Op. 15. The players had the Opera House stage to themselves; it was a Saturday afternoon, not another soul about. In quintet and quartet alike, Barbirolli 'led' from the 'cello against the traditional order of precedence. Nobody minded this. 'J. B.', as they generally called him, had earned seven-and-six a night in entr'acte pits before he started shaving; gloried in his tough beginnings; was as much the comrade of his players as their (sometimes) sharp-tongued master. Also he was a tenacious teacher who had exceptional funds of experience to draw on. In the Debussy, breaking off now and then, he would pom-ti-pom-pom the rhythm to one or other of his co-players who seemed to be malforming it. That night he led his men into Schubert's 'Great' C major Symphony as to a famous victory.

What other classical conductor is there of such eminence whose passion for music not only keeps him unremittingly at it but also makes friends of his subordinates? What conductor has there been who, while knowing full well how to crack the disciplinary whip, never rode the high horse? Physically he was small (5 ft. 5 in.), a fact that may have irked him superficially at times. Here again musical passion compensated, conferring a stature upon him which no tape could measure but which gave him dominance none the less.

That he would have conducted music better if he had loved it rather less is a thought that crops up occasionally in, or is suggested by, notices of his concert and operatic performances from the 1920s to the end. Sometimes he so genuflected before beauty or 'drama' of detail that this part and that tended to outweigh the whole or even make it run aground. In the eyes of aesthetes such malproportion is more than error. It comes near to cardinal sin. Yet the passion which sometimes may have bemused him led at other times to performances that were touched with grandeur. For such happenings 'perform-ances' is, indeed, too pallid a word. 'Occasions' is fitter.

As I have tried to bring out in my narrative, on one rostrum or another (it did not matter much where) he could give tang and a greatness to some favourite late-Romantic or neo-Romantic symphony which (so the listener felt in his bones) would never recur. Weeks or years later he might touch great-ness again in the same context: but the greatness would have a different flavour or accent. A great Barbirolli night was unique independently of time and place, its greatness a thing of his own making as well as the composer's. He was not the only conductor with this power. Thomas Beecham had it conspicuously. A great Beecham night was a wonderworker's hour, all iridescence and bloom and glitter, with a touch of imp superadded and hints of tongue-in-cheek. A great Bar-birolli night, on the other hand, smacked a little of the cathedral close; whether the issue was Schubert or Mahler, Bruckner or Beethoven, Debussy or Nielsen, we were there, as he was there, to kneel and be fervent. Up to a point and in so far as music can yield anything of the kind, his purpose was ethical, a word he rarely used, still less traded, and which has nothing to do with frumpish.

My last meeting with him was in the year before his death. I told him I had some such book as this in mind. At that time he was still (as he explained) under contract to write his autobiography: which precluded further co-operation with me for literary purposes. Already I had a Barbirolli archive the size of a hillock. It is a bigger hillock now. I wished him well in any writing enterprise he might have in mind and, after further months of research, got on with mine.

ACKNOWLEDGMENTS

In amassing my archive I had help for which I am warmly grateful from many persons and institutions.

The account of Barbirolli's schooldays in Bloomsbury derives from The History of *St. Clement Danes Holborn Estate Grammar School 1552-1952* (privately published) and supplementary material afforded by the author of that monograph, Ralph B. Pooley, M.A., senior history master and Housemaster of Clement House; as also from the researches of a retired colleague of his, William H. Kipps. Mrs. Marjorie Barbirolli, Sir John's first wife, contributed lively memories of his and her adventures in English opera long before the era of State subvention. There was help in similar matters from several others, among them Dame Eva Turner and Gladys Parr, the mezzo-soprano. From two leading violinists of note, Samuel Kutcher and the late André Mangeot, came accounts or records or both of Barbirolli on chamber music platforms in boyhood and youth; and from Kenneth Wright, O.B.E., sometime Head of Music Programmes, B.B.C. T.V., and before that an eminent deviser and director of classical music on B.B.C. sound radio, much about his earliest conducting engagements and his readiness to take on contemporary music. On these and like themes Victor Olof, an entrepreneur-violinist of those times and later a celebrated recording director, added insight and many an anecdote.

Mention has been made of orchestral players who served either alongside Barbirolli on symphony platforms or under his baton from the remote days of the Barbirolli Chamber Orchestra. I am greatly beholden to many of these. But, since some prefer not to be named as sources, it has been decided—with the object of avoiding speculative attributions —not to identify the rest, apart from a few whose names occur in the narrative. Among the 'named' is David McCallum, a former principal violin and leader for Barbirolli and also of Beecham, whom he similarly served for spells as leader of the London Philharmonic Orchestra before the war and the Royal Philharmonic Orchestra after it. Without Mr. McCallum's

memories—and those, incidentally, of another string player
of note both then and later, Eileen Grainger (Mrs. Wilfrid
Parry)—Barbirolli's decisive years with the Scottish (National)
Orchestra could not have been given the scent of actuality
which I strove, at any rate, to achieve. On this aspect: further
thanks to a past member, Douglas Shanks, of the S.N.O.
board, a sitting one, Hugh Marshall, and the orchestral
manager, Miss Jean Mearns.

After Scotland in Barbirolli's career came his seven years
with the New York Philharmonic Orchestra, whose managing
director, Carlos Moseley, and archivist, Miss Carlotta Wilsen,
as well as certain veteran players, greatly facilitated me. I
benefited, too, from the advice of Harold C. Schonberg,
music-critic-in-chief of the *New York Times*. After New York:
Manchester and the Hallé Orchestra, whose successive managers, the late Kenneth Crickmore, T. Ernest Bean and Clive
Smart, dug deep into their records at my behest and at various
times over twenty years or more. Concerning his work with
Our Lady's Choral Society of Dublin and especially his
poignant final concerts with them in May 1970, I had much
help from the Society's director, the Reverend Andrew Griffith
of Bohernabreena-Tallaght.

Barbirolli's career in this country on recording floors lasted
for sixty years. There have been few gramophone careers to
touch it. Most of his recording was for the H.M.V. and other
labels of what is now Electric and Musical Industries Ltd.,
whose David Bicknell (International Classical Repertory
Liaison Manager) and Ronald Kinloch Anderson (Senior
Recording Producer, International Artists Department) helped
me to relive the incidents and atmosphere of many an outstanding recording session. Also of E.M.I. is Douglas Pudney
(Promotion and Repertory Manager, Classical Division). It is
to him that I owe the list of Barbirolli's postwar recordings for
the Company which appear as Appendix Four.

Other archives from which I have drawn material and
succour are those of Michael Goold, of North Harrow, whose
hobby for many years has been compiling historical data
about leading British and other orchestras; the Royal Opera
House, Covent Garden; Rediffusion Television Ltd.; the Royal
Festival Hall; the musical section of the British Council; and

those of the B.B.C.—especially the Corporation's reference library, gramophone library, library of sound/television transcripts or scripts, Concerts Management (which were supplemented valuably from personal memory by the B.B.C. Concerts Organiser, Miss Freda Grove) and those of Radio Three under Barrie Hall.

After archives (or before them), libraries. The Henry Watson Music Library (Manchester), the library of the Royal Academy of Music, that of the Press Association (London) and the British Museum's unique Newspaper Library at Colindale: these and their staffs are warmly remembered. As also are a handful of books which, although most are acknowledged in the main text, I gladly list here:

Two Centuries of Opera at Covent Garden, Harold Rosenthal, Putnam, 1958.

Bloomsbury Fair, Mrs. Robert Henrey, Dent, 1955.

The Life of Kathleen Ferrier, Winifred Ferrier, Hamish Hamilton, 1955. Also the foregoing with *A Memoir* edited by Neville Cardus, the whole in one volume, Penguin Books in association with Hamish Hamilton, 1959.

The Hallé Tradition, a Century of Music, Michael Kennedy, Manchester University Press, 1960.

The Works of Ralph Vaughan Williams, Michael Kennedy, Oxford University Press, 1964.

Philip Godlee by His Friends edited with an introduction by Charles Rigby, Dolphin Press, Sale, Manchester, 1954.

Donald Francis Tovey, Mary Grierson, O.U.P., 1952.

Chords and Discords, Malcolm Tillis, Phoenix Books, London, 1960.

The Orchestra Speaks, Bernard Shore, Longmans, Green, 1938.

The World of Carnegie Hall, Richard Schickel, Julian Messner Inc., New York, 1960.

Dictators of the Baton, David Ewen, New York, 1943.

The Philharmonic Society of New York. Its First Hundred Years, John Erskine, New York, The Macmillan Company, 1943.

The American Symphony Orchestra, a Social History of Musical Taste, John H. Mueller, John Calder, London, 1958.

Toscanini, Howard Taubman, Odhams Press, London, 1951.

Virgil Thomson, Virgil Thomson, Weidenfeld & Nicolson, London, 1967.

One Hundred Years of the Hallé, C. B. Rees, Macgibbon & Kee, London, 1957.

Mrs. Patrick Campbell, Alan Dent, Museum Press, London, 1961.

CHAPTER ONE

ANTONIO AND LORENZO

JOHN BARBIROLLI, Knight Bachelor, Companion of Honour, Sir John for short, Commendatore of the Italian Republic, bearer of the Star and Collar of Commander First Class of the White Rose of Finland, Honorary Academician of the Accadèmia Nazionale di Santa Cecilia, Officier de l'Ordre du Mérite, and much else, was born on December 2nd 1899 over a baker's shop at 12 Southampton Row in the sub-district of Bloomsbury St. Giles South, first son and second child of Filippo Lorenzo Barbirolli, native of Padua, then thirty-five and documented variously as musician and professor of music; and of Louise Barbirolli, *née* Ribèyrol, once of Bordeaux and latterly of Paris, aged twenty-nine, who, thirty years later, on hearing her son tell friends about the baker's shop in Southampton Row, corrected him thus: 'Not over a baker's shop. It was a highclass con*fec*tioner's shop.'

Over the high-class confectioner's shop the Barbirollis had six rooms on two floors, and most of the rooms were big; which was well, since already the family circle was big (and destined to grow), the new baby being its seventh member. Three generations lived under one roof. As well as father and mother, Lorenzo Barbirolli and Louise Barbirolli, there were Grandpa, Antonio Barbirolli ('Nonno'), and Grandma, Rosina Barbirolli ('Nonna'); also their unmarried daughter, Elisa; and (sixth on the list) Rosa, the new baby's small sister.

The baby was baptised Giovanni Battista and for long was called Giovanni by relatives and friends in London's Italian colony. Throughout his school life he was Giovanni on school registers also. It will be more convenient in this account to call him by his adoptive name, John, that most English of names. As he often pointed out with amused wonderment, however, there was no drop of English blood in his veins; he grew up in a tightly-knit immigrant household with Italian as his first language in the order of learning, French his second, English his third.

A fourth language was music. Father and grandfather were fiddlers who had settled in Soho in the mid-1890s. Between them they kept house at one point or another within the same square mile or two for thirty or forty years; in general the theatre pits and restaurants where they habitually played were within ten minutes of their doorsteps. They came from Northern Italy, province of Veneto; to the last they spoke the Venetian dialect and bore the stamp of their origin in many other ways. Grandfather Antonio had been born in the sizeable market town and sometime provincial capital of Rovigo but, when married, settled in the cathedral city of Padua fifty miles away. There had been Barbirollis in Padua before; one of them is said to have been the organist of a noted church there. Following up ancestral traces, John Barbirolli opened a volume of Canaletto and came upon a picture of the Casa Corleto on the Piazza dell' Erba as it looked in the middle of the eighteenth century. This house, which is no more, was his paternal grandmother's house.

'Here's a strange thing,' Barbirolli used to say. 'The print of the Casa Corleto, like others reproduced in that book, is at Windsor, the property of the Queen. The Queen of England is the only person today who has a picture of the house where my father was born.'

When he went to Padua, Antonio did not shake off the dust of his birthplace for good. Rovigo had a lovely old theatre. From time to time Antonio returned to its pit as first violin and leader. Later on his son Lorenzo joined the second violins there. Around 1884, the theatre took on a talented and tense stripling as principal 'cello. The stripling's name was Arturo Toscanini. Between rehearsals Toscanini would put aside his 'cello, take over the rehearsal piano and accompany Lorenzo in violin sonatas. After they had been through an unfamiliar sonata once or twice, Toscanini knew the music by heart and could play it from memory. 'This,' Toscanini said when John was introduced to him in London forty or fifty years later, 'filled your father with wonder. It was nothing really.'

As will be seen, one of John Barbirolli's signal traits was filial reverence. When, in 1968, he conducted Verdi's *Otello* for the first time* the profound artistic satisfaction he felt was supplemented by a more intimate glow: the knowledge that his father and grandfather had played in the Scala (Milan) pit at the *Otello* première in February 1887. *Otello* did not merely come his way contractually. In a sense he inherited it; the score had ancient Barbirolli fingerprints upon it. The fingerprints were those of musical nomads. Antonio's and Lorenzo's talents became increasingly prized outside their native province. And they wandered accordingly. By the early 1890s they were on tour in France with an Italian opera company: a cheap way of getting to Paris. Paris took their fancy. There they played cafés-concerts, hotel lounges, small theatres. For a while Lorenzo was with a self-styled Hungarian band. Its conductor was a Belgian, its payroll polyglot. What of that? The players wore a Hungarian uniform. This convinced everybody.

While a 'Hungarian', Lorenzo chanced upon a restaurant in the Faubourg St. Honoré. A girl of twenty or thereabouts was helping the *patron*'s wife to serve. She caught Lorenzo's eye and fancy on the instant. From this to making himself known and falling in love with her were the interim of another meal or two merely. Louise Ribèyrol had lost her father, a machine-maker by trade, at the age of twelve. The restaurant in the Faubourg was owned by an uncle. At seventeen she left Bordeaux to give a hand there and get a little money. Lorenzo's advent turned her thoughts in quite a different direction. Whenever they could snatch time together he would take her out. He gave Louise her first smattering of Italian. Then the Hungarian band moved on to London, having been booked for the lounge of the Cecil, a lavish new hotel in The Strand. On coming out of Charing Cross station the Barbirollis were confronted by a startling placard which made them wonder whether they ought not to turn back: ENGLAND COLLAPSES. It took them a while to learn that the language of Test cricket is more lurid than the reality.

Before leaving Paris, Lorenzo had told Louise that he

* Not publicly but on the recording floor for E.M.I.

would come back soon and take her away and marry her. Everything fell out as he had said. He brought Louise over from Paris as soon as he had made himself professionally secure. They married according to the rites of the Roman Catholic Church on January 2nd 1897 at St. Peter's Italian Church in Clerkenwell Road, the core of London's 'little Italy'. The bride was twenty-six, the bridegroom thirty-two. Lorenzo and his father were described on the marriage certificate as 'professors of music'.

The first Barbirolli household was in Wardour Street, the second in Drury Lane. From the start Antonio and Lorenzo had no difficulty in finding work. Gaps between morning rehearsals and evening dates in theatres and restaurants were increasingly given over to teaching; between them they gave violin, piano and mandoline lessons. There wasn't a great deal of money in the house, however. Lorenzo's regular pay was not much over two pounds a week. 'To eke out,' John explained, 'we took in a lodger or two. But the lodgers were always *artists*.' The most illustrious of them had been Arturo Pessina who, at Covent Garden, sang London's first Falstaff (*Verdi*) as well as Iago opposite the great Tamagno. Pessina got 85 guineas a performance. Having no English, he didn't know how to pay his guineas into the bank. The bank he used was over the way from the Royal Opera House. Lorenzo, whose English was just about equal to the task, used to interpret for him. The sight and sound of coins, many gold ones among them, shovelled and weighed on the teller's counter moved Lorenzo to awe. He often told the infant Giovanni about it; and the infant stared in solemn wonder.

In his middle sixties he looked back affectionately on his Edwardian upbringing. His childhood, he said, had been very happy, 'considering'. By later amenity standards he and his sister and younger brother might be thought to have been brought up, to all intents and purposes, in the 'workhouse'. How wrong such notions were! 'In fact, we were much better off than [the general run] of people are now. Father, mother, Italian grandfather, Italian grandmother, all under one roof: ... a happy, devoted, rather Italian family—which we remained.' By nature he was 'very nervous, sensitive', however;

avid of new sensory impressions; given to locking himself in his dreams. At the same time he needed a hero. He found a hero to hand: his father. Lorenzo Barbirolli had the well-built and stately presence which, in middle life, often goes with a gentle temperament. He was attentive to his beard and moustaches, which were of imperial cut, carried his cane with aplomb and chose his greatcoats, neckties and bowler hats with care. In regard to John, when John was little, he had one quirk (Barbirolli later called it a 'mania') which—whatever gloss latter-day psychoanalysts may put upon it—is remembered as, on the whole, harmless and amiable. That quirk was for dressing John up as much like himself as could be managed. From the age of four John was given the same type of overcoat and bowler hat to wear and the same sort of cane to carry when the two of them went out together. His mother strongly disapproved of the overcoat and cane. She would have disapproved of the bowler hat more strongly still if she had known about it. Alonzo bought these hats in secret, smuggling them in and out of the house. Louise must have thought that John came and went bareheaded.

Lorenzo was tallish. Even in his miniature bowler hat John only just came up to his elbow. Those were the palmy days of the Hippodrome Theatre, Charing Cross Road, a house noted for spectacular water shows, with waterfalls, a lake on the stage, foundering ships and a one-legged diver who plunged into the deeps twice nightly from high up in the 'flies'. These delights were supplemented by recurring tit-bits, including a Dwarf and Giant act. Walking past the Hippodrome on their way to church one Sunday morning, father and son became aware that they were being tailed by facetious urchins. Obviously the Barbirollis were the Dwarf and the Giant in person. The urchins were in no doubt of that, as their catcalls made clear. They followed their quarry along the street and round a corner to the threshold of Notre Dame de France, the French church in Leicester Place. There they let them go.

Usually the Barbirollis went to church in strength on Sunday mornings. Father always chose a pew as far back and as near to the exit as possible. The priest would go up into the pulpit, say 'Mes chers frères en Jésus-Christ', clear his throat and start upon the sermon. The curé had been at Leicester

Place for many years. Lorenzo knew his repertory well. After the first few sentences he would whisper, 'Oh, we know that one', then tiptoe his children out of church and to a French pastrycook's a short distance away. After éclairs or madeleines he would tiptoe them back for the Credo and the Canon of the Mass. His timing was immaculate. On the way home from church he often ushered his brood into some delicatessen, usually a renowned one in Old Compton Street, to buy oddments for the Sunday table. Pointing to a sequence of salamis or hams he would inquire, as if he didn't know already, whether this one or that was up to much. 'But try it, try it, Professore', the shopman would say, for Lorenzo was 'Professore' to Soho at large and many places beyond. His samplings and tastings in Old Compton Street often amounted to a meal in themselves.

What John derived from his father, whether musically or in wider human domains, cannot readily be calculated by the outsider. One thing emerges, however: the tenacity of affection. Thirty years after Lorenzo's death John Barbirolli spoke of his father's great wisdom and gentleness; of the much he had learned from him beyond music. 'My gratitude', he said, 'is boundless.' Again: 'My Dad* was a man to whom I owed *and still owe* an awful lot.' It is as though Lorenzo did not really die. His son spoke of him secondarily as a fine musician and mentioned the beautiful sound he got from the violin. Under potted palms at the Queen's Hotel in Leicester Square Alonzo led two ensembles at different times of the day or on different days of the week: a trio, which played while people were eating, and a septet or octet for 'after dinner' concerts. These latter were on Sunday nights only. John was taken to them in knickerbockers or a sailor suit.

'There,' he said, 'I heard Dad play piles of operatic selections, all with authentic phrasing. That was the heyday of Italian opera. So, as a child, I was trained in the best school.' One of the lessons he remembered best from that school was the laceratingly sweet prelude to *La Traviata* Act III. Afterwards Lorenzo asked him, 'Do you know who wrote that music?'

'No, who did?'

* As a child, he never called his father 'Daddy', as he would have done if born in the next social layer above Southampton Row.

'God, my boy. It was written by God.'

Lorenzo used to put on singers in and among the bits of *Cavalleria, Traviata, Samson and Delilah* and such. One of his singers was a beginner from Ireland whose tenor was to win much fame and money, John McCormack. It was for Lorenzo at the Queen's that McCormack sang 'I hear you calling me', an Edwardian ballad then in manuscript which presently riddled the country. McCormack was paid a guinea for this début.

The Queen's used to put on a three-and-sixpenny theatre supper, not in the grill room but in the 'grand hall', a less splendid place for all its grandeur. Much was made of this theatre supper—as might have been expected, for there were theatres on all sides. Two of them are part of our story. Next door to the hotel stood the Empire. A little downhill, on the eastern side of Leicester Square, stood the Alhambra (pulled down in 1936) with its clustering minarets, stars and crescents and fake orientalism. At one theatre or the other you could see or hear lady gymnasts, troupes of trained cockatoos, a Mr. Vanderfelt reciting 'Jameson's Raid (from the Poet Laureate's pen)', inimitable jugglers, burlesque wrestlers, 'soubrettes danseuses', Tschernoff's dogs, whoever Tschernoff may have been, and much else of a trifling sort. While John was in the cradle the Boer War threw a blare of jingoism on to both stages. Led by hip-swaying choruswomen, bandsmen, fife-players and drummers from thirty regiments marched back and forth on the Alhambra stage, giving everybody patriotic goose-pimples. For the same management Mr. (later Sir) Landon Ronald, whom John was to meet in later decades as a fellow-conductor, composed music for a spectacle in four scenes and a prologue called *Britannia's Realm*. A marvel called the Animatograph flickered impressions of troop trains and horse-racing on to a crumpled screen. When John was in his third year a superseding marvel, the Imperial Bioscope, showed the coronation procession of Edward VII. Both theatres had resident dance troupes headed by maîtres-de-ballet and put on lavish ballet entertainment. It was this, rather than the performing dogs, that brought the hansom cabs rolling to Leicester Square.

Even as 'inserts' to music-hall programmes, ballet entailed a sizeable orchestra. The Leicester Square pits were apt to be crammed. At the Alhambra there were up to fifty players. So, at least, the advertisements said. The Empire advertisements said the same. Music-hall had known nothing like it. Thirty years later Colonel Blois gave Barbirolli no bigger an orchestra when he took grand opera from Covent Garden into the provinces.

Back now to his elders. Sometime in the 'nineties Antonio was taken on as leader in the Alhambra pit. Lorenzo joined him as sub-leader. Later, they migrated to the first desk at the Empire. When John was four, Antonio started taking him to the Empire for ballet rehearsals. He would plump the child down in a stall, telling him to be good and to watch and listen. Often there would be a new production on the stage with scenery fresh from the paint shop giving off a characteristic smell.

'That,' Barbirolli used to say, 'is when and where I first got the smell of size into my nostrils. It has been in my nostrils ever since. The smell of newly-"sized" scenery and the sound of music: for me they've always gone together. It was those mornings at the old Empire, then the greatest vaudeville house in the world, that helped to make me a good opera conductor. I began to adore everything to do with the stage.'

The bigger ballets put on in Leicester Square ran to four 'tableaux' and were commonly billed as grand spectaculars; it is unlikely that the Diaghilev public, then waiting in the wings, so to say, would have prized either the choreography or the aesthetic message of the Square's *Bluebeard*, or *Don Quixote* or *Monte Cristo*. It is true that the Empire rose as high as the *Coppélia* of Delibes. This was put on for the Empire's première danseuse Adeline Genée. Genée came from her native Denmark to London as a girl two years before John was born and left when he was seven. As the Empire's star, she gave the house a prestige that echoes still. Whenever he mentioned her, Barbirolli put on the solemn look and used the earnest tone that is usually reserved for legends on two legs. For many shows on both sides of the Square, whatever music the producer needed was composed by the house conductor, or musical director, as he was officially styled. In the Barbirollis' time the conductor at the Empire was Leopold Wenzel. The bills called him Mons. Wenzel, since he was said to come from Belgium. This was considered to show a nice feeling. Among other things he composed the music for *Under One Flag*, a sprightly 'divertissement in two tableaux', and conducted it between a trapeze act and the Marvellous Craggs, acrobats. When conducting Wenzel wore white gloves. To say that these gloves engrossed John would be understatement. They monopolised him. 'I don't think I noticed anything else,' he would say.

Next day he rooted about at home and found a pair of white or light-coloured gloves belonging to his mother or his sister. Shutting himself in a room—'for there was no exhibitionism in this. I didn't want to show off'—he sat on a chair, hummed a tune and beat time. From that moment it was his settled purpose to become a conductor—as well as a doctor. For medicine was his first ambition or, at any rate, his parents' early ambition for him. They had to renounce it. To make him a doctor would have meant putting him to medical school and years of training. This they could not afford. As will be seen, Giovanni had to start earning his living in orchestra pits at fourteen. To console himself against frustration, he began reading medical books, a hobby which he kept up ever afterwards. While his two ambitions were still in the balance he would wander in Lincoln's Inn Fields. In good time he became aware that demigods called the Royal College of Surgeons had something called a museum there. Perhaps when he grew up he might be granted a look inside it. Sometimes he heard bands play in the Fields. Walking with his father one day when the bandstand was empty, he climbed up into it and gave the beat to imagined players as he had done at home.

When he heard about this Grandfather clapped his knees enthusiastically and laughed to the ceiling. Antonio had watched the boy's first musical stirrings with gruff pride. He made it his business to encourage them. As compared with Lorenzo's, his was an exuberant, almost boisterous nature. The tendency among fellow Italians was to regard him as a 'card' in Arnold Bennett's sense. Although his later career was committed to this country he could never be bothered to learn English. When the family took on a Cockney servant

girl he talked her into picking up more than enough Italian for
day-to-day domestic needs. Naturally her Italian, such as it
was, smacked of Veneto. He had a warm heart and its frequent
concomitant, a quick temper. John he adored (John adoring
back)—and occasionally exploded at him: 'One minute he
would smash a fiddle over my head. Next minute he would
take me over the road to a toyshop, a scruffy little place, where
I always bought a whip.' Why a whip? Because the world of
his childhood was a world of horse buses. Small boys not
fascinated by horse buses were hardly considered to be small
boys—or any sort of boy—at all. In the dining-room at
Southampton Row John would play at driving one. This
entailed piling chair on chair on chair. Climbing to the
precarious top, he would thrash away at an imagined team,
fancying himself at trot with a full pay-load along High
Holborn.

When, fifty or sixty years after the event, he spoke of Grandpa's smashing a violin over his head he may have been speaking
figuratively. It is certainly the case that his violin playing
failed to bring out the best in Grandpa. He started on the
violin at six or seven. Practising made him restless; while
playing he would wander from room to room all over the
house. This infuriated Grandpa. In the end, during one of
John's unmusical rambles, he jumped up and left the house
without a word. Twenty minutes later a hansom cab pulled up
at the door. From it emerged Grandpa with a quarter-size
'cello which he had bought impulsively at Edward Withers'
shop in Wardour Street. Putting his hands on the boy's
shoulders he pushed him down on to a chair, put the 'cello
between his knees and barked: 'Now you'll *have* to sit. You
can't walk about playing *that*.'

'Which', explained Barbirolli, 'is how I became a 'cellist.'

His first 'cello teacher was a bizarre German who used to
turn up with a little bag. He did not require the boy to play
scales or exercises. Instead he would open a book of traditional
tunes arranged for the instrument, point to one of them—
usually it was 'Bluebells of Scotland'—and say 'Play that'.
While the boy was grumping away as best he could, he would
take off his shoes and socks, open the little bag and take out a
towel and a fresh pair of socks. Wiping his feet with the towel,

he would put on the fresh socks and stow the discarded ones. 'The scent of bluebells', Barbirolli remembered, 'had nothing to do with the case.' Such were 'cello lessons with the bizarre German. He used to come to the house of an evening, when Lorenzo and Antonio were at the theatre. The boy did not think much of his method and complained accordingly to Lorenzo, who sacked the man. Genuine 'cello lessons came a little later.

Before dealing with these let us take a look at Giovanni Barbirolli the schoolboy. For it was as Giovanni, not as John, that his parents had him entered, in September 1907, on the (junior) register of the St. Clement Danes and Holborn Estate Grammar School. Two years later he was admitted to Dane House in the senior school and stayed there nominally until the summer of 1914. There were fees to pay. In the early 'nineties these were four pounds ten a year. Not long after John left they were up to ten pounds.

So far as this story is concerned the immediate point of the St. Clement Danes school, an indirect offshoot of the 'Oranges and Lemons' Church in The Strand, is that it took a little Italian and turned half of him into a little Englishman: which remained the Barbirolli pattern for ever. His mother, true, was from France. Louise Barbirolli was as close to him (and he to her) as were Lorenzo Barbirolli and Antonio. She taught him her language. He spoke it fluently and revered her memory. But nobody, apportioning his acquired and inherited traits, would have called him one-third French. He was known to repudiate the idea himself, insisting that he was Venetian on one side and Cockney on the other and that racially there was no room for anything between. When asserting his Cockney origins (this he did with pride), he would cite an old tag: 'A Cockney is one born within the sound of Bow Bells'. It may be that on a quiet Sunday morning with the wind in the right quarter the bells of Bow Church in Cheapside can be heard in Southampton Row. 'Cockney', however, is a quality not of bells and birthplace but of speech and vocabulary. Barbirolli's habitual English was cultivated. His slight drawl had pleasant Edwardian overtones. But his Cockney, whenever he chose to put it on, sounded equally authentic. 'That,' he would say after giving a sample of it, 'is somewhat how I talked as a boy, I suppose.'

That first accent he picked up in the swarming streets of Bloomsbury and the parish of St. Giles.

School was an early corrective; and the grammar school of St. Clement Danes was a very good corrective indeed. Few schools like it remain in the heart of London today. It stood in that part of Houghton Street, off Aldwych, which had survived the tumultuous clearance and rebuilding schemes of John's infancy.* Although the charity which controlled it dates back to the middle of the sixteenth century, the school that John knew did not open until 1862; and that is precisely how it looked. The frontage on to Houghton Street had a pious-looking arcade with six pillars and florid capitals and arches which were neither Gothic nor Norman but a creepy variant on both. It was a small, snug school with poky classrooms and one Big Room, as it was called, which, to the remembering eye, seemed the size of a railway station. It was long and lofty, its tent roof and skylights supported by ornate semicircular girders. White-globed gaslamps hung from brackets two by two; there was a clock on the wall with soporific tick and, in the facing wall, a fireplace with coal scuttle alongside. Comfortable smells came up faintly from a coal-fired cooking range in the underground kitchen. The asphalted playground measured thirty yards by ten, which wasn't conducive to team games. (For inter-house football and cricket the school used Regent's Park and far-off Clapham Common.) Until some genius introduced five-a-side netball, the great diversion during break was climbing a wall that divided the boys' school from the girls' playground, which was of exactly the same shape and size. Peeking at the girls during break was against the rules. Boys who persisted in it were liable to get a 'swishing'. Not that St. Clement Danes made much of the rod. To the contrary. In John's day the headmaster, recently installed,

* During John's first six years, acre upon acre of streets and small property, much of it slum, between the Barbirollis' home and The Strand were pulled down to make way for two great new thoroughfares (Aldwych and Kingsway); three new theatres, a big hotel; a prodigious underground tramway to link North London with South London; and other improvements which incidentally displaced 3,172 of the 'working-class population'.

was the distinguished W. P. Fuller. It was Fuller who introduced the house system, the prefectorial system, inter-house sports and a school magazine that carried on its front the school's new-found motto, 'Loyauté m'oblige'.

Like most of Barbirolli's early memories, those of the school in Houghton Street had a cosy glow and comic glints. In general the masters were 'characters' or, in minor matters, amiably odd. There was the master who, as he remembered, wore the same green necktie and the same mock-pearl tiepin for seven years. 'For anything I know,' he reflected half a century later, 'he is wearing them still.' Another whom he remembered was Arthur Robson, bald and gravely bearded, who 'took' history. For all his gravity, Robson was incapable of keeping order. When agitated in class he curbed himself by biting on his fountain pen. At last, said Barbirolli, he bit it through. The pen had a big barrel and was full of red ink, which poured down Robson's beard to macabre effect. Then there was the master who could not put up with street pianos. One of them used to jangle regularly beneath the windows of his classroom. He would rush out and give the piano-grinder a penny to go away. By the time he got back the grinder was at it again, bribed to return by boys who, clubbing their halfpennies together, had slipped out to a sidestreet and given him twopence. A fourth master was reputed to spend lunch break in Fleet Street pubs. Coming back one afternoon with a suspicion of slur on his tongue, he was perplexed by a boy's cap which seemed to be moving across the floor of its own accord. On learning that the boy's tortoise was underneath it he laughed in a relieved way.

To one master young Barbirolli always remained grateful, for signal help of a personal kind. James Oswald Francis, who taught English among other subjects, was a high-spirited and imaginative young Welshman fresh from Oxford and the Sorbonne; something of a dandy with his high-cut velvet waistcoats and elegant watch-chain. Observing that John was hampered by 'certain hesitancies of speech', he went out of his way to help him master them.* Francis was editor of the school magazine, *The Dane*. It was probably he who, in the

---

*Barbirolli warmly acknowledged this in a prize-giving day speech at the school in 1954, referring to 'a kindly master's personal interest'.

issue of April 1913, wrote this in noticing a school concert the
previous December: 'Of Barbirolli's 'cello solos what can we
say but that Barbirolli played them to his sister's fluent
accompaniment in his usual charming way and responded to
a rapturous *encore*?' There was a lot of excitement among
the boys when rumours ran of animosity between Francis
and the renowned H. H. J. Lee, master of Clement House,
who had taught at Houghton Street for thirty years. The
truth, which didn't come out until a file of the headmaster's
confidential papers came to light decades later, was even more
piquant than the rumours. During a confrontation in the
headmaster's study, Francis accused Lee of manipulating
school sports points in favour of his own house.

'You are an unspeakable cad, sir,' said Lee.

Francis punched Lee on the nose, breaking his spectacles,
and, when asked to apologise, said 'To hell with that!'
Not long after this Francis shot out of John's orbit and the
school's. Joining Kitchener's Army, he served with home
defence units, had plenty of leisure, scribbled industriously
and, by the end of the Kaiser's war, had made his mark as a
playwright, especially on amateur stages, where his *Birds of a
Feather* and *The Poacher* were highly regarded. Francis had a
lot to do with bringing out the English half of young Barbirolli
and consolidating it.

It does not follow that young Barbirolli was much of a
scholar in the conventional sense. His school record card for
1911–14 chances to be among the handful which survived
second-war evacuation, bomb damage and a later removal to
new quarters. Superficially it makes dismal reading. He is
usually at or near the bottom of his form. For 'conduct' (i.e.,
an assessment of how hard he tried) one marking survives; he
got a 4. An old 'Dane' comments: 'The higher the mark the
worse the "conduct". When a boy got a 3 it meant he hadn't
tried at all. In my day 4 was unheard of.' One re-reads the
record hopefully. Hope is rewarded. Here are details which
explain everything. John was on the senior-school roll for
seven terms in all. For four of these he is marked either as
'Not placed' (meaning that he did not sit the end-of-term
examination) or as 'Absent'. The truth is that he was leading a
double life, burning candles at both ends, trying to be in two

places at once. We find him from September 1910 to July 1912, a scholarship holder on the students' register of the Trinity College of Music in Mandeville Place, miles away. From July 1912 he is registered as a scholarship holder at the Royal Academy of Music.* That he should have put in any appearances at all in Houghton Street is something to marvel at.

By the time he left the grammar school he had not only made his début as a concerto soloist at the Queen's Hall. He had also cut his first gramophone records and seen them on public sale. Some terms earlier he had been auditioned for the school choir. The music master, Reginald Johnson, known to the boys as 'Ginger', had turned him down as not good enough. This worried him at the time. It was now something to laugh about.

* 'Barbirolli, who is one of the most promising musicians we have ever had in the school, has made a stride forward in the musical world by winning a 'cello scholarship at the Royal Academy of Music'—*The Dane*, December 1912. That same month he is reported as playing two 'cello solos (Squire's *Slumber Song* and a Scherzo by Van Goens) at a school concert 'by permission of the Royal Academy of Music'.

CHAPTER TWO

THE PIT

LORENZO cast about in some perplexity for a successor to the bizarre German. He knew little about academic string-pulling in the land of his adoption. Some friend in the profession suggested that John should try for a 'cello scholarship at the Trinity College of Music. John went round to Mandeville Place, passed an examination, was admitted to the register and remained on it, as has been said, for two academic years. He played in the students' orchestra, took part in the chamber music classes, had theory lessons from one man, piano lessons from another and 'cello lessons from old Edmund Woolhouse who, as well as being a 'cello teacher, was a chapter of musical history personified.

Half a century earlier Woolhouse had been in the last 'continuo' team, or one of the last, at the Covent Garden theatre (then and for long after the Royal *Italian* Opera House), playing in recitative accompaniments with double-bass and harpsichord according to an archaic convention. At the end of a big aria one or other of the team would improvise a cadenza. Woolhouse remembered his own cadenzas well and used to play samples of them for John's benefit, ending with flourishes that dated back to Queen Victoria's childhood or earlier. Barbirolli affirmed that Woolhouse picked up these devices and tricks and the style that goes with them as a young pupil of Robert Lindley, who led the 'cellos at Covent Garden from 1794 to 1855.

It was during his time with Woolhouse that John made his recording début. Years before this there had been an Edison-Bell phonograph. It played cylinders of black wax which were beautiful to behold; musical titles were printed in white on the bevelled ends, and in certain lights the playing surface had an iridescent sheen. A cylinder that especially fascinated

John was an excerpt from the ballet music in Gounod's *Faust*;
he could not hear enough of it. Cylinders had now been
superseded by discs; Edison-Bell had opened a London branch
with recording studios at the Elephant and Castle; and they
were keenly recruiting new names and new talents for their
Velvet Face label—'No scrape, no scratch, all music, smooth as
velvet, three shillings each', according to the blurbs. John's
growing reputation as a prodigy 'cellist came to the ears of the
London manager, who approached Lorenzo and arranged
that the boy should cut four numbers on four sides: *The
Broken Melody* (van Biene), 'O! Star of eve' (Wagner), *Tre
Giorni* (Pergolesi) and *Simple aveu* (Francis Thomé). He was
to be accompanied on the piano by his sister Rosa, who was
thirteen and a half.

He and Rosa went down to the Elephant and Castle by
horse bus, so far as he remembered—'We certainly couldn't
afford a cab.' In the studio, a 'primitive, poky place', they
were put on a high and uncomfortably narrow platform on
which stood an upright piano. In front of the piano and
John's 'cello two small recording horns were rigged, each with
a cross-gartering of tape against intrusive vibration. Thus
began a recording career which, in John's case, went on for
more than sixty years. When first copies of the discs came to
Greville Street, a pleasant Georgian house to which the family
had moved from Southampton Row, the Barbirollis and friends
gathered round the gramophone, listening avidly. 'There were
tears of joy and pride,' he recalled. His fee from the recording
company was two guineas.

When inquired after some years ago the original discs were
said to be 'under lock and key' at Walton Lodge, Barbirolli's
home in Salford. One of the four numbers, *The Broken Melody*,
was transferred to another early label, Winner, which showed a
racehorse passing the post. Twenty years ago a copy of this
was found by a discomane in the collection of a seventy-seven-
year-old at Finchley and acquired by the British Broadcasting
Corporation's gramophone library. There the present writer
listened to it by courtesy of the B.B.C. and made the following
note: 'A slithery performance. *Portamento* all the time. He slides
from note to note.' This was quoted to Barbirolli. He commented thus: 'That was in the fashion of the epoch. It was

not only Woolhouse's style. You hear, or heard, the same type of *portamento* in Ysaÿe, Willie [William Henry] Squire, Beatrice Harrison. It's not surprising that my 'cello playing of 1910 sounds dated. There was little or none of the "electric" *vibrato* you have today. It was a slower kind of sound. But my intonation! Those jumps in *The Broken Melody*—how accurate they are!'

As well as lavishly praising 'Master John Barbirolli', 'a really marvellous executant for one so young', for his phrasing, delicacy and finish, all of which are pronounced perfect, Winner's publicity gives the date of Master John's concerto début at the Queen's Hall. This happened on December 16th 1911, a fortnight after his twelfth birthday, the occasion being the annual concert of Trinity College. The orchestra was a hundred strong, all students; the chosen 'cello concerto that of Georg Goltermann (German; 1824–98) 'frightfully difficult thirds, octaves, double-stopping, glissandos, harmonics, the entire bag of tricks'. Having an insurmountable aversion to the velvet jackets and lace collars that were customary wear among musical prodigies, he appeared on the platform in a sailor suit, tiny and self-possessed, his black hair immaculately parted. (A year or two later he discarded the sailor suit for a silk-lapelled dress jacket and white waistcoat, with knee-breeches, Eton collar and white bow tie.) Among good judges who heard him that night was Herbert Walenn, 'cello professor at the Royal Academy of Music and founder of the London 'Cello School across the road in Nottingham Place, in some sense an unofficial offshoot of the Academy. On the strength of John's concerto feat, Walenn introduced him to his 'Cello School and put him in for an Academy scholarship, which the boy won, and continued as his teacher for five years. Walenn is among those mentors of whom Barbirolli spoke with fervour: 'From him I learned not only about 'cello playing but about an immensity of things. A really great man; another to whom I owe a great debt.'

The Academy was the root of his external training and, to a great extent, the making of him as a professional musician. At this point a summary of what he did there will not be amiss. He entered as an Ada Lewis Scholar (1912–13) and continued as a Broughton Packer Scholar (1914–16). In addition to the

Academy's bronze medal, silver medal and certificate of merit, awarded for progress in his principal study, he won three prizes for 'cello playing in 1914 and 1915—the Charles Rube, the Bonamy Dobrée and the Piatti. Certificates of several of these awards hung framed years later alongside the piano in the study of Walton Lodge. He was elected an associate of the Academy at the age of thirteen. Up to this point he had figured on the Academy's concert programmes as Master Tito Barbirolli, for 'Tito' was the name by which he was called at home. After the associateship he was listed as Mr. Giovanni Barbirolli. During his student days the Academy never knew him as 'John'. Master Tito was noted for his bustling energy: never a minute to spare; always hastening along corridors with serious, introspective eyes, half-size 'cello slung over his shoulder; no time off for student larks and loungings; no thought for anything whatever but the immediate musical task. Outside the classroom and lecture hall he was gradually getting the 'feel' of audiences on public and semi-public occasions. At the annual concerts of the Academy, usually held in the Queen's Hall, Sir Alexander Mackenzie (Principal) conducting, and at official chamber music concerts in the Academy itself (these were held in the Duke's Hall), he played solo 'cello or with chamber ensembles in seventeen works or single movements* from the standard and virtuoso repertories which covered such diversities of style and technical difficulty that the mere fact of the youngster's tackling them at all in public speaks well for his skill and coolness.

So much for what may be called first-line Academy concerts. There were others besides of a more venturesome and less official kind. Early in 1916, Barbirolli and three fellow-students got up Ravel's String Quartet in F (composed 1902–3; revised and published 1910), by no means an aggressive piece as to idiom when compared with such established path-breakers as Stravinsky's *Petrushka*, or the tone poems of Scriabin, or those even of Richard Strauss, but dubious to many influential though insular ears on account of its 'impressionism', so-called. On seeking to have the Quartet included in one of the Academy's officially sponsored chamber-music programmes, they were

* Listed in Appendix One.

told that this could not be. If they were to play it under the
R.A.M. roof they must do so 'on your own responsibility' at
one of the Academy Club's Branch B concerts (for students and
their friends); it could not be given at a Branch A concert (for
ex-students and ex-staff members only). The performance duly
came off on May 23rd 1916 before a hundred and fifty Branch B
members and guests, Ravel being the centrepiece of a programme that included these additional contemporary works,
all for string quartet: *Three Idylls* by Frank Bridge, Three
Pieces by J. B. McEwen and an Elegy by Hugh Priestley-
Smith in memory of a former student who had been killed in
the Neuve Chapelle battle the previous year.

Nobody is reported to have been corrupted morally or
musically by these excursions into what were regarded by
staider tastes as wilfully esoteric styles. Of the Ravel performance Barbirolli claimed: 'So you see, I was a bit of a pioneer
in my way. You could never call me a stick-in-the-mud.'

At home of an evening the pursuit of music went on until
bedtime. To the Greville Street house during this time came a
regular visitor, the late Alfonso Gibilaro, a talented young
Sicilian musician who was to marry Rosa Barbirolli. He first
knew Tito as a reserved (rather than shy) eleven-year-old who,
after the dinner table had been cleared, habitually sat in a
corner with his head in some score, sealed off from the talk and
amiable disputes and laughter of the family circle, deep in
newly mastered, newly imagined worlds of sound. It was to
be the same three years later when he began playing in
'legitimate' theatre pits. During intervals and long breaks,
when other players went out to the 'theatre pub', he would
stay in the bandroom, score on knee, with absorbed eyes, the
ears of his mind hard at work.

When he was twelve a score of the *Tristan* prelude came his
way. He annotated it passionately and wrongheadedly. He
was to smile indulgently later at his annotations, especially the
'tremendous rubatos' he introduced. 'But,' he ventured, 'it
was only because I felt the music so intensely then that I can
conduct it now with serenity and insight which, in any case,
can only come with the years.'

Another acquisition was Debussy: 'I adored Debussy's

La Mer when little more than a child and have adored it ever since. Dad bought me a score when holidaying in Paris. At that time Debussy scores were dear to buy in this country. *La Mer* is one of the great classics of modern music and one of the most difficult to play, because every particle of it is playable and *must* be played. You know, there are some works where playing all the notes spoils the effect. That occurs particularly in Wagner and Richard Strauss. In *La Mer* every note can be played and has to be played. Even with the greatest orchestras in Europe and America I wouldn't dream of performing it without intensive rehearsal, no matter how often or recently they had played it. There's always work to be done on *La Mer*; and that's one of the fascinating things. The full beauty of this music cannot be achieved without the most scrupulous technical accomplishment.'

Between twelve and fourteen, then, he fell in love with Ravel and Debussy; also with early Stravinsky—and was regarded by some of his elders as 'fit for the asylum. This music was completely misunderstood. Pundits quarrelled about it. It had to be fought for. And as a boy I fought for it.' There did not have to be any fighting for the classics. He revered and loved them nevertheless. And they were his staple. At ten he began studying the Bach 'cello suites. By twelve he had played 'cello in all the Beethoven string quartets—'a liberal education in itself'. Haydn was another early and abiding loyalty: 'He is a much more adventurous composer than Mozart. He wrote eighty-three string quartets. None of us know more than half of them yet. Whenever I get the chance to play a bit of chamber music nowadays [mid-1960s] I always fly to Papa Haydn.'

Barbirolli's purpose in stressing his classical upbringing—he went so far as to call it an austere one—was perhaps to correct the once popular fallacy that any conductor with Italian antecedents or merely with an Italian name must in his heart of hearts be committed wholly and solely to Italian opera. He admitted that when he came to Italian opera and began conducting it, he felt he had stumbled upon something that had been with him all the time. 'Inbred' is the word he used. His championship of Puccini dated from a time when the composer of *La Bohème* and *La Fanciulla* was looked down upon by the musical snobs (there were many of these), largely because

'Your tiny hand' and 'One fine day' were played in all the
teashops and on every street piano. At the same time he let it
be known that he did not study any Puccini score until he was
in his twenties, with a dozen or so years of musical austerity
behind him. By that time much Bach and Beethoven was
engraved on his heart as well as upon his memory. As a
comparative latecomer to his affections Puccini somehow
survived a furnace of comparisons and standards.

Adventures were coming his way as a listener, some of them
indelible. From the age of twelve he started going to the
Promenade concerts at the Queen's Hall on his own. Sir
Henry Wood, knighted the year before, had been ruler of the
Promenades for nearly twenty years and was to continue for
another thirty. His Queen's Hall Orchestra was the one
which, every summer, endured unaided a season of seven to
ten weeks, playing a fairly high percentage of unfamiliar music,
on appallingly skimpy rehearsals, as they seem by later
standards.

Every member of the orchestra was given an admission pass
which he could lend to friends. The Barbirollis were on good
terms with many of Wood's players. John used to post himself
on the pavement near the band entrance half an hour before
starting time and, when the players came along, would ask
those he knew: 'Have you a pass for me?' He always got one.
On an evening in 1913 he heard an orchestral piece called
Night on a Bare Mountain. The programme said it was by Modest
Petrovitch Moussorgsky, a name as good as new to him.
'Fifty or sixty years ago,' he said, 'Moussorgsky was a revelation.' A flame was lit in his mind and in the minds of thousands
more. He said to himself: 'I must hear something more of this
chap'.

On the way home he met the revelatory name again.
Posters outside the Theatre Royal, Drury Lane, for Sir Joseph
Beecham's season of Russian ballet and opera* announced
forthcoming performances of Moussorgsky's *Boris Godounov*,

---

* The season ran from 24th June to 25th July 1913. For singing in
Boris, *Khovantchina* and *Ivan the Terrible* Chaliapin got £400 a night. Sir
Joseph Beecham was Thomas Beecham's father and the funder of many
of his son's musical enterprises.

opera in four acts, with Fedor Chaliapin in the title part.
Chaliapin meant nothing to him, the composer all. That night
he mentioned the posters to his mother. 'You must take me,'
he bade. 'All right, then,' she promised. Six or seven hours
before the performance they queued up for the gallery at
Drury Lane and got seats. *Boris* multiplied the revelation of
Night on a Bare Mountain; and Chaliapin was as much a part of
that revelation as if Moussorgsky had himself specified and
created Boris with Chaliapin in mind.

We shall meet Chaliapin again at closer range, as Barbirolli
was to do twenty years afterwards.

Now the Kaiser's war. In tracing Barbirolli's professional
and other experiences during the next five years an occasional
zigzag in chronology will be helpful.

Our first jump is to 1916. Two years earlier scores of German
musicians had vanished overnight from orchestras and theatre
pits and restaurants throughout the land. Some of them had
got back to their homeland in the nick of time; others were
interned. Meantime the ranks of English players had been
thinned by recruiting and the first 'call-ups' under what was
known as the Derby Scheme. All this meant unusual openings
and exceptional opportunity for young players of promise
even before they had left college.

John sought an audition for the Queen's Hall Orchestra
while still on the Academy register and was called before
Henry Wood who, having heard his 'prepared' piece, put him
through a number of what he supposed were sight-reading
tests. In crafty anticipation Lorenzo had provided his son
beforehand with an anthology volume which contained the
most difficult 'cello passages in the standard orchestral
repertory. By the time he went before Wood the boy had the
entire collection almost off by heart. As had been calculated,
the bits that Wood required him to sight-read were familiar
ground. After this excerpt or that 'Timber' would ask, Was
he *sure* he hadn't played it before? A delicate challenge. Long
afterwards Barbirolli argued that it was *almost* true to say he
hadn't, since only fragments were in question, and he had
never played the complete 'cello parts from which they came in
orchestral performances. As the audition proceeded Wood

B *

looked more and more astonished. Later he wrote a charming
letter of invitation. Thus at sixteen, John Barbirolli became
a back-desk 'cellist in Wood's orchestra and the youngest
member of it: 'a really great event', as he assesses it.

Before long he was in the thick of Promenade concerts.
From player acquaintances he had heard much about under-
preparation and the nightly struggle this involved. Now the
struggle was his. For every six concerts there were only three
rehearsals. Today, eighteen rehearsals for six Promenade
concerts are not unusual. For years the B.B.C. Symphony
Orchestra, on whom the main burden falls, has, into the
bargain, had a week of preliminary rehearsals before the
season begins. There was nothing like that half a century ago
or for long thereafter. Nor was there any burden-sharing. As
well as the B.B.C. orchestra we hear nowadays a dozen or so
relief orchestras, some of them from other countries. In
Barbirolli's day Wood's orchestra took on the lot, playing
every night but Sunday in a season that went on for eight
weeks or more. Barbirolli said: 'We had to sight-read half the
stuff when the time came. But old Henry J. was a master at
keeping us on the rails.'

Of all the musical revolutions or evolutions London has
known, none is more striking than the history of the Promenades.
Programmes were at one time divided into a serious symphonic
first half and a homely, rather inane second half dotted with
sheet ballads which the commercial promoters looked to sell
more briskly over the counters after an airing or plugging at
the Promenades. The odd thing, said Barbirolli, was that
audiences then, so different from those of today as almost to
suggest a different race, swallowed everything with relish, say
Brahms's Symphony No. 1 or Strauss's *Don Quixote* before
the interval and, after it, Charles Tree, a baritone in great
demand, singing, say, 'That Fat Little Fellow with his Mammy's
Eyes'. As Barbirolli remembers these occasions, Brahms and
Tree always got the same reception; that is to say, both
were cheered to the echo. At that time Tree was nearing
fifty and wore stiff, pointed moustaches like an old-fashioned
sergeant-major. It was during Barbirolli's inaugural season
that Tree, in deference to prevailing patriotic sentiment or
perhaps to vindicate the cut of his moustaches, followed up the

Pagliacci prologue with Florence Aylward's 'Khaki Lad', of which a textual sample is given below to satisfy the curiosity of a more fastidious generation of Promenaders.*

Slog and pressure at the Queen's Hall toughened him and did much for his technical resource. Professionally he had to prove himself as a 'cellist in other ways, however. The most important of these other ways was a public début at one of London's two main recital halls, the Wigmore in Wigmore Street and the Aeolian (now a B.B.C. outpost) in Bond Street. Until a young singer or instrumentalist had given a concert on one or other of these platforms, winning quotable notices from *The Times* and the *Daily Telegraph*, he could not consider himself or be considered by anybody else as launched and truly fee-worthy. Young Barbirolli gave recitals at both places. 'Wonderful notices!' he claimed a generation later. 'They said I was the future Casals.'

His Aeolian recital was on the thirteenth of a month; 13th July 1917. (The date did not scare him. On his sixtieth birthday he said he had never been superstitious about 13: 'I got a scholarship on 13 June, when I was 13 years old. It's my lucky number.' He was superstitious in other ways, however, as is noted in a later chapter.) On that day the Germans staged one of their first big daylight raids on London, Essex and Kent, their bombers coming over in groups of five. The raid on London began at lunchtime while he was rehearsing on the Aeolian platform. That afternoon 162 people were killed, 432 wounded. Next day the anonymous *Times* critic spoke of the young man's technique as above the average, found his Locatelli variations 'masterly', praised his Boëllmann Sonata in A ('well managed pianissimo effects and excellent intonation') and demurred on one point only: in the Boëllmann the strings 'did not always speak as the player wanted them to'. There were private encomiums in plenty. As things then stood, however, a future Casals who could not be cosseted financially had poorish prospects. 'I had to earn my living,' he says. 'I couldn't do

---

* I saw a lad in khaki, in khaki, in khaki,
 With braided star upon his sleeve
 And a little cane to swing
 He walked down Piccadilly so proudly, so proudly
 He walked down Piccadilly as though he were a king.

that on the Wigmore and Aeolian platforms.' His immediate recourse was 'gigs', as they would now be called, in 'straight' theatre pits and in 'silent' cinemas.

At fourteen he surprised everybody, including, possibly, the musical director who took him on, by getting into the entr'acte band at the Duke of York's Theatre, St. Martin's Lane. Up to then he had worn nothing longer than knickerbockers. His mother rushed out and bought him his first long trousers. They fitted him 'somewhere under the armpits'. On one and the same night, therefore, he made his début both as a theatre bandsman and as a 'grown-up'. His fee was seven shillings and sixpence a session—'not bad for 1914. That was my beginning in the theatre. And a very rich experience it proved.' During the three years that followed his fee went up to twelve and six a night which, at six shows and two matinées weekly, brought in five pounds a week, high earnings for an adolescent at that time. He did not relinquish 'straight' theatre pits until the early 1920s and claimed to have played in every London theatre built before 1923. When he wasn't score reading during breaks he would stay in the theatre if the play was of moment and played by eminent actors. He remembered with zest such names as: Robert Loraine, Martin-Harvey and Mrs. Patrick Campbell. His first sight of Mrs. Campbell was during a return engagement at the Duke of York's in the autumn of 1917. She played a spiritualist medium in *The Thirteenth Chair* by Bayard Veiller; and, as though the sight were before him still, he wrote of how formidable she looked when seated and impassive and how 'all the temperament we have heard about was very much in the air.'* Earlier there had been an encounter with George Bernard Shaw. A revival of *Arms and the Man* was in rehearsal. Shaw attended every session and put in his fillings and quips while Barbirolli, in the four-piece pit band, devoured him with eyes and ears; he had never come upon a being so fascinating to watch and hear. During a pause Shaw leaned over the rail and said pleasant things to the band about some Hungarian rhapsody they had played—'His words were much kinder than his writing as a music critic!'

Between theatre jobs he would resort, if nothing better

* Quoted by Alan Dent in *Mrs. Patrick Campbell*, Museum Press, 1961.

offered, to cinema pits, at that time the poorest paid work
that came a musician's way. For a five-hour session, six to
11 p.m., he got seven and sixpence: no more than his 'probation'
fee as a fourteen-year-old at the Duke of York's. Each new
programme was preceded by a morning session called 'fitting the
film'. As the week's feature-film was given a demonstration run,
the musical director would watch analytically, emitting spur-of-
the-moment decisions which somebody at his elbow noted
down: 'Two or three bars of *La Bohème*, opening of act three,
will come in nicely here', 'Now we'll have a touch of *Poet and
Peasant*', 'Marching soldiers? Schubert's *Marche militaire*,
obviously', 'Moonlit kiss? Some slow, sweet Chopin', and so on.
For a feature-film an hour and a half long Barbirolli would
find scores of pieces of music on his stand or stacked on the
floor. In the ordinary way nothing more than snippets were
played, three to five bars at a time: 'The conductor would tap
or stamp his foot, and we turned over. You never knew what
was coming next. It was all good training. I wish youngsters
today had such work to do. I'm sorry those days have gone.
Some of the young people who come into orchestras today
shelter behind the mass for a long time. But there, in the
cinema pits, there was no mass to shelter behind. You had to
do your stuff. If you didn't they'd throw you out like nobody's
business. Wonderful way of improving your sight-reading and
quickening your mind.' It was a handy and sure way also of
getting to know what sort of people workaday musicians were:
'By now I've conducted all the great orchestras in the world,
and I've never had any trouble with any of them, because I
know them from the bottom rung, having started down there
myself—and they *know* that I know.'

'Oh yes,' he would add, 'I have played everywhere except
in the street: dance halls, restaurants, cafés, even in "panto" at
the old Surrey Theatre.'

From such labours to grand opera was something to take in
one's stride and, given a certain aplomb, almost for granted.
He was inducted, after a fashion, during his eighteenth year at
the old Shaftesbury Theatre where the Carl Rosa company
were playing. For decades 'the Carl Rosa' had been great
popularisers of operatic classics throughout Britain. For all
their loyal and widespread following, however, they never had

money to throw about; as the years went by and competition sharpened, their doings had an air of chronic penury. On alternate Saturday nights Ben Davies, a tenor upon whose every note multitudes hung, sang in *Maritana* and *The Bohemian Girl*, giving backbone to the box office. The orchestra had been augmented for the season, 'which meant two 'cellos instead of one. I was one of the augmentations or "extras", as we were called.' For the 'extras' there were morning rehearsals from ten until one; he and one piccolo, one horn and one clarinet, say, would sight-read their parts act by act, producing eerie skeletons or residues of what the composer had in mind. He swore that he waded once through the *Tannhäuser* Overture on his own with an assistant conductor beating time. After three hours of rehearsal he would speed home and practise from two until evening on his own account, preparing for recitals and chamber music. Between half-past seven and eight he was back in the Shaftesbury pit for the night's performance, which usually went on until eleven.

Although nobody on casual meeting could have read it from his features, those of an introspective and sensitive youth, the drive to get on in music and the need to conquer more and more of it—for the music's sake as much as for the sake of a career—were uncommonly fierce in him. He never lazed; could not have done so if he had tried. The mere concept of lazing was grotesque; it made him wrinkle his nose in repugnance, much as the idea did later in his life of eating a five-course meal or even a three-course one or even a sizeable beefsteak.

His true induction to grand opera came when, in the summer of 1917, not long after his Aeolian Hall recital, Sir Thomas Beecham, who had been making do off and on with the Shaftesbury and Aldwych theatres, where he had to lift out a row or two of stalls to house a scratch orchestra of forty or fifty, moved to the Theatre Royal, Drury Lane, which had room for more players as well as for a much bigger public. There happened to be a vacant 'cello seat. It went to Barbirolli. With his team of co-conductors, Beecham did Englished versions, sung by English artists in the main, of many operas, including Russian ones, which had been sung in their original texts during his pre-war seasons. The first piece Barbirolli played in was Rimsky-Korsakov's *Ivan the Terrible* under the baton and venerable beard of Eugene Goossens senior. There was another Goossens on the conducting strength, Eugene junior, whose career was in some ways parallel to John's and whose senior he was by six or seven years. Reared professionally in the second violins of the Queen's Hall Orchestra, he left his desk there for good soon after Barbirolli joined the 'cellos and, in the next four or five years, was to conduct (mostly for Beecham) sixty or seventy operas as well as a multitude of symphony concerts. His and Barbirolli's paths were to run closer during the 1930s and later, when they were respectively conductor-in-chief of the Cincinnati and New York Phil-harmonic-Symphony orchestras. Goossens appeared as a guest conductor with the latter during Hitler's war while Barbirolli was still associated with it.

After the Russian nights: *Tristan*—for Barbirolli the apogee. What made it momentous for him as a novice was the opening bars: 'After all, it starts on the unison 'cellos'—and he would sing the Love's Longing motif, which is so hard to get just right in shape, pitch and homogeneity of tone. In October 1917 there was a *Tristan* performance (or, more exactly, a projected one) which carries grotesque memories. The first act was under way, with Frank Mullings (Tristan), Rosina Buckman (Isolde) and Edna Thornton (Brangaene) on the stage, singers who had a fervent following in theatre, concert hall and oratorio. Among them appeared an assistant manager in dress clothes who said: 'We have just been informed that enemy aeroplanes have crossed the coast and that an air raid is about to take place.' He invited people on upper levels to come down for safety into the stalls, where there were more than enough seats for them. In the upshot, as Barbirolli remembered it, the entire company (and others, probably) spent most of the night under the stage; they were there when a bomb fell calamitously in Long Acre, not far away.

The war was coming closer. He decided to go meet it. To avoid being conscripted, as would have happened after his eighteenth birthday, he volunteered for the Army late in 1917.

But first a word about his début (as orchestral player) with the Royal Philharmonic Orchestra for the illustrious Royal Philharmonic Society, who long afterwards conferred their gold medal upon him for his services to music. The night was November 26th, 1917, Beecham the conductor, the programme an unimpressive Beechamesque ragoût,* the occasion as a whole not much worth remembering except for young Barbirolli's presence among the 'cellos. The R.P.S. has a long memory and did not forget. Fifty years later they dined him ceremonially in remembrance. Then khaki. He found himself Private 52537 in the First Reserve Garrison Battalion of the Suffolk Regiment, stationed on the Isle of Grain—'a patch of mud at the mouth of the Thames', he called it—where unforeseen things happened to him. For the first time in his life he wore a signet ring. It was from his mother. On the day he left for the war she gave it to him as a token and talisman.

* Overture *Prince Igor*, Borodin; Symphony No. 40, Mozart; Symphonic Variations, César Franck; Orchestral Drama, *Fifine at the Fair*, Granville Bantock; *Clair de Lune*, Debussy-Goossens; and *España*, Chabrier. Arthur de Greef played in the César Franck and solo pieces by Bach and Scarlatti.

CHAPTER THREE

QUARTET

THE patch of mud was 'terrible' (his word) not because of the mud but because the people on it had little to do. He became anti-gas instructor to his unit, not an exacting job; there was still an aching emptiness. Several musicians, professional or amateur, were dotted about the island in this company and that. Some had brought their instruments with them and, for want of a centralising hand, played them solo in canteens and dormitory huts. When Private Barbirolli returned from his first leave he brought his 'cello back with him. Soon afterwards the scattered musical particles coalesced: 'We decided to form our own orchestra as a way of passing the time.' It became 'really quite a good orchestra', he insisted.

He said at least this about almost every orchestra with which he was connected. No musician was ever truer to his own; with him professional bonds could be timeproof, like family ones.

Before launching itself the orchestra sought the Colonel's permission to do so. The Colonel was 'a very bad amateur violinist' and, like most of his kind, enthusiastic in forwarding good musical works. His answer was favourable. 'But,' he said, 'you mustn't expect time off for this. You must call yourself a Voluntary Orchestra.' One of the officers happened to be a qualified Army bandmaster. During the week he rehearsed and on Saturday nights conducted them at concerts in the main canteen. They played overtures, suites and 'bits of symphonies'. Barbirolli's utter immersion in music and his professional sureness won him deference and one exuberant compliment, the latter from the oboe, ex-Regular (Indian Army), often drunk and 'the most enchanting person you ever met', who said: 'You're an Irishman loik me, an' your name's

Bob O'Reilly.'* Turning up for rehearsal one Saturday afternoon, the Voluntary Orchestra learned that their conductor was sick. The rehearsal was cancelled and the players dispersed to other duties, but not before some of them—'all pals of mine who knew about my conducting ambitions'—had gone to the proper quarters and said: 'The rehearsal's cancelled, sir, but the concert isn't. What about Barbirolli conducting tonight?' That afternoon, Private 52537 Barbirolli was on fatigue in the officers' mess scrubbing floors. Somebody tapped him on the shoulder and told him the concert was his. A story used to circulate that his first conducting chance came years later when, in a like emergency, he was called to the rostrum from his 'cello desk in a grand opera pit on tour. 'Nothing of the kind,' he said. 'I was summoned not from the pit but from my knees.' His main piece as stand-in was Coleridge Taylor's *Petite suite de concert*. It retained a nostalgic charm for him. 'When he heard that I had conducted the concert and had been a great success, our officer-bandmaster got over his illness remarkably quickly.'

Except when pretending as a child he had never before used a baton or given a beat. 'That night,' he affirmed, 'I conducted technically as I do today. I have a more than strong belief that conductors are born, not made. From the first time I picked up the baton I had the same facility as I have now. I'm not really boasting, because all this has nothing to do with John Barbirolli. The good Lord, or whatever the thing is, put this facility into my arms. Once I've learned music mentally, the translation of it into physical terms for the eyes of the orchestra is absolutely unconscious. That has been so from the start. I'm speaking only of the physical side of conducting, of course, the one which has a direct effect on the orchestra. The other side, the musical and psychological side, is a different matter'—a matter which will be touched on later in this narrative in so far as it concerns Barbirolli's nature and development as an artist.

Within a year of his joining the Suffolks the war ended. He

---

* Thirty-four years later he was jocularly referred to as Bob O'Reilly—'which places a man's origin well within the shores of Ireland'—by the professor who presented him at Iveagh House, Dublin, for the honorary degree of Doctor of Music, conferred by the National University of Ireland.

had one spell of authority. Fifty years later, when presented by the British Ambassador to Marshal Castelo Branco, President of the Brazilian Republic, in Rio de Janeiro during a tour of Latin South America, he said: 'I also have been a military man, though my rank was somewhat junior to yours. The war ended before I could be sent abroad; but for three glorious weeks in 1918 I was an acting unpaid lance corporal in the Suffolk Regiment.'* Awaiting demobilisation, he and his 'cello were out of the Army in the middle of 1919. So, back to band-room, concert platform, theatre pit.

His first assignment that summer was with the *Ballets russes* of Serge Diaghilev at the Alhambra, Leicester Square, one of the theatres to which he had been taken by his grandfather as an infant. He played through a repertory which, whatever the provenance of this score or that, was intensely of the 1920s: *Petrushka* and *Firebird*, *The Good Humoured Ladies* and *La Boutique Fantasque*, the *Polovtsian Dances*, *Scheherazade*, *Thamar*. . . . The dancers' names in themselves are the scroll of an epoch. Karsavina, Lopokova, Lydia Kyasht, Tchernicheva, Sokolova, Massine drew full-throated roars at curtain-fall. The season in which Barbirolli took part was the middle among three Diaghilev seasons at neighbouring theatres—Coliseum, Alhambra and Empire—which amounted in effect to one long and sumptuous season from the autumn of 1918 to the end of 1919: fifteen months of exaltation and dazzlement. Since the company's first visits, before the war, London had not known anything that remotely compared with the *Ballets russes*. Diaghilev's mating of salty, elegant movement or mime with disturbingly powerful stage designs and racy, opulent music easily outbid all other aesthetic 'musts' of the period. At his 'cello desk Barbirolli thus helped along the cultural making of a privileged generation.

The Alhambra season ran from the end of April to the end of July. The last week of it saw the first performance anywhere of Manuel de Falla's *The Three Cornered Hat*. Diaghilev had two conductors at the Alhambra, one of them a newcomer from Geneva, Ernest Ansermet, who made his mark with a number of Stravinsky premières, including that of *The Soldier's Tale*. Clearly he was the man for the new de Falla

* Quoted by Sir Leslie Fry, *The Times*, August 8th, 1970.

ballet. Diaghilev had a whim, however, He ruled that, whenever it was practicable, composers—*his* composers, especially
—were to conduct their own works. Accordingly he brought
de Falla along to an orchestral rehearsal of *The Three Cornered
Hat*—virtually dragged him there, indeed. Barbirolli recalled:
'All the way down the aisle poor little de Falla was pleading (I
can see him now): "Mais, mon cher Diaghilev, je ne peux pas,
je ne peux pas!"' Diaghilev was obdurate. He got de Falla on to
the rostrum. 'We were all agog to play for him because we
admired his music a lot. So he started. The moment he got to
one of his cross rhythms he'd stop, and we'd stop, too. After
five minutes he turned it in. The man who physically devised
those rhythms,' added Barbirolli, 'couldn't physically beat
them.' (He often cited this case as illustrating the conductor's
special function and faculty. Some composers do well with the
stick, he allowed. 'Others are foxed by what they have written.')
De Falla stood down and, a substitute having been called in, sat
out the rest of the rehearsal in the orchestra pit alongside
Massine and Picasso, who had designed the sets. After *The
Miller's Dance*, a new number which de Falla had composed
within twenty-four hours for the Alhambra first night,
Massine, who was to dance the Miller, gave him a congratulatory hug. Ansermet saw the first night (22nd July 1919) to
clamorous success on the musical side.

Three months later Barbirolli was present at a contretemps
of a more humiliating kind. As a back-desk 'deputy' with the
London Symphony Orchestra he was booked for the rehearsal
of Sir Edward Elgar's Concerto for Violoncello and Orchestra.
The première was to be at Queen's Hall on October 26th 1919.
The idea was that Elgar should conduct the première, Felix
Salmond playing the solo part, in a programme which, as to
the rest, would be conducted by Albert Coates, one of music's
ardent slavophils. There were many of these about in 1919.
Coates's main pieces were to be Scriabin's *Poem of Ecstasy* and
Borodin's Symphony No. 2, questionable bedfellows, one
would have thought, for big-scale Elgar. Coates rehearsed
first—and went on rehearsing for an hour beyond the time at
which he should have stepped down for Elgar and Salmond.
Elgar, as we know from his biographer, Dr. Percy Young, 'was
almost inclined to throw his hand in'. Consideration for

Salmond seems to have been the only thing that deterred him.
On the night an obviously under-rehearsed performance drew
a thunderbolt from Ernest Newman. The London Symphony
Orchestra, wrote Newman, made 'a lamentable public
exhibition of itself'.* A harsh judgment. Failing some dis-
criminatory clause, it implied that the L.S.O. players had
been as 'lamentable' as Coates and the L.S.O. management.
All were lumped together in sin. One thing is sure. Young
Barbirolli—and probably some of his fellow-players, too—
burned with Elgarian zeal.

The following autumn at Worcester—'in those days a
lovely country town still, with Elgar's father's music shop
standing'—he again played under Elgar as an L.S.O. back-
desker in the first post-war Three Choirs Festival. *The Dream of
Gerontius* was the business in hand. Elgar conducted his
oratorio from memory. ('He was the antithesis of Vaughan
Williams, who couldn't remember a note of his music.') Judged
by the highest professional standards, adds Barbirolli, nobody
could have called Elgar a great conductor. (Nobody of moment
ever did.) 'But,' he goes on, 'it was extraordinary how he
could make players feel what he wanted—if they were in
sympathy with him.' The art of conducting is in itself of
relatively little account, however. The music conducted is
what matters. It was Elgar's music, not his modest ability
with the stick, that made young Barbirolli's zeal burn. Many
in the 1920s thought such zeal misplaced. Elgar's works and
even his person—'. . . with his grey moustache, grey top hat
and frock coat, he looked every inch a personification of
Colonel Bogey'†—were to become aunt sallys for every
modish and self-appointed arbiter of taste in the land. Or
arbiter of *dis*taste. As a rule people are more cowed when told
what they mustn't like than what they must. Barbirolli's
reverence for Elgar's music, his response to its detail and
substance, will emerge more fully when we come to his
adventures with the E flat Symphony and *Gerontius*. An interim
point is that his reverence and response were none the less
deep and acute for his being of Latin stock and, as to early

* *Sunday Times*, December 1919.
† Elgar at seventy as described by Osbert Sitwell in *Laughter in the
Next Room* (Macmillan), London, 1949.

upbringing, at any rate, as far removed from standard Anglo-Saxon ideas and inculcations as could be imagined. He was by no means the only conductor of his generation who remained true to Elgar during the quarter-century or so when the composer of *Gerontius* was given over to the mockers. Another champion who comes to mind is Malcolm Sargent. But Sargent saw into Elgar's art as a person of roughly the same stock, social forces and emotional loyalties. Barbirolli saw into him as a demi-Italian. It may be that he saw into him the deeper for that. In the beginning Elgar's music was, for Barbirolli, an exotic thing—and therefore not to be taken for granted. Taking any music for granted is a sure way to performing it bloodlessly and toothlessly. When, on the other hand, music comes to us from off the edge of the ancestral map, bringing other melodies than those of our cradle, we are all wonder and marvel and thirsting curiosity. Our performances of it, if we happen to be performers, benefit accordingly. This hypothesis (it is nothing more than that) may perhaps be illustrated by the impact upon two personalities of Elgar's symphonic study *Falstaff*, whose 'programme' derives from the chronicle plays of Shakespeare. Barbirolli came under the spell of *Falstaff* long before he had the chance of conducting it. Meeting Landon Ronald, to whom the score is dedicated, Barbirolli exclaimed how wonderful *Falstaff* was. 'I can't make head or tail of it!' Ronald replied. Of Ronald's sapience as an Elgarian and of his devotion to the corpus of Elgar's music there can be no doubt. When it came to *Falstaff*, however, that most English of compounds, in which Elgarian thought is shot through with Shakespeare's pathos and grandeur, Giovanni Battista, son of Lorenzo, grandson of Antonio, showed greater acumen and imagination than either Ronald or the generality of English aesthetes.

Barbirolli's regard for Elgar did not go unreciprocated. Elgar seems to have heard him conduct early on in his career, although Barbirolli knew nothing of this at the time. At some music club function not long afterwards, Landon Ronald presiding, Elgar, the chief guest of the evening, said: 'As long as we have conductors and musicians like Barbirolli, this country has nothing to worry about.' Whereupon, said Barbirolli, he felt like falling through the floor. A second and much later compliment reached him through a friend to whom Elgar, apropos an early Barbirolli recording of his Introduction and Allegro for Strings, is said to have said: 'I didn't know that this was such a big work'. From this avowal Barbirolli was known to argue that he and Elgar must have had 'a natural affinity'. About his music Elgar was gruff, reticent or evasive as a rule; often his attitude seemed perversely tinged with self-mockery. During the last phase he was perhaps a little more open with Barbirolli than with some—'because he knew I loved his music so much that I couldn't gush about it. He felt that what I said about it was really true.'

Their last meeting was late in 1933, four months before Elgar's death. Elgar invited him to tea at Marl Bank. He showed him the view of Worcester's towers and steeples from his bedroom window. That, he said with satisfaction, was what he saw on wakening up in the morning. Downstairs he played a *Falstaff* recording and seemed to enjoy every note of it. In the fourth section ('Near Westminster Abbey') a triumphal march is interrupted by what Barbirolli called, with relish, 'this wonderful bit . . ., this terrific crash for bass drum and cymbals'. After the crash Elgar said, 'Well, that's a good bit, anyway'—just as if (commented Barbirolli) he'd dismissed the rest of it!

Back to 1920, a crowded year. His Easter was a working holiday. Victor Olof, an enterprising young violinist of Swedish stock (thirty years or so later he became an eminent recording director) had charge of music at a fashionable Minehead (Somerset) hotel: which is to say that he led a piano quartet—two violins, a 'cello and piano (the management called them a salon orchestra) in set programmes picked by himself. Bits from opera, operetta and musical comedy were the staple. He took on Barbirolli as his 'cellist for the Easter season at seven pounds a week. They played in the hotel lounge twice a day: 4.30 p.m. to 5.30 and 8.30 to 10, a total of three hours' work. Mondays were free. With varying degrees of vacuity and dreamy attention, they were listened to by hunting people, polo people and occasional celebrities, among them the Bernard Shaws. There was much talk above stairs and below about Mrs. Shaw; how she used to go into the hotel kitchen and cook vegetarian meals for her husband. It was the second time Barbirolli had played before Shaw, a fact of which Shaw was probably less mindful than he. The pianist of the quartet was a Scot from Inverness, Rae Robertson, who had been a fellow student of Barbirolli's at the Royal Academy of Music; they and Robertson's wife, Ethel Bartlett, likewise a pianist, were to see more of each other in years to come on chamber music platforms or on a conductor-performer basis. Meantime the aim was to bring Barbirolli out of himself a bit. He was serious, pale, devout (during Eastertide he made a point of going daily to 6 a.m. Mass) and, except when playing, inclined to be tense. Olof and Robertson took him for walks on Exmoor. He was an obstinate teetotaller. They tussled with him accordingly. At length they persuaded him into a moorland pub and into drinking a pint of cider. This was accounted a triumph.

Holiday ended. The theatrical round resumed. Anna Pavlova, the Russian ballerina, gathered about her a troupe of dancers and settled at the Theatre Royal, Drury Lane, with commotion, mystique and a repertory designed primarily to show what a wonderful mover Pavlova was and how fragile and poetic her personality. Her orchestra was twenty or thirty strong. Barbirolli led the 'cellos, what there were of them. His big chance was when Pavlova danced *The Swan* to Saint-Saëns' bland, best-selling 'cello solo. At the end of *The Swan* the first-night audience roared its head off. A footman brought on a sheaf of tiger lilies. Pavlova meltingly took the sheaf, divided it and strewed one half on Barbirolli, who in the meantime was taking his bow in the pit. He put one of the lilies between the pages of a book. It was there still in the library at Walton Lodge fifty years later.

From Drury Lane he moved a stonesthrow to the Royal Opera House for Beecham's third post-war international season. This kept him lucratively busy from early May until the end of July. The especial excitement that summer was the first hearing in this country of Puccini's latest, the three one-act pieces (*Il Tabarro, Suor Angelica* and *Gianni Schicchi*) which were then played as *Il Trittico*, a triple bill. The conductor, Gaetano Bavagnoli, was from Italy. As usual in mid-season the Opera House was bursting at the seams from morning until night.

For want of a better place Bavagnoli was obliged to take some of the *Trittico* rehearsals in the theatre foyer. While they were working on *Schicchi*, Barbirolli, out on the orchestra's perimeter at the rear 'cello desk, sensed someone standing behind him. He looked round and saw Puccini. The composer was in London to supervise the production rehearsals. Barbirolli had a crestfallen memory of that day: 'Puccini was once very close to me. But only literally. There he stood behind my chair, listening to Bavagnoli conduct. Bavagnoli was a fine musician from Rome Opera. And, you know, although I had bought all the scores of his operas and admired them passionately, I was too damned shy to speak to the great man. I have regretted it ever since.'

With Ambrose Gauntlett, a rear-desk partner in the L.S.O. 'cellos, he went on to a recording floor and played in Arthur Bliss's *Rout*. At thirty, Arthur Bliss, future Master of the Queen's Music, was looked upon, not altogether without reason, as a harum-scarum dog, always up to musical audacities that got his name into the papers and had to be listened to —if you wanted to keep in the swim—whether you could make sense of them or not. *Rout* (first performed in 1920) is for ten instruments and a soprano who sings meaningless syllables strung together for their abstract sound value. The thing Barbirolli remembered most vividly of this occasion is 'the devil of a job' he and Gauntlett had in getting over their 'pizzes' (plucked string passages) to the satisfaction of the recording manager: 'We ended with bleeding fingers, literally.'

They bled in an unexceptionable cause, that of the 'English musical renaissance'. At a time when, in Paris, Vienna and Budapest, musical ideas and, more to the point, music itself were being reshaped, touched with new beauty, re-aerated and generally stirred up by Igor Stravinsky, Arnold Schönberg, Alban Berg and Bela Bartok, there were some at home who, often a little touchily, maintained that contemporary English music was every bit as good and 'seminal' as foreign—or, anyway, would be if English composers were given a comparable chance, fair deal, crack of the whip and so forth. In support of this thesis a round dozen of new or newish names and established ones were cited either early in the decade or as time went on. Bliss was one of the first newcomers. Walton and Constant Lambert were imminent. Among established names Vaughan Williams and Frederick Delius were uppermost. (Elgar didn't have a look in. A zealot minority of the recently founded British Music Society, a body with irreproachable aims, positively blushed for Elgar, never mentioning his name except to chide others for praising it.) High hopes were cherished for less familiar gifts or talents: those, for example, of Arnold Bax, Gustav Holst, John Ireland, Granville Bantock, young Eugene Goossens (who, as well as conducting, composed irrepressibly), Balfour Gardiner, Frank Bridge, Josef Holbrooke. Time has done much winnowing among the foregoing and their works. A few had something of note to say in music and the technique to say it with. For the rest, England's 'musical renaissance'—a phrase that incautiously evoked the genius of Henry Purcell and the glory of the Tudor polyphonists—is remembered by this writer (and not a few others) as a porridge of folk tunes and modalism with contradictory oddments floating on top—bits of whole-tone scale, *Petrushka*-type 'wrong notes', a clatter of xylophones here, a length of seven-to-the-bar there. Pearl-grey mists straight from Debussy turned out to be Celtic twilights. Thematic pertnesses in the manner of a new French 'wunderkind', Francis Poulenc, were perpetrated by some who might better have gone to school with Arthur Sullivan.

Such was the scene, or an important part of it, on which Barbirolli found his feet and expanded his reputation as a player in chamber music and as a brain behind many 'forward-looking' chamber-music programmes. During a single year, June 1924 to June 1925, he helped to promote (as well as taking part in) first or early performances (some of which he and his platform colleagues repeated during the same season) of at least fifteen contemporary English pieces, most of them by composers listed above and ranging in calibre from 'cello and piano sonata to string sextet and piano quintet. These tasks were cheerfully undertaken and attended to with scruple. Some of them may have been thankless tasks. Alongside Barbirolli's preferred classical repertory, few of them can have been emotionally rewarding. What the case does argue is an insuperable passion for chamber music media in Barbirolli and his fellows of the Kutcher Quartet, for this was the ensemble in which he worked. He could claim, indeed, to be the original begetter of the K.Q. Here a retrospect.

As an eleven-year-old at Trinity College he fell in with another eleven-year-old, Samuel Kutcher, who was learning the violin. They took to each other at once, each agog about the other's budding musicianship, and remained friends as well as colleagues for the next sixty years. With a third eleven-year-old who played the piano they were picked to do the *Molto allegro* from Mendelssohn's D minor Trio during a banquet interval at De Keyser's Hotel (long since vanished) on the Embankment. The banquet was for musical examiners. The venerable Sir John Frederick Bridge presided over it. Bridge had first become a cathedral organist in the year public executions were abolished and, as Master of Music at Westminster Abbey, was that very month (May 1911) perfecting musical arrangements for the coronation of King George V. Bridge spoke graciously about the boys' Mendelssohn, which meant a lot. Afterwards they were given as much ice-cream as they could eat, which meant more. When the time came Kutcher went out into the world with his violin to earn a living. Until the end of 1923 or thereabouts his career as a violinist roughly ran parallel with Barbirolli's as a 'cellist. Both played in orchestras and were highly considered as soloists. And both felt beckoned as musicians to matters of higher moment and authority.

The Barbirollis now had a flat in Marchmont Street, Bloomsbury, over a chemist's shop. Kutcher was a frequent caller. They talked avidly about their newest enthusiasms and ambitions. During one of their talks they hummed and thumped favourite themes and rhythms at each other. Barbirolli suddenly broke off and said: 'Why don't we start a string quartet?' Within a week or two a quartet had been provisionally formed with Kutcher as its leader. Rehearsals began around a standard lamp in the Barbirollis' music-room. At its début and throughout Barbirolli's connection with it, the K.Q. had George Whitaker as second violin and Leonard Rubinstein as viola. Whitaker not only played in chamber music; he composed it as well. His Theme and Variations in E were in the Kutcher repertory. So, in a manner of speaking, was his celebrated dress suit, shiny from wear. Barbirolli thought the world of Whitaker and tactfully 'nannied' him. Before a concert at Woking he went round the hem of Whitaker's dress jacket with a pair of scissors, snipping away pendant shreds of lining. Before any pizzicato movement he always made sure that George had trimmed his nails.

The quartet gave pilot concerts as early as March 1924. For the South London Philharmonic Society at Goldsmiths' College, New Cross, for example, they played Mozart's No. 17 in C and, with Lily Henkel as pianist, Schumann's E flat and Dvořák's A major (Op. 81) quintets before a smallish audience who had booked ahead at 4s. 9d. each or paid 1s. 7d. at the doors. A writer in the *Daily Telegraph* felt that Barbirolli's bass line was perhaps too restrained. However, the quartet presented a united front—'a hard secret to discover'. What Kutcher regards as his quartet's true début came in June. Platform: the Aeolian Hall. Programme: César Franck in D major, the Delius and (again) Mozart in C. For this there were ten rehearsals at Marchmont Street, says Kutcher. In moments of hyperbole Barbirolli was known to confess that they rehearsed the César Franck alone for six months twice a week. The Franck opens with a chord for second violin, viola and 'cello. This left Kutcher free to leave his desk and check balance from the far end of the room. 'A touch more viola,' he would advise. 'That's just right, second violin. . . . Keep it down a bit, John. . . . Now, let's try it again, shall we?' On the night, all being set for the opening chord, John gave a signal to Sam that he wasn't ready and stooped to readjust his 'cello peg. Kutcher didn't see Barbirolli's signal to 'hold it', and Barbirolli didn't see Kutcher's signal to start, although the other two players did. The upshot was that the famous opening chord, on which so much time had been spent, went off with the 'cello part missing. Everybody wondered, a little fearfully, what *The Times* would say next morning. It said this:

We cannot speak too highly of the Kutcher Quartet's work . . . [Intonation was] flawless throughout. . . . The violoncello is an ideal quartet player, as steady as a rock, quite unobtrusive and thoroughly alive. When he was playing a sober counterpoint in the Mozart and the leader hurried him the least little bit, he raised an eyebrow in the gentlest of protests. . . . All three quartets were models of what such things should be.

Kutcher drew Barbirolli's attention good-humouredly to the raised eyebrow dig. Barbirolli laughed. So did Kutcher. And all was well.

During that first year the Kutchers repeated the César Franck at the King Cole Club's annual dinner and in an ethical society hall off Holborn. They and the tenor John Coates packed a grammar school assembly hall in Surrey with Dvořák, Debussy and Schubert's *Erl King*; took Beethoven and Delius to the Victoria and Albert Museum with acclaim; and were made much of when, with young Leon Goossens, they did Arnold Bax's Quintet for Oboe and Strings at Marylebone Courthouse, Marylebone Lane, since replaced by a residential hotel. From a cramped studio on Savoy Hill (2LO) the infant B.B.C. broadcast their Beethoven in F major Op. 18, Mozart in D minor, Balfour Gardiner (Quartet in One Movement) and Chausson (Piano Quartet in A, with Ethel Bartlett at the piano). A note in the wireless trade press complimented Kutcher and Barbirolli and rejoiced that, despite the sneers and pressures of the jazz faction, classical music was 'coming on' at 2LO. Cordial reports came in from afar. Somebody at Batley, Yorks, linked a seven-guinea loudspeaker to his six-pound receiving set in the next room and reported every note as clear as a bell.

In a snug at the York Hotel, Berners Street, the Kutchers put on seven programmes drawn from the contemporary English, French, Italian and Russian schools for subscribers who paid five shillings each and sat in armchairs. A coy leaflet said that the consumption of alcohol would not be discouraged. Fifty years ago music lovers were chary of letting themselves go. By way of encouragement Josef Holbrooke and Granville Bantock played a set of Brahms's Hungarian Dances for piano duet while smoking cigars. After this the room regularly hazed up with tobacco smoke, and glasses clinked uninhibitedly to music which, it must be said, was

not of a particularly convivial kind. The range was from
Max Reger's Op. 133 through Paul Juon's Sextet Op. 22
and Giacomo Orefice's *Riflessione ed ombre* to reams of
Holbrooke, including his *Pickwick* Quartet. It is probable that
Holbrooke's cigar-smoking act had, up to a point, been self-
promotion.

From late 1923 until well into 1926 Barbirolli played from
time to time with a second ensemble which, although successively known as the Music Society Quartet and the International
Quartet, is better named the Mangeot Quartet from its
French-born founder and leader.

At this time André Mangeot was forty or a little over, a
distinguished recitalist and teacher. Lean, twinkling and
vibrantly energetic, he had originally settled in London as a
young man with training and a personality that fitted him for
musical explorations off the humdrum track. In 1920 he set up
not only the Music Society Quartet but also the Music Society
itself. His announced aim was to present chamber music,
including 'all works worthy of performance, whether new or
old, British or foreign'. Subscribers paid two guineas for a
season of six concerts in what was variously described as, or
likened to, a crypt, a bare-walled cellar, a tobacco-clouded
vault, the hideout of some proscribed sect and a cave of
enchantment. The address was a narrow street behind Westminster Abbey. Not an easy place to find. The best way of
getting there was to skirt the Abbey, turn into Dean's Yard
and go through the archway in the south-east corner. On a
foggy night few were equal to this who had not done it before.
Deck-chairs were the only seating, and the place was dimly lit
—except when there were no lights at all; for the electricians
were amateurs and apt to be vague about switches. Yet the
crypt pulled people in. Some arrived in the afternoon for the
rehearsal and afterwards took tea with the players. The concert
proper usually ran from 5.15 to 7 p.m. The players were thus
freed for any evening job they might have with symphony
orchestras, theatre bands and what not. For their first concert
Mangeot led his fellow players to Britanny for practice in
congenial surroundings. It is remembered that Barbirolli wore
what looked like a schoolboy's blazer and an engulfing panama
hat and that his family came down to Waterloo to see him off.

The party journeyed across Britanny by motor-coach. Often the others called out to him: 'Look, John! Look at the view!' But no. John sat in a corner seat, his panama helping to insulate him from the outside world, read scores all the way and never glanced at the Breton countryside.*

For all the informality and want of starch, or perhaps because of these things, music was tended in the Westminster crypt with sobriety, concentration and style. For the César Franck piano quintet Mangeot brought the great Alfred Cortot over from Paris. At rehearsal Barbirolli and the others found yellowing music-sheets on their stands. They turned out to be parts used at the first performance of the quintet under Saint-Saëns in Paris half a century earlier. They had been given to Cortot by Madame Chausson, who had been left them by her husband, the composer Ernest Chausson, secretary of the society that promoted the concert. After the première, Chausson picked them up from the piano where they had been snubbingly left by the original players; they had found the piece 'terrible', or so asserted Mangeot, who had it from Cortot.

Into the Music Society's doings and atmosphere Barbirolli fitted admirably if not easily. He was never easy about concerts. Waiting for them to begin was mild torment. At any rate that was the impression he gave. In the artists' room at Westminster, as in those used by the Kutchers, he would sit in tension with legs crossed, jigging his free foot as ceaselessly as he tapped ash that wasn't there from his cigarette. The signal to go on transformed him instantly. He would come on with his 'cello, make his bow and take his seat with the unflurried calm of a man moving about his breakfast room on a cheerful morning. Once the music began, even when not on top form, he invariably looked in tranquil control of himself, of his instrument and of every attendant circumstance except, for better or worse, local acoustics. On two Music Society occasions, one a Rameau night when he companioned two flautists, Mangeot and a harpsichord, the other a performance of the Bax oboe quintet, critics found his bass line indistinct or swamped in rapid passages. The fault was not in Barbirolli but in the new

* André Mangeot told of this in the BBC's 'This is Your Life' programme, January 21, 1957.

platform drapes. Once the crypt had had a baneful echo. Now it wore a mute.

On an August night thirty years after these events Mangeot, looking not a day over sixty, and a spry sixty at that, gave a supper to mark his seventieth birthday. With him he brought the young 'cellist Amaryllis Fleming, whom he had been conducting that same night in her concerto début at the Promenades. It had been arranged that after supper Mangeot should lead Miss Fleming and two of his Quartet colleagues in Ravel's F major. One of the colleagues, the violist, failed to turn up. At 1 a.m. there was still no sign of him. Barbirolli said: 'André, you have a viola. Lend me it.' Mangeot brought out a viola of exceptional size with a lion's head carving instead of the usual scroll. Ysaÿe, he said, used to call it 'Zeppelin'. The other players took up their positions, and the Ravel began, Barbirolli playing the viola line 'cello fashion, with 'Zeppelin' upright on his knee. When the performance was over the doorbell rang. It was the violist. He had been having transport troubles. A second performance began at 2 a.m. This time Barbirolli was a listener. With him listened Augustus John, the artist. After the second Ravel the two of them resumed talk about old times: Chelsea poets and painters and art shows and one especial gallery where there were variegated and elegant goings-on, some of them by John Barbirolli and the Barbirolli String Orchestra.

CHAPTER FOUR

BOW INTO BATON

H IS early orchestras were small string orchestras. Woodwind and brass he knew by ear and theory but was still
chary of them technically; they would have to wait.
Strings he rejoiced in and was confident about: 'Of course I'm
an expert on strings. I play all fiddles from double-bass up-
wards. From the start I insisted on uniform bowing, not
because it looks nice, although that has its own importance.
Uniform bowing is the only way of producing uniform tone.
You produce one sound with the heel of the bow, another
with the middle, still another with the point. A mixture of
string timbres is disagreeable.' He has always held the string
choir to be the making of any first-class orchestra: 'No amount
of rehearsal will make a bad oboe play well. . . . But a lot of
rehearsal will make a string section—and, *per se*, a string band
—play well.'

We first hear of him on a public rostrum in October 1924.
His friend Lily Henkel, who sometimes played piano with the
Kutchers in chamber music, ran a Guild of Singers and
Players. At the Court House, Marylebone Lane, which we have
looked in at before, she put on six concerts during the winter of
1924–25 at five shillings a seat. Barbirolli appeared at the
first concert of the series, conducting what was called the
Guild String Orchestra. Forty years later he was asked what
they played and couldn't remember a thing. His true London
début came a year later. The old Chenil Galleries (opened
1905), in the King's Road, Chelsea, rebuilt and expanded,
had become the New Chenil Galleries, with a domed hall for
sculpture; five rooms for paintings, engravings and the like;
two restaurants with windows that gave on to a bowling green
and a biggish floor to house chamber-music audiences. After
music the floor was sometimes cleared for dancing. The

chairman of the new board was a brigadier-general. He let it be known that the New Chenil Galleries were to become *the* artistic, literary and social centre of the borough. Eight or nine hundred artists, a few established, the rest 'unknown', lived in the precincts or not far off. If the unknowns had talent enough the walls of the Chenil would be as much at their disposal as anybody's. Inaugurated with a speech by Augustine Birrell, better known to Chelsea as an amiable bellettrist than remembered as a discomfited Secretary of State for Ireland, the opening festivities lasted for three days, and the Kutchers were among ensembles, including singers of madrigals and old English drinking songs, who, at intervals, made music while viewers went on tiptoeing round the exhibits. Among these the most talked of were an Augustus John sketch of the film cowboy Tom Mix, Orpen's 'Changing Billets, Normandy', Lady Lavery's portrait of Bernard Shaw and Sir John Lavery's of Lady Lavery. The Kutchers' share included Vaughan Williams's G minor, Balfour Gardiner's A flat major, Haydn's Op. 74, No. 3 and folk song arrangements by Holbrooke. The scene as one imagines it is as remote from our day as the daguerrotype: yet the 1920s seemed extraordinarily up to date at the time.

Barbirolli made his entry at the Chenil as conductor when the new regime was four months old. He brought with him ten strings, Sam Kutcher leading again: four violins, three violas, two 'cellos and one double-bass. He explained about the lone double-bass to young Kenneth Wright, later head of music productions, B.B.C. Television, who then, as assistant to the musical director at 2LO, was arranging live broadcasts of contemporary music from the Chenil Galleries. 'One double-bass,' he said to Wright, 'is better than two, because two are never in tune, and better than three, because three cost too much.' His first programme, which opened the Chenil's concert season that autumn, and his second a month later, took in a Vivaldi concerto, a Purcell suite (*The Gordian Knot Untied*), a transcribed Bach prelude and fugue, Mozart's *Eine kleine Nachtmusik* and smaller things by McEwen and Percy Grainger. Nothing could have been defter or, within reason, more improving. A conducting career, however, is based on more than music or the way in which it is played. There is a third thing, made up of several subordinate and highly irrelevant things: the cut of the conductor's face and his clothes, how he bears himself, the quality of his smile and of his frown. In short, what sort of human being—or, better still, demigod—does he give the impression of being?

In Barbirolli's case the irrelevancies were irresistible. He was diminutive, as some emperors have been diminutive; and pale and unperturbed and a bit stern; and, in vigorous music, given to savage down-beats that made his thick hair rise and fall like a rook's wing. What of the smile? It is doubtful whether, on the platform, he used one. Music was a matter too deep, too toilsome spiritually, to smile about even when triumphantly over and people were clapping their hands off. It was his frown that denoted what music demanded of him and what it took out of him. In the 1920s, as in the 1950s and later, he had a way, when confronted by some work of high genius, of coming on to the platform with hand laid upon his heart as though overburdened by the task ahead and, while meaning to be brave, fearful of it. After the last bar he would take his bow, panting a little, with the pallor and removed gaze proper to a mortal who has been wrestling with angels.

All this wasn't music, to be sure. But it did not get in the way of the music, for it bore the music's impress and was fine in its own right, not to say astonishing. It astonished because, in his twenty-sixth year, Barbirolli looked a boy. It is not every day in the week that a boy grapples with angels. Nor, in the ordinary way, are boys expected, stick in hand, to keep an astute, evocative beat and elicit the right sort of sound. On these last points Barbirolli and his players had clearance from on high. *The Times* said their playing had precision and 'that keen and refreshing tone which is the special charm of a small string band'.

The time had not come, but was nearing, for him to put aside his 'cello. There were still sonata recitals to give up and down the country with Ethel Bartlett, everything played from memory, not a sheet of music in sight. And a splendid, resonant afternoon is remembered at Kingsway Hall. Immaculately spatted and tailcoated, he led one hundred 'cellos, pupils of his old mentor, Herbert Walenn, in transcriptions—the more

important of them his own work—of five Bach pieces: Air for
the G string, Prelude to the First Suite and three movements
from the Sixth Suite, with a Pablo Casals sardana as tailpiece.
After which, back to the stick. A fancy-dress supper took him
to the Gargoyle Club, Soho. Hosts and guests in eighteenth-
century costume drank champagne and ate wild boar. Barbirolli
and his twelve, Victor Olof leading on this occasion, played
Mozart divertimenti. They, too, had champagne and wild
boar. They, too, wore eighteenth-century costumes. These
were from Willie Clarkson's theatrical wardrobe: embroidered
coats, knee breeches, buckled shoes, wigs and what not. The
clothes fitted after a fashion and were too cumbersome to play
well in. The wigs tickled. And everybody was desperately
hot.

In April 1960 this writer had a talk with him in the room
overlooking Kingsway which he used for a while as musical
director of a commercial television company. In the dimness he
was wreathed in cigarette smoke, a haggard elf with sharp,
dark eyes. It was a bright morning. Lattice blinds were
drawn against the brightness. We talked among other things
of his drudgery in theatre pits as a youth. This is from notes
made that day.

Barbirolli: 'I was earning five pounds a week. That was good
money for 1917. And I didn't squander it. You know how
theatre bandsmen, when they have a "rest" or an interval,
slip out to the stagedoor pub? Well, I never did that. I spent
my free time in the band-room reading scores—the Beethoven
symphonies, Tchaikovsky, *Tristan, Tannhäuser.* I used to
imagine how I would phrase these works if given the chance,
how I'd shape my beat, what I'd do with my left hand.'

Reid: 'You first wanted to be a conductor at the age of four
or five. Your infant ambition hadn't been blunted by the
theatre treadmill, then?'

Barbirolli: 'Not in the least. You see, Reid, a man has to be
ready when the opportunity comes. People say I have been
lucky. Luck isn't the thing. Opportunity comes to everybody.
Be ready when it comes. That's the secret.'

Opportunity of the kind Barbirolli had in mind, that is to
say, specific opportunities which determine the rest of a career,

came to him thrice. The first two occasions didn't look much at the time. Both can be dated. The first was 14th December 1925. On that day he conducted two singers and an unnamed chamber orchestra at Wigmore Hall in excerpts from a one-act opera, *The Tailor*, words by Robert Nichol, music by a highly individual composer of Dutch origin, Bernard van Dieren (1884–1936). The entire programme was devoted to van Dieren's music. It had been promoted by a selfless admirer of his, 'that remarkable singer John Goss'. The quoted phrase is Barbirolli's. It hardly meets the case. Goss (1874–1935) was remarkable not as a singer (his baritone was of the serviceable rather than enrapturing sort) but primarily as a musical mind and will. His origins were unpretentious. After attending what was then called a council school, he worked successively as errand-boy, golf-caddy, 'bell-hop', cotton factory hand and fitter's mate. In and among these callings or later on he rounded himself off at an educational 'settlement' in Birmingham and at Ruskin ('the working man's') College, Oxford.* Taking up music with pioneering vigour, he became a professional singer in 1920. Within five years he was ensconced as the most talked-of recitalist in his chosen fields, which extended from Marcello, Hugo Wolf and unfamiliar Schubert to composers of the 'English renaissance', Elizabethan rounds and catches and traditional sea shanties, those 'coarse and vulgar songs of seamen'. Probably he was the only baritone extant who could sing shanties in a tailcoat and white tie without making his audience squirm at the incongruity of it. In much of his repertory he was supported by a male voice quartet which he was to tour with success in the United States and Canada. 'Little Johnny Goss', as he was called, not because of his compact figure but out of affection, gave much thought to others. The researcher gets the impression that when he chanced to think of himself he did so incidentally. He had sung on the same platform with Barbirolli both at the Chenil and, nearly two years earlier, at Goldsmiths' College; and from 'in front' at various times he had watched him

---

* Ruskin College, facilitated by Oxford University although not part of it, was founded to provide liberal education 'for working men and women, especially those associated with trade unions . . .' and who were financed during their studies in large part from trade union funds.

conduct. He knew a 'score-breaker' when he saw one. The
Tailor excerpts were tricky. He was relieved when Barbirolli
took them on.

The Wigmore concert began at an awkward, fashionable
hour, 8.30, and went on until 11.30 p.m. By later standards
and currency values the seat prices were stiff: 3s. to 12s.*
The programme was not of a kind that packs a house. For
the *Tailor*, Goss, who sang the baritone part himself, had
hired a second singer of repute, Megan Foster, as well as the
Barbirolli ensemble and, for other van Dieren pieces, an
established pianist, Kathleen Long. The programme entailed
much rehearsal; and rehearsals cost a lot unless performers
are friendly and merciful. From a notice (*Musical Times*,
January 1926) by Goss's friend Philip Heseltine† we gather
that Goss promoted the concert single handed, incurring
'heavy financial responsibility. . . . A quixotic act'. Goss's
reward was of the sort Don Quixotes usually reap. Next day
but one, *The Times* threw up well-bred hands. Its characterisation of van Dieren's music contained these phrases: 'Festoons of
melody which often tie themselves in desperate tangles. . . .
His trick of writing melodies in cipher. . . . Instead of writing
the notes he means he will substitute others for them and let
them stand uncorrected. . . . Piano pieces that are completely
unintelligible to the uninitiated. . . . This music has serenity,
yes—but the serenity of a fainting fit. . . .' Of the *Tailor*
excerpts Barbirolli remembered the complicated recitatives.
They were 'all very difficult', he said.

Frederic Austin (1872–1952) was in the audience: urbane
principal baritone of Beecham's opera company during the
Kaiser's War and now even more in the public eye because
of *The Beggar's Opera*. For Nigel Playfair's production at the
Lyric Theatre, Hammersmith, he 'realised', that is to say,
arranged, harmonised and orchestrated, Pepusch's skeletal

* Such fees and ticket prices, etc. as are quoted in this narrative from
the period mid-1920s to mid-1930s should be read in the light of devaluation
and, for their equivalents at the end of 1970, be multiplied progressively
from $3\frac{3}{4}$ times (1925), 4 times (1930) and $4\frac{3}{4}$ times (1935). Generally speaking,
concertgoers then had to pay a lot more. Musicians were reasonably well
paid—when they had work.

† Better known by the pseudonym Peter Warlock, which he used as a
composer.

score (1728). The production ran for 1,463 consecutive nights, was revived several times, and is still accounted the most successful in the opera's two-and-a-half centuries' history. While in the first flush of widened fame Austin was made artistic director at its founding of the British National Opera Company; and this was the capacity in which he came to the van Dieren concert. At the end he went to the artists' room.

'On the strength of my performance that night,' said Barbirolli, 'he decided I was a born conductor of opera.' Austin made him an offer on the spot. He needed an extra conductor for the B.N.O.C. If Barbirolli was interested the job was his. Barbirolli accepted there and then. For the next ten years or so he was known to the English public as an opera conductor first and foremost.

The development of his concert career must therefore be set aside for the rest of this chapter and the whole of the next.

Here a glance at British Opera as Barbirolli had known and, until the mid-1930s, was to know it. In this context British Opera means opera of any school or sort sung (whether in English or not) and staged by a company or companies of British artists (as to the regular majority) under British administration and with British money. During the decades with which we are dealing British Opera, as defined, achieved much artistically. The hopes it raised were mirages none the less. The glittering Beecham company lasted for five years (1915–20), ending in liquidation; the cumulative losses were equivalent to well over half a million sterling of 1971 money. The British National Opera Company, artistic heir to the Beecham company, lasted for seven years (1921–28) and ended up the same way. Its liquidation cast one of the minor but symptomatic glooms of the age.

Barbirolli was under no illusions. Before his first and only complete season with the company he knew it was 'on the verge of bankruptcy and that I couldn't expect anything lavish in the way of rehearsals. No matter. I saw it as a great chance. About rehearsals I wasn't far wrong. In one week on tour I did *Romeo and Juliet* (Gounod), *Madame Butterfly* and *Aida*, each of them for the first time in my life, on three and a half hours' rehearsal for the lot. It comes back to conducting as a physical gift. If I hadn't been a born opera conductor I shouldn't have survived one act, let alone up to five acts a night. We started with *Romeo*. If I hadn't had this physical gift we shouldn't have got beyond the first ten bars.' His salary rose and fell with the box office 'take' wherever they happened to be. One week he drew £12 10s., another week £18, the week after that £20. His London début with the company (January 1927) was at a noted 'perimeter' house, the Golder's Green Hippodrome. Here, as junior baton to Aylmer Buesst and Eugene Goossens, sen.,* he did a *Romeo and Juliet* and, four days afterwards, a *Madame Butterfly*, both casts being headed by Miriam Licette and Tudor Davies. The *Butterfly* was a Saturday night sell-out, with no one on stage or in the pit afraid of being sentimental—'least of all the conductor', rejoiced *The Times*. Was Barbirolli experienced enough to handle the big climaxes and 'the more rhythmical passages' dexterously enough? asked the writer. Perhaps not. He did nicely by the lyrical melodies, however, phrasing them expressively. *Romeo* won him a bouquet from the same quarter if not from the same hand. A 'spirited, expressive and precise' performance, we are told. Then: 'Barbirolli has abandoned his staccato style and improved his technique enormously. He is now able to obtain from his singers and players the effects he wants.' By 'staccato' style the writer may have had in mind impulsive over-emphasis of a kind which, as has been noted, made his hair lift like a rook's wing. Whatever *The Times* said, this idiosyncrasy, if it was the one in question, had by no means been abandoned. It took Barbirolli many years and some tribulation, perhaps, to mellow himself free of it.

Meantime there were provincial cities to visit; new operas to study and rehearse and conquer in all too little time. Birmingham, Manchester, Liverpool, Newcastle, Sheffield, Bradford: between the latter part of 1926 and the spring of 1928 all had their first sight of Barbirolli in the opera pit and sometimes on the stage at the end of a performance, linking hands for curtain calls with his principal singers to applause that ran

---

* Eugene Goossens II, aged fifty-nine, father of Barbirolli's former colleague in orchestral strings, Eugene Goossens III, at this time in the U.S.A. as conductor-in-chief of the Rochester (N.Y.) Philharmonic Orchestra.

from middling to 'thunderclaps'. (This last was a word used of the ovation after his *Barber of Seville* at the Theatre Royal, Newcastle, in September 1927.) Occasionally he would conduct a *Barber* matinée for schoolchildren. A story went the rehearsal-room rounds that after one of these a small girl was heard to ask: 'Who was that little boy who came on the stage when it was over?'

At twenty-eight he was readily mistaken at a glance, in the wrong sort of light, for twenty or even eighteen. He was highly conscious of this and did all he could by way of tailoring, owlish spectacle frames and the swing of his cane to make himself look older. On occasion he was helped by his tongue. It could be noticeably cool. One morning he found himself rehearsing a new Aida, the American soprano Rachel Morton.

'You're a bit young, are you not?' she asked. He replied: 'Not *too* young, I think.'

His casual way of throwing off such things put ten or twenty years on his seeming age. On the other hand, there was nothing his tongue could do about his stature: five feet five. A professional intimate who saw him in the presence of six-footers and knew how to read his face judged that he would have dearly loved another three inches and that this was always a matter of regret to him.

Possibly because of the Italian in him, the *Barber* and much else by Rossini were always among his especial delights. Before taking the *Barber* into the provinces that year, he tried it out during July and August, the theatrical 'dog days', at Wimbledon and the King's Theatre, Hammersmith, a week at each. A dwindled remnant of B.N.O.C. contemporaries remember his rehearsals and talk about them exclaimingly: how hard he was to please on rhythm; everything to be exact yet spontaneous; everybody (especially the chorus) watching out for dotted notes followed by demi-semiquavers. 'Watch those dotted notes! Don't come off them until the very end! And I want every demi-semiquaver like the crack of a whip!' He worked the chorus at their 'dotteds' and 'demis' until people sitting in on his sessions were on the point of wincing. Then he said they'd do. 'One thing John knows,' said an observer, 'is exactly how much to over-rehearse.' People began to call him The Rhythm King. By this time he was beginning

C*

to enjoy authority and use a tart tongue. He pulled up his Basilio during some concerted number. 'Was I flat?' inquired the Basilio, twice Barbirolli's age and one of the household names of British vocalism. 'Not more than usual', he replied. Opera in the dog days, even *opera buffa* with a text that Frederic Austin had translated, patently asked for box office trouble. Barbirolli's luck held. His *Barber* fortnight was rainy. With outdoor diversions cancelled right and left, the public would go anywhere to be out of the wet—even to opera. *The Times* called Barbirolli's *Barber* the best musical comedy of the season.

Back to the provinces, this time with an important addition to his repertory, *The Mastersingers*, which had hitherto been entrusted to Aylmer Buesst. This he conducted in Glasgow and Birmingham. In both cities there were critics who spoke their minds and were not easily pleased. The *Glasgow Herald* man was delighted. *Mastersingers* showed the company and Barbirolli at their best, he said; how splendid J.B.'s grip of singers, stage, orchestra! Seven months later (spring 1928) his *Mastersingers* reached the Prince of Wales Theatre, Birmingham (packed for the occasion). The first act came in for a slating. 'One's memory is racked in vain,' wrote the *Birmingham Post* critic, 'for recollection of a performance of the Overture so rhythmically dislocated as between strings and brass. During the first act we feared for what would follow, because Mr. Barbirolli overstressed many points and in consequence often dislocated the flow of the music.' On top of which the brass tone was strident. This was not Barbirolli's fault, however, but that of the theatre, which had no well for the orchestra.

On Easter Monday he conducted *Aida*: big house despite glorious holiday weather. The Radames was Frank Mullings, an actor-singer of genius, nothing less, as many testified, among them Beecham. Mullings off form could sing a semitone flat for minutes on end or for a whole night and rarely got through a performance without occasionally misproducing a voice which at its best was a trumpet of silver. The *Birmingham Post* critic wrote testily. It was an evening, he said, in which 'the niceties of intonation and rhythm precision were not to the fore. . . . Mr. Barbirolli conducted most ably and with care and finesse. . . . Had his indications been followed we might have had a memorable performance. . . . There were many moments

when the performance did not go at all comfortably.' Of the
chorus: 'Poor singing . . ., especially by the women. . . . There
seemed to be elements in the chorus neither ornamental nor
useful.'

A dispirited troupe, clearly. They had reason to be dispirited. Not only was this the fag-end of an exacting spring
tour. It was also the fag-end of the B.N.O.C. itself. For months
Sir Thomas Beecham had been stumping the country with
his scheme for an Imperial League of Opera. For the funding
of British Opera, opera lovers were invited to pay a pound
down and a subscription of ten shillings ('tuppence a week')
yearly. There were at least 150,000 ardent opera lovers in the
country, or so Beecham estimated—except on days of hyperbole, when he put the figure at 250,000. Frederic Austin in a
curtain speech at Birmingham was openly sceptical about his
company's future but cited Beecham's scheme as possible
salvation. A reporter asked Barbirolli for his views. Barbirolli
obliged: 'The chief trouble facing us is that support is naturally
spasmodic . . and gives no assured guarantee of anything like
permanence. We have to face difficulties that arise from
industrial depression. . . . Perplexing and often discouraging
worries . . . beset us on every side.' About Beecham's League
he was reticent. Off he went, interview over, to the Prince of
Wales Theatre and, this being Saturday (it happened to be
the concluding day of the run), conducted a double bill:
Butterfly in the afternoon (large audience) and, at night, the
Barber, 'winning the last ounce of vivacity from the gay and
sprightly music and revelling in its joyous humour'. Thus the
Birmingham Post. He had reason to rejoice if not to revel.
Although it did not go into liquidation until the following
year, the B.N.O.C. was doomed, and known to be doomed,
for want of subsidy which, whether private or public, has been
the breath of opera if not its birthright down the ages. The
year 1928 might have seen the breaking of Barbirolli as a
conductor of opera. It was, in fact, the year that led him to
the company of the great, multiplied his prestige, gave him
new professional weight and ultimately an office in which he
could throw some of that weight about.

Within a month or two of the Birmingham *Barber* he walked
into the Royal Opera House, Covent Garden, for the 1928

international season, a junior conductor still, it is true, and one among a total of eight. But several of the other conductors were of attested international rank: and one of them, Bruno Walter, like Toscanini, belongs now to the century and to musical history, an apotheosis that rarely befalls an executive musician. Barbirolli's youth and the rapt intensity of his conducting had taken the fancy of Lieutenant-Colonel Blois and his advisers. Managing director of successive Covent Garden opera syndicates for eight years from the mid-1920s on, Eustace William Blois was one of those amiable and slightly improbable figures who, during post-Edwardian epochs, held administrative reins and did their best not to run anybody down in the uncertain terrain that separated fashionable society from the arts. He came of an old Suffolk family with a baronetcy, though he was not the bearer of it, dating back to James II. His father before him having been a lieutenant-colonel, he went from a crammer's into the Army and served six pre-1914 years with the Rifle Brigade. His true love was music. Music gnawed at him. After six years he resigned his commission, studied singing and composition in Leipzig, Florence and Milan, composed *Juliana*, an opera, had it produced by the Moody-Manners* company and conducted it more than once himself. In 1914 he rejoined his old regiment, served with Salonika Force and, before being invalided home, occasionally conducted a French military band. It was through Samuel Courtauld, the rayon millionaire, that he found his way to Covent Garden. In 1925 he happened to be Courtauld's private secretary. When Courtauld decided to finance international seasons at the Royal Opera House and formed a new syndicate to that end, Blois moved into the recently vacated managing director's seat and stayed on after Courtauld decided he had had enough and others took over the headship of the syndicate. One original thing about Blois was that he looked every inch his name: tall and lean and tanned, with cropped moustache and blue eyes. The eyes might have given people an impression that he was very shrewd and a little hard

---

* The title sounds like a joke, but the company it denoted was serious enough and in business from 1897 to 1913. It was named after its founders, both operatic singers, Fanny Moody and Charles Manners (stage name of Southcote Mansergh).

but for his urbanity and charm, which were in evidence all
the time. He roved European opera houses regularly in quest
of new voices. Some did not consider him much of a judge. He
had no reason to repent his taking up of Barbirolli. Nor, so long
as the regime lasted, had anybody else. For five years the two
of them pegged away at a fearsome problem: how to make
the British at large, as distinct from the 'patrician' minority,
an opera-going and opera-loving lot.

But we are getting ahead of chronology. Back to Barbirolli's
début during the London international season of 1928.

In a season which rose, under other batons, to a *Boris
Godounov* with Chaliapin, Gluck's *Armide*, *Turandot* and two
cycles of *The Ring*, his tasks were relatively modest. With
Vincenzo Bellezza he shared five *Bohèmes* and five *Madame
Butterflys* which rang the changes on foreign singers and a small
minority of English ones. In one of his *Butterflys* a former
B.N.O.C. artist, the distinguished Miriam Licette, sang
Cio-Cio-San 'opposite' a German Pinkerton, Hans Clemens.
This happened on a 'popular' Saturday night. Box divisions
had been removed from the grand tier. Lounge suits were
seen in the stalls. And the world did not come to an end. On
the strength of Barbirolli's success, Blois extended the season
for a week at popular prices, putting on extra performances of
Bohème and *Butterfly* (with Barbirolli again in charge) and of
Aida and *Turandot*. Barbirolli had gained an envied toehold.
The critics were kindly. He came back to the Royal Opera
House a year later, again for the international season. This
time his charge was more onerous: three *Don Giovannis* sung by
names from the four corners of the operatic world: Stabile as
Giovanni; Anna Roselle, of Dresden, as Donna Anna; Elisabeth
Schumann as Zerlina; Miriam Licette as Donna Elvira; Fernando
Autori as Leporello; and Heddle Nash as Ottavio. The notices
suggest that Barbirolli got lively and true ensemble from his
variegated cast and real Mozart from his orchestra. For any
beginner but an over-confident fool, *Giovanni* is a peculiarly
intimidating work. Barbirolli's 1929 performances of it are to
be accounted the first triumph of his career.

The passing of the B.N.O.C. had left a gap which Carl Rosa,
a much older touring company and chronically penurious,

could not hope to fill. The most calamitous financial crisis in
history, or at any rate the opening phase of it, was but a few
months off. The spectres of worklessness, poverty and want
were in the wings. Who divined anything of this in the summer
of 1929? With the happy insouciance of passengers dressing
for dinner in an ocean liner that is heading for an iceberg,
entrepreneurs generally were scheming and blueprinting
away at great enterprises—operatic ones among them—as
though the world's riches were enough to go round and round
self-renewingly and for ever. The 1929 international season at
Covent Garden ended without a loss. Blois and his principal
backer—now Frederick Alexander Szarvasy, a naturalised
Hungarian financier girded with anthracite mines, cotton
mills and bank directorships—were happily startled into
setting up what purported to be a genuine national opera
company which, headquartered in London, was to supplement
the brief international seasons at Covent Garden by going out
on tour, thus providing grand opera in one part or another
all the year round, a thing for which (it was imagined) the
millions pined without really knowing it. Who was to be the
musical director and conductor-in-chief of the new Covent
Garden touring company? Obviously somebody fervent,
energetic and young, an artist to the finger-tips, somebody
who knew all the ropes and technical tricks. The choice was
inescapable: John Barbirolli.

The international season had been followed by a month's
respite. In Barbirolli's case this took the form of score-reading.
He bent and pored over scores everywhere and anywhere,
bus tops preferred, blind and deaf to what was going on about
him. At the beginning of August he and his aides, both the
musical ones and people with hammers and saws, took over
the Royal Opera House from ceiling to cellarage and prepared
for the company's first tour. They knew they were making
history and were jubilant about it. They were to take twelve
operas to eight cities* for either a week's or a fortnight's stay,
Aberdeen being the farthest north. The twelve operas were
*The Mastersingers, Lohengrin, Turandot, La Bohème, Madame
Butterfly, The Barber of Seville, Tosca, Falstaff* (Verdi), *Faust*

* Halifax, Glasgow, Edinburgh, Aberdeen, Leeds, Birmingham,
Liverpool, Manchester

(Gounod), *Cavalleria Rusticana, I Pagliacci* and *Il Trovatore*. Although under Barbirolli's supervision, 'Cav' and 'Pag', *Lohengrin* and *Faust* were allotted again to his associate conductor, Eugene Goossens, sen. Barbirolli was to see to the rest, most of the repeat performances included. In the carpenter's shop and paint rooms replicas of Covent Garden sets and backcloths were being built and painted to fit the smaller provincial stages. Puccini's *Turandot* was an exception; everything in this case was copied from models of the Milan production, the first anywhere, three years earlier. The costumes were the Milan originals. Barbirolli was very proud of that. He had with him as coach for the tour a voluble and valuable little man who, as an actor-singer of character parts (with the emphasis on acting), touched genius. Nobody who saw Octave Dua, a familiar of Covent Garden seasons back to 1907, is likely to have forgotten his Spoletta (*Tosca*), his Landlord Benoît (*Bohème*) or his Mime (*Siegfried*). On tour with Barbirolli in 1929 and later, while leading the Ping, Pang, Pong trio in *Turandot* and doing an occasional Benoît, he kept an eye on what everybody else was up to; he succeeded in giving a bit of life to the acting of many a singer whose natural bent was to turn the operatic stage into an oratorio platform with something by Mendelssohn or Spohr afoot. Overworked and delighted because of it, Barbirolli rehearsed the 'band' and the singers, sectionally or together, for nine hours a day on a sandwich and black coffee to the tinkle of upright pianos in foyer or crush room while chorus-master and repetiteurs went to work in other makeshift retreats from basement to 'flies'. A touch of the autocrat was beginning to show. A morning is remembered when the chorus confessed to not knowing their parts. The principals knew theirs and were waiting to join them in some act finale. Barbirolli was furious. Clapping on his hat, he walked out of the theatre and wasn't seen for the rest of the day. The big table from which he directed rehearsals had room for a travelling clock as well as the conductor's score. A tenor came puffing on to the rehearsal floor with alarm in his eyes and a mouth full of explanations. The time was 10.10 a.m. Barbirolli, says one who was there, looked at the clock, then looked thunder at the tenor. 'If I can be here at ten o'clock,' he told him, 'so can you!'

Occasionally a dignified, attentive old gentleman came with
him to rehearsal. When Barbirolli was ready for the rostrum
the old man would help him off with his greatcoat, a massive
'motoring coat' with outsize patch pockets, and keep it on
his knees during the music. At the break he would put the
coat over John's shoulders lest John, sweating from his exer-
tions, should take cold.

'Who's that?' whispered those who weren't in the know.

'That's John's father, Lorenzo Barbirolli,' whispered those
who were.

After five weeks of preparation a mountain of scenery was
stacked in railway trucks and hitched to the saloon coaches of
a northbound special train. Aboard it were singers, orchestral
players, stage staff and the like to the number of nearly two
hundred. Most of the principal singers and much of the
chorus were from the dead B.N.O.C. The company had not
been on the road long before sharp eyes were noting that out of
seventeen principal singers constituting the 'new' *Mastersingers*
cast, twelve had performed in the old one for the B.N.O.C.
eighteen months before. Then as to *Falstaff*. Barbirolli boasted
that they had spent four months preparing this. Yet the 1929
cast, headed by Arthur Fear, was practically the same as the
B.N.O.C.'s in 1928. It was put about, not unnaturally, that
the B.N.O.C. itself had been taken over by the Covent Garden
syndicate. Covent Garden spokesmen were at pains to squash
this technical inaccuracy. Barbirolli himself took a hand in
denying what came pretty close to the truth.

Then as to the orchestra. Advertisements up and down the
tour route made much of the fact that there were fifty players
in it. Barbirolli claimed it was 'quite the best opera orchestra
that has ever been taken out on tour in this country', no small
claim bearing in mind the best touring standards of Beecham
and, say, the B.N.O.C.'s *Ring* orchestra. He had had the pick
of first-rate instrumentalists recently robbed of work by the
'talkies', an innovation which killed hundreds of cinema bands.
Yet his jubilation has an odd ring today. What were fifty
players, however good, when pitted against scores of heavy
symphonic calibre? Later on his tone was more sober. He was
to say: 'The first opera orchestra I ever toured was, as to
strength, no more than a chamber orchestra.'

The method at that time, as it had been for long before, was to enrol a strong orchestral cadre in London and recruit 'extras' from provincial pits as you went along. Since some of the theatres played by touring opera were music-halls, music-hall pits were among the company's favourite recruiting grounds. Many a side-drummer or violist who had unoffendingly accompanied comics, equilibrists and contortionists all the year round for twenty years or more found himself translated overnight to *The Valkyrie* or *Trovatore*. Despite these augmentations the size of the Covent Garden 'band' did not always live up to the advertisements. For *The Mastersingers* even fifty players is short commons. We read of an Edinburgh *Mastersingers*, however, when Barbirolli made do with forty-five. The orchestral performance was accounted good. But that was put down to Barbirolli's 'magnetism'.

Halifax had been chosen for the start of the 1929 tour. Why? Because the local Theatre Royal seated 2,500, exceptional for the provinces, and happened to be unbooked at the time. On getting off the train few in the company could see any other good reason for the choice. Halifax proved, for those who had not seen it before, to be a hollow among the hills (Pennines) set with textile mills and their chimney stacks, palled by their smoke and made melancholy before dawn and after dusk by the wail of their sirens. Any building more than forty years old was soot-black. The hills immediately overlooking the town bore no blade of grass; fumes from below had stripped them to the clay. A town, if ever there was one, with the calloused finger of the Industrial Revolution upon it. One of the most bizarre things ever written about Halifax came from Eustace Blois: 'As I have said on many occasions, Halifax during the opera season is the nearest approach we have in England to a German Festspiel town such as Salzburg.'* At the time of the first Barbirolli tour it had just under 100,000 souls. Some of them were musical souls. They relished singing and did a lot of it, mostly in choral societies. From *Messiah* and *Elijah* to the Covent Garden repertory was something of a step. They proved equal to it. In its unpretentious way, Halifax assimilated opera—unless it was opera that assimilated

* Letter to the president of the Halifax Music Society, quoted by the *Yorkshire Observer*, 5th December 1931.

Halifax. The town showed that it could fill its Theatre Royal night after night for a fortnight on end, and this at a time when, owing to the Great Depression (which hit Halifax as severely as any community in the land), certain of the great cities were turning faint-hearted in the company's regard. The town's loyalty warmed many professional hearts, that of Barbirolli among others. He made return in two ways. He would journey to Halifax out of the season to give lectures at the Ebenezer School about operas which had not yet been produced locally. His second return took the form of chamber music. Twice he gave concerts for the local Music Society with a string quartet which he had got up from the Covent Garden orchestra. Of this more in the next chapter.

His opening night at Halifax, Monday, 23rd September 1929, was also his public début as musical director and conductor-in-chief of the Covent Garden touring company—or salvaged B.N.O.C. He was twenty-nine years old. Most of the London critics had come to hear him. Every seat was taken; hundreds were turned away at the doors including many who, refusing to take 'No' for an answer, had to be dealt with forcibly. The inaugural piece was *The Mastersingers*. Barbirolli was ready to tap the rail for the overture when latecomers made a noisy incursion to the gallery. He put his stick down and waited until the house was quiet, not to say cowed, before beginning. From his earliest conducting days he was skilled at letting an audience know what was what and who the master.

That night's performance was hard on the words. The difficulty of hearing them, complained *The Times*, was aggravated by 'the almost uniform loudness of the orchestral playing'. John Barbirolli, it was added, 'rarely gives us a *pianissimo*'. (Twenty or thirty years later his *pianissimi* had become the least audible in the business.) The *Daily Mail* man wrote of coarse brass and of strings that were hardly ever heard. He granted Barbirolli animation and talent but found him inclined to press the pace. It cannot be said that *The Mastersingers* was proving to be his lucky piece. A month later A. K. Holland, already among the musical arbiters of Merseyside and the North, wrote in the *Liverpool Post* after Barbirolli's conducting of it at the Empire Theatre:

We expected more than we got in the way of polished orchestral
playing. . . . The woodwind and the brass left much to be
desired in quality and cohesion. . . . An acutely disappointing
performance. Possibly we expected too much from the magic
name of Covent Garden. Mr. John Barbirolli's reading is
based, as it were, on the view taken at German headquarters,
that is to say, on a German performance. It is very questionable if a performance in English will stand so deliberate a
tempo, though what Mr. Barbirolli lost on the swings he
was apt to make up for on the roundabouts. The pace of the
German language is slower than ours. . . . English translation
draws attention to the fact.

In general the critics of 1929 and throughout his touring
career were admiring and cordial. He was allowed to have
drive and fire and rarely reproved for misapplying either.
Meantime the ticket-buying public—who do not always wait
to be told what to think—were making up their minds at
first hand. From the ovations he gathered at curtain-fall and
the festive stir which usually attended his appearance at the
rostrum, it was evident that the picturesque little man had
made his mark on the popular imagination. Having heard
him once, the towns and the cities did not forget; they looked
forward to his return. Especially the city of Glasgow.

Barbirolli was to bring his company to Glasgow thrice
during the first eleven months of its short existence. And there
were other good and important things in store for him on the
Clyde. In 1929 he opened at the Theatre Royal with *Turandot*.
Something of a gamble, said the faint-hearted. This was
Puccini, true, but Puccini with important differences: posthumous, completed by another hand, massively spectacular
and, thus far, unquoted (if there was anything worth quoting
in it) by teashop bands of the sort that dispensed Musetta's
waltz song four times a day. On 'the night' there were two
formidable competing lines. At the McLellan Galleries the
distinguished Budapest String Quartet was starting a week's
season with Smetana and Haydn. St. Andrew's Hall was
billing a recital by Maria Jeritza, who was blonde, opulent-
looking and by far the most photographed, written of and
talked about operatic soprano of her day. The evening turned

out gusty and wet. Who would want to be abroad in such weather? That night Jeritza sang, among other numbers, Santuzza's aria from *Cavalleria Rusticana,* Elsa's Dream from *Lohengrin* and fragments from Ponchielli and Massenet. She was accompanied by a young lady on the piano. Encores were in lively demand. She announced their titles in diffident, ingenuous English. Nothing could have been more winsome. Even so there were enough empty seats for comment in the press. Barbirolli's *Turandot,* on the other hand, drew 'an immense audience' and made 'a brilliant beginning to the season'. Jeritza confided to an interviewer how sorry she was she couldn't be there—'But I shall be there in spirit!' That *Turandot* had drawn such an attendance and aroused such enthusiasm 'in spite of the great counter-attraction of Jeritza' was very gratifying indeed, admitted Barbirolli, and, he said, reflected credit on Glaswegians' taste.

The 1929 tour lasted for twelve weeks and comprised eighty-seven performances, most of them conducted by Barbirolli. In a last-night speech Colonel Blois said: 'We set out to discover if the public wanted opera, and the results have been very satisfactory'. This non-committal sentence was taken to mean that the tour had been a financial success. Blois packed Barbirolli off to Italy for a busman's holiday over Christmas. He was to visit the 'principal Italian music-centres' on behalf of the Opera Syndicate and spot English-speaking singers talented enough to deserve a chance at Covent Garden or on tour who might be studying under Italian teachers or cutting their professional teeth in Italian theatres. In and among talent-hunting he went sight-seeing and looked up theatres and halls (including those of Rovigo) where his father and grandfather had played. The ovations which had come his way in English theatres still rang in his ear. He found Italian audiences 'curiously apathetic' as compared with English ones. Also they were smaller.

Already the capitals of the world were in the grip of financial crisis, but the effects of it had not begun to bite home. Blois had another tour lined up for him. Life seemed set fair.

CHAPTER FIVE

MARJORIE BARBIROLLI

During the next two years he went out with the Syndicate's touring company, most of the time as its chief, on six further provincial tours, taking opera in English, sung by a prevalence of British singers, to all except Aberdeen of the eight places visited in 1929 and to seven fresh ones: Streatham Hill, Golder's Green, Brighton, Blackpool, Bradford, Wolverhampton, and Southampton. A full-length tour ran to eighty or ninety performances. At first these were spread over one-week 'stands', but later Blois divided them over a smaller total of theatres into local seasons of a fortnight each, sometimes called 'festivals': e.g., the 'Midland Opera Festival' (Birmingham), the 'Yorkshire Opera Festival' (Halifax). Sooty workaday cities did not find it easy to be festive, especially on the brink or morrow of a murky winter. Nor, in towns with a lingering puritan tradition, was festivity always encouraged. Consider (say veterans) what happened at Halifax in 1929. At that time the local theatre had a 'soft' drinks café. In honour of grand opera the management thought to dismantle it and set up a liquor bar for the benefit not only of incoming opera-lovers but, more to the point, of sixty or seventy singers, fifty orchestral players and thirty stage hands. An application for a liquor licence went before the magistrates, who turned it down without comment. Drinking choruses, 'brindisis', even champagne carousings might be very well on the stage. In real life a line had to be drawn.

When it came to extending the repertory there were always the Covent Garden wardrobe and 'props' store to draw upon. With the B.N.O.C. in liquidation, operatic costumes were going elsewhere for a song. While the company were in the train for Glasgow the *Golden Cockerel* wardrobe fetched sixty pounds. It had cost £3,000 at a time when the pound sterling was relatively unsapped. More than one B.N.O.C. veteran wept tears of exasperation on learning of this.

To the twelve productions he and Goossens, sen., had taken out in 1929, Barbirolli added an operetta, *Die Fledermaus* (Johann Strauss), by which he set great store, *The Bartered Bride* (Smetana, another 'light' piece), *Rigoletto, Gianni Schicchi, Aida, Der Rosenkavalier, Hansel and Gretel, Carmen* and *The Valkyrie.* (The most momentous addition to the company's repertory and to his own, *Tristan,* came when, although he was still doing most of the conducting, the artistic supervision of the tours had passed to other hands.) At most times he had two associate conductors, on whose work he kept an eye and ear, allocating their rehearsal time and, to judge by one episode, making himself answerable *vis-à-vis* his managing director if there was any falling off in their work. Apart from the two associates he took on occasional 'guests'. The company's first *Valkyries,* for example, were conducted by Dr. (later Sir) Adrian Boult. The pressure of recording and other conducting engagements, which (as will be detailed later) ran neck and neck with his operatic work, sometimes whipped him away overnight from the provincial round. At the end of performances there was much dashing for the night train to London and cutting it fine. A conductor could not afford to be precipitate when the house was still applauding. Curtain calls were to be cultivated rather than skipped. More than once, leaping into a taxi which waited at the stage door, engine running, he beat the train guard's flag by half a second. There was a *Mastersingers* night in Glasgow when he exceeded his last previous playing time by three minutes and missed the train by roughly that margin.

By this time the Barbirolli public was beginning to be vocal. His absence irked. In the autumn of 1930 the company spent a fortnight in Birmingham. His name did not appear on the conducting rota until the tail-end of the visit. He was busy hundreds of miles away. Disappointment at his non-appearance was bruited in the newspapers. He returned to the Prince of Wales Theatre, a frowning whirlwind, on the Friday morning of the second week, perturbed by reports that, while he was away, some of the performances had not been up to the mark. He put *Rigoletto* into rehearsal at once. The theatre quivered to his keenness and scruple. That night's performance packed the place. On taking the rostrum he had a tremendous reception. 'It was as if the audience thought a deliverer had come', reported the *Birmingham Post*. The following March he compensated his Birmingham public further by conducting all fourteen performances of another fortnight's season (two of them matinées)* —a self-imposed feat which, when morning rehearsals and 'touching up' sessions are taken into account, leaves the researcher, as it left contemporaries, with an impression of fathomless energy.

It is in the nature of opera, especially touring opera, to breed casting emergencies; and it is in the nature of born conductor-administrators to rejoice in the scope such emergencies give for quick expertise. Over tea and cakes at a civic reception, Gladys Parr, the contralto, who had thought her night was free, learned three hours before *Aida* that Constance Willis, cast for Amneris, had lost her voice. 'You'll have to go on tonight,' she was told. 'See John in the theatre a quarter of an hour before the show.' Miss Parr knew the Amneris music but had not sung it since her début phase with the Carl Rosa company years earlier. Before going down to the theatre she spent two hours with the score. Amneris was in her head, note perfect. In such a situation the notes are only part of the battle. The question was whether Barbirolli's tempi and 'stick' technique would have pitfalls for her. In her dressing-room before curtain-rise he whipped through the score of the first act. From time to time he would pause on an Amneris line, jab a finger at some phrase, hum it, then say: 'I beat this [making an illustrative gesture] here'. Another pause, jab, hum and gesture: 'And I beat this there'. The 'rehearsal' was over in a matter of minutes. 'You'll be safe as houses,' he said. 'See you again before act two.' Before act two and again act four (act three being omitted because it gives Amneris almost nothing to do) he put her through summary coaching on similar lines. The performance went well.

This incident was one foundation stone among several of the early Barbirolli legend. Another was the effect theatrical crowd scenes could have upon him. Occasions were known

---

* *Aida* (two performances), *Falstaff* (2), *Fledermaus* (3), *Trovatore*, *Hansel and Gretel* (2), *La Bohème*, *The Barber of Seville*, *Rigoletto*, *Tosca*.

when, at rehearsal, if things were going with especial zest, he would climb on to the stage and take part in the crowd's goings-on. This was to occur during preparations for a R.A.M. students' season of *The Mastersingers* at the Scala Theatre in Charlotte Street, London. Geoffrey Dunn, who was the young producer, remembers a piano rehearsal of the second act with full cast. Barbirolli suddenly dropped his stick and, out of high spirits, joined the rioters in the riot scene. (When this happened he was in his middle thirties. 'But,' witnesses Dunn, 'he looked younger than most of the students, and the average age of those on the stage would be about twenty, I suppose. And they adored him. Partly because he looked—and *was*—so young. Partly because of his boundless energy.')

A rehearsal of the Syndicate's *Fledermaus* brought a similar incursion. This time, however, he had a practical point in mind. During the big waltz scene he dashed on to the rehearsal floor and, taking a girl partner by hand and waist, showed the rest what sort of rhythm and swing he was after. The producer, whoever he was, cannot have been much pleased. There are, however, borderline cases where the action so fuses with the music that it may be hard to know where one writ runs and another stops. He took such relish in *Fledermaus* as to become earnest about it. Stiff-necked people overlooked that the work had been pioneered at the Royal Opera ('grand' season 1930), against some internal opposition, by none other than Bruno Walter. For such people the thought of *Fledermaus* gallivanting in high-minded provincial cities and Barbirolli revelling in it was not altogether edifying. There were murmurs against the Syndicate for taking up operetta, and a waltzy operetta at that, as a matter (it was supposed) of box-office expediency. Henceforth Barbirolli had his knife into the 'highbrows'. As will be seen, he took to trouncing them publicly. *Tristan* remained his central ambition; he was to realise that ambition and conduct *Tristan* in two years' time. Meantime he saw no reason why he and his public should not have a little pleasure without tears. On *Fledermaus* he and his team spent 'eight weeks of intense work from morning till night'. Everybody seemed pleased with the outcome except the tiny stiff-necked minority—and, for quite different reasons,

Neville Cardus (now Sir Neville) who, after a performance at the Manchester Opera House, wrote:

> ... good fun in a romping English way. But the poise, the intriguing manner, was missing. . . . The violins did not allure. . . . Too much weight in the rhythms. . . . The brass often crashed coarsely through inadequate strings. . . . And Mr. Barbirolli is frankly not the conductor for Johann Strauss. His beat is too deliberate, being either languorous or brutal, in the style of Puccini. A conductor of Italian origin is no more likely to know the Viennese secret than an Englishman. The waltzes were frequently hoofed, so to say, to the earth.*

Cardus did not define the nature of the Viennese 'secret'.

Much has been written of Viennese string tone and its heady sweetness. Barbirolli is on record as saying in 1957 that the celebrated Viennese tone 'happens to be one of those historical myths'.† Certainly his newly conquered public seemed to get along happily without it. From Glasgow he wrote ebulliently on how things were progressing to his managing director, still 'Dear Colonel Blois' but soon to be 'My dear Blois'. By all accounts, he reported, the second *Fledermaus* night at the Theatre Royal was eighty per cent better than the first, the production having acquired the flow and facility which only continued performance could impart. A very big audience had been 'almost delirious' with excitement. Everybody who had seen the production in Glasgow talked of nothing else. Could Blois see his way to sponsoring a run of *Fledermaus* in London independently of the 'grand' season? Why not put it on at Covent Garden for four weeks around Christmas as a special holiday run? The sheer novelty of the undertaking would cause much stir. It would be a pretty safe proposition financially, he thought. Blois was not prepared to go as far as a special season but shared Barbirolli's faith to the extent of giving him five *Fledermaus* nights in the touring company's English season at Covent Garden in the autumn of 1931.

These performances were momentous for Barbirolli in a

---

* *Manchester Guardian*, 5th November 1930.
† *Chords and Discords*, by Malcolm Tillis, Phoenix, London, 1960.

double sense. They showed London a new facet of his musicianship, bracketing him in a sense with *Fledermaus*'s pioneer,
Bruno Walter. And they marked the Covent Garden début of
his fiancée Marjorie Parry, who sang Rosalinda.

A note here about the charming and accomplished artist
who became the first Mrs. John Barbirolli. Marjorie Parry
was about the same age as he but had forestalled him as a
member of the B.N.O.C. by a season or two. Her experiences
during the mid-1920s and later tell much of the summary and
sometimes hand-to-mouth way in which English opera seasons
were got together and, indirectly, what Barbirolli and others
were up against when trying to get aesthetic results on a
shoestring.

On the strength of a year at the Royal Academy of Music,
private lessons from a professor of the Royal College and an
inborn passion for singing, she put in for an audition when
touring talent-seekers from the B.N.O.C. set up at a music
shop in her native Bristol. She was heard by the company's
chorusmaster and after a test piece or two was taken on. The
chorusmaster asked hopefully whether she knew any operatic
rôles. No? Well, would she mind being in the chorus? Not at all.

Soon afterwards she was called by telegram to a bleak
rehearsal room off Shaftesbury Avenue. To the usual tinkle of
upright piano and a lot of leaping about by the producer, a
season was preparing for His Majesty's Theatre (July 1924)
during which Vaughan Williams's *Hugh the Drover* was to have
its first public performances and Thomas Beecham was to
return to the opera pit after four years' absence for *The
Mastersingers*.

Hugh is an exacting score. It gave the chorus and everybody
else so much to think about and took up so much rehearsal
time that there wasn't much left for anything else. Other pieces
in the repertory were apt to get summary treatment. The
chorusmaster would pick out a 'key' phrase in this chorus or
that. Sometimes he would content himself with a single note:
the top A natural in 'Wach auf!' (*Mastersingers* Act III), for
example.

'Whatever else you *don't* sing,' he bade, 'be sure you sing
that!'

Of the Triumph in *Aida* he said: 'I know you've not had time to get the words off. When in doubt sing *Glory, glory!*'

A number of seasoned chorus singers had been recruited from the Carl Rosa company. Their heads were full of different English translations, and they often sang their own words from their own side of the stage. The chorus wage was four pounds ten a week. But Miss Parry and several others, although in the chorus, were not accredited members of it; they sang in the back row, got three pounds a week pending promotion and did their job while learning it.

Limited casting lists led to casting emergencies, and these in turn often gave a chance to new talent. During her second season she was brought out of the chorus to sing Lauretta in *Gianni Schicchi* at less than forty-eight hours' notice. She spent one evening with her head in the score and throughout the following day was coached by Aylmer Buesst until the time came to change and go on. This was in Manchester. Manchester took to her. She was good to look at; might have stepped out of a Botticelli. 'O, my beloved Daddy' stopped the show, as Puccini intended it to. . . . Then *Falstaff*. The rôle of Mrs. Ford had been given to a soprano of some fame who, no longer up to it, withdrew after three performances. Again they turned to Miss Parry, now out of the chorus and singing leads as considerable as Elisabeth in *Tannhäuser*. No rush this time. She had all of four weeks in which to get up Mrs. Ford; and it was John Barbirolli, a relatively new face, who took her in hand, coaching her first in the solo 'line', then inducting her to Verdi's complex, hairsprung ensembles.

After *Falstaff*: *The Mastersingers*. She was a fresh-voiced and comely Eva on his opening night at Halifax and at many performances that followed. During a Covent Garden season that remains to be detailed she sang a 'boy' part, that of Jack, in a revival of Dame Ethel Smyth's *The Wreckers*. Barbirolli took rehearsals in the foyer as usual, and, characteristically, Dame Ethel insisted on attending all of them. Having listened avidly she rushed over and gave the new Jack a hug, exclaiming, 'Thank God! At last there's a singer who knows the difference between a crotchet and a quaver.'

Then *Rosenkavalier*. She made a radiant yet fiery Octavian in Act II. Of her 'Mariandl' in the *louche* restaurant scene, Act

III, somebody said that a woman has to be uncommonly
clever to impersonate a man impersonating a woman, and that
Marjorie Parry was one of the few who managed it without
seeming either or neither. One night in the first Act, during a
dialogue with the Marschallin, she came in a bar too soon.
Nothing of the kind had happened to her before. She glanced
down apprehensively at Barbirolli, who in the meantime, with
conductor's sleight-of-hand, had brought her and the orchestra
abreast. He was smiling all over his face. Afterwards she told
him how horrified she had been. 'That's all right,' he said.
'I had to smile. It proved that even *you* can make a mistake.
You're human like the rest of us!'

On all musical matters he and she thought alike; or so those
judged with whom they worked from day to day. Professionally
their affinity was complete. (Later he pressed her into service
for a whole season of symphonic rehearsals in Glasgow; he
had her sit at tactical points in the hall and let him know how
timbres were blending or balancing in passages that needed
nursing.) Soon they were spending all their time together.
'John', it was said, 'doesn't let Marjorie out of his sight.'
Clearly the affinity went beyond music. In the autumn of
1931 it became known that they were engaged. During their
courtship someone heard him say with emphasis that Marjorie
Parry was the most beautiful woman in England.

Increasing professional calls were made upon her. Blois
contracted her to sing on tour during that same autumn five
times a fortnight and to have the following fourteen rôles in
readiness: Eva, Elsa (*Lohengrin*), Mrs. Ford, Lola (*Cavalleria
Rusticana*), Rosalinda, Octavian, Musetta (*La Bohème*), Jack,
Nedda (*I Pagliacci*), Liù (*Turandot*), Margaret (Gounod's Faust),
Leonora (*Il Trovatore*), Gerhilde (*The Valkyrie*) and one of the
Flower Maidens in *Parsifal*. In one town or another she sang
for the Syndicate all rôles on this list apart from Liù and
Leonora. For her five performances a fortnight she was paid
fifteen pounds a week (increased in a later contract to twenty
pounds), each performance in excess of the basic five bringing
in an extra six pounds.

Although not negligible in terms of 1931 money, her fees
and those of everybody else with the company reflected the

financial disarray of the outside world; as did also a letter confirming her appointment which she received from the management and which is of sufficient general historical moment to warrant quoting at length.

Dear Miss Parry, . . . As you are no doubt aware, there exists at present a very severe financial crisis which has considerably limited the public spending capacity; this is likely to cause lower receipts during our opera seasons.

In addition, our Syndicate has incurred very severe losses in recent tours, even before general conditions had reached the present low ebb. In spite of this it has been decided to continue operations, provided all concerned do their best to co-operate in reducing expenses. Certain savings are being effected such as a lighter load on the railway, concessions on the part of the orchestra regarding rehearsals, etc., etc., but it is also necessary to reduce the weekly total of artists' fees. This has already been carried out on the Continent, particularly in Germany and Austria; it is being done in England in the Theatre and Music Halls and also in the Industrial Concerns; it will therefore be seen that it is an economic necessity resulting from the bad times through which we are all passing.

I feel confident that this will be realised by everyone and that the terms we are in a position to offer will be accepted. . . . . I would point out that the attached offer to you is conditional on the acceptance of the new terms by sufficient of the other Artistes to make it possible to carry out the season, as it must be clearly understood that these terms can in no way be increased.

In June 1932 Marjorie Parry and Giovanni Battista Barbirolli 'otherwise John Barbirolli' married at the Bath Register Office. They settled at Woburn Court, off Russell Square. The places where he was born and grew to manhood and lived during his first years of celebrity were close at hand, round this corner or that. He was as much a 'citizen' of Bloomsbury as Barbirollis before had been.

Lorenzo was gone. During one of the opera tours he had sent a postcard to John saying that when the company got

back to London he would be at the railway station to meet
him. John was met instead by other members of the family.
They were in tears. That morning, a Sunday, Lorenzo had
got up in good time. While dressing to go out he suffered a stroke.
They took him to the Italian Hospital in Queen Square, Holborn, where he died without coming to. John treasured
Lorenzo's last postcard. Ten years later he took it out of his
wallet to show his brother-in-law Gibilaro and said that he
would always carry it with him.

Lorenzo was gone. But Louise remained—tenacious in
affection, possessive and self-sacrificial in the same breath, set
upon keeping the entire Barbirolli clan under a matriarchal
wing. Her own flat was in a block near Woburn Court; she
had a key to John and Marjorie's flat for use when they were
away. Whether they were away or not, she was often in and
out. Not only was she Mamma. She was also 'Nonna', with
two generations to watch over. Her first grandchild, niece to
John, had been born fifteen years earlier.

No families are, or were, more tightly knit than those of
Latin stock and of modest-to-middling social origin. Usually
it is the grandmothers who keep the family circle intact and
tight. In this matter Louise Barbirolli typified a whole race or
region and its notions of domestic hierarchy. She saw to it
that under her own roof things went on in the kitchen, at table
and at the fireside precisely as in Lorenzo's day and Grandma
Rosina's and Grandpa Antonio's and Aunt Elisa's day. As a
young Frenchwoman she had been inducted to the Venetian
dialect by Lorenzo and the others. So, when the time came,
were the younger Barbirollis. In 1932, as for the preceding
thirty or forty years, Venetian continued to be the staple of
small talk and most kinds of talk when the Barbirollis got
together.

Nonna knew nothing of music, just as Grandma Rosina and
Aunt Elisa had known nothing of music. But all three were
passionately concerned about it by proxy. Season after season,
into extreme old age, Nonna would make the double journey
between Streatham and Manchester, often alone, to be with
her son on the Hallé Orchestra's opening night. Those about
her in the hall made sense of and drew magic from sounds
which must in the main have been cabalistic to her. For

Nonna the small, swallow-tailed figure up on the rostrum exuded magic enough. What need had she of Debussy's tone-scapes or the instrumental tale-telling of *Don Quixote*? When the audience thundered its affection at the end, their dins were sweeter in her ear than anything the orchestra and choir had been up to.

In her heart and to her eye, John remained, in some odd way, the engrossed thirteen-year-old in knickerbockers who had queued with her for six hours outside the Drury Lane theatre to hear *Boris Godounov*—not because he knew anything about the opera, still less because Chaliapin was singing in it, but because *Boris* was the work of Modeste Moussorgsky, who was the man who had composed *A Night on a Bare Mountain*, about which he *did* know a thing or two—transfixing, incredible things.

Such, although Nonna may not have worked it out quite like that, is musical faith. She knew John had something of the sort. And she knew, or imagined, that there were things that his musical faith and, still more, his faith in himself (a more vulnerable gift) should be protected against. One Sunday all the Barbirollis were with her for lunch. Afterwards John made off to a far room with a stack of parts to bow. Somebody asked where *The Sunday Times* had disappeared to. Nonna put her finger to her lips and said in a hissing whisper: 'Zere was a bad notteece about John. I hev put it away. It opsets 'im so.'

He was beginning to plump up, as persons of new-found consequence often do. He worried about this a little and watched his eating in the hope of getting weight off. There were days when he looked almost as old as he was. Posed photographs showed him glancing from under his brows. This gave him something of profundity, as well as a certain air of forensic penetration; it was the glance of a man who isn't to be fooled. If people—or cities—were slack, retribution must follow. In the spring of 1931, a Barbirolli tour being imminent, Manchester, of all provincial cities the one most courted by opera impresarios, became unhappily aware that it had been left off the list.

'No, we have not been to Manchester,' Barbirolli told a reporter towards the end of the tour. 'Manchester does not

deserve any opera. It has not given us sufficient support in the
past. We cannot afford to throw money away.' He expatiated
on the contrast between little Halifax, where they could afford
to spend a fortnight, and the world-wide musical reputation of
a city over seven times the size which didn't justify a visit at
all. He did not return to Manchester until the next tour
but one.

This was a time of castigations and lashings out. It has been
mentioned that he had his knife into highbrows. He railed
against musically 'superior' persons, 'highbrow cant and
criticism', and those 'chosen spirits' who, self-nominated,
wanted to wall-about the great things of music and make
them their 'sacred preserve'.*

Why the scorn? Because he felt that such people and their
pseudo-intellectual antics were all too likely to scare the plain
man from opera as something too deep or too lofty for his
understanding. The plain man was all too often given to
understand that he was beneath contempt. Let him content
himself with musical comedy, suggested his 'betters'. About
the lighter entertainments he had conducted at Covent
Garden or on tour he sounded an almost bitter note. Warning
his hearers against derogatory things which certain London
critics (unnamed) had written about *The Bartered Bride*, he
went on:

'These critics have done a lot to prevent the Syndicate
from enlarging the operatic repertory. When we tried to
produce some very pleasant works at Covent Garden and
provide a simple evening's entertainment, we were told by
some of these critics that we were wasting our time!'

It was only through simple, readily understandable works
that ordinary people could attain to the mountain peaks of
music. Yet there were influential folk who sneered at ordinary
ones for preferring, before they had time to know better,
Butterfly to *Tristan*, Gounod's *Faust* to *Pelléas et Mélisande* and,
in the concert hall, the 1812 *Overture* to, say, the Brandenburg

* The summary and quotations which follow are from an address to
the Halifax Women's Luncheon Club, 25th February 1931; an article
which he contributed to the *Birmingham Weekly Post*, 5th December 1931;
and a lecture to the Halifax Music Society on *The Bartered Bride*, 15th
November 1932.

Portrait study late 1920s, when making his name in English
opera pits and as concerto–conductor for H.M.V.

With Laurance Turner, former leader, Hallé Orchestra, 1949.
Sir John played all stringed instruments but when illustrating a
point on the violin preferred to use the 'cello position.

Concertos. '*Butterfly*? *Faust*? The 1812 *Overture*?' these people would say. 'My dear fellow, you don't call that sort of thing music?' How well he remembered the day when the 1812 *Overture* first bowled *him* over! It was from the 1812 *Overture* and such that people got the impetus to greater things. But suppose the ordinary man really went out of his way. Suppose that instead of going to Verdi's *Rigoletto* he went to Verdi's *Falstaff*. The likelihood was that he would be rebuked in his newspaper next morning for laughing at Falstaff's 'vulgar' clowning instead of smiling a connoisseur's smile at Verdi's scoring for the bassoons. (It seemed that, not long before Barbirolli unburdened himself thus, some critic had actually rebuked some luckless *Falstaff* audience in these terms.) Why, he asked, should not the plain man be permitted to enjoy *Falstaff* in his own way? Why should he be required to relish the ins-and-outs of Verdian orchestration? (A possible answer to this is that being 'educated up' doesn't serve; that the beauty of Verdi's orchestration speaks for itself to those with ears and that *Falstaff* isn't the business of anyone without ears.) A thing which Barbirolli realised and the 'superior' people overlooked was that the Syndicate only kept *Falstaff* in the repertory at 'great financial loss' (Barbirolli's phrase).

There were, he conveyed, too many people about in opera foyers who flipped dismissive hands at the mention of anybody whose stature dwarfed their own. He mimicked their drawlings: 'Chaliapin? Well, yes, but his voice isn't what it used to be.' ... 'Beecham? He conducts like a dancing dervish.' ... 'Heifetz? Never heard such expressionless fiddling.' ... 'Kreisler? Too sentimental by half.' ... 'Paderewski? If only he wouldn't thump and play wrong notes!'

There had been talk of Beecham's return to Covent Garden and of his collaborating with Szarvasy and Blois. Whatever the approaches, they came to nothing. The gossips turned to other themes, among them Barbirolli's reappointment (summer 1930) by the Covent Garden Syndicate as musical director. This was regarded as confirming Barbirolli's whip hand and as putting Beecham somewhat in his place. Of Beecham the artist he always spoke warmly, however. They happened to get on well with each other professionally. It did not follow that he was committed to the League of Opera. Beecham and his lieutenants were canvassing this project as sonorously as ever. Sometimes they gave the impression that their feet were not altogether on the ground. Barbirolli publicly praised the Covent Garden Syndicate as the breath of opera-goers' and operatic artists' nostrils and lauded the Syndicate's chairman, Szarvasy, who, he disclosed, had 'put his hand in his pocket to the extent of £50,000. What did some of the critics do? They practically insulted Szarvasy. Beware of insulting this gentleman. If you go on insulting him you'll have no opera at all. If we go you'll have nothing. . . .

'There has been a lot of talk lately about another organisation, talk of a rather grandiose and nebulous sort. . . . It is time somebody stopped it. I refer to the League of Opera. I was present at a meeting some time ago when people were told—and they cheered heartily—that instead of entrusting themselves to people like us they could have something marvellous and magnificent in something under five years. They were told that the promoters of this scheme would produce seventy-five new operas. If you stop to think, that means producing fifteen operas a year. If the organisation plays for twelve months of the year—which has never been done by any opera company in any country of the world so far—it means producing more than one opera a month. Frankly it is nonsense. *Die Fledermaus* took us eight weeks of intense work from morning until night, *Falstaff* at least four months. We must stop talking nonsense and get down to the real facts. In this jazz and cinema debauched age, the Syndicate not only keeps the works of the great masters alive; it is also keeping British artists and musicians alive. . . .'

The lean, bewildered years were come. Bills were going unpaid. Belts were tightening. Even so, opera went on travelling, at the expense of its backers. It could not hope to make money or even ends meet without playing to something like full houses. In the provinces during 1930–31 the Syndicate played to four, or nearly four, empty seats out of ten. Most of the empty seats were the higher-priced ones. Things looked black. Blacker was to come. In a fumbling way Whitehall tried to help. The Syndicate were promised £17,000 from the G.P.O.'s wireless licensing revenues provided their box-office takings exceeded certain minima. In short, the less money they took from the public the less they were likely to get from the Government. Even if the subsidy had been unconditional Barbirolli would not have been impressed. Much had been made of Whitehall's generosity, he commented, in 'these terrible times'. But the subsidy, if it happened, would be just about equal to what the Syndicate had paid in entertainment tax, a mere remission. Let it not be forgotten that entertainment tax bills of £78,000 had, in effect, been the death of the B.N.O.C. As taxpayers, opera companies helped to pay for other arts. Did people, he asked, reflect upon the National Gallery? Upon the £100,000 of taxpayers' money spent yearly on the upkeep of 'a place used by people to court in because of its emptiness'?

In mid-September he took what was ordinarily the Syndicate's touring company to Covent Garden for a six weeks' season of opera in English. Let the snobs look down their noses as much as they pleased. Most English people, Barbirolli maintained, wanted opera sung in their own language, just as most cultivated Germans preferred Italian opera in German and cultivated Italians German opera in Italian, whether our own snobs were alive to the fact or not. There were forty performances that season. He conducted twenty-seven of them. One guest conductor (Adrian Boult) and one associate conductor saw to the other thirteen. Only one piece was heard which the company had not sung before. This was Ethel Smyth's *The Wreckers*, cited earlier in this chapter, well-made, unmemorable music to a sardonic though turgid libretto about a Cornish village where the profession of wrecking was practised and enjoyed as a social and moral duty. It had been heard under Beecham at His Majesty's Theatre a generation earlier. The original scenery had been exhumed from some cellar and eighty pounds spent on adapting it. Barbirolli conducted three performances of *The Wreckers* and was told by the *Birmingham Post* after the first one that the very foundation of a good operatic performance, namely fine orchestral playing, had been sadly wanting. The notice went on: 'In spite of Mr. Barbirolli's tremendous efforts—or was it possibly because of them?—the playing was terribly rough and unready.' Such strictures were rare, the critics for the most part being

benevolent—and wistful. The wistfulness was accounted for by
the disheartening attendances; the most case-hardened writers
of overnight notices could not but feel a pang. Seat prices
were half the usual 'grand' season prices, and commentators
conceded that seat buyers were getting performances which
were more than half 'grand' season value. But who, asked one
of them, could in times like those afford to pay fifteen shillings,
twelve-and-six or even eight-and-six? One good thing was to
be said, in spite of all, for the highbrows, the superior people
and the snobs. Once *they* were on your side and vocal about
you, people anxious to do the fashionable thing would come to
you in droves, even under the sign of social calamity, because
scared to ignore the highbrows and stay away. The trouble
with the English season was that 'No one hears of it. . . .
Nobody pays any attention.' The report ran that most nights
Covent Garden was half empty. Even this was more than the
fiscal truth. Receipts turned out to be only 25 per cent of
capacity. The season had been a disaster.

Back to the provinces without respite: a fortnight each in
Glasgow, Edinburgh, Birmingham, Liverpool. Then, in the
opening months of 1932, a fortnight each in Streatham Hill,
Golder's Green, Halifax, Manchester. Complaints came in
from needy, frustrated opera lovers. An Edinburgh example:
'At *Die Fledermaus* the other night the gallery of the King's
Theatre was only a quarter full. What do you expect? Half-
a-crown and two shillings seem stiff charges for the pleasure of
sitting on a plank and must have deterred many. One can have
comfort in the upper circle for three-and-six, but how many can
afford to attend as often as they would wish at that price?'
The Syndicate showed every sympathy. They deserved a
little themselves. On the autumn tour alone they lost £8,000.

What Covent Garden needed, whether at home or on the
road, was a name, a face and character-flourishes known not
to coteries and specialists merely but, of long date, to the
country at large. The need, to put it briefly, was for Thomas
Beecham. The Syndicate had long hankered after his collaboration. At first his mind was excludingly set upon his League of
Opera. If the League prospered he would not need to col-
laborate with anybody. But for all his drummings and
optimistic devisings the League went haltingly. Early in 1932,

Blois having made another approach, he yielded and, during
the summer, returned to Covent Garden as its principal
conductor. He was to stay on as artistic director until the
outbreak of Hitler's war.

His first season (May–June 1932), a short Wagner festival
with a much stronger infusion than usual of English talent into
polyglot casts, comprised two *Ring* cycles, *Der Fliegende Holländer*,
Tannhäuser, *Tristan und Isolde* and *Die Meistersinger*. Of this last
there were four performances, and Beecham shared them with
Barbirolli. In grand seasons, of course, everything was sung in
the original texts which, according to the lie of the words and
the syllables, had different musical phrasings and demanded
different 'breathing' as compared with the English translations.
Beecham having defected from one of his *Meistersinger* through
indisposition, a substitute had to be found. That is where and
how Barbirolli came in. He did so at very short notice—a
matter of hours, not days. He had never conducted a German
Meistersinger before and felt trepidation at the prospect. The
one who, in what time could be snatched, helped him over the
linguistic and other technical stiles was his Eva, the adorable
Lotte Lehmann, to whom he was for ever grateful. Always she
took her expertise lightly, laughing at it, as great artists will.
About the Quintet, Barbirolli had more misgivings than ever.
'Where,' he asked, 'do you "breathe" in the Quintet?' She
replied with the gayest of smiles: 'I breaze everywhere all ze
time.' After that nothing seemed very menacing. Barbirolli
not only survived his double-harnessing with Beecham. He
also won many compliments. But his sway over the touring
company was nominally curtailed. It had been put out by
the Syndicate that Beecham would generally supervise the
tour as artistic adviser and conduct occasional performances.

They were on the road again in October: Glasgow, Edinburgh, Halifax, Manchester. On the opening night of the
tour, in Glasgow, Barbirolli conducted *The Rosenkavalier*.
During an interval Beecham appeared on the stage and made
a jaunty speech about the new operatic peace pact, which
looked like lasting for a week or a couple of minutes at least,
and about the great things they might expect from the League.
The following night he was to conduct *Tristan*, a prospect
which Glasgow had been breathless about for weeks. Yet this

opening night was distinctly Barbirolli's night and almost a
gala occasion. An uproarious ovation at the end was so graded
that, while the *Rosenkavalier* principals and the orchestral
players got their meed, the crown went indubitably to the
conductor. Beecham might belong to the nation but Barbirolli
was peculiarly Glasgow's, a fact which was to be illustrated
even more strikingly within weeks.

Beecham's *Tristan* left the cognoscenti in a dream: rather a
troubled dream when it came to the stolid pseudo-acting (as
distinct from the lustrous singing) of the new Isolde, Florence
Austral, and the Tristan, young Walter Widdop. *Tristan* was
sung again during the second Glasgow week, and this time the
stick was Barbirolli's. Here was the heady privilege he had sighed
after from boyhood. Again the two voices had strength. And
they shone. But what did their owners know of Isolde and
Tristan and Richard Wagner in the sense that Barbirolli knew
these three? As he gesticulated and toiled in the pit, the gap
between his conception and their relative imperviousness pointed
a moral at his own expense. He had said that if a man could
play an instrument well it was up to the conductor to turn that
man into a good player. What applied to instruments applied
also to voices, surely? Not in this case, apparently. His toil
was judged to be in vain. It evoked little or nothing to match
from the stage. And the fault was not in him. What he did
evoke was fine orchestral playing, despite an undermanned
string choir. 'From the very first bar of the Prelude, rendered
with a slight *rubato* which increased its poignancy to remarkable
effect, it was evident that Barbirolli would extract the last
ounce of eloquence from the score.' Thus the *Glasgow Herald*
critic. The clamour at the end was as fervent as after *Rosenkavalier*; as after Beecham himself, in fact. That night was one
of the marker-posts of his life. Remembering it thirty or
forty years later he would say, 'I shall never forget' and,
falling silent, smile upon the past.

The sands were running short, and not many knew it.

Two weeks in Edinburgh were followed by two in Halifax,
with a repertory of seven pieces, all of them sung twice over.
The theatre sold out every night, a preternatural thing; the
town seemed slump-proof. On the first free Sunday night he
took his quartet, calling it the Royal Opera String Quartet, to

the assembly hall of a smart new 'Secondary' school and, as a treat for the local Music Society, played the Haydn No. 5 in D, the Kreisler in A and the Dittersdorf in E flat. During the preceding week they had rehearsed this programme for thirty hours on top of regular morning rehearsals, six evening shows and one on Saturday afternoon. 'I don't think,' said Barbirolli, 'that I ever worked harder or kept more disreputable hours or felt better in my life!' The season ended with *Butterfly*. His curtain speech said how happy they had all been in Halifax, in a sense the touring company's cradle. He added: 'I don't know what the future holds for us.'

He had a pretty good idea what it held all the same. On reaching Halifax the company had received a circular letter from the Syndicate saying there would be a six weeks' spring tour starting at the end of January 1933. A few days before they left Halifax a notice went up on the call board saying that the spring tour would not take place and that the contracts of all the artists would terminate at the end of the current tour. The news did not become public until after the terminal night in Manchester something over a week later. It caused consternation. The better part of two hundred musicians and technical staff were thrown out of work. In pinched, oppressive times a fount of beauty and marvel had been cut off which, although accessible to relatively few, stood for many born without the taste for it as a symbol of what was called, a little hopelessly, the good life.

Soon after the last night in Manchester he was back in Glasgow. He had momentous business there. It did not look much at the time. The Choral and Orchestral Union had posters out giving their arrangements for the 1932–33 concert season. There were to be two conductors: Albert van Raalte, a Dutchman, and John Barbirolli. The Union ran the Scottish (now the Scottish National) Orchestra, and this was the more important part of their purpose. On the last night of 1932, van Raalte having concluded his half-season, Barbirolli opened the second half-season by conducting one of 'the usual popular orchestral concerts', in St. Andrew's Hall. His programme, which began with a Purcell-Barbirolli Suite for Strings, had Brahms's Symphony No. 2 as its centrepiece, the *Blue Danube* Waltz as a sweetmeat and Berlioz's *Roman Carnival* as its 'curtain'. A comfortless night of rain and mud. Classical music has strong counter-attractions in Glasgow on Old Year's Night. Attendances at Saturday night 'pops' had not been up to much latterly. The audience for Barbirolli, however, was 'big', 'unexpected', 'gratifying'. Those were the reporters' words. Old Year's Night 1932 marked a new beginning. The rest of his career was a logical unfolding from it.

CHAPTER SIX

VICE BEECHAM

IT is time now, retracing four or five years, to give some
account of his beginnings and early laurels as a conductor
of symphony orchestras and, especially during the 1930s,
of concerted recordings which involved him with instrumentalists and singers of the first eminence. The making of 'symphonic'
conductors has rarely if ever been a matter in this country
of academic qualification and foreseeable promotion. Self-help
and luck enter into the matter; and, often enough, luck means
somebody else being taken ill or breaking a leg or missing the
last train. So it was in Barbirolli's case.

Sir Thomas Beecham was to have conducted the London
Symphony Orchestra at the Queen's Hall on Monday, 12th
December 1927 in the following programme: Symphony in
C major No. 37, Mozart; Concerto for Violoncello and
Orchestra in D, Haydn (with Pablo Casals as soloist); and
Symphony No. 2 in E flat, Elgar. In his day Beecham had
ruthlessly hacked Elgar's No. 1 (A flat) in performance,
reducing its playing time from an average of fifty minutes to
thirty-five, and had derisively likened Elgar's music generally
to the façade of Euston Station,* this at a time when Euston's
famous portico still stood. All things considered his choice
of the E flat was challenging, almost piquant. Did he, perhaps,
repent it? Five days before the concert it was announced that
during the afternoon (Wednesday) he had suffered a fall in a
West End street. Although painful, the accident was not
serious, but he had been ordered a complete rest for a day or
two. He spent much of the day or two orating publicly or
privately about his Imperial League of Opera. Who was to

* Not long before his death he committed this absurdity to video-tape.
It is said that he sometimes varied the simile, mentioning St. Pancras
Station.

conduct Monday's concert in his stead? From Wednesday
evening onwards the L.S.O. management cast about in some
consternation for a substitute. The notice being short and the
season at its height, they had some difficulty. They were
hunting still the following day. At length somebody mentioned
Barbirolli—'Why not give young John a chance?' As a deputy
(i.e., not as a regular member of it), Barbirolli had played
'cello in the L.S.O. from the age of seventeen until his middle
twenties. Since the L.S.O. was a self-governing body, he was
on personal terms with most of the director-players who ran it.
'Why not give young John a chance?' was a friendly, natural
and highly audacious question. It is to be admitted that the
London Symphony Orchestra had much to be audacious
about. A lunatic system then prevailed under which regular
players, having attended sparse rehearsals—and scored up pay
for them—could, if a more attractive assignment offered,
absent themselves 'on the night' and send along unrehearsed
'deputies' to sit in for them. Thanks to this abuse and to
chronic financial stringency, orchestral playing in London
was at low ebb. Ernest Newman had written of the L.S.O.,
'our premier orchestra', that it compared not unfavourably
with the orchestras in some of the New York picture houses.
This gibe, nearly three years old, had some truth and therefore
some sting in it still. How a symphony orchestra could and
should sound had been electrifyingly proved that very winter
(November–December 1927) by the Berlin Philharmonic
Orchestra, the first German orchestra to visit Great Britain
after the Kaiser's War. The Berliners' playing under a new-
found genius, Wilhelm Furtwängler, had timbres and a precision
beyond most London concertgoers' dreams. Piqued and
spurred by a unison of adulation which they regarded as
an implicit snub for home talent, the L.S.O. directors said to
themselves and each other: 'The Berliners aren't the last word.
Let's show 'em what an English orchestra and a young
English conductor can do.'

On Thursday afternoon the Barbirollis' telephone rang. It
was an old-fashioned telephone fixed to a wall in the vestibule.
It had a separate earpiece and a little desk for making notes on.
Because of the part it played in his life Barbirolli could see
every detail of it two generations later. A voice at the other

end said this was the L.S.O. and could John stand in for
Sir Thomas on Monday? For the moment John could do little
more than gulp, stammer and temporise. He checked over the
programme and reflected rapidly. Mozart's No. 37 in C? Not
insuperable. And not essential. If necessary he could get them
to substitute a Haydn symphony. He knew all the 'known'
Haydn symphonies inside out. Nor would the Haydn 'cello
concerto be any great trouble, even with the great Casals on
the job; he had often played solo in it himself. But Elgar's
E flat? *There* was the rub. He had played in this long and
complex symphony more than once as an orchestral 'cellist.
But he had never seen the score. He was completely without
conducting knowledge of it. No, the thing was impossible. He
began explaining to the voice at the other end just how impossible. Then he became aware that Lorenzo Barbirolli was
at his elbow, whispering Italian swear words. Lorenzo had
taken in the situation and was furious. His son put his hand
over the mouthpiece to hear him more freely. 'Don't be a fool,'
hissed Lorenzo. 'You'll never get another chance like this.
Take it!' John did as he was bid. As he put it later, 'I capitu-
lated'.

One change only was made in the Beecham scheme.
Mozart's No. 37 in C was taken out and Haydn's No. 104 in D
(the 'London') put in. There were to be rehearsals on Sunday
morning and on Monday morning. Before the first rehearsal
he had three nights and two full days to get the E flat into
his eyes and memory, analysing its 'meaning' as he went along.
In fact he had it off by heart in less than forty-eight hours.
To manage this he went practically without sleep for two
nights.

While he had his head down that week-end Beecham hobbled
with two sticks on to the Queen's Hall platform at an Opera
League rally, got a great laugh by saying he could stand up
but not sit down—'a curious sensation I have not experienced
since I was a small boy at school'—and, after praise for his
pre-1914 Beecham Symphony Orchestra, 'described by every
foreign musician visiting this country as the finest orchestra in
Europe', asserted that in the whole of Britain there was not
now a single orchestra whose members were earning their
living by playing good music. (As everybody knew, they were

earning it in part by playing inferior music in cinema pits and elsewhere. How many potential ticket-buyers did this cold douche keep away from the concert he was to have conducted three nights later?)

At Sunday's rehearsal it was clear that Barbirolli had mastered the text of the symphony. By Monday morning he had ideas of his own about the symphony's emotional purport and the dynamics it called for. When veteran players thought to give him certain technical wrinkles, W.H. ('Willie') Reed, the L.S.O. leader, a man of high professional prestige and a familiar of Elgar, said to leave well alone—'John already knows what he wants to do. Elgar might even *like* it!'

The concert ended in enthusiasm and cordial noise. Barbirolli took his calls and walked off into the Queen's Hall wings. A little man with a congratulatory smile and shrewd eyes behind spectacles was waiting for him among the rear desks of the first fiddles. He said: 'My name is Gaisberg. I am from H.M.V. Don't sign any contract. I'll see you in the morning.'

Fred W. Gaisberg is a name that echoes still down the corridors of recording directors and recording accountants the world over. A quarter of a century before Barbirolli's conducting début at the Queen's Hall he had prevailed upon the tenor Enrico Caruso to sign a contract which, in twenty years, made Caruso one million pounds and what was known then as the Gramophone Company two million pounds. By this time he was the world's busiest gramophone impresario—and as intent on new talent as any beginner. It was naked anxiety not to let Barbirolli slip which had driven him to sentinel duty among the fiddle desks. He needed 'a first-class orchestral accompanist for opera as well as concerto recording. I knew I had found in John Barbirolli a gifted and practical man.'*

The talk with Gaisberg, which had been fixed provisionally for the following morning, must wait a little. Before attending to it Barbirolli had other matters to digest; and so have we, namely what the newspapers said about his conducting of the L.S.O.

There are few professions whose members see eye to eye on all matters all the time. If doctors disagree it is usually under

* This and other relevant quotations are from Gaisberg's memoirs, *Music on Record*, Hale, London, 1948.

the cloak of professional secrecy. When pleading lawyers disagree they commonly do so in public. Disagreement is, indeed, expected of them, and they are usually well paid for it. With music critics the case is different. Although as much in the limelight as pleaders they rarely get paid as well, and when they disagree radically, as sometimes happens, much offence is taken, especially by musicians of the impulsive sort, who sometimes swear they'll read the critics no longer, a threat they rarely persevere in. It is certainly the case that if he takes critiques in pairs the reader sometimes wonders, despite coincidence of time and place, whether the writers are writing about the same concert. It fell out thus in Barbirolli's case. The critiques in the *Daily Telegraph* and *The Times*, both anonymous but clearly by senior hands, are so dramatically at variance that I print the essence of them in parallel columns for direct comparison:

The opening of the Haydn Symphony in D . . . gave us hopes of a really good performance. But these hopes were unhappily dashed when we arrived at the *Allegro*. A not unnatural nervousness may explain Mr. Barbirolli's excessively jerky manner, although we know that this is not a new fault of his. The result was a lack of flow in the playing and, moreover, a lack of modelling in the details. The absence of these two things was even more disastrous in Elgar's symphony, where the phrases need the most careful shaping, and the general current of the music must be kept moving steadily onward by means of a nice adjustment of the parts, both vertical and horizontal. That is to say, the balance between the various sections of the movements, especially in the matter of *tempo*, must be thoroughly studied. The *tempi*, especially in the first movement, had not been given this consideration, with the result that the music sounded heavy and

Haydn's 'London' Symphony was at once finished and vigorous. From the moment when the violins turned the opening subject of the *Allegro* with a suave, easy beauty . . . one realised that Mr. Barbirolli knew what he wanted and was able to get it. But there was no mere point making, and a fine performance left one admiring the youth of the conductor and not oblivious of the maturity of the composer. The Elgar E flat Symphony . . . presented a more difficult problem. It is a long work, heavily laden with what one may call emotion, and to make it tell as a whole a conductor has to keep a tight hand on the orchestra and himself. Mr. Barbirolli came through the ordeal successfully, moments of special beauty being the brilliant climax of the first movement and the *diminuendo* which marks the coda of the finale. His skill in keeping his forces in control also showed up well in the third movement, where the complicated rhythms were admirably turgid instead of being, with all its faults, vigorous and brilliant. For the first time in one's experience the most magnificent pages in the slow movement went for nothing. —*The Times*, December 13th 1927.

brought out. Mr. Barbirolli has few personal idiosyncrasies, and his beat is always indicated in a straightforward way. With more experience he will doubtless make greater use of his left hand, for a modern conductor has to be ambidextrous.
—*Daily Telegraph*, December 13th 1927.

Somewhere between these extremes comes a note in *The Musical Times* (January 1928):

Mr. John Barbirolli, hitherto unknown on the Queen's Hall rostrum, stepped into Beecham's shoes at short notice— a piece of daring on the part of a young man, for the symphony of the evening was nothing less than Elgar's in E flat. But Mr. Barbirolli proved himself to have the confidence of ten.

The performances were a series of brilliant improvisings. A young man who can pull off such an event should go far. Judged without allowances, Mr. Barbirolli's Haydn was brutal and his Elgar a torrent. Mr. Casals gave us the only serene moments of the evening in his concerto. But the young conductor let no one go away without knowing he had talent, audacity and a remarkable will of his own. It is good that youth should now and then be allowed a fling. The world in general is all too much in the hands of middle age.

How did the incomparable Casals come out of the battle? According to Gaisberg, Barbirolli regarded him from the rostrum 'with misty eyes eloquent of a lover who can never aspire to attain his love'. It is not certain, however, whether Gaisberg was writing here of the 1927 concert or some performance on the recording floor. *The Times* gave the performance short shrift: 'Of the concerto we prefer to say no more than that the conductor had evidently not had the opportunity of absorbing the soloist's views of the work and that Mr. Casals attempted to conduct it by proxy.' Richard Capell (*Daily Mail*), while complimenting this 'bright young man' upon his magnetism, upon his knowing the Elgar well and upon having

well-defined views about it, found his touch in the Haydn
symphony 'military and drastic'. Casals' solo-playing, he
added, was a soft and smiling reproach to the dashing young
conductor's parade-ground style.

Elgar did not get to the concert; but Barbirolli gave this
account of a sequel to it: ' "Willie" Reed must have written
or telephoned to him about it, because two or three days
later I got a large envelope superscribed "The Master of
the King's Musick, Buckingham Palace".* Inside it was a
note from Elgar saying: "I must thank you for what I hear
was a magnificent performance".'

With the challenge over and assorted verdicts, flattering,
middling or adverse, taken to heart or discounted, Barbirolli
retained one great good that outlived them all: a mystic regard
for the E flat Symphony. What its peroration meant to him
he summed up most eloquently:

> I am always very deeply affected by the last movement. I
> can never reach the end of it without shedding a tear or two,
> be it at morning rehearsal or in the afternoon or at the
> performance in the evening. There is a nostalgic feeling in
> this music, as of the end of an era. It is a full close. It tells of
> a way of living that is no more, a way that I knew something
> of as a child. During those closing pages I think of Sir
> Edward Grey's words the day before the '14 war was
> declared: *The lamps are going out all over Europe. We shall not
> see them lit again in our lifetime.* For me, infallibly, those lamps
> are fleetingly relit by the flame of Elgar's genius every time
> we reach the end of the E flat symphony. A sublime piece of
> music. It is part of my heritage and my life.

Something over a year later a conducting engagement
came his way which was in the nature of a minor public
honour. The venerable Royal Philharmonic Society, who had
been patrons of Ludwig van Beethoven during Beethoven's
lifetime and of Felix Mendelssohn during his, awarded him
the fourth concert (out of eight) of their hundred-and-seven-
teenth season. This fell on January 17th 1929. The Society's
first approach stunned him somewhat as the L.S.O. telephone
call had done. This time, however, he made up his mind

* Elgar succeeded to the Mastership in May 1924.

gleefully and without delay. The Society gave him to under-
stand he would have some say in what music he was to conduct.
The following programme was fixed: Concerto in E minor for
Strings, Vivaldi; Concerto for Violoncello and Orchestra,
Delius (soloist: Alexandre Barjansky), Symphony in G (the
'Oxford'), Haydn; and Suite, *La Mer*, Debussy. 'And the last
shall be first.' *La Mer*, needless to say, was his own choice.
As will be remembered from Chapter Two, he had known and
adored this score since adolescence. The moment the concert
was bruited he said to himself: 'Ah-ah, the Royal Philharmonic!
Here's my chance at last to play *La Mer* and get it out of my
system.' (It was to stay in his system and pervade his programmes for forty years.) He was allowed two rehearsals only
for the entire programme. 'At that time,' he said, '*La Mer* was
still practically unknown to English orchestras. To do anything
like justice to it on a two-rehearsal basis was out of the question.
So I asked, could I have an extra rehearsal for strings only? The
strings are the greatest problem in *La Mer*. The wind, after all,
are soloists, and if you've got a good crowd you don't need to
work on them to anything like the same extent. But the string
backgrounds must be absolutely unblemished. To get unblemished strings takes time. I explained all this to the Society.
They said, Sorry, an extra rehearsal was financially impossible.
A thought struck me. I inquired what the cost of an extra
string rehearsal might be. It came to almost exactly my fee.
So I grandiloquently—and perhaps rather impertinently—said:
"Well, I will pay for the rehearsal". Which I duly did—and
had the great joy of preparing and playing one of the *miracles*
of music, for *La Mer* is no less.'

In sprucing up the string parts of *La Mer* he showed a
watchmaker's care for minutiae. He took apart and put
together tirelessly. There is a longish passage near the beginning
for divided second-violins and divided violas, the whole
producing a supple, quick-running pattern in four-part
harmony. Other things are happening on other instruments
at the same time, including an important tune-line; but the
other things, he argued, do not properly tell unless the accompanying *divisi* are polished, fluent and exact. To get what he
wanted he always worked separately on the two halves of
second-violins. Then he fitted the two halves together and

worked on them as a section. The two sections of violas were rehearsed in the same way: one at a time, then together. 'Finally,' he used to say, 'I take the four parts together. You know, orchestras have been playing this passage for years. [He was speaking thirty-five years later.] But when they hear it absolutely as it's written they give a gasp of surprise—and I give a gasp of relief.'

Such was his joy in the Society's strings that he retained the lot of them for Haydn's 'Oxford' Symphony, a work which, to some tastes, invites a smaller body. 'The privilege of hearing ten double-basses, supported by ten 'cellos, thunder out the bass line of a Haydn minuet is a rare but hardly enviable one.' That is how Ferruccio Bonavia saw the case next morning in the *Daily Telegraph*. For the critics in general *La Mer* was the piece that came out best. It was this that 'proved his talent' (Richard Capell, *Daily Mail*); evoked the best playing of the evening, evoking spirit and 'a wide range of colour' (Bonavia); 'got vigorous direction from him, as a result of which the music's orchestral effectiveness was well displayed' (*The Times*). The grumbles were of a sort that had been heard or hinted at before. Here was a young man addicted to rigour and emphasis. He ran some danger of having critical labels gummed on to him. Capell felt that Haydn's 'Oxford' Symphony had been kept on much too tight a rein. Of the Vivaldi concerto for strings, Bonavia complained that the players seemed to lose sight of stylistic considerations; an 'uninspired performance' gave the bare bones of the music, nothing more. Of the same performance *The Times* said: 'It reminded us of a fault which has been noticed before in Mr. Barbirolli's handling of the classics, an insistence on accent rather than on outline. He makes his mark with a dig of the stick to produce a strong entry or an emphatic chord. What lies between these points may have to take care of itself.' It was clear that the young man had a long way to go before subordinating impulse to the eloquence of symphonic form.

On the whole, however, he was doing well for himself. What is more, he was doing it in the traditional manner. Teaching others (e.g., teaching string players about bow techniques) was a means of teaching himself; which is what most English conductors did and do. Towards the end of 1929

Capell commented on a Brahms D major Symphony of his with
the L.S.O. 'An equivalent performance by a violinist or a
pianist,' he wrote, 'would have been called spirited but crude;
but then, violinists and pianists can master their art in private,
while conductors have to learn theirs in the full public gaze.'
There were plenty who had faith in the learner, none the less.
Early that year the converted Empire Theatre, Leicester
Square, retained an orchestra of forty-five, a not unusual
strength in 'super cinemas' before mechanisation made its
clean and final sweep. The Empire management invited
Barbirolli to take charge and conduct three orchestral interludes
a day. The task didn't look onerous. A typical interlude
consisted of one concert overture. And the pay was £3,000
a year—'absolutely untold wealth!' A family council was called.
'No,' said Lorenzo, 'you have conducted the London Symphony
Orchestra. You have conducted for the Royal Philharmonic
Society. They have done you that honour. We have never
had much money. So we can get along comfortably without it.
It would be betraying the confidence placed in you by these
great organisations if you took any such job.'

John Barbirolli felt the force of this consideration and said
No to the Empire Theatre. Within ten years he was to do
vastly better than £3,000 a year. If anybody had predicted
as much at the time of the Empire offer he would have scoffed.
So would most other musicians with their heads screwed on
the right way. There would have been no scoffing on Lorenzo's
part, however. He had always known that his son's good
professional repute would swell to fame.

We return to Gaisberg and the morrow of Barbirolli's
'stand-in' concert with the London Symphony Orchestra.

At their first meeting they talked money among other
matters. Of this Barbirolli said later that he thought Gaisberg
rather did him down. According to Gaisberg's account of these
or later contractual dealings, Barbirolli was elusive in negotia-
tion: 'I very nearly lost him, as my terms were below those offered
by a company which, however, could not give him the world-
wide publicity I had to offer'. Many a recording director
might have been put off by the cleaver which The Times had
used on the young man's Elgar performance. Gaisberg's faith

in Barbirolli's specialist talent and the uses to which he could
put it remained unruffled. As has been said, he wanted him
for operatic excerpts and concerto 'accompanying'. He had
seen him at work in the opera pit and diagnosed a wideawake,
fluent musical mind. Barbirolli commented: 'I always had a
great facility with the stick. A lot of people don't realise that,
to be a fine accompanist, you need a tremendous technique
and judgment. In opera a soprano has to open a door, let us
say. The door jams. She can't make her entrance. The conductor dallies. He holds his orchestra until the door "unjams".
The soprano comes on. He gives a beat accordingly. Well, I
could manage such things. It was rather a gift of mine.
Gaisberg spotted it.' He was aware at the time and freely
acknowledged long afterwards what a rare chance it was that
Gaisberg gave him. During the next eight years or so his
recordings for Gaisberg's company won him prestige of an
exceptional and productive kind on both sides of the Atlantic.
None of this could have happened as it did and might not have
happened at all except for his assignment with the L.S.O. on
December 12th 1928, a date which is therefore to be coupled
with that of the Goss-van Dieren concert (December 14th 1925)
as one of the opportunities which determined the rest of his
career. Astonishing things ultimately came of his early recording output and the professional friendships it bred.

So, with an eager Gaisberg at his elbow, again learning as
he went along, he entered upon the exasperating craft of
conducting for a relatively newfangled thing, the recording
microphone—not, as yet, on to electronic tape but on to old-
fashioned wax discs which, if anybody played a wrong note
in the last bar or sneezed immediately after the last note, had
to be scrapped for remelting; in which case a fresh disc was put
on the turntable and the '78 r.p.m.' side (duration: four and a
half minutes at the most) 'cut' all over again. In retrospect,
typical 'wax' sessions are apt to smack of slow martyrdom.
There were occasional leavenings of the grotesque or comic,
however. During Barbirolli's first 'grand' season (1928) a highly
considered Italian baritone, Giovanni Inghilleri, sang Iago
at Covent Garden, although not under Barbirolli's baton. It
was decided to record him in the act-one drinking scene, which
Iago leads. Not only did Barbirolli bring along the Covent

Garden chorus. With them he brought their Italian chorus-master, a conscientious and vital little man, Signor Conca. In the theatre Conca would dress up, go on with the chorus and mingle with them throughout a scene, giving cues and, if the cues gave signs of failing, hissed exhortations. . . . 'You very rarely hear the Brindisi [drinking chorus] in *Otello* well sung,' said Barbirolli. 'Usually the rhythm is weak. Not enough emphasis is given to the second beat in the bar. I had this little fellow in attendance at the recording. He went round pinching chorus singers' bottoms to be sure of getting that second beat right.'

There were days of waking nightmare when every wax seemed doomed. During the 'grand' season of 1931 Barbirolli lined up a distinguished team headed by Elisabeth Schumann and Friedrich Schorr for the third-act Quintet from *Die Meistersinger*, an opera 'rested' at Covent Garden that summer but one in which all five singers—including the leading tenor—had repeatedly sung. As it happened, the leading tenor, one of the most illustrious operatic artists of his time, was badly off form that day. The other four sang superbly from the first test run onwards. Mr. X, however, repeatedly muffed his entries and went off pitch. Soon the entire studio was in a state of jumps. Even Gaisberg, usually a man of aplomb, forgot himself in the end. When Miss Schumann, a great charmer as well as a singer of genius, stood up, presumably to make some healing suggestion, he lost his temper and bade her sit down, shouting 'You shall not sing at all today!' After this Barbirolli concentrated all his efforts on the distraught tenor and finally had him sound in note and phrase. By this time the session was nearly over. Another wax was put on. The Quintet began again—'and,' as a veteran technician remembers, 'it all came off splendidly in the last few minutes'. Sessions ordinarily began with a stock of forty-eight waxes in thermostatically heated cupboards which made them workable under the stylus. Extra waxes were called up by tele-phone as needed. The total used on the *Meistersinger* Quintet (two 12-inch sides) was not a record (this was put up by Artur Schnabel, who got through sixty-five waxes in one day on two sides of the 'Diabelli' Variations) but ran it pretty close.

Another singer of uncommon lustre whom Barbirolli had fallen in with at Covent Garden was Frida Leider, a German soprano who is thought of generally as a singer of Wagner but whose repertory took in Mozart and Verdi as well; she had sung Donna Anna in one of his three *Don Giovannis* during the 1929 season. He convoked her to Kingsway Hall, then as now a Methodist mission on Sundays and a recording studio during the week. She was to record Leonora's sublime and taxing aria 'Abscheulicher! wo eilst du hin?' from *Fidelio*—'a terrific job for conductor, orchestra and singer'. The orchestral accompaniment is admired—and professionally feared—for its elaborate horn writing. For this Barbirolli had recruited the finest horn quartet in London. Aubrey Brain, who led it, was of a family which had been eminent on London orchestral platforms for decades. Leider put her whole heart into Beethoven's music and was technically on the dot:

'A great artist. No hysterics. Just the music. We rehearsed like the devil. Finally we decided everything was in order. We got what we thought must be two absolutely perfect waxes. That was quite "something" in the 78-rev. days in a piece that has such orchestral hazards. [Nobody could ever be sure whether any recording except a test wax was altogether as good as it seemed whilst it was being made. What were thought to be the best ones went straight to the factory for processing. There was no question of playing them back; that would have damaged the grooves.] We all sat back with a sigh of relief. Came a telephone message. Gaisberg was in a state of collapse. The performance was supposed to have been transmitted from Kingsway by landline to a studio miles away [actually off Leicester Square, where Gaisberg super-vised two engineers and a pair of recording machines that worked in relay to maintain continuity]. There had been some transmission defect. Not a note of our perfect "Abscheu-licher!" had reached the machines! We couldn't resume at Kingsway for technical reasons. As it happened the Lesser Queen's Hall was available. Gaisberg decided that the session should be resumed there. [The Lesser Queen's Hall was upstairs at the big Queen's Hall and on the far side of central London, a failed cabaret with plush benches and vestigial dining tables round the walls. A good deal of recording history was made there around the turn of the decade.] Gaisberg joined us pretty quickly at Kingsway. He went out into the

road and stopped every passing taxi. Leider, myself and the
orchestra reached the Lesser Queen's Hall in driblets. We
started again at two-thirty. There were only two sides to make.
Only nine minutes of music. We finished at six o'clock. And
the performance we got in the end was flawless. After the
Kingsway disaster many a singer would have been unnerved
for days. Not so Leider. She was a first-class professional.'

Another who came to the Lesser Queen's Hall was Fedor
Chaliapin, then in his sunset years, grand seigneur and
whimsical tyrant, as much the actor off-stage as on it. Tales
were told, most of them true, of his lordly caprices and huffs.
For a set of Russian folk numbers and proletarian songs which
he was scheduled to 'cut' Gaisberg rounded up a balalaika
band from Soho. They rehearsed agitatedly. Turning up an
hour and a half late with his voice in poor shape, Chaliapin
promptly dismissed the conductor, took over the stick and fell
foul of the recording engineers. The session dissolved unhappily.
Staying on with Gaisberg and one or two other chosen souls,
he began talking of his early days in Russia. Suddenly he
found his voice. Without accompaniment—or waxes—he
sang and mimed all the songs he should have been recording
with unmatchable artistry. When test waxes did not take his
fancy he was capable of slipping out unnoticed while they
were being played. There would be a hunt among the streets
of the neighbourhood. Passers-by would be asked if they
had seen a tall handsome man in a blue suit, bareheaded and
with fair hair. In the end he would be winkled out of some
teashop, gesticulating in three languages. As has been seen, on
good days he was still capable of splendid sound. On bad days
his voice was heavy and intractable. It was on one of his bad
days that he came to record 'Madamina', the so-called
Catalogue Aria from *Don Giovanni*. The session should have
begun at two in the afternoon. He appeared at three—'with
Sacha Guitry and joint retinue. Guitry wore a flowing bow
tie and a flamboyant personality.* Chaliapin was known to be
a "difficult" character: 'Everybody had the dithers. He brought

* I am indebted to Mr. David Bicknell, Gaisberg's principal assistant
then and later his successor as chief of E.M.I.'s international artists'
department, for a supplementary and vivid impression of Guitry's relation-
ship with Chaliapin around this time. See Appendix Two.

with him several kinds of pill. They were set out on a table.
Also a bottle of brandy. The pills and the brandy were to
coax his voice. It had to be "awakened". When I stood on the
rostrum alongside the giant my head was about level with his.
He put an arm around my shoulder and was very charming.
We did two rehearsals, and his voice began to roll up. We had
a good orchestra, the cream of London. I had brought along
my favourite players. When we were satisfied the balance was
right we made a couple of waxes. We got one which we thought
we could venture to let the old man hear. We play it. He
listens. Then he draws himself up majestically as if he were
Boris on the stage. "I sing with all my voice," he says. "I
sing with all my heart. And what comes out?" Here he made a
grandiose gesture. "And what comes out? *Un pet!*" '

They went on to other tests. The voice began to 'live'. At
last they got a 'Madamina' that went simultaneously into the
English and American catalogues. It delighted—and shocked.
Barbirolli said of it: 'What a performance! Chaliapin made
"Madamina" sound frightful. He made it filthy. But filthy in
an aristocratic way.'*

A succession of concerto recordings interwove with the
operatic snippets, soon outnumbering and outweighing them.
His vogue and ramifying celebrity as a concerto conductor,
as an 'accompanist', that is to say, of concerto soloists—a
function which in the long run was to irk him rather—
stemmed from the most lucrative 'box office' piece of its sort
and day: Tchaikovsky's for piano in B flat minor, *the* concerto,
as many were to call it. He recorded this with Artur Rubinstein and the London Symphony Orchestra at H.M.V.'s

---

* Barbirolli was not putting it high. H.M.V. DA 994 (1, 'Madamina',
2, 'Nella bionda') is now a rarity. By courtesy of the B.B.C. gramophone
record library the writer recently heard a tape of it. On phrases ingeniously
selected from Da Ponte's text, Leporello, through Chaliapin's mouth,
conveys his master's lechery now droolingly, now caressingly, sometimes with
fire, sometimes with impudent rhythmic stresses. For the line about
Giovanni's 'passion predominante, . . . la giovin principiante', he falls not
into a *parlando* but into outright speech of the confidential, buttonholing sort.
There is a quick passage where he gets a bar ahead of Barbirolli, whose
nimble orchestra, nevertheless, is one of very few Mozartian things about a
performance which may be described as Chaliapin plus Da Ponte multiplied by Maupassant.

studios in St. John's Wood, London. 'Artur,' said Barbirolli, 'was above all things very musical. We started on a run-through before making tests. We had only played a few bars when he jumped up and shouted, "Oh, what a man! At last I can *play* this concerto." He found he could play just as he wanted to play. It wasn't that I was "following" him. Never "follow" a soloist. You're sure to be left behind if you do. The point is, I felt the music in the same way as Artur felt it. I had the same *warm* approach as his.' Afterwards he did the two Chopin piano concertos and the Mozart in A (K 488) with Rubinstein. But the decisive product was the Tchaikovsky: 'After that I started accompanying other big artists. They had either heard what Rubinstein had said about me at the run-through, or they had heard the recording itself, and they said to Gaisberg: "Could we have this John Barbirolli for *our* recordings?" I made a big series with Jascha Heifetz. Heifetz always wanted me. Then there were Casals, Schnabel, Horowitz, Cortot, Suggia, Mischa Elman, Edwin Fischer, Wilhelm Backhaus. . . .'

About Backhaus he told another gratifying story. Together they recorded the Grieg piano concerto with 'Anonymous Orchestra', as a discography puts it. 'We were doing a test of the slow movement. You remember that wonderful opening tune for muted strings? Before coming in with his D flat arpeggio, Backhaus looked up from the keyboard and said, "What a pity the piano has to come in and spoil that!" Wasn't that a charming thing?'

After three or four decades the Heifetz list has rather the look of bric-à-brac with a stray dinosaur here and there. There were Tchaikovsky's violin concerto and Mozart's A major K 219, to be sure. But what heart today (or then) beat the faster at the thought of Sarasate's *Ziegeunerweisen*, or the *Havanaise* of Saint-Saëns, not to mention the same composer's Introduction Rondo and Capriccioso, or Glazounov's Concerto Op. 82, or Wieniavsky's No. 2 Op. 22, or the Vieuxtemps No. 4 Op. 31? Of the Vieuxtemps it may be argued that its special function at any time is to make the hearts (and batons) of those professionally involved in it beat not faster but miss beats altogether.

In 1935 Barbirolli had business abroad which entailed a

tiring return journey. At 11 a.m., having had no sleep the night before, he got off the boat train at Liverpool Street Station looking forward to a restful, recuperative day. Gaisberg, whom he had supposed to know nothing of his timetable, was there to meet him. In any other impresario this would have been startling. Since it was Gaisberg, Barbirolli showed nothing more than mild surprise. Gaisberg said: 'Welcome home. You have a session with Jascha Heifetz at two this afternoon to record the Vieuxtemps No. 4'. Barbirolli murmured that he had never heard the work, much less seen a score. In any case, he asked himself, why should anybody want to hear or see a piece so desperately out of fashion? However, Gaisberg was Gaisberg, a mover of mountains. Barbirolli allowed himself to be shooed into a taxi and to the Berkeley Hotel: 'There we found Jascha. He had a piano score of the Vieuxtemps. Also a full score, yellow with age. The pages crumbled as you turned them. Where did he get that score from? I've often wondered. He had his accompanist with him, a Hungarian called Sandor. They played it through for me. I was all eyes and ears. There was a fearful, frightening one-in-a-bar Scherzo. I must say that alarmed me rather. At the finish I said resignedly, "All right, let's have a go". By this time we were on the recording floor. The orchestra was the London Philharmonic. We started at two o'clock sharp. To my astonishment we were through in three hours. The Scherzo, once we started on it, went well enough—which was more astonishing still. The old opera training of the quick stick served me well. . . . Years later Jascha told me he had never played the Scherzo since. Nor have I ever conducted it!'

The crowning glory of those years, as he styled it, was two violin concerto recordings. They were Beethoven's Op. 61 and Brahms's Op. 102. The soloist in each was Fritz Kreisler, a name which, to anybody remembering the epoch, even if tone-deaf or stone-deaf, more than warrants Barbirolli's metaphor. Kreisler himself had worn a crown of glory for years. Anybody chosen to conduct him automatically acquired a crown which, although of much smaller size, was widely envied. With Kreisler's crown went what amounted to a financial halo. Had he not signed a five-year contract with an American recording company that guaranteed him $150,000 a

year? So it was whispered (and is whispered still) in the St.
John's Wood corridors. He would arrive at the studio half an
hour early, carrying two fiddles, one a Stradivarius, the other
a Guarnerius, and put a pocket hydrometer on the piano.
Taking off his shoes, since the best-made shoes in the world
could not be relied on absolutely not to creak, he would put
on a pair of carpet slippers and play in those, having first
determined by hydrometer reading which of the two fiddles
to play that day. He did not sweep across recording floors
like a pillar of fire and confusion as Chaliapin did: but his
smile, word and wish had at least as much weight and a more
tranquil charm.

Of the two concertos he did with Barbirolli, and the London
Philharmonic Orchestra, the Beethoven ran to a dozen
12-inch sides, after the manner of those days; and who was not
exasperated by eleven turnings of the 'pancake' and eleven
interruptions when 'so golden a stream of noble tone' was
in question? This image again was Barbirolli's. It referred not
to the recording but to Kreisler performances of Beethoven's
Op. 61 four years later in Carnegie Hall, New York. Again
Barbirolli was 'accompanying' him. The orchestra was the New
York Philharmonic-Symphony, Barbirolli its musical director.
The war was savagely on. Barbirolli's career had changed
preternaturally and as in the twinkling of an eye. The world
had been stood on its head. Kreisler's feet stayed on the ground;
his art still went up towards the stars. In the slow movement
his golden stream of noble tone made time stand still, as it
seemed to Barbirolli. That performance, a performance which
he helped to mould, 'was, by a trick of fate, perhaps the
finest I ever heard him give'. In what manner a trick of fate?

Some months later, while hurrying against the lights over a
Madison Avenue crossing towards Carnegie Hall, Kreisler was
run down by a dairy truck and lay unconscious for days
with head injuries which, although he recovered from them,
were considered by some to have adversely affected his career
when he resumed it. His performance of the Beethoven concerto, Barbirolli conducting, in Carnegie Hall on November 14th
1940 was to be his last.

CHAPTER SEVEN

THE SCOTTISH YEARS

A CHAPTER ago we saw him on to the platform of St. Andrew's Hall, Glasgow. It is time to rejoin him there. Without Glasgow there could have been no New York, as it were. Nor could there have been any Sir John Barbirolli as we watched him grow and knew him in the end. The Scottish Orchestra was the first orchestra he could call his own. It gave him reserves of keen young playing talent; lunatic work schedules of a kind that would scandalise any other profession; and, best of all, the chance to build up a symphonic repertory wide and diverse enough to qualify him for any rostrum in the world.

He had made the orchestra's acquaintance first in 1930. For their 1930–31 season the executive of the S.O. engaged five conductors of whom four, although not top-notchers exactly, were internationally known and of established or growing reputation: Robert Heger (German), van Raalte (Dutch), Nikolai Malko and Issai Dobrowen, the last two being ex-patriate Russians. Against this company Barbirolli was picked to open the season: something of a plume in the cap of a relatively unproved thirty-year-old. In November he broke away from one of his provincial operatic tours and conducted six S.O. concerts, four of them in Glasgow, two in Edinburgh. His inaugural in Glasgow was a Saturday 'Pop': the César Franck symphony, a movement from a Mozart cassation, trifles by Grieg, the Wedding March from *The Golden Cockerel* and a soprano from the Warsaw Opera (she was billed as The Polish Nightingale) whom he accompanied in 'Ah! fors' è lui'. A full house lifted up the directors' hearts. Times were bad, full houses a rarity. If only they could keep this up, they told each other, their troubles would be at an end. Two nights later he made his Edinburgh début. Here the audience was smaller. Its fervour more than made up for the sprinkling of empty seats. During Brahms's Symphony No. 2 he kept his hearers on a tight rein, shortening the intervals between movements and holding his baton at the ready to obviate premature applause. The enthusiasm at the end was like a dam bursting.

In the same hall, four nights earlier, Edinburgh's own orchestra, the Reid Symphony, and Edinburgh's own conductor, Donald Francis Tovey, professor of music at Edinburgh University, who industriously composed music on his own account and, to more lasting purpose, lectured about that of others, had done Brahms's No. 1, a performance of characteristic gravity and warmth. Allowances made for the aesthetic differences between the C minor and D major symphonies, it was generally felt that Tovey's Brahms was one thing, Barbirolli's another, each having its special insights. As we shall see, tacit rivalry between the Scottish Orchestra and the Reid Symphony flared into something like musical politics a few seasons later. This was the doing of touchy partisans rather than of the two conductors, who got on together with easy humour. Long before his analytical essays had become a reading vogue throughout the English-speaking world and beyond it, Tovey was always 'the great Professor Tovey' in Barbirolli's mouth and writing. (Their first meeting had been in the spring of 1929, when the Edinburgh Opera Company [amateur with a professional stiffening] put on a week's triple bill at the Empire Theatre, Tovey conducting his *Bride of Dionysus*, Barbirolli two *Bohèmes* and a *Pagliacci*. Barbirolli's leading tenor was the dazzling Joseph Hislop, then in the first flush of international acclaim. Hislop, a native of Edinburgh, had not sung there before in opera. On Hislop-Barbirolli nights the theatre sold out at double prices.* Inevitably *The Bride of Dionysus* wore a homely look in this context. Tovey took the situation lightly but, in talking with Barbirolli,

---

* On one of these nights Sir Thomas Beecham appeared before the curtain and, as usual, spoke up for his Opera League. Incidentally he described Hislop as one of the greatest artists of the world and made much of his belated recognition by his compatriots. France, Germany, the United States and Scandinavia, he said, were Hislop's true spiritual homes.

permitted himself this: 'One day Edinburgh may be made a fit place for musicians to live in.')

Barbirolli's programmes with the S.O. in 1930, although drawn from a small repertory, had a fairly catholic look. At one end of the scale came the Mozart cassation music, a Handel concerto grosso, Haydn's Symphony No. 97 in C and Mozart's 'Jupiter'. The other end took in Arnold Bax's Symphony No. 2, which had piano, xylophone, glockenspiel and celesta in its percussion department—aggressively modern 'colour' in some ears; and Ravel's *Bolero*, 'orchestration without music', then two years old and new to Scotland, an entertainment that everybody revelled in whether owning up to it or not. *Bolero* was repeated later in the season by Heger. Musical wiseacres mulled earnestly over which reading was the better. In both cities Barbirolli mustered a following who paid little attention to wiseacres whether academic or literary. (What leading Scottish critics thought of him will be examined in the next chapter.) From the first it was a love match between Barbirolli and his Scottish audiences; no lesser image will serve. Many in his following knew him from his work in the opera pit; they were captivated by his frown and tenacity and drive. His round-off concert that year in Edinburgh was on a night of heavy fog, the inside of Usher Hall a muggy blur. After the César Franck and 'Jupiter' symphonies and Delius's *In a Summer Garden* he received a standing ovation, as later jargon has it. In the Edinburgh of forty years ago newspaper language was statelier. 'Deeply pleasurable satisfaction,' we read, 'was written on the countenances of the audience as they stood to greet and bid farewell for the season to Mr. Barbirolli.' Barbirolli converts were reported to be asking why he had not been engaged for more than a 'measly' six concerts out of forty. A few days later, between *Rigoletto* rehearsals, he wrote to Eustace Blois from Birmingham, where he had rejoined the touring Covent Garden company. His concerts with the Scottish Orchestra, he said, had been 'a really big success'. They had had 'the biggest audiences for years . . .; 3,000 at my first concert'.

Undoubtedly he had been a tonic. The Scottish Orchestra needed something more than a tonic, however. What did six relatively well-attended concerts amount to out of forty which,

considered as a series, were going downhill persistently? The
Great Depression was becoming greater and more depressing.
Individuals and institutions alike were chronically hard up.
Season by season the S.O.'s box office 'take' and subscription
revenue dwindled progressively. It was officially admitted
that attendance at the supposedly 'popular' concerts was
deplorable. It was certain, said the directors, that if the decline
was not checked the Scheme (this was their word for the S.O.
concerts) must come to an end: which would be nothing short
of calamity. By the beginning of 1932 the end seemed at hand.
Everybody knew that even in prosperous times the Glasgow
concerts alone were not enough to keep the S.O. alive. Its
Edinburgh engagements were an equally important part of
the financial lifeline. A point came at which the Edinburgh
Concert Society, the body which hired the S.O. for the Usher
Hall 'Mondays', paying substantial fees, began to entertain
doubt as to the orchestra's future. In such a situation doubt
can be a death warrant. To make sure of their 1932-33 season
the Edinburgh people secured an option on the services of the
Hallé Orchestra of Manchester. They let it be known that if
the Scottish Orchestra could not, by a certain Friday in
January, give them a firm assurance that it would be available
to them the following winter, the option would be taken up
and Edinburgh henceforth be served by Manchester.

To prevent Glasgow from being wiped off the map sym-
phonically speaking, the S.O.'s friends and office-holders
went to work determinedly. Despite the penury of the times
they enrolled new guarantors at five pounds a head and
increased the guarantee fund to something over £3,000: a tiny
sum to an age that takes orchestral subsidies from public funds
for granted but one which, in 1932, meant the difference
between symphonic life and death to a city of over a million
souls. On the Wednesday before what might have turned out
to be a fatal Friday the orchestra's guarantors and subscribers
had an ebullient meeting at which they resolved not only
that the orchestra should carry on, alike in Edinburgh and
Glasgow, but also that Scotland should some day set up a
National Orchestra to serve the country as a whole. Nobody
at this stage committed himself publicly to the notion that the
Scottish Orchestra of Glasgow was tantamount to a national

one already and needed but funds and goodwill to become
national in good earnest all the year round. When that notion
was put up and canvassed three years later it gave rise to sore
feelings here and there in Edinburgh, birthplace and home of
Tovey's charge, the Reid Symphony Orchestra. To this we
shall return.

More guarantee money was on the way, then. (So was an
extension of the loathed entertainment tax, now applicable for
the first time to 'serial' subscriptions.) But money was not the
only consideration. What the S.O. needed to make its concerts
'go' was musical excitement emanating from the top. It
needed more Barbirolli, in short. In planning for 1932–33
the directors fell to discussing Barbirolli as a possible saviour.
One of their number was deputed to go up to London and
invite him to a bigger share in the 'Scheme'. He needed no
coaxing. An orchestra of his own, a public of his own and the
chance to build himself a copious symphonic repertory had
long been his daydream. He accepted the Glasgow invitation
with alacrity. His first charge, as we have seen, was a half-
season. At the end of 1932 he took over from van Raalte and
directed the 1933 half, which ran into mid-February. He was
given a tolerably free hand in programme planning. The
governing committee had furnished a general directive. It
said that programmes were to be 'as acceptable as possible,
having regard to our duty to be discreetly adventurous in the
introduction of works not hitherto performed in Glasgow'.

Subject to this he played pretty much what he wanted to
play. The 'discreet adventures' of 1933 were Bax's Symphony
No. 4, Elgar's No. 1 in A flat, Sibelius's No. 2, Vaughan
Williams's *Job* suite and the set of Vivaldi concertos known as
The Four Seasons. All these novelties except the Vivaldi, which
went to van Raalte, were done by Barbirolli. He converted
Glasgow on the instant to Sibelius's No. 2. For the Bax and *Job*
he got respectful attention; for the Elgar little, if anything,
more. To his players at rehearsal and to friends at convivial
after-concert parties which, thanks to his tireless and eager
loquacity, had a way of going on until dawn, he preached
Elgar with an awe and wonder which in their absoluteness
were almost sacral.

'What people haven't begun to realise,' he would say, 'is

that with Elgar's death the great line of symphonic composers
came to an end. I will "bracket" him for you without hesitation:
Bach, Beethoven, Brahms, Elgar. There's the great line.'

Scotland responded tepidly. In Glasgow and Edinburgh—as,
for that matter, in London and other great English cities—
Elgar's music lay under chilling shadow still. After thirty-five
years or more, S.O. veterans remember how penetrating and
privileged an experience it was to play under his baton in the
two symphonies, the *Enigma* Variations, the violin concerto
and the Introduction and Allegro for Strings. One says: 'He
was always "selling" Elgar. No conductor could have "sold"
Elgar more devotedly.' Another veteran: 'And Scotland
wouldn't "buy". A big Elgar piece always meant a lot of
empty seats.'

During the 1933 half-season he conducted the S.O. at
twenty concerts in eighty or ninety items big and small, the
big items including nine symphonies apart from those already
named: two Beethovens (Nos. 5 and 8), two Schuberts (the
'Unfinished' and No. 8 in B minor), Mozart's G minor and
'Jupiter', the Brahms No. 2, Tchaikovsky's No. 4 and Dvorak's
No. 8 in G. Outside the symphonic repertory he drew upon
familiar Debussy, Strauss and Delius; and, while revelling
himself, made everybody else revel in Wagner overtures,
preludes, interludes and excerpts. To the usual helpings from
The Mastersingers he added (during a later season) the Procession of the Guilds with its comic choral strophes for bakers,
shoemakers and what not: a memorable hit. The half-season
ended with the customary plebiscite concert, that is to say,
with a programme chosen by audience-votes from the season's
entire repertory. The night began with the *Leonora* No. 3
Overture and ended with the Overture to *The Mastersingers*.
In between came Schubert's Symphony No. 8, *Eine kleine
Nachtmusik* and the 'Blue Danube' Waltz, each piece having
proved the most popular in its category. The 'Blue Danube'
meant much to Barbirolli. He was among those who think it's
a poor musical heart that doesn't rejoice in Johann Strauss.
There is more than one way of playing him, however. There is
the so-called 'symphonic' way, with free manipulation of
rhythm and climax. And there is the way of the strict dance
measure. The strict way was favoured by some of the 'more

With his French-born mother, Louise Barbirolli, then 82, after
a London concert, 1953.

Dr. Ralph Vaughan Williams O.M. discusses his new *Antartica Symphony*, 1953, with 'glorious John', as he named Barbirolli in a dedicatory note.

venerable members' (the phrase was Barbirolli's) of his Glasgow public. They put in a request that he should beat 'The Blue Danube' accordingly. To oblige them he did precisely that a year later—and was reproved by the critic of the *Glasgow Herald* for 'an artistic offence . . . Authorities tell us,' frowned the writer, 'that toying with the pulse in the playing of the music was part of the Viennese tradition and that the Viennese dancers were quick to follow all pace modifications as they danced.' Barbirolli was adept at either mode. He brought the house down with both.

At the end of his first plebiscite concert the crowd boiled over affectionately. Glasgow had taken him to its heart. He thanked Glasgow in general and his players in particular for 'six of the happiest weeks in my musical career' and looked forward to meeting them all again. What he did not mention, since it would have been premature to do so, was that he had accepted an invitation to return for the 1933–34 season as conductor of the complete series. The Scottish Orchestra was now his. In announcing the appointment some months later the committee of management claimed that under John Barbirolli the S.O. had attained a standard of performance that made it comparable with the best orchestras in Britain. 'Comparable with' is not the same thing as 'equal to' or 'every bit as good as'. These latter were the assessments on which Barbirolli's sights were set. Less than two years later he was to tell an Edinburgh gathering:* 'Although we do not, as an orchestra, bear the name of Berlin or Vienna, I can assure you that you will hear as fine playing from the Scottish Orchestra as you will hear anywhere in Europe today.'

A sizeable claim. It ranked the S.O. not only with the Berlin Philharmonic and the Vienna Philharmonic but also with a formidable home product, Beecham's London Philharmonic, before which musical mankind in general was beginning to genuflect. Undoubtedly, however, great and gratifying changes had been worked in the spirit and technique of the Scottish Orchestra. Let us see how these changes were brought about.

The S.O. was a well considered and fully professional body

* The Scottish Women's Club, Edinburgh, 3rd December 1934.

E

of between seventy and eighty players, eighty being the complement for such massive scores as *Götterdämmerung* excerpts and Strauss's *Ein Heldenleben*, which could have done with more. It had been founded in 1891 and used St. Andrew's Hall as its home base. St. Andrew's had a drab auditorium. Edinburgh's Usher Hall was considered dashing and elegant by comparison. But the acoustics are claimed to have been 'magnificent'. Caruso said he had never come upon anything better. It is impossible to check such claims now. Fire gutted the hall in the 1950s, and at this writing it had not been restored; the concerts of what is now the Scottish National Orchestra take place elsewhere. In Glasgow and Edinburgh the S.O. had been conducted in their day by illustrious guests, among them Hans Richter, Henry Wood, Richard Strauss and Serge Koussevitsky. Each conferred upon the S.O. a badge of prestige, although one of them started off on the wrong foot. Koussevitsky's first piece with the orchestra was Tchaikovsky's Symphony No. 5. At rehearsal he put down his baton after five minutes and, speaking in German, said: 'I am surprised at the inferior quality of the playing. I cannot understand it, because this is a *recognised* orchestra.' The orchestral leader, who understood German, having studied at Leipzig, interpreted what had been said to his colleagues, then explained to Koussevitsky: 'We have only just met. Give us a chance to "collect" ourselves and become a unit under your baton.' Koussevitsky resumed; seventy-five players technically coalesced and, as one of them remembers, 'were galvanised into a fantastically good performance'.

Visiting luminaries were well enough. Their light and stimuli soon passed, however. Down the decades the S.O. had had full-time conductors before Barbirolli, but there hadn't been enough of them, or they had not been sufficiently compelling to tighten the orchestra's technique and give it lustre. Nor was this the only disadvantage. Like most British symphony orchestras outside London, although in greater degree than any other, the S.O. laboured under two exasperating handicaps. The basic handicap was a ludicrously short season. During Barbirolli's first seasons the S.O. crammed a minimum of three concerts a week in Glasgow and Edinburgh —as well as a fluctuating total in other Scottish towns—into thirteen winter weeks. In opening-night or last-night speeches Barbirolli often referred to this absurdity in terms which, although restrained, betrayed impatience. After his 1933 concert-round he said: 'In presenting so many important programmes in so short a season, the Scottish Orchestra performs feats that are not asked of any other orchestra in the world'. And on the eve of the 1935–36 season, now extended by a fortnight: 'The work before the orchestra this season is eighty-six concert engagements in fifteen weeks'. At other times he spoke of his players working 'superhumanly' or 'like niggers'. As the playing schedules developed, two concerts a day—an afternoon one for schoolchildren and another in the evening for grown-ups—became a commonplace. Many of these tandem programmes took the orchestra far outside the two big cities and entailed train or motorcoach journeys which, in the depths of the Scottish winter, could be quelling. Rehearsal sessions were shoehorned into otherwise vacant hours as they went along.

There are three main types of orchestral rehearsal: routine-soporific, nag-sessions and root-and-branchers. Barbirolli's were of the third sort. To begin with he would take a score apart with the deftness of a champion carver; then, having meticulously attended to the bits, fit them together, every chord and phrase chiselled or moulded as he wanted it on the night. Already a typical Barbirolli rehearsal was more tiring than any Barbirolli concert. Yet, even towards the end of a session, when lips in the brass department were getting sore and backs and bow arms were beginning to ache, the players were at one with him and content. For him every detail in every score, *Molly on the Shore* as much as Beethoven's Ninth, was momentous: and, thanks to his will and fervour, everything became momentous for his players, too. What with Barbirolli's genial drive and the economic factor (in the penurious 1930s seven pounds a week, the rank-and-filers' pay rate, was a lot of money), the players bore the breathless winter concert schedules cheerfully enough. David McCallum, who became principal violin in 1932 and left three years later to become Beecham's leader with the London Philharmonic, offers his own footnote to those strenuous, anxious and happy days: 'All that hard work, concert crowding on concert! I often

wonder how we got through it. Well, we were all young and
healthy. That's what pulled us through. It was the survival test.'

It is said above that the S.O. suffered two handicaps. The
second handicap was bred of the first. At the end of a season,
S.O. players, who were from many parts of Scotland, with an
increasing few from England, dispersed widely and, during the
rest of the year, eked out in teashop bands, theatre pits,
restaurants and seaside concert pavilions. Nobody could
pretend that ekings-out alternating with massive overwork
were conducive to a consistently stylish orchestral ensemble.
There seems little doubt that at its best, namely, under a
'galvanising' conductor, the S.O. pulled off some noble performances. The list of great instrumentalists who played in
concertos with the orchestra during Barbirolli's years is in
itself strong evidence of its dependability and all-round
quality. Schnabel, Horowitz, Artur Rubinstein, Heifetz,
Thibaud, Hubermann, Feuermann: such a roll speaks much
for the mettle of the players who accompanied them. But 'as
fine as anything in Europe today . . .'? Most authorities,
recording impresarios included, obstinately stuck to it that
the Berliners, the Viennese and Beecham's Londoners led the
Scots by at least a point or two. Barbirolli was always a great
one for praising his own. This may be a fault. If so it is a good
one.

Before taking full charge in November 1933 he worked over
the players' list and did a bit of weeding out: not the most
agreeable of jobs. Twenty old players went, twenty new ones
came in. Fifteen of the replacements were in the string choir.
They included a new first 'cellist and a new leader of the
second violins. The string strength was only forty-four as
compared with sixty or so in most symphony orchestras of
standing. His first and second fiddles, great melody carriers in
the sort of romantic and neo-romantic music that was near his
heart, totalled twenty-two as against a norm of thirty. With his
string choir undermanned, he had to be sure of getting the
last ounce of effective tone from every particle of it. After the
replacements he redeployed some of the old players, moving
this man forward from his former desk and that man recipro-
cally to the rear.

The first vacancy of consequence after his refurbishing of the orchestra happened at the end of the 1933 half-season and caused a stir backstage that reached many outside ears.

In the beginning his first oboe had been a Belgian in his early fifties, Léon Dandoy, who had won a first prize with honours at the Royal Brussels Conservatory when seventeen and had gone on purposefully from there. At one of his early rehearsals Barbirolli took mild exception to Dandoy's phrasing of some melody, saying, 'I don't think that's exactly the way I want it . . .' Before he could get any further Dandoy muttered something disobliging.

Barbirolli put down his stick with deliberation and said: 'When I came to Glasgow it was my intention, as it still is, to treat everyone in the orchestra like a gentleman; and I expect everyone in the orchestra to treat *me* as a gentleman.' Dandoy retorted that if that was how Barbirolli felt it was all the same to him. Taking his oboe apart and packing it up, he walked off the platform but was back for the concert and stayed on until the end of the season. Then he left.

Barbirolli's head was a positive card-index of players worth winning over in the event of vacancies. He had already leafed through his index and made up his mind. He sent for Evelyn Rothwell, a player with London and other orchestras. She accepted his offer and was installed as first oboe for the beginning of the 1933–34 season.

She was twenty-three years old. As we shall be seeing a good deal more of Evelyn Rothwell, something had better be said here about how her path and Barbirolli's had come to converge. In 1931, when an oboe student at the Royal College of Music, Miss Rothwell had taken it into her head to apply for an audition with the Covent Garden Opera Syndicate. From the Royal Opera House she had a letter asking her to bring her oboe along and was so excited that she could not make out the signature. It looked rather like 'John Barkworth'. She showed it to Leon Goossens, brother of Eugene III, her oboe teacher. He said that John Barbirolli was the name. She knew Barbirolli by repute already and 'was more thrilled than ever'.

Her audition was in the crush room at Covent Garden. An upright piano was in readiness under the lustre chandeliers. She played through a Handel sonata. He said :'You have a

lovely tone, very musical.' She replied ('being very green')
that she hadn't had much experience.

He smiled and told her not to bother about that. 'The rest,'
he said, 'is the conductor's job. If a man—or a girl—can really
play an instrument it's up to the conductor to make him or
make her into a good player.'

She was to hear him say the same thing to many auditionees
down the decades. He appointed her to the second oboe desk at
the Royal Opera, and she played with the touring company
on most of its remaining tours as well as at the Glyndebourne
opera festival and with the London Symphony, among other
concert orchestras.

In Scotland she not only led the oboes. She was also to make
several concerto appearances. One was in a concerto for oboe
and string orchestra which Giovanni Battista Barbirolli had
devised from Giovanni Battista Pergolesi's trio sonatas and
'Stabat Mater'. Another was by Pergolesi's senior and contemporary Benedetto Marcello. For this Miss Rothwell,
already something of a musical scholar, wrote the programme
note. She explained that, Marcello's manuscript not being
accessible and a printed score impossible to come by, she had
made her own arrangement for string orchestra from a German
piano transcription. Later on, with a girl second oboe, she used
to lead the oboe duet in The Entry of the Queen of Sheba from
Handel's *Solomon*. Whenever and wherever Barbirolli put on
this piece it caught the popular fancy. There would be a storm
of applause at the end. Modestly declining it for himself, he
would wave up the girls to rise and bow. The applause would
continue. The piece would be repeated. Again the girls would
be waved to their feet. In some of the smaller Scottish towns
it was only with reluctance that audiences turned their minds
to the next piece.

There were ten other young women besides Miss Rothwell
on the new S.O. strength. One of them was Eileen Grainger
(Mrs. Wilfrid Parry, as she presently became), whom we have
met as violist in his Royal Opera String Quartet. How she came
to join Barbirolli and how she fared with him professionally
are matters that throw a further sidelight on his quickness in
diagnosing talent and the loyalty with which he made use of it.

Miss Grainger came out of the Royal Academy of Music, where she learned viola, a year or two later than Evelyn Rothwell left the Royal College. At a time when the musical profession was wounded and bleeding still from the 'talkies', she looked around, not very hopefully, for a first job. Violists, like instrumentalists of all other persuasions, were, typically, people who couldn't pay their rents or uncertain where the next quarter's was coming from. Surprisingly, however, she learned from an acquaintance in the Covent Garden orchestra that a viola seat was vacant for the forthcoming autumn tour. The upshot, after a telephone conversation with Woburn Court, was a meeting with Barbirolli in the conductor's room at Covent Garden. He asked her to play bits from *Tristan* and *Mastersingers* and the viola part of the Arnold Bax sonata for viola and piano. There was a grand piano in the room. He did not touch it but sat in an armchair, his head buried in the scores.

At the end he said, 'That will do. Thank you very much. Do you know what this is for?'

'Well,' said Miss Grainger, 'I know it's for your opera tour.'

'Yes, I want a principal viola.'

'But I don't know these operas.'

'Don't bother about that. My second viola will look after you. He's not keen on being leader himself. He's experienced, and he's a nice chap. The pay is twelve pounds a week.'

On returning home she told her mother she had accepted. 'How much did you say they are paying you?' asked her mother. 'Twelve pounds a week.' 'They must be mad,' concluded her mother, happily.

What Barbirolli had said about his second viola turned out to be true. Sharing first desk as sub-principal he plied his new leader, raw girl though she was, with *sotto voce* advice throughout her first rehearsals about Barbirolli's way of looking at things and doing them and his pet cares and phobias on points of tempo, phrasing, tone quality and the like.

Barbirolli made no comment on her playing. She survived *Rosenkavalier*. After that they rehearsed *Tristan*. From *Tristan* onwards she knew she was 'all right'. In it there are important viola solos. Her first performance of these in public brought her a compliment much prized by section leaders, namely,

the 'orchestral shuffle', a quiet sliding by fellow-players of
their feet on the pit floor. Occasionally there were mild rebukes.
At the end of a *Mastersingers* act one night, Barbirolli put a
benevolent hand on her shoulder after stepping down from
the rostrum and, in passing, said to her and the sub-principal,
'Don't be excited. You're running.' Through keenness she had
been getting ahead of his beat.

When a seat fell vacant among his Scottish violas Barbirolli
at once thought of Eileen Grainger. He persuaded her north
without much difficulty.

Then, as always, it was his policy not to bank exclusively on
visiting stars but also to use his leaders and other outstanding
players as concerto soloists. In appointing Miss Grainger he
had this very much in mind. To start with, however, she
contented herself with a modest place in the viola section. At
the end of her first season he asked her to stay on as sub-
principal.

'I hope you'll say Yes,' he said. 'If you do I'll get you another
pound a week.' This was no small promise. The S.O. had to
count its pounds carefully. He put in for the extra pound to
the committee of management.

'That,' objected one of the committeemen, 'would mean
paying Miss Grainger eight pounds a week. Why should we
pay that money to a girl?'

There were murmurs of agreement.

'I'm not bringing you a girl,' countered Barbirolli. 'I'm
bringing you a viola player.'

The Committee paid up and looked pleasant.

Back to November 1933, the month when he entered into
full possession of the Scottish Orchestra. Before the opening of
the season he rehearsed for three days, dissecting, magnifying,
burnishing, putting the bits together again and 'galvanising'
them. Breaking off for a reception in his honour by the Lord
Provost, magistrates and city fathers of Edinburgh—who (as
some speaker mentioned) were putting up guarantees for the
Glasgow orchestra as well as for the orchestra on their doorstep,
the Reid Symphony—he made a speech of acknowledgment in
which he spoke up for his own, naming the Scottish Orchestra
as the one truly permanent orchestra of its size in Scotland.

He added that by 'permanent' he meant an orchestra that rehearsed as an entity every day of the week. It may have struck some of his hearers that this definition came near to claiming national status for the Scottish Orchestra. So much (implicitly) for the Reid orchestra.

For his opening in Glasgow, a Saturday 'Pop', St. Andrew's Hall was filled and agog. Until the last minute—and after—there were queues at the box offices. The opening piece started late because people were streaming in after the advertised starting time. All standing places were taken. Latecomers had to go without programmes. Supplies had given out. It was long since St. Andrew's Hall had known such a Saturday night crush. Perhaps the new prices had something to do with this. Half the area seats had been cut to one-and-nine. There were some at a shilling.

Nearly everybody in the hall wore a Flanders poppy, and at the end Barbirolli received a basketful of them (in the Usher Hall, Edinburgh, two nights later they gave him poppies in the form of a harp), for it was November the Eleventh, Remembrance Day, when the dead of the First World War were ceremonially invoked; and nowhere with greater solemnity than in the Scottish cities. With its banging maroons, its two-minute standstills throughout the land, its sorrowing skirl of pipes and its processions of bemedalled veterans, Remembrance Day always coincided with S.O. inaugurals or came sufficiently near to mark them off from the generality of musical occasions. Not that the programmes were in any sense memorial programmes. Even so, these nights that were spotted as with the blood of battlefields gave an urgency and dimension of their own to great music and even to small: as much on this night of the Eleventh, 1933, to Jarnefelt's Praeludium and Percy Grainger's setting of *Shepherd's Hey* (which went so well that it had to be played twice) as to Tchaikovsky's fourth symphony and the third Brandenburg concerto of J. S. Bach.

To the four items named here were added the *Mastersingers* overture, the Hungarian March of Berlioz, 'Ombra mai fu' and the Four Serious Songs of Brahms, the singer of these being Maria Olszewska, whose 'encores' brought the night's spread to a dozen items when the repeat of *Shepherd's Hey* was reckoned in. What is the point, Barbirolli used to ask, of a Saturday 'Pop'

E*

if you don't give everybody too much?* Lavishness did not preclude style, however. In the Brandenburg concerto he had his violins and violas stand, maintaining that they had better command of their instruments than in the sitting position and were likelier to produce richer tone.

On the following Monday, in accordance with long-established weekly routine, everybody got into a train for Edinburgh and an evening date, preceded by rehearsal, in Edinburgh's Usher Hall. The players in general travelled third class, as all cheaper seats used to be labelled. Up in front a first-class compartment was, as usual, reserved for Barbirolli and David McCallum, his leader. On this Monday, which typified many a Monday, the party took with them the core of the previous week-end's 'Pop' programme (i.e., the *Master-singers* overture, Tchaikovsky's No. 4 and the Brandenburg No. 3) plus Schubert's 'Unfinished' Symphony (which was to come before the Tchaikovsky) and Delius's *A Song before Sunrise* as the round-off piece. Thus did the S.O.'s programmes, pair by pair, in the process of travel, switch, slim, change a little and remain rather the same. It rarely happened, however, that current programmes preoccupied Barbirolli and McCallum in their first-class compartment. Usually their thoughts ran further ahead. The run from Glasgow to Edinburgh took about an hour. Never was an hour put to better musical purpose. They used to sit together on one side of the compartment and litter the opposite seats with string parts and full scores of pieces scheduled for later concerts, even much later ones. With some 'unproved' string part open before him McCallum would play through crucial bits of it, Barbirolli listening with micro-phonic ears and the eyes of a hawk. They devoted several journeys to Berlioz's *Fantastic* Symphony and the *Fledermaus* Overture, to name two instances out of many. Passage after passage was subjected to alternative bowings and phrasings

* What Barbirolli and his men could get through in a night is illustrated by a concert which he conducted in aid of the local unemployed at Leith Town Hall in February 1934. The scheme was as follows: *Merry Wives of Windsor* Overture, Nicolai; Fantasia on *Carmen*, Gibilaro; the Grieg piano concerto; Tchaikovsky's 'Pathetic' Symphony; group of piano solos; Jarnefelt's Praeludium; *Shepherd's Hey*, Grainger; The Cachuca (*Gondoliers*); Keel's *Salt Water Ballads* for solo baritone; *Tales from the Vienna Woods*, J. Strauss; and *The Mastersingers* Overture.

before Barbirolli pencilled in definitive ones. As well as listening to McCallum's trial shots he sought his advice and sometimes adopted it. Of a given note-grouping McCallum might say: 'Shouldn't this be done with the heel of the bow? Let's try it with the heel.' Barbirolli: 'No, try it in the middle.' The middle would be tried to no purpose. Then McCallum: 'Frankly I think it's going to be better at the point after all.' So the point had its turn and, after much replaying and ear-cocking, would probably be adopted.

Barbirolli was already noted and soon became almost a byword for his obsession (as some considered it) with 'point playing' and his passion for *pianissimos*. But in this as in other technical matters he never, while in Scotland, imposed his views and rarely made arbitrary decisions. He listened to what other people said. He was prepared to accept that other people might know better or have a better idea. Not all conductors are as open-minded as this. In the eyes of some, to know better than they may be presumptuous, even offensive. There was nothing factitious about Barbirolli's comradely and (on suitable occasions) egalitarian attitude. Undoubtedly it made him something of a hero with the orchestra.

Of his first six weeks with the S.O. he said that they had been among the happiest of his musical career. His full term with the S.O. ran to nearly sixty weeks spread over five years. The sixty weeks were as happy as the six.

CHAPTER EIGHT

LION RELAXES

His middle thirties brought out a dozen latent characteristics, as happens with most men, although less markedly, and so expanded his personality that those who remembered the ferociously hard-working youth of fifteen years earlier, pale, prudent and a little withdrawn, might have been excused for asking where the real Barbirolli had been hiding all this time. He worked ferociously. There was a Friday night when he should have been the guest of honour at the Glasgow Art Club. During that week he rehearsed and conducted a total of seven concerts—three in Glasgow, two in Greenock and one each in Edinburgh and Sheffield. The following week he was down for nine more. These were equally widespread and entailed eighteen hours of rehearsal. When the Friday came, drooping with overwork, he turned in the Art Club engagement with apologies and went to bed for a recuperative sleep. At rehearsal next morning he was all bounce and pertinacity.

Such interstices as there might be in his winter schedules with the Scottish Orchestra were for the most part filled by recording sessions, London concerts and concerts in English towns. Of concurrent provincial commitments—and achievements—the most striking were in Leeds. Early in 1933 the Leeds Symphony Orchestra (later the Northern Philharmonic) was on the point of putting its shutters up for want of support. Barbirolli was invoked to the rescue. This involved cutting the schedule from seven concerts a year to four. In 1933–34, his first full Leeds season, he put on three symphonies (Mozart's No. 34 in C, Beethoven's No. 8 and Sibelius's No. 1), the second Brandenburg concerto (violin, flute, oboe and trumpet) and Mossolov's *Music of Machines*, a Soviet confection which *had* to be done because everybody else was doing it. Among concertos that season or the next were the Schumann piano with Myra Hess, the Rachmaninov C minor with Moiseiwitsch, the Tchaikovsky for violin with Jelly d'Aranyi and that of Elgar with Albert Sammons: high-ranking artists all. The top price of a serial ticket was only a pound. You could get a seat behind the orchestra for a shilling or one in the 'back area' for sevenpence if you turned up early enough. The concerts were given in a mid-Victorian hall with names of the great and less great inscribed in gilt under its cornices. Spohr and Sullivan were on equal terms with Handel and Beethoven. On symphony nights the place had often been painfully under-populated, with seasonal losses running to hundreds of pounds. Barbirolli's first full season ended with a modest profit; and so matters went on under his baton for two seasons and a half more. During that time the schedule went up from four concerts a year to six. Most of them fell on Sunday nights, slotting between his Glasgow Saturdays and his Edinburgh Mondays.

Again he had revived a corpse or, at any rate, set a moribund on his feet.

When it was time to relax and be lionised he relished both. At table he talked unendingly—and not about music only; cricket came into it, too; and Georgian glass; and the hansom cabs of old Bloomsbury; and his hobby interest in medicine and surgery; and how unschooled he was as a young man in the world and its ways. He would remember effervescent first nights as seen from the entr'acte pit. The first night of Somerset Maugham's *Our Betters* at the Globe Theatre in 1923, for instance: 'A naughty play. But I was an innocent. So much of an innocent, although I'd been in the Army, that I didn't always know what the point of the naughtiness was.'*

While talking, or in and among his talk, he did not neglect his food. People who knew him thirty-five years ago as well as in his later years, said: 'In those days John *ate*'. As he grew older, his sparse diet bewildered them as much as his ability to do with little sleep. In the late 1950s this writer talked with him at the end of a tough morning rehearsal in Manchester. He had been at it on the rostrum for three hours. That morning

* *Our Betters* would not raise an eyebrow today. Desmond MacCarthy, a leading critic of the 1920s, wrote that it was about a smart set whose habits were luxurious, standards cynical and love affairs 'canine'.

he had got to bed fairly early (i.e., at something after two) and, on rising, had put in three or four hours among his current scores or at his 'cello. Throughout the morning he had taken nothing but coffee. It was put to him at 1.30 p.m. that a steak with half a bottle of claret would be no bad thing. A look of pained nausea came over him. He waved the idea aside as one replete. During the old Edinburgh days he took steaks and much else with unflagging relish and would choose a matching claret with scholarship. Like all true gourmets, he liked to see others eat well. He is remembered as guiding a diffident young player by the elbow to the buffet at some well-found official reception. 'For heaven's sake grow up!' he adjured. 'Have something to drink! A glass of sherry at least! And a breast of chicken! . . . That's better!'

He was full of Italian and French kitchen lore, acquired at home from his parents and grandparents. In the Charing Cross district of Glasgow, which has been largely rebuilt since then (he was later to exclaim wistfully at the radically changed scene), he had a suite of rooms with kitchen. There he would cook ancestral dishes at which he considered himself a dab. His cooking was often for visiting friends as well as himself. (Much later it tended to be for friends only; often he did little more than taste what he had cooked.) To spaghetti bolognese he brought niceties comparable with those of the rehearsal rostrum. Before a ten o'clock rehearsal call for *La Mer* or, say, *Verklärte Nacht* he would put some recondite sauce on to simmer which had been nuanced as knowingly as he was about to nuance Debussy or Schönberg. Exotic dishes are not for all palates. Often he invited S.O. leaders and other players to his table. 'You like spaghetti?' he asked one guest, a little absently, while spooning a big helping on to her plate. The player didn't like spaghetti at all but was so awed and abashed that she mumbled something like 'Yes' both then and at subsequent parties where exactly the same thing happened. The truth as to her inhibition came out at last through another woman guest, Evelyn Rothwell, who *did* like spaghetti bolognese. And there was a lot of confusion and jollity about it all.

The problem at parties, whether his own or others', was how to persuade him to go to bed. When he was carried away by

his fervours and his memories and his pet aesthetic theories as
to this score or that, time went unregarded. On programme
music he could be amusingly sceptical. Strauss's *Don Quixote*
was in preparation. A piece which often rates an imported star
soloist was to be played as to its 'cello and viola solos by
Glasgow's own Mr. Meert and Mr. Nichols. (A crowded and
elegant concert, as things turned out. Artur Rubinstein was
there. Before the Strauss he played in a Saint-Saëns piano
concerto and Falla's *Nights in the Gardens of Spain*.) According
to programme notes that derive from Strauss himself, the
'cello stands for Quixote, the viola for Sancho Panza. Some
naïve person asked Barbirolli whether it was true that
Strauss's music 'told' Cervantes' story? He replied: 'Yes. But
only if you've been primed. It's just about impossible to
write music which makes people think right away of a spring
morning, or an elephant, or falling in love. There's a variation
in *Don Quixote* which is meant to be Quixote riding along a
road and charging a flock of sheep under the impression that
they're a hostile army. We hear him riding along the road,
then we hear the bleating sheep and the shepherd playing on
his pipe and Don Quixote attacking the poor things and
putting them to flight. It's all enormously clever as descriptive
music—if you know what it's about to begin with. We've got
to admit that music cannot "describe" without the help of
words. Given verbal aids, music has marvellous powers of
adding something of its own, the unique *something*, to the mental
pictures we have already formed.'

Such talk made the hours speed not only unregarded but
also unregretted by everybody within earshot except those
who happened to be jumpy about their commitments of the
morrow or, to be exact, of that same day. At the last Edinburgh
concert of the 1933–34 season McCallum led a heavy programme that ended with Tchaikovsky's Symphony No. 5,
having earlier played solo violin in Bach's second Brandenburg
Concerto. The following night he was due to lead the season's
last Edinburgh concert, ending with Strauss's *Ein Heldenleben*.
This, too, carries a part for solo violin, a very exacting one.
His one thought at the end of the Edinburgh concert was to
get back to Glasgow by late train for a good sleep before the
ten o'clock rehearsal. While he was packing his instrument

and the *Heldenleben* solo part—on which he had been working
as opportunity served in odd snatches during the day—
Barbirolli put his head round the bandroom door and said:
'We're going to a party'.

McCallum: 'No thanks. There's *Heldenleben* tomorrow. I
must catch the train.'

Barbirolli: 'That's all right. We are being taken back to
Glasgow by road. Why don't you relax? Come on, now.'

McCallum yielded with misgivings and went along. So did
a few other players. The party was at a big house in that
stately quarter of Edinburgh which has been known ever since
the era of tie-wigs as the New Town. There were lots of food,
lots of people (several of them 'big' people) and lots to drink.
Everybody lionised Barbirolli. Each of us loves being lionised
if the chance comes his way. As has been said, Barbirolli was
no exception to a sound rule. Whether being made an especial
fuss of or not, however, he always had a taste for reasonable
conviviality. 'Sitting and drinking with friends after a concert
has always been John's idea of heaven.' One has heard this
or something like it from a dozen intimates. The malt whisky
could not have been bettered. But McCallum wasn't much of a
drinker. He kept looking at the clock. At two in the morning
he vanished. Wishing to bring him into some story about
fiddle technique, Barbirolli turned to where he had been
sitting and found he wasn't there. The cry went up: 'What's
happened to David?' His hat and coat were still in the lobby.
A search began. Hearing the notes of a fiddle from afar,
Evelyn Rothwell tracked them down to the butler's pantry.
There she found McCallum among the silver, working away
at the *Heldenleben* solo. He broke off, rejoined the party for a
spell, then returned to the pantry for another *Heldenleben* bout,
explaining regretfully that he had no mind for anything else.
Towards four in the morning the Barbirolli party, five in all,
got into the promised motor-car. It belonged to the S.O.'s
tuba player and was a small one. It was never quite understood
how he contrived to get his tuba in, the tuba being a buxom
instrument, as well as four passengers. McCallum turned up
at rehearsal that morning after a catnap feeling dreadful and
found Barbirolli busy and bright. Late hours never had any
effect upon him.

Another such party followed an S.O. concert at Stirling. The hostess was a woman of cultivated taste who is said to have 'literally worshipped John'. Again a big house (Barbirolli and McCallum were taken to it in a spacious motor-car); magnificent supper; glasses plenteously refilled; and plenteous Barbirolli talk, the company hanging on his every word. Once more McCallum had anxious eyes on the clock: 'Are you watching the time, John? We've got to get back to Glasgow, you know.' Barbirolli reluctantly asked what time the late train left. With equal reluctance their hostess rather thought it was 'about now'. She had Charles, the butler, put in a call to the railway station. Charles came back from the telephone and was afraid the train had gone. The situation was the same as after the Edinburgh party but a degree worse: rehearsal at 10 a.m. and no train back to Glasgow until 8.30. McCallum went on worrying. Barbirolli went on talking. His hearers went on listening, laughing, exclaiming and twinkling their admiration. At last to bed—except that, owing to some domestic exigency, there were no beds free; they slept beneath eiderdowns in their underclothes on shakedowns. At eight they were driven to the station in the spacious motor-car, leapt into a taxi at the other end and reached St. Andrew's Hall late for the rehearsal. Barbirolli used never to come on to a platform, whether at rehearsal or performance, until all the players were seated, the leader included. McCallum went on first. He was in full evening-dress. His white tie was less than pristine. Ribald exclamations and sallies greeted him. The S.O. knew David McCallum as an assiduous professional whose life and all its routines were built around his calling. The bare notion that he might be a rake—which he obviously wasn't—struck everybody as highly comic. Two minutes later Barbirolli came on. He, too, was in tail-coat and a less than pristine tie. The only thing he had discarded from the night before was his carnation buttonhole. This time the sallies swelled to ironical cheers. Barbirolli took them with great good humour.

It is unlikely that any other eminent conductor of the day, especially an English one, ever found himself in a like situation but, if it had happened, none would have been rallied in so friendly, not to say affectionate, a spirit.

In Scotland, as later in Manchester and elsewhere, his

relations with orchestral players put him rather apart from other conductors and perhaps made some of them mildly envious. As the years went by, lack of responsiveness at re-hearsal, especially among the strings, could goad him to exasperation and to slammings down of the baton or even of the score. Most conducting scores are heavy objects and make an intimidating thud when slammed. Slams and thuds were usually succeeded by brief, thundery silence. Then came minatory words. On this we have vivid testimonies fifteen years apart. Both are from players who brought to rehearsals a quick eye, a good memory and a talent for writing down what they saw and heard. The first dates from the mid-1930s, and is by Bernard Shore, formerly first violist of the B.B.C. Symphony Orchestra and a teacher of renown. Barbirolli raps the rehearsing orchestra to silence. Exasperation point has been reached. Shore reports him thus:

> 'I've never heard anything like it! Can't you play at the point of the bow, eugh? ['Eugh' was Mr. Shore's notation of a questioning or condemnatory grunt that Barbirolli was given to using in these situations.] What's the matter? I've already asked you three times to play it at the point, and some of you are still sawing away at the middle, eugh! Now don't let me have any more of this nonsense, please!' Smack of the baton on his desk, emphasising his irritation.*

On to 1953. In that year Malcolm Tillis, another violist, joined the Hallé Orchestra. At his first rehearsal the chief business was Beethoven's Symphony No. 7, whose opening:

> . . . caused more trouble and exasperation than any symphony in the repertory except Sibelius's Second. Bets were often taken on the number of times it would have to be repeated. I think the record stood at eleven. . . .
>
> The eagle eye of the conductor missed nothing. If one player's bow was not in the right part of the stick, let alone not going in the same direction as all the others, he would stop the orchestra. Wearily flopping into the high chair which is always placed on the rostrum for rehearsals, his two arms hanging limp, he would remonstrate: 'But we have

* *The Orchestra Speaks* by Bernard Shore, Longmans Green, London, 1938.

played this section at the point for years. Some of you can't remember anything. It's enough to try the patience of a saint.'

His score was always open but his eyes seemed to be continually fixed on the players. There was a definite time-lag between his beat and the response from the orchestra. He alternated sarcasm and insults freely and without the slightest fear: 'Most of you seem *incretinated* this morning', 'I shall try giving you feeding bottles tomorrow', 'I wish the bio-chemists would invent some rhythm pills—I would buy them by the score and distribute them freely.'*

When a master scolds the whole class, keeping his cane, his tongue and his glare off individuals, the class, if it has quality, will take his tantrums without offence, provided he is a master with character and (what cannot be taken for granted) a human being into the bargain. A point made by Tillis and other witnesses to Barbirolli's goings-on is that as soon as a rehearsal break came the lashing words were forgotten; if he happened to be free of business during the break he would mix paternally with his players, exchanging jokes, gossiping about the newest concerto star, talking colour photography to one, asking after another's newborn, enthusing with a third about a certain restaurant in a certain back street near the Rialto bridge in Venice with *pasticcio maccheroni* that would take some beating and where a singer, flanked by accordion and fiddle, would oblige with Venetian folk songs on call. 'If you go there, mention my name,' he would add. (At least two player friends found their way to the Venetian back street and did as he advised; they were greeted with festive smiles and wine on the house.)

These later testimonies chime exactly with what the Edinburgh veterans say *unisono*: 'He was one of us. All stories about John or anybody else in music reached John as soon as anybody, or nearly so. If they were funny stories (I don't remember any ill-natured ones about him), he was literally one of the first to laugh. This sort of thing could never have happened to Sargent. To Beecham, occasionally, yes. *He* was a god who descended once in a while and deigned to notice what was going on. Sargent was the god who stayed upstairs; he didn't

* Malcolm Tillis, op. cit,

have a clue about what was being said. John was downstairs most of the time. He didn't miss a thing.'

He was judged by certain of his Edinburgh admirers to be something of a poseur. And his poses were among the things they admired. For special occasions he put on what was called his 'learned mien'. Glasgow had an amateur orchestra which rehearsed in the galleried hall of a club. One evening he paid an unannounced call. The players became aware of a small, lordly person up in the gallery who was not so much looking at as surveying them through what may have been alternatively pince-nez or an eyeglass but which certainly had a broad black ribbon. When the music halted there were gratified nudgings and whisperings on the rehearsal floor: 'Look who's up there!' The broad black ribbon made a great impression. His way of whipping off his spectacles, if that is what they were, made an even greater one. And was no doubt intended to. 'That was John all over,' judges a contemporary and professional witness. 'We saw through his poses. And we loved him.' Whipping off his spectacles became a mannerism at rehearsals also. He would pick up the score and scrutinise it at nose length with the naked eye.

'That,' said the knowing ones, 'is a Toscanini trick.' (He had attended Toscanini's first concert in London. This was in 1930, when Toscanini brought over his New York Orchestra. After the concert he was presented to the Maestro at a reception given by a pre-eminently musical peer, Lord Howard de Walden. This was the occasion when Toscanini, struck by the young man's name, established that he had known Barbirolli's father in Rovigo decades earlier.) There were other imputed mimicries. When the horns had a great unison tune of the Strauss-Mahler type he would raise his clenched fist, a signal for them to lift the bells of their instruments and produce the last ounce of *fortissimo*. 'The raised fist was Mengelberg* to the life'—just as his trick, before the opening beat, of smartly shooting his cuffs, was (again according to the knowing ones) 'pure Tommy Beecham'.

Those who, while playing under him in Glasgow and Edinburgh, noticed these things and put them down to

* Willem Mengelberg (1871–1951), conductor of the Concertgebouw Orchestra, Amsterdam, who often visited the U.K.

unconscious imitation, thought none the worse of him. Their regard and their loyalty were rock-solid. They accepted his authority and disciplines eagerly. This for a simple reason. When he first came to them they had been loose-knit and dispirited. Now they were welded. A whole had been made out of disjunct parts. Their spirit was back; and, with the spirit, pride.

He began to speak of the 'rebirth' of the Scottish Orchestra; of the remarkable revival of enthusiasm for orchestral music in Scotland; of the extraordinary fashion in which the musical scene had been transformed; of the young people now coming to S.O. concerts in numbers that hadn't been seen for years. There was no overstatement in all this. The S.O. had escaped dissolution early in 1932 by recruiting new guarantors and doubling its guarantee fund. Less than two years later the S.O. had doubled its guarantee fund again. This was Barbirolli's doing more than that of any other person or factor. More tickets were being sold; which made it possible to keep the prices down. With more money coming in or at call, it was possible to hire the Horowitzes and the Heifetzes, the Schnabels and the Rubinsteins oftener than had hitherto been dreamed of. At the end of Barbirolli's first full season the call on the Glasgow guarantors was cut by two-thirds. This was made feasible partly because there were more guarantors to call on and partly because of increased takings. Before the end of his tenure the Glasgow call was down to four shillings in the pound, or one pound a head. In Edinburgh S.O. concerts cost more to promote. Here, too, however, the guarantors' burden was lightened: after his second season, for instance, from sixteen and three in the pound to nine and six.

His last nights were ebullient and full-hearted. More than once enough people were turned away from a crammed St. Andrew's Hall for a substantial overflow meeting if there had been any place to overflow. At the end the audience would be on its feet, faces shining. Barbirolli would be given a laurel wreath and would bow his thanks for the happy clamour. Then came three sung farewells—'For he's a jolly good fellow', 'Will ye no come back again?' and 'Auld lang syne', with the orchestra joining in.

Between concerts and between seasons he was made much of as a public speaker. He affected not to take himself seriously in this rôle. 'My career of spurious public oratory', he used to say. In the mid-1930s there were things that needed to be said about music. He said them without mincing words. As when speaking up for English Opera, he assailed insidious misconceptions. First: the notion held by many people clever enough to know better that music is a purely emotional as opposed to intellectual art: 'These people are inclined to look upon our most distinguished performers as superior performing animals. Let me tell them that to elucidate the full score of a composition by Strauss or Stravinsky requires just as much brain as to elucidate certain statutes of the lawyers—and makes a damned sight more sense when you've elucidated it.' A second misconception: That all foreign manifestations of art, music especially, were to be exalted above our own: 'In reply to that I say there is no such thing as a musical nation or an unmusical one. People are musical or unmusical in accordance with the opportunities afforded them. If Germany or Italy had had to get their music under the same conditions as we get ours, that is, by private enterprise and the munificence of a few isolated individuals, I doubt whether they would have worked so well and purposefully for music as we have done.' This brought him to the Grand Indictment: the cold shouldering of native music by the State. While other arts were officially recognised and cosseted, music was left to struggle and survive as best it could: 'At the mere mention of subsidies for music worthy people throw up their hands in horror, as if one proposed to snatch bread from the mouths of the unemployed. What of the musician's bread? Instead of helping music, Government has penalised it excessively.' He invited his hearers' attention to an Iniquity known as the Entertainment Tax. This was in the autumn of 1934. It was made known soon afterwards that the Scottish Orchestra had been granted exemption from the Iniquity. Since the tax was first imposed it had accounted down the years for £13,000 out of the S.O.'s aggregate deficits of £17,000. A thorn was out of Glasgow's musical flesh at last.

Those who ran the orchestra were encouraged in their dream of national status. They put before the Edinburgh Concert

Society proposals for 'closer co-operation and an amalgamation of interest'. In making this approach publicly known, a spokesman of the E.C.S. mentioned that the men who had founded the S.O. forty years earlier, although themselves Glaswegians, intended it as a national institution and not exclusively as a Glasgow affair. This was interpreted by certain other Edinburgh music-lovers as another way of saying: 'There's only one orchestra for Edinburgh, namely Glasgow's, and to hell with Edinburgh's own, the Reid Symphony'. Sore feelings resulted and a blaze of debate in newspaper letter columns. Reid apologists made no bones about the proportion of amateurs in the Reid ranks. They made much of the auditions these amateurs, as well as the professionals, underwent at the hands of the B.B.C., who were already feeling their way towards the setting up of a Scottish wireless orchestra. They had sharp things to say also about the traditionally exotic and foreign appearance of the Scottish Orchestra's players, people collected from 'all quarters', and the extreme rarity in its annals of conductors who could claim a purely British ('to say nothing of Scottish') name or origin. Money entered into the case as well. People who had studied the accounts of the Glasgow Choral and Orchestral Union, the S.O.'s parent body, contended that the average cost of an Edinburgh concert was out of all proportion greater than that of a Glasgow concert, mainly due to the high fee charged to Edinburgh by the orchestra's directors. No blame to the latter, wrote one apologist, if Edinburgh was 'willing to be used as a milch cow to keep down the price of Glasgow seats and the call on Glasgow guarantors'.

In this hullabaloo one thing tended to be lost sight of, namely that good orchestral playing is better than the not-so-good, highly professional conducting preferable to picturesque amateurism. One of Tovey's most eloquent champions has given an affectionate account* of the great man's odd ways on the rostrum. During slow movements he used to let the music flow with the lightest of beats while grasping a rostrum knob in his left hand and gently crossing right foot over left. A beat ungainly at the best of times became a 'shovel action' on climaxes. He was incapable of covering up a mishap. Slips

* In *Donald Francis Tovey*, Mary Grierson, Oxford University Press, 1952.

which would have passed unnoticed by most concert-goers were brought to general attention by his 'immediate and involuntary reaction, which often made matters worse by drawing attention to the player concerned'. Setting out to rehearse a symphony billed for an imminent concert, he would become so immersed in a single movement as to devote much of the three-hours session to it, often pausing to lecture on the music's finer points for the benefit of students, who flocked to his rehearsals as to orchestration lessons.

No amount of essay prose—and Tovey's prose was, in its department, uniquely sage and penetrating, that of a master among masters—could make up for such impracticality and the gaucherie that went along with it, especially in the eyes of people under the spell of Barbirolli and his businesslike yet passionate way of going about things. Tovey himself had too much good sense and propriety to embroil himself in the general tit-for-tat between Reid supporters and S.O. supporters. Privately he was watchful, a little touchy, perhaps a little hurt. There were people, he said, who, in the national orchestra debate, wished to undermine or ignore the Reid. Any suggestion that the Reid 'is not *de facto* the nucleus of a national orchestra' was impudence and should be damned accordingly. A national orchestra, he added, was what he had been aiming at with the Reid Orchestra ever since 1916.

Long before achieving permanence and national status, the S.O. staked claims in nine communities outside the two 'home' cities. Some were far off, some were fairly near. Some were big, others small. These towns and their populations in the mid-1930s are listed below.* During ten biting and snowy days at the end of his appointment Barbirolli took out the S.O. at reduced strength (sixty at best, sometimes fewer) and played twice in each of them. There would be an afternoon concert for children; whole schoolfuls came in by motor-coach. Usually some lecturer was on hand to explain what an orchestra was and say something mildly analytical about pieces that were to be played, from Tchaikovsky's No. 5, Beethoven's No. 7 and the *Mastersingers* Overture to *the* Minuet

---

* Dumfries (pop. 22,795), Elgin (36,565), Fraserburgh (9,720), Inverness (22,582), Montrose (10,196), Motherwell (64,708), Paisley (86,441), St. Andrews (8,269), Stirling (24,593).

(that of Boccherini), *the* Pizzicato (that of Delibes) and (of course) the Queen of Sheba music with its two young women oboists. The concerts were given in town halls, theatres, assembly halls. At the start questions would be put by the lecturer:

'How many of you boys and girls have seen the Scottish Orchestra before?'

A few hands would go up.

'How many of you have seen any other orchestra?'

Fewer hands still.

'How many of you have heard the Scottish Orchestra over the wireless?'

This time a forest of hands.

After the dialogue would come solos on various instruments to show off their range and 'colour'. The tuba usually played 'Rocked in the Cradle of the Deep'. The bassoon would run a bar or two of 'Hush-a-bye-Baby' into Tosti's 'Goodbye'. The cor anglais' choice was 'Charlie is my darling', the clarinet's a fragment of Laurel and Hardy, the American film comics' signature tune, always good for a titter. The evening concerts for grown-ups drained the countryside for miles around, packing hall after hall despite the forbidding state of the roads. A bus strike in Stirling accounted for a hundred or two empty seats in the unreserved part. The eight other halls did splendid business. Sometimes Barbirolli got five-minute ovations between items. Percy Grainger's 'Molly on the Shore' was an infallible concert-stopper.

It was put about that these nine-town itineraries were to be annual and that they could be extended; to qualify for a S.O. visit all a town had to do was put up a fifty-pound guarantee and pay for hall-hire and local advertising. Owing to the war the Scottish Orchestra did not become the Scottish National Orchestra until 1950. Tovey was dead by then. His orchestra had given up the ghost. Mary Grierson's comment was rueful: 'Edinburgh has . . . decided that nothing but the best from elsewhere will suffice her and remains incapable of judging whether or not that best is better than what her . . . native talent, fostered and encouraged, could have provided'.

At his hundreds of concerts with the S.O. during his three

full seasons and two half seasons in Scotland Barbirolli conducted about 800 performances of particular works. On account either of their popularity or because what Glasgow heard on Saturdays and Tuesdays Edinburgh heard or was apt to hear on Mondays, a high proportion of these performances were repeats. Deducting repeats we are left with a solid repertory of 400 or 500 pieces of varied sizes, many styles and widely different technical challenge. The span was from Mozart divertimenti, Corelli's Concerto for Christmas Night and the *Siegfried Idyll* (which at that time he insisted on playing with what he cited as Wagner's original specification: seventeen players, including one double-bass and two each of first violins, second violins, violas and 'cellos, a total of nine strings*) to Beethoven's Choral Symphony, Schubert's 'Great' C major and such exotics (for that time and place) as the Adagietto for strings from Mahler's Symphony No. 5, Stravinsky's *Pulcinella* suite and the complete *Petrushka* ballet score. Symphonies were the backbone of his work. He had about forty in his repertory at this time, and he gave nearly eighty performances of them. This does not mean two performances of each. A few came up once and were then shelved. Of the Beethovens, No. 5 and 7 returned oftenest, as might have been expected. Of the Brahmses each except No. 3 (once only) had a good innings; and so it was with Tchaikovsky's Fourth, Fifth and Sixth. Sibelius's No. 7, the two Elgars and Berlioz's *Fantastic* were all doubles.

Altogether, his schemes were solid, lively and reasonably wide in outlook. Subject to a little trimming of the Saturday night programmes, they would have done credit to any metropolitan orchestra with a middle-of-the-road policy. Listening to them while they were, so to say, on the simmer must have been agreeable enough for sensitive and keen concert-goers. But few laymen can have suspected the intellectual sweat that went to their preparation. Most of the 400 to 500 pieces which, by the end of his term, comprised

* Which is all there was room for on the stairs at Triebschen, Lucerne, says Ernest Newman, for the first performance, on Cosima Wagner's birthday in 1870. Newman adds that for a performance at Mannheim a year later Wagner specified 31 to 35 players, including 23 to 27 strings. (*The Life of Richard Wagner*, Vol. IV, Cassell, 1947.)

Barbirolli's repertory had had to be analysed, assimilated or re-assimilated and technically mastered in a matter of three or four years. The theatre has a phrase for actors who get up parts in next to no time. They are said to be 'quick studies'. As a conductor Barbirolli was one of the quickest studies and perhaps the most insatiable that English orchestral rostrums have known.

Some account has been given of one feat of memory, his mastering of Elgar's E flat Symphony in forty-eight hours. He brought off a more startling one which, although it reached the ears of the Incorporated Society of Musicians at their annual conference in 1937,* was little canvassed either at the time or later. In March 1930 he had been billed for his second concert with the Royal Philharmonic Society. He was to conduct Casals in the Schumann 'cello concerto and two new English works. Of the latter, one was a *Fantasia on Sussex Folk Songs* by Ralph Vaughan Williams, who was to receive the Society's gold medal at the interval. In this score, too, there was a part for solo 'cello. Casals attended to it. The other novelty was a triptych, *Overture, Elegy and Rondo*, by Arnold Bax.

For days Barbirolli burrowed into the new scores, carrying them with him wherever he went. On bus tops (always favourite workrooms of his) he never lifted his head out of them. Jacques Thibaud, the violinist, with whom he was on cordial terms, happened to be staying at the Park Lane Hotel. He called on Thibaud. That day he had the Bax under his arm. He put it down in the lounge and went to the reception desk. When he came back the score had gone. Nothing more was heard of it. It can only be concluded that it had been stolen, though with what motive is unknown. So far he had not heard a note of the piece. It was not a lightweight work. Its size and complexity, Barbirolli used to say, were those of a three-movement symphony. That night he sat up till dawn, writing it down in short score from memory. From this he not only conducted the rehearsals but also corrected the orchestral parts, which were in manuscript and unchecked. To spare Bax tenterhooks, he told him nothing of what had happened until after the concert.

* It was mentioned briefly and incidentally by Frank Howes, the musicologist and critic, in a paper that dealt with the *chant intérieur*.

With players he always had a great reputation as a teacher; a teacher who devoted little time or attention to aesthetics, much to the brass tacks of technique. His preparing of William Walton's viola concerto illustrates his appetite for thoroughness and his talent for getting hard work out of others.

The Walton had come out in 1929, with Paul Hindemith as its first soloist. It was still a newish work, therefore, and for conservative ears something not so much to enjoy as to puzzle out. The S.O. committee had not forgotten their policy of 'discreet adventure'. They knew, as did Barbirolli, that the concerto was something which *had* to be done. One day he said to Eileen Grainger: 'It's been decided to do the Walton, and I want you to do it.' Miss Grainger blinked. She had done the same when invited to lead the Covent Garden touring violins. She was little more than a girl. She was still a very junior player. 'But,' she objected, naming the greatest of English violists, 'that is a job for Lionel Tertis, surely?' Barbirolli: 'That's what somebody on the committee said. I told them I'd got my own girl in my own orchestra. And that was that. There's no time to lose. Now about coaching . . . .'

It was mid-November. The performance was listed for a Tuesday in mid-January. Between these dates fell eight clear Saturdays. On each of these Miss Grainger took her viola to Barbirolli's flat in the afternoon. From the start he concentrated on the quick or otherwise difficult passages. He had sorted these out and marked them in readiness for her first session. He took her through them at very slow tempo. At the end he said: 'Go home and practise at that tempo during the week: *that* tempo—no quicker, mind!' The following Saturday afternoon he had her take the same passages a shade more quickly. During the week she practised at the new speed. And so it went on week by week. Gradually accelerating, they reached Walton's metronome markings eleven days before the performance. In and among they had, of course, coped with the concerto's slower and sweeter pages. Miss Grainger went on to the platform feeling technically sure of herself and gave a well-considered performance. After Walton came Balakirev's symphonic poem *Tamara* and Elgar's E flat Symphony. A distinguished programme kept hundreds of people away; from the platform St. Andrew's Hall looked half empty. In those times an Elgar symphony on top of an English novelty was not Glasgow's idea of a musical night out. Mrs. Wilfrid Parry, as she now is, remembers Barbirolli's reading of the concerto as intensely romantic, the sort of approach which would not do at all for the young people of a later generation—and would not have done perhaps for the latter-day Barbirolli. One clue to his attitude thirty-five years ago is a signed photograph of himself which he gave his soloist in memory of their collaboration. In the margin he notated the viola's opening entry and over the top wrote: *Vibratissimo!!!*

Before we leave Scotland, let us glance at two of its leading music critics, what they made of him and how one diagnosed chalk where the other proclaimed cheese. Neither man had a personal 'byline'. William Daly was with *The Scotsman* and wrote on music for that newspaper from 1918 to 1944. Not only had he no personal byline. He had no byline of any sort. Percy Gordon was the *Glasgow Herald's* man. All his notices were headed: 'By Our Music Critic'. Daly and Gordon were not required to cover the same concerts. Daly's concern was with the S.O.'s 'Mondays' at the Usher Hall, Gordon's with its 'Saturdays' and 'Tuesdays' at St. Andrew's Hall; but they listened to roughly the same Barbirolli-S.O. repertory, even if in slightly different conditions. Both halls were acoustically good, although each may have brought out certain orchestral strands or tints that didn't 'speak' to as good effect in the other. Then again, depending on where they fell in either repertory, some pieces may have been better prepared and therefore better performed in one city than in the other. The essential difference, however, was of a more radical sort: a difference of mental temper and emotional 'tuning'. As in the case of *The Times* and the *Daily Telegraph* after Barbirolli's first concert for the Royal Philharmonic Society, their readers may have wondered at times whether the two men were writing about the same orchestra and the same conductor in the same pieces.

Daly's notices were all praise, or nearly so. Of Tchaikovsky's No. 5 he might hint that the finale went at a quicker pace than he was accustomed to but that the effect was 'very stirring' just the same. Almost every notice was a paean. He

heard a fine dignity and beauty of melodic line in Barbirolli's
Handel; loveliness and a massive solemnity in his Brahms
No. 1—'a great performance', one that 'could not readily be
surpassed'; glitter, brilliance and superb 'line' in Elgar's
E flat; in Mozart, Beethoven, Mendelssohn and much else
all or just about all the grace, elegance, polish, tone-breadth,
seductive colour, climatic magnificence and whatnot that the
ear could wish for, the whole justly shaped, balanced and controlled. Daly was no fool. He did not, as ignoramuses sometimes
will, make a point of crying up everything so as to be on the safe
side. In any case *The Scotsman* employed critics, not flunkeys.
On the evidence of his notices, Daly knew his way about
music. His praise of Barbirolli clearly came from the heart,
and his heart was a musical one. For string playing he had a
good ear. 'What a joy it is,' he exclaimed, as soon as Barbirolli's
remodelling of the S.O.'s string choir took effect, 'to hear a
body of string tone with such volume and of such fine quality!'
Taking into account also improvements in the brass and
woodwind, Barbirolli (he wrote) had made of the S.O. a
powerful, brilliant and flexible instrument. Listening one
night to a 'vivid and startling' account of Berlioz's *Fantastic*
Symphony, he suddenly realised 'how valuable a *national*
possession the Scottish Orchestra has become' (italics mine).
Can he have been on the side of Glasgow against the
Reidites?

Percy Gordon was on nobody's side except, perhaps, the
composer's, and sometimes he gave the impression that even
the composer had better mind what he was about. A small
man with a goatee beard and eyes that were either big by
nature or seemed so because of his spectacle lenses, he was
said jokingly to look rather like William Shakespeare and had
the humour to laugh at this himself. In private life he twinkled
companionably and had a taste for drollery. As soon as he
picked up a pen a change came over him. Criticism was a
professional sideline. In Glasgow he had a church organ,
looked to a church choir and took pupils in harmony, counterpoint, theory and composition.* The lessons he proffered, the

---

* He appears to have been a good teacher. Before coming up to the
Royal College of Music, the late Gavin Gordon (not a relative), composer
of that excellent ballet score *The Rake's Progress*, had lessons from him.

ferrule he wielded, in the *Herald* on Monday and Wednesday mornings and any other mornings of the week that followed straight upon concerts or operatic performances were reproving or corrective more often than not. Many a musician went in fear before the event and licked his wounds after it.

On Barbirolli and the S.O., their programme building and their standards of performance Gordon trained an ear which, when affronted, did not readily forgive. There was the unlucky Saturday night when Mr. Wood, the leading bassoon, did handsomely by Mozart's concerto K. 191 for that instrument, winning uncommonly warm applause and, according to the custom of those times, an 'encore'. Before passing on to Delius's *Walk to Paradise Garden,* Barbirolli announced that Mr. Wood and the orchestra would oblige with the *Lucy Long* variations. By an older generation of Saturday Pop- and Prom-goers, *Lucy Long* is remembered as one of those facetiae which music has learned it can live without quite comfortably; its effects included an isolated note, loud and low, which always transported the simple hearted. An unfortunate choice, exclaimed Gordon: 'From the musical point of view *Lucy Long* is no more than a music-hall turn. On Saturday night it repeated many a previous success. The audience laughed; and the bassoon's appointment as the Orchestral Fool (no wit demanded) was confirmed.'

Exactly a week later he brought his guns to bear again. The annual 'plebiscite' concert ended with a *Scottish Fantasia,* a work especially composed for the S.O. by Alfonso Gibilaro which had had its première at the S.O.'s hands some weeks earlier. On neither occasion did the programme mention that Alfonso Gibilaro was John Barbirolli's brother-in-law. That would have been gossip; and S.O. programmes were nothing if not sober and analytical. On the strength of published voting figures, Gordon held that those responsible for the plebiscite programme had departed from the expressed will of the 'electorate' by leaving out the *Fledermaus* Overture and putting in the Gibilaro *Fantasia* which, he added, was not, strictly speaking, a fantasia at all 'but merely a selection of Scots airs, a class of work which belongs to an entirely different department of music from that associated with symphony orchestras. It should be left for military bands or the numerous small combinations that broadcast light afternoon programmes. While effective as orchestral scoring, the *Fantasia* must be challenged on the artistic side, since it robs the airs of their fundamental simplicity. In doing this it continues a falseness of expression which too often kills the folk element in music and of which Scots, if they really appreciate their unique heritage of song, should be the first to complain.'

Between 1930 and 1937 Barbirolli conducted one hundred and nine concerts in Glasgow. So far as can be ascertained, given the anonymity of his notices, Gordon 'covered' practically all of them. It is notorious that no prose tastes more like yesterday's tea than the staple of yesteryear's music criticism in daily newspapers: and it must be admitted that Gordon's aggregate on Barbirolli in the *Herald*, something near a hundred thousand words, is no easy draught for the researcher. In the light of criticisms which had seen print earlier and others which were to come, however, certain of his strictures are worth weighing.

Roughly a third of his notices were approving, though not exactly cordial, and couched as a rule in general terms that do not lend themselves to quotation. Of the remaining two-thirds many were adverse in what may strike the reader as too subjective and finical a way. That the 'inner grace of many of Haydn's phrases was only partly revealed' is an indictment that gets us nowhere. That a performance of *Till Eulenspiegel* 'lacked spiritual abandon' gets us no further. There may have been something, however, in the charge of undue deliberation: 'The Till whom we heard whistling in the street was not impudent enough; he performed thoughtfully and carefully, as if at a competition, and in his replies to the judges [the reference here is to the penultimate section of Strauss's tone poem] he was not so much defiant and impertinent as inclined to argue the matter on legal grounds.'

Gordon would often describe a performance as brilliant. Sometimes this meant he had been well pleased. At other times 'brilliant' in his first paragraph warned of whippings to come. Thus of Tchaikovsky's No. 5. Brilliantly performed, to be sure. But didn't Barbirolli take Tchaikovsky's symphonies too seriously on their emotional side? Over-insistence on the music's wildness and excitability had resulted in the audience going through 'as strenuous an experience as the conductor himself. Mr. Barbirolli seemed to be raising the temperature of the whole work. Even the quieter periods took on the quality of exaggerated and almost distressful personal expression. . . . The timpani often startled the listener, dominating the situation instead of simply adding pulse to the vigour of the music.' This was not the only case, in Gordon's opinion, of over-drumming. It happened also, he complained, in Tchaikovsky's *Pathétique*, where 'the percussion was allowed to be too important'; in Beethoven's No. 7, where Barbirolli was disposed to demand 'too much energy of the timpani whenever a full-toned excitement was called for,' the drums 'occasionally taking command of the score'; in the finale of Schubert's 'Great' C major, where 'he allowed the drums to dominate the situation in several places, turning what should have been a rich excitement into something like melodrama'; and in the Brahms No. 4, where 'the unmusical emphasis he required from the timpani was at times disturbing. . . . Such activity from the drums is not part of Brahms's scheme.'

There were chidings, too, as to speeds and styles. We read (again of Schubert's 'Great' C major) that Barbirolli 'is inclined to be restless in his idea of pace, altering it slightly in the course of a steadily moving period. There was not enough of simple greatness of expression'. And (again of Brahms's No. 4): 'It does not help the expression to slacken the pulse without a direction from the composer. . . . In giving too big a presentation to the gentler periods Mr. Barbirolli . . . often weakened his result. . . . In broadening the pace for a chord or two at strong cadences . . . he was, so to speak, turning an extra limelight on what Brahms had already fully illuminated. The symphony calls for a classic steadiness of pulse . . . without which Brahms's careful provision of variety cannot be made effective.'

In Beethoven's No. 2 Barbirolli was reproached for choosing a big frame for a small picture; into the bargain he sometimes made the music sound 'quiet without being restful'. In Beethoven's No. 4 his first movement 'suggested hurry rather than geniality'. In Beethoven's No. 5 he failed to bring off the right balance between the 'drama' of the first movement and the excitement and brilliance of the last. Sibelius's No. 5?

F

Some of the 'power and onwardness' of the great final theme
was lost by being done too slowly. Sibelius's No. 7? Not quiet
enough. Some of the music's profound simplicity was missed.
'A general bigness of result clouded the score at times.'
Mendelssohn's 'Scotch' Symphony? Too warmly treated. 'He
put more passionate romance into the music than is really
there, thus taking away lucidity and emotional balance. . . .
Mr. Barbirolli was thinking of Scotland too much. . . .
Mendelssohn's melodies were tempted to sing of feelings
beyond their experience.'

Thus Percy Gordon went nagging on. His naggings are not
to be dismissed as bile. They point to what appear to have
been at this time recurring marks and limitations of Barbirolli's
musicianship. No matter. Gordon might nag himself blue in
the face. Scotland loved Barbirolli none the less. He had been
heard of in other places, one of them an extremely important
place. And so another curtain rises.

CHAPTER NINE

NEW YORK PHILHARMONIC

THE cablegram from Arthur Judson, manager of the New York Philharmonic-Symphony Orchestra* and executive secretary of its parent society, reached Barbirolli on an April morning in 1936, knocking the breath out of him. He had looked forward to spending that morning, by way of diversion, in the museum of the Royal College of Surgeons, Lincoln's Inn Fields; a doctor friend had promised to show him round. The cablegram asked whether he would be interested in going over to New York the following October and guest-conducting the first ten weeks of the Philharmonic's 1936–37 season. From 1926 until his break with the Society that same Spring, the Philharmonic had been Arturo Toscanini's august fief; and Toscanini was 'by almost universal consent the greatest conductor of his time, *perhaps of all time*.'†
With the aura and the glory of Toscanini wrapped about it still and for ever, the Philharmonic was widely accepted, not least by many who had never heard it, as the world's greatest orchestra. In 1936 Barbirolli, when measured against such prestige, looked small indeed. 'Yet it was obvious', he said on looking back, 'that they wanted to try me out for the permanent conductorship in succession to Toscanini. And it sounded crazy.'

Cancelling his visit to Lincoln's Inn Fields, he hastened to his agent, Harold Holt, an impresario with branch agencies in

---

* A cumbersome but transient title dating from the merger of two New York orchestras in the 1920s. Henceforth, in this narrative, the New York Philharmonic or, for brevity, the Philharmonic.

† Everyman's Dictionary of Music, compiled by Eric Blom, C.B.E., D.Litt., third edition. The italicised phrase illustrates the unreason to which a leading musical savant could be tempted by Toscanini's extraordinary spell.

a dozen capital cities who traded astutely in old careers and new. Already his heart was in his mouth. On his way he said to himself again and again: 'This is *the* moment of your life. You've got to face up to it.' (Later he preferred to put it thus: 'I told myself: "This is a great challenge. However great the challenge it must be accepted." ') After his talk with Holt he cabled acceptance to New York. Everything from then on was negotiated by cable. No emissary came to see him. So far as he was aware, nobody connected with the Philharmonic Society had ever set eyes on him. Later he gathered that Judson, visiting Britain a season or two earlier, had seen him at work on what Americans call the podium. As the orchestra's administrative head, Judson was the breath of nostrils without number; forty years after his prime he was spoken of by greyheads in the Carnegie Hall precincts as the musical Czar of his day: and a long day it was.

'What', Barbirolli was asked a quarter-century later, 'made Judson and his board pick you?'

'I can only assume', he replied, 'that all those great artists I accompanied in the recording studios or on the concert platform—Heifetz, Elman, Horowitz, Rachmaninov, Casals and, above all, Fritz Kreisler—I can only assume that one or more of them recommended me in New York when the Philharmonic people were looking for somebody to follow Toscanini. Their recommendations remain the great pride of my life. Or perhaps "recommended" isn't the right word. It's truer to say they brought me up in conversation; they mentioned my name in the right quarters at the right time. What they said was something to this effect—"If there's no established conductor to fill the post, try Barbirolli. If you're looking for a *young* man, he's the one." '

It was not so much that New York imperatively needed somebody young. Anybody was welcome to the Society's rostrum, whatever his age, who had (1) the musicianship, (2) the personality and (3) box-office pull or (4) enough potential under the second and third of these headings to fill what nobody had the pluck to admit was an unfillable gap. Ever since the late summer of 1935 the Society had been in a poor way. In America 'depression' had bitten hard. The Maestro's music-making (Toscanini's, that is to say) was godlike, to be sure. But even the Maestro could not be sure of filling Carnegie Hall every time. Saddled with a season's deficit equal to over £100,000 of today's money, the Society was driven to appealing for funds over the air. For some reason this had offended the Maestro. Nor was this the only thing that did. When the Society paid him $100,000 for a season's work he alleged that they owed him $2,000 more. The Society thought to mollify him by paying him not $2,000 extra but $10,000. He refused to be mollified. Another thing. When he decided that he could not conduct certain concerts which he had been listed for during the 1935–36 season, the Society turned the dates over to Sir Thomas Beecham. They neglected to consult the Maestro before doing so. That, for the Maestro, was (pending a new beginning) the end. He telegraphed the board of the Philharmonic Society not to count on him for the 1936–37 season. 'Very good,' replied the board in effect, 'we'll skip 1936–37: but why not return and direct a Toscanini Festival in 1937–38? We should be happy to put one on for you.' The Maestro did not budge.

At his last Philharmonic concert of the current season (Wagner excerpts and the Beethoven violin concerto with Heifetz) five thousand persons, some having come hundreds of miles, mildly rioted for one hundred and forty standing places. Breaking through police cordons, they were dealt with by a clatter of mounted patrolmen. Impostors led a string of gullibles up a fire-escape on the Fifty-Sixth Street side, promising standing-room at the top for two dollars a head. At the end of the concert a press photographer let off a flash bulb point blank in Toscanini's face and was instantly reported over the air to have almost blinded him. Carnegie Hall and radio stations and newspaper offices had their switchboards blocked by anguished inquirers, many of whom would have been hard put to it to distinguish between *Leonora* No. 3 and the Liebestod from *Tristan*, both of which had been heard within the hour. No matter. Those things were mere music. Toscanini amounted to much more than that.

The Philharmonic Society picked up the mantle he had shrugged off and unhappily cast about for other shoulders to put it on. Their first thought and that of many others was Leopold Stokowski. No conductor was more unquestioningly adored. He was almost fifty: just the age, so far as conductors are concerned, for adoration. It was not to be, however. Stokowski let it be known that he was relinquishing much of his work with the Philadelphia Symphony Orchestra to Eugene Ormandy and devoting himself increasingly to musical research. What of dissident Germans? An invitation was cabled to Fritz Busch, former musical director of the Dresden State Opera. Busch was forty-six. He had renounced German citizenship when the Nazis came to power in 1933 and now directed the Danish State Radio Orchestra and Glyndebourne Opera, England. He cabled back that, while the invitation flattered him, his present commitments obliged him to turn it down. What of not-so-dissident Germans? Wilhelm Furtwängler, for instance?

Furtwängler was another fifty-year-old. A great conductor, undoubtedly, but not, perhaps, a hero. He chose to live on and make music in a land where that of Mendelssohn, Mahler and Meyerbeer were under racial ban and had accepted honours from a regime which imposed that ban and savagely maintained it. On the other hand he had incurred Hitler's frown by speaking up publicly for great Jewish artists, whom the Nazis were casting out, and by arguing for freedom of artistic expression against a repressive ideology. And had he not, to mark his dissidence, resigned his directorships of the Berlin Philharmonic Orchestra and the Berlin State Opera?

Another cable went out from New York. It reached Furtwängler in Vienna. At the end of February the Philharmonic Society announced that they had appointed him musical director for 1936–37; he was to conduct the first twelve weeks of the season starting in November. Uproar resulted. Newspaper letter-columns were avalanched with protest. An anti-Furtwängler committee was set up to keep protest on the boil. Many long-term supporters of the Philharmonic threatened to cancel their subscriptions unless the appointment was rescinded. From Berlin came officially inspired reports that Furtwängler had been rehabilitated by the Nazis and would soon be back in the musical commands which he had relinquished: in other words, that he was a Nazi pet once more. Fury redoubled. The Society tried to allay it with dignified phrases. Any attempt to make it appear that Furtwängler's appointment involved recognition of the Nazi dictatorship or approval of its artistic policies was unwarranted and misleading. Furtwängler, it was added, had risked and sacrificed his prominent position in Germany by waging 'single-handed, earnestly and persistently' a contest for tolerance and broadmindedness towards executant musicians as well as composers.

The Society might have saved its breath. After a fortnight's storm Furtwängler backed out. The cable in which he did so was that of a superior person whose art, of its nature, rode high and conveniently immune from all human battles: 'Political controversies disagreeable to me. Am not politician but exponent of German music which belongs to all humanity regardless of politics. I propose postpone my season in the interests of Philharmonic Society and of music until the public realises that politics and music are apart.' The executive committee gave a last deprecatory cough. The political implications which had been read into the abortive appointment were, they felt, greatly to be deplored. With that they dismissed Furtwängler from their minds. They had plenty else to worry about.

On the assumption that the 1936–37 season, if it came off, would see a further falling off in box-office revenue, they decided to cut their Carnegie Hall series from thirty weeks to twenty-four. Lest the musicians' union should jib at this, possibly forcing a disbandment of the orchestra, it was agreed to pay the players as much for twenty-four concerts in future as they had been paid for thirty concerts in the past. This placated the players without altogether ending their anxieties. Among contenders for the chief-conductorship were certain bold rebuilders, professional new brooms, who, after a trial run with an orchestra, were given to turning it upside down or inside out and sacking and replacing anything up to a third of the personnel. One such 'possible', resident already in the United States, they particularly feared. Which among them were destined to lose their jobs? Who was going to move up, who down? The air of musicians' clubrooms was electric with unease.

Barbirolli's appointment was announced by the Philharmonic Society's directorial board on 7th April 1936. The musical world rubbed incredulous eyes.

Barbirolli, said the announcement, was to open the forth-coming season, conducting ten weeks out of a total of twenty-four and twenty-six concerts out of a season's total of eighty-four. The other fourteen weeks and fifty-eight concerts were to be divided between three composer-conductors—Igor Stravinsky, Georges Enesco (Rumanian) and Carlos Chavez (Mexican) —who were to have a fortnight each, and Artur Rodzinsky, of Polish origin, conductor of the Cleveland Symphony Orchestra, who was to take the last eight weeks. Although Barbirolli was to be a 'guest' like the others, there could be no doubt as to his priority.

In much newspaper comment the following day surprise verged on perplexity. Nobody had heard of John Barbirolli. The official statement carried a hundred or two words of biographical matter which fed without satisfying. Not a line in the newspaper morgues. Not a word in the *New York Times*'s elephantine index, a fact about which the *New York Times* did not omit to exclaim. The New York Philharmonic was the greatest orchestra in the world. Every New Yorker knew that. There were people in Vienna, Berlin, London and Milan who knew it as well. What sense was there in giving the New York Philharmonic to a man who had never been on an American front page before or, so far as could be made out, on any front page of moment anywhere? Under a London dateline Ferruccio Bonavia, formerly an orchestral violist and now a leading English critic, explained that if Barbirolli played mostly in the British provinces that was because Henry Wood, Beecham, Landon Ronald, Adrian Boult, Malcolm Sargent and Hamilton Harty conducted so much and so regularly for the London concert societies that not much room was left for 'guests' however accomplished they might be. For a touch of 'colour' the gossip writers had recourse to his friends from student days, Ethel Bartlett and Ray Robertson, the piano duettists, who were now settled in California. Americans began to read of Antonio Barbirolli and Lorenzo Barbirolli in the Milan pit on the first night of *Otello* and how Toscanini had been a comrade of theirs.

Beneath the puzzlement were occasional rumbles of dis-content. From his magistral chair in the *New York Times* office Olin Downes, a kind of Percy Gordon perfected and multiplied by ten, made short work of the Society's arrangements and had little of comfort to say about the Society's designee:

When he comes here Mr. Barbirolli may conceivably reveal unexpected and phenomenal capacities, but there is nothing in the available records to indicate such a likelihood. The question therefore arises as to what justification there may be for giving this musician the lion's share of the new Philharmonic-Symphony season. There is not an American-born conductor in the whole group of visiting virtuosi; and the only one who has earned a Philharmonic-Symphony invitation by service and accomplishment in our midst is Rodzinsky. . . .

Mr. Barbirolli is not a bit more of a box-office attraction than a baker's dozen of conductors in this country who would have gone down on their knees for the opportunity which has been given to a foreign conductor of no exceptional reputation. . . .

Who, under these circumstances, will be the director of the orchestra? Who will be able to hire and fire, a condition absolutely indispensable if discipline is to be maintained and the best results secured? Will this power be given to the newcomer who is to be made responsible for the largest part of the season? One wonders. Or is nobody to have final authority at rehearsals and concerts? The need of such authority has been glaringly shown in recent months, when indifference approaching insolence was shown by certain players to certain of the guest conductors. Or shall we just roll along?

As a young man Downes spent a year or more at a New Jersey military institute before addressing himself to piano, harmony, theory, solfeggio and other mysteries at the National Conservatory of Music, New York City. Extolling discipline and deploring insolence came more naturally to him, perhaps, than to the generality of critics. There was much in his attitude to music and its performers that suggested the bluff brigadier. At this time he was fifty years old. First in Boston, then in New York, he had been writing 'overnights' and week-end features about music for thirty years and had another twenty

F*

years to go. A formidable gentleman. In what he wrote about
the Philharmonic's prospective virtuoso troupe one certainly
hears the thwack of riding crop on riding boot. But the sense
was sound, the tone warranted.

Nor was it all jubilation at home, even among Barbirolli's
admirers, especially the sage ones. The Royal Academy of
Music was presided over now by old William Wallace, one of
the less trumpeted originals of British music: exuberant
composer in his day of romantic tonepoems (Beecham had
taken him up before the first world war), writer of books on
musical aesthetics and on the Wagner-Liszt circle, surgeon and
(again in his day) a practising eye specialist. Writing in the
RAM magazine of how the musical world had been taken by
surprise when Barbirolli's appointment came out, he owned
that the New York Philharmonic's 'departure' had been
regarded with misgiving. 'It is impossible for us here', he
added, 'to appreciate the conditions that prevail in New York
or what influences determine a policy ... but we may conclude
that Barbirolli, with his quick and observant mind, rests
secure and may remain unshaken in our confidence.'

Nearly seven months passed before he sailed for New York:
'Throughout those months I went through hell. Nerves isn't
the word for it.' There were over a hundred names on the
New York orchestral strength: thirty more players to get tone
out of than he normally handled in Scotland. Of the hundred
he knew only two. One of these was a 'cellist; the other a
contrabassoonist whom he had served with in the Queen's
Hall Orchestra twenty years earlier. The rest would be new
faces which, when the time came, he would try to read for
some idea whether the thoughts behind them matched what
the mouths were saying or, more pointedly, not saying. Would
they take to him? Or take from him? He had many things to
lose, the most important being that spring in the heel and in
the heart that comes from confidence and tranquil energy.

While waiting he immersed himself in score-study for the
battle ahead. At his twenty-six concerts he would be performing
well over a hundred programme items, not all different ones;
many were to be played two or three times over to different
audiences during the same week. In this aspect New York

was Glasgow-Edinburgh over again but more so. There were series on Thursday nights and Saturday nights, with interlocking series on Friday afternoons and Saturday afternoons. In most cases each Thursday programme was repeated wholly or in part at two succeeding ones. His 1936–37 repertory, as it came to be agreed with New York, was little more than an echo of what he had been doing in Scotland, and a cautious echo at that. He spent a lot of time reading with more hope than relish through new American music, picking out a concert overture here, a symphony or tonepoem there. Whether one considers typical programmes or his scheme as a whole one gets an impression of things thrown together, a criticism occasionally voiced at the time. Perhaps nothing better could be expected of a season confected across three thousand miles of water.

The Scottish Orchestra was loth to see him go but made no bones about releasing him for an assignment regarded as an indirect honour to itself. At the end of the previous season it had been announced that he would conduct the whole of the 1936–37 one; this would have been his fourth as the orchestra's permanent conductor. His ten weeks at Carnegie Hall, entailing an absence of thirteen weeks altogether, made a gap in seasonal arrangements for Glasgow and Edinburgh which was filled by bringing in the late Georg Szell, conductor subsequently of the Cleveland Symphony Orchestra, two years older than Barbirolli and already well established on German rostrums, including that of the Berlin State Opera. Barbirolli was to come back in mid-January 1937 for over thirty concerts in the two Scottish cities and the nine Scottish towns named in the previous chapter. No sooner had these plans been rounded off than a request came from the Minneapolis Symphony Orchestra that he should take over in the New Year from Eugene Ormandy who, in the symphonic general post then going on, was to relieve Stokowski in Philadelphia. Barbirolli decided that his Scottish commitments came first and turned the Minneapolis offer down. That the offer had been made was one of the sweets of his New York appointment. His name was being bruited in many a far-flung orchestral boardroom.

At Pagani's restaurant late in October he was given a

send-off dinner and a silver presentation tankard by fellow
musicians, among them Adrian Boult (now Sir Adrian), who
took the chair. 'They knew I had taken something on,'
reflected Barbirolli. Then he sailed with a load of current
scores and for leisure reading—if there was to be any leisure—
a small library of books about cricket. He sailed alone: in
other words, without Marjorie Barbirolli. They had parted
company eighteen months earlier.

For his first full season with the Scottish Orchestra (1933–34)
they had travelled north together and kept house in Glasgow
where, as in Edinburgh, she appeared at some of his concerts.
To Parry Jones's Siegmund she sang Sieglinde in a performance
of Scene 3, Act 1, *The Valkyrie*, which got agreeable notices.
After Scotland they returned to Woburn Court. The end came
a year later. It had long been obvious to many who mixed
with them professionally that the marriage was not going well.
Had John become overmarried to music or, at any rate, to his
vocation? Had Nonna been over-solicitous for his welfare or
too much the matriarch? There were many diagnoses and much
speculation. Early in 1936 Marjorie petitioned for a decree—
which was granted by Mr. Justice Langton, with costs—for the
restitution of conjugal rights. The petition was undefended. In
it the petitioner alleged that the respondent had left her in
March 1935 'without just cause' and that he refused to return.
To anticipate: the marriage was dissolved in June 1939 at a
session of the High Court (Divorce Division) presided over by
Mr. Justice Bucknill. The decree nisi stated that the respondent,
'Giovanni Battista (John) Barbirolli deserted the Petitioner
without cause for a period of at least three years immediately
preceding the presentation of the petition.'

Marjorie Barbirolli presently resumed her career in British
opera and went on with it for a decade or more before retiring.
She has not remarried. Nor did she ever see John Barbirolli
again. She speaks cordially of his personality and his gifts.
Whatever of bitterness there may have been had passed long
before his death. 'All the tears were shed long ago.' Exceedingly
few among Barbirolli's vast post-war public had heard of
Marjorie Barbirolli or knew that he had married twice. To an
older generation of opera-goers she is remembered indelibly.
In his mind's eye the present writer sees her Octavian as

plainly, with all the scene's glitter and pomp, as if the years had rolled back, the curtain were up and she there on the stage again, handing the silver rose to Sophie while watching (without appearing to watch) her husband's beat down in the pit.

People from the Philharmonic Society were waiting for him on the pier when *Aquitania* docked in New York. Rooms had been taken for him at Essex House. They took him there and saw him settled in. There were one or two things to talk about which it had not been feasible to clear up in correspondence. One thing especially had preoccupied him. He had heard much about America's preference—if that was what it amounted to—for conductors who conducted from memory. He and his new friends mulled the point over.

Stokowski was a conspicuous no-score man. He was a conspicuous no-baton man into the bargain. Somebody brought up a story told by Stokowski's wife. At a concert in Boston, conducted by some colleague of her husband, she had a seat in front of a Fat Lady and a Thin Lady. This is what she overheard:

Fat Lady: Oh, what a relief to see a great conductor using the score!

Thin Lady: Yes—so different from that upstart Stokowski.

Fat Lady: Well, my dear, surely you know why *he* doesn't use his notes?

Thin Lady: I didn't know that. Why doesn't he?

Fat Lady: He doesn't use his notes because he can't read music.

Barbirolli at length decided in favour of score-on-desk, as well as score-in-head. He was complimented on this by the dread Downes who, when the time came, found it pleasant to record that the new man did not conduct from memory 'in the ridiculous way in which certain conductors find it necessary to imitate Toscanini.* It was evident that . . . Mr. Barbirolli could at need have led [conducted] without the score. He did

---

* Toscanini had no choice in the matter. He was so short-sighted that he studied scores with his eye almost touching the page and conducted from one of the uncanniest musical memories ever known.

not choose thus to exhibit himself and thus to make matters more risky and less certain for his players.' Nine concerts later, presumably to show he could walk this particular tightrope with the best (not necessarily as hazardous a feat as it looks), he did *Eine kleine Nachtmusik* from a blank desk. 'This was Barbirolli at his happiest,' someone wrote.

On that first day he took his first look at Carnegie Hall, outside and in. The conductor's room was bleak and impersonal. For years it had harboured during longish terms or short a succession of great batons, worthy batons and merely celebrated ones; nobody's aura clung there. The Philharmonic had had no permanent conductor since Josef Stransky (from Bohemia), incumbent for a single season, 1920–21. Into this anonymity came The Unknown, one guest baton out of five. What of future terms and tenures? Would there be any? . . . He put his head round the door of the players' clubroom. It was empty yet 'human'. Photographs of conductors made a great wall display; they were patterned around that of Arturo Toscanini, whose myopic eyes looked as penetrating as drills. Then to the auditorium. He liked the look of it; for all its three-thousand capacity, it gave him 'a sense of intimacy' and didn't look far away. So far as he could judge from a cursory trial, the acoustics were excellent. His first rehearsal call was for ten o'clock the following Monday morning, six days ahead. From Carnegie he was taken to meet reporters. He wore a brown tweed suit with exceptionally wide lapels and was smoking a cigar which he 'chewed on vigorously' between phrases. The matter of the succession was in all minds, in none more than his own:

'How does it feel to be following in the footsteps of Toscanini?'

A pre-ordained question. For a moment, nevertheless, he looked startled. Then, glancing with a quizzical smile at the questioner, he spoke emphatically and with deliberation:

'I do not intend to follow in the Maestro's footsteps. No one can do that. Toscanini is unique. His going marks the end of an era for the orchestra. It was a great era. And it is past. Unfortunately things have to come to an end. But music must go on. You will find me a very simple person, passionately fond of music. I serve it in the best way I can. I hope you'll like me. . . .'

In his seventieth year Toscanini had a prodigious amount of conducting left in him. The New York Philharmonic Orchestra had not seen the end of him. He was to conduct thirteen orchestras in one part of the world or another that were as yet unborn. Even so, Barbirolli's answer pleased because of its tact, patent sincerity and reverence. Modesty, simplicity, honesty: these were qualities that shone out of him. The celebrity scene had had enough of brassy, tortuous egocentrics. His first day in New York was a breath of new air.

At Carnegie Hall the working plan was five rehearsals a week, each two-and-a-half hours long, for four concerts a week, each concert lasting for less than two hours. Sometimes there were out-of-town concerts to work in and Saturday morning concerts for young people who, with attendant adults, usually crammed the place. More concerts might mean extra rehearsal sessions. Playing in the Philharmonic and conducting it were not jobs for the indolent. For a 10 a.m. rehearsal-call the players began arriving as early as 8.45 a.m.; instruments had to be tuned or warmed up, and in any case orchestral players of mettle find it a good thing to make a last run-through of especially stiff passages in their parts. These latter were supplied well in advance of rehearsal for study and practice at home.

On Barbirolli's first morning the first bell sounded as usual at 9.45. The players went to their seats and settled down. Buzz of talk. Discordant tangle of bits played against other bits, possibly from different works, by most of a hundred men. At the second bell the din stopped. The orchestra waited in silence for the new man, excited, even apprehensive about how things were going to turn out. The new man came on briskly, almost cockily, head back, left hand poised near his chin, a mannerism with which New Yorkers were to become familiar. The hell of which he was to speak later—the minor hell of anticipating the worst, the major hell of not knowing how he was to come out of it: all this persisted until a few minutes before his entry. Then it characteristically stopped: 'By the time I got on to the platform I was the calmest person in Carnegie Hall.' Arthur Judson came on with him and said a word of introduction. Barbirolli acknowledged this. He said how great an honour it was to 'lead' the Philharmonic. He

went on: 'Gentlemen, I may be a good conductor or a very
bad one. I know you to be members of a magnificent orchestra.
... I can do nothing without your friendly help and encouragement. With it I think we can deliver the goods.' There were
cordial murmurings from the orchestra. He shot his cuffs and
held his baton at the ready. The baton quivered. So did his
baton arm. This was noticed and speculated about not only
that first morning but throughout his time with the Philharmonic. (Not in much later years, however, when he returned as a guest. By that time the quiver had gone or was no
longer noticeable.) His first piece at rehearsal was that most
genial of gateways whether into a night's music-making or
into a new rostrum career: the *Roman Carnival* Overture of
Berlioz. On the Carnegie rostrum he looked a good deal less
Italianate than he had done on Scottish platforms. In front of
him sat so many men of Latin or other European stock and
descent that what Anglo-Saxons thought of as exotic profiles
and complexions were no longer worth remarking upon.*
From the *Roman Carnival* he passed that morning and at four
succeeding rehearsals to the other pieces in his début programme: Arnold Bax's *The Tale the Pine Trees Knew* (which he
had done in Scotland but was new to America), Mozart's
'Linz' Symphony and Brahms's No. 4. He worked as he had
worked with the Scottish Orchestra: that is to say, intently,
hypercritically and tirelessly. In the light of his concerts with
them during the 1950s and 1960s, Philharmonic veterans
realise now, whether or not they did so at the time, that in
the 1930s he had something still to learn in rehearsal techniques. At sixty and later he no longer to the same extent
experimented his way towards what his mind's ear had conceived.

* Here is a list of Philharmonic section leaders during Barbirolli's first
seasons. The names strikingly show American music's debt to other than
Anglo-Saxon cultures: Mishel Piastro (principal violin), John Corigliano
(deputy principal), Imre Pogany (second violins), Zoltan Kurthy (violas),
Joseph Schuster ('cellos), Anselme Fortier (double-basses), John Aman
(flute), Bruno Labate (oboe), Simeon Bellison (clarinet), Benjamin Kahon
(bassoon), Ernest Wagner (piccolo), M. Nazzi (English horn), E. Roelofsma
(bass clarinet), Bruno Jaenicke (horn), Harry Glanto (trumpet), Mario
Falcone (trombone), Vincent Vanni (tuba), Saul Goodman (timpani),
Theodore Cella (harp), Lloyd Strafford (piano and celesta) and Melchiore
Mauro-Cottone (organ).

Whatever effects of phrasing and tone-colour and refinements of balance he wanted in later days were achieved more quickly and economically. It was evident from the start that he was a great man for strings. His insight into the genius as well as the executive mechanics of stringed instruments is said by seasoned players who served under all three to have matched the insights of Fritz Reiner, Bruno Walter and Toscanini himself. Could it be said that he specialised in string training to the detriment of woodwind and brass? Or was it truer to say that the Philharmonic woodwind and brass were of such quality as not to need equivalent working on? The issue is still debated by old Philharmonic hands.

A thing that nobody dreams of debating, for nobody has ever questioned it, is the personal success he had with the orchestra. His warmth of spirit, the awe and worship engendered in him by great music and his easy talkativeness at rehearsal made for contentment all round and, as time went on, allayed fears of what the new broom might sweep away. It was true he had done some weeding-out and seeding-in after his first Scottish season. Yet he was not by nature a sacker. That was pretty clear. At the final rehearsal for his début several of the section leaders went over to Bruno Zirato, then associate manager of the Philharmonic and later Judson's successor. Barbirolli overheard them say: 'We have found a conductor. Don't lose him!' When he stepped down from the rostrum at the end he was applauded.

Philharmonic concerts began at the lordly hour of 8.45 p.m. Barbirolli walked on to the Carnegie platform for his début concert, Thursday, 5th November 1936, at eight forty-five sharp. The decisive challenge had come. It worked upon him in the usual fashion. For the second time in four days he was the calmest person in an excited Carnegie Hall.

He had come a long way from the flat over the baker's shop in Southampton Row. The community whose guest he was to be for seven years and the particular company into which he was now stepping were the hardy survival of a plutocracy whose monuments had been scarred and certain of whose economic myths had been exposed by its own greed, muddle

and panic. The worst of the Great Depression was over. Some
private fortunes had sunk beyond salvage. Others which had
listed heavily were righting themselves. More money was
finding its way to the Carnegie box office. The amount which
came the Philharmonic Society's way from other than box-
office sources was staggering by English standards; and
Barbirolli staggered accordingly. But the days of pyramidal
riches were receding into history. Barbirolli had watched
something of the same kind happen at home. Here, however,
the scale was more rhetorical.

In the chairman's box that night sat Clarence Hungerford
Mackay and his friends. Mackay was the principal signatory
to various public statements by the Philharmonic Society
which had to do with Barbirolli's services and how happy the
Philharmonic were to have him. He was a great layer and owner
and amasser and interweaver of international cables and home
telegraphic networks and radio stations; something of a
musician; 'desperately' fond of the 'cello; given to shooting
grouse in Scotland and quail in North Carolina; and the
builder of a great house (1902: cost, $840,000) on Long
Island where he gave resplendent parties for the Prince of
Wales and Charles Lindbergh, the transatlantic flyer, and
showed people around roomfuls of mediaeval armour. One of
his immense cable corporations had gone into receivership
the year before, and another was going the same way. He still
had more money than is good for anybody and showed no
sign of taking his hand off the Philharmonic tiller. In other
Carnegie Hall boxes for Barbirolli's opening and on Philharmonic boards and auxiliary boards during contractual
dealings with him were men of even more versatile attainment.
Warburg the banker, for example. Felix M. Warburg and his
associates had six leading American railroads among their
clients. He loved business much and fiddle-playing more. He
had been taught the fiddle as a boy in his native Hamburg.
When he had a lot of money he lavished some of it on babies'
hospitals, playgrounds for slums and a set of Stradivarius
instruments which he bought not for vainglory but for the
pleasure of lending them out to worthy chamber music
players. Richard W. G. Welling was another in the Philharmonic's inner counsels: marksman, master mariner and,

at one time, a teacher of evening classes on New York's lower East Side. Profession: the law. As a lawyer he leaned to reformist causes. No man had a keener nose for electoral frauds. He had made his name professionally by collecting 'in the public behalf' $30,000,000 in rates from thirteen gas companies. But the loftiest name the Philharmonic board could show was Nicholas Murray Butler's. Butler towered above the rest of mankind not so much as president of Columbia University but because he had met or was to meet everybody destined for heavy type in the history-reference books: Bismarck, Kaiser Wilhelm II, Lenin (with whom he had conversations long before the world at large had heard of him), Benito Mussolini (with whom he quarrelled in a friendly way), and most English prime ministers from Gladstone to Winston Churchill. Butler was the one who prevailed on Pope Pius XI to put out an encyclical endorsing the Pact of Paris (1929) whereby sixty-three nations renounced war as an instrument of policy: pathetic memorial to the hopes and mirages of a generation which had survived one cataclysm and was sleepwalking towards another. The scene on to which Barbirolli had, in a manner of speaking, been pitchforked is not likely to be remembered as one of the high plateaux of human achievement; but the trends and events of which he now had a close view were so much bigger in stimulus and scale than those of the English scene that inevitably he found himself living at new velocities and with a new effervescence.

The night of Thursday, November 5th, 1936, was brilliant, festive and, in most of its immediate sequels, of good augury. The best of the auguries was Lawrence Gilman's account of it in next morning's *New York Herald Tribune:*

Mr. Barbirolli walked resolutely on to the Carnegie platform. . . . [After three hours it was clear] that he had won the respect of knowing ones among an audience that had doubtless gathered to hear him in a mood politely sceptical, waiting to be shown. Mr. Barbirolli came to us almost unknown, meager of reputation, a wholly unsensational apparition. He has disclosed himself as a musician of taste and fire and intensity, electric, vital, sensitive, dynamic, experienced: as an artist who knows his way

among the scores he elects to set before us, who has mastered
not only his temperament but his trade. He is already, at
36, a conductor of impressive authority, delicacy and
imagination, with a power of control and stimulus before
an orchestra that exerts itself wholly upon the music to be
revealed—a conductor who forgets his audience until they
remind him that they have been stirred and persuaded and
taken out of themselves into the presence of the composer
and his vision and his voice.

Mr. Barbirolli had not proceeded through more than
a dozen pages of *The Tale the Pine Trees Knew* before we
became aware that he had mastered the first and last secret
of the fine interpreter's ability to lead us to the heart of the
music: the ability to discover and to release the melodic
impulse that gives it life and direction and coherence. . . .

He made the Philharmonic's sumptuous and enamoring
strings sound at times like musing and introspective lovers,
again like bardic rhapsodists and poets. Indeed, the whole
magnificent orchestra, strings and wind alike, sang with a
clarity and depth and lusciousness of tone, an imaginative
choiceness of phrasing and of style, giving emotional and
characteristic utterance to Berlioz in the dramatic brilliance
of his *Roman Carnival;* to Bax in the shadows of his Celtic
twilight; to Mozart in the crystalline exquisiteness and
gaiety of the relatively 'little' symphony . . .; to the soaring
immensities and glories of that Gothic passacaglia (or, if
you will, chaconne) that brought last evening's programme
to a close. . . . A devoted yet free-voiced and impassioned
performance of the great E minor Symphony of Brahms . . .
set the seal of musical piety and eloquence upon Mr.
Barbirolli's gifts as an interpreter and commended his self-
effacing modesty and his fine integrity as an artist to the
gathering that applauded him as though they welcomed
him as companion and as friend. For Mr. Barbirolli, to
judge from his achievements of last evening, is something
better and rarer and finer than a conductor of power and
sensibility. He permits us to think that he is akin to those
uncommon interpreters who give us a measure of 'that inner
standard of distinction: refusal', which an incorruptible
artist once defined as the gift of those who have sifted from

experience 'all that seemed beautiful and significant and have treasured above all things those savings of fine gold'.

The point is made earlier in this narrative that the bulk of overnight music criticism makes poor reading in after years. Much of it, for that matter, does not seem particularly bright the morning after. There have always been exceptions, however, and Gilman was one of them. The flame for music that burned in his heart and brain imparted a persisting glow to prose written with an eye on the clock. His writing meant much to Barbirolli. We shall be reading more of it. Therefore a note about him.

As an adolescent in the 1890s he saw a conductor's score of *Tristan and Isolde* in a shop window. The price was eighteen dollars. He saved up and bought it. While working as cartoonist, journalist and short story writer he devoted the spare time of three years to musical studies: theory, harmony, composition and orchestration. He composed among other things a full-length opera which, since it derived all too obviously from Wagner, he did not seek to publish. His loyalties and passions in music extended to Debussy and Richard Strauss and a little beyond. That his response to music *was* passion as distinct from professional duty or attitudinising is illustrated by what he said to somebody who had said of a third party that he was 'passionately' fond of music: 'But will he forgo leisure, forget to eat, face poverty? Will the blood leave his face as he listens to the third *Leonora* overture or the finale of Schubert's C major Symphony?'

What Barbirolli performed in New York, how he performed and what Gilman and others wrote and said about him will be touched upon in a general survey of his New York seasons. For the moment it is enough to say of his probationary season that standard symphonies which he conducted included another Mozart (B flat K319) and another Brahms (No. 2) in addition to those already mentioned, Schubert's as yet unfamiliar No. 2 in B flat ('a jewel', wrote Downes, 'which Mr. Barbirolli is to be thanked for bringing to the notice of the public'), the first symphony of Haydn's 'Salomon' set, Beethoven's second and fourth, Tchaikovsky's fourth and fifth, the César Franck, Mendelssohn's 'Italian' and Sibelius's

No. 1. There were Brandenburg concertos and Vivaldi concertos and the Sibelius violin concerto with Heifetz and the Beethoven violin concerto with Szigeti. These and other concerted performances consolidated his reputation as an uncommonly deft and tasteful accompanist. As in Scotland he often brought his section leaders to the fore: his assistant concertmaster (or leader) for Max Bruch's D minor violin concerto for instance; his first flute for a Chaminade flute concerto; his first double-bass for a movement of Koussevitsky's double-bass concerto; his first 'cello and first viola for Strauss's *Don Quixote;* his first oboe for the Pergolesi-Barbirolli oboe concerto; and, for Mozart's *Sinfonia Concertante* K. 297b, his leading oboe, clarinet, horn and bassoon. His principal English 'offerings', to use a word much favoured in American concert notices, were (in addition to Bax's *Pine Trees*) Vaughan Williams's *Job* suite, Delius's *On Hearing the First Cuckoo* and the *Enigma* Variations. New music by Americans was a required preoccupation. The Philharmonic Society had an amiable habit of offering from time to time a thousand-dollar prize for competition by native symphonists: which meant a lot of hard work for many people and not a little trouble. That season he did three American pieces which had not been heard at Philharmonic concerts before: Charles Martin Loeffler's tonepoem *Memories of my Childhood*, a symphony by Anis Fulheian, and Philip James's *Bret Harte* overture. None of his nights, then or later, gave more elation than his Wagner ones. For his second Thursday concert (and for a repeat the following Sunday) he brought a young Australian singer, Marjorie Lawrence, over from the Metropolitan Opera, where she had caught the general fancy as Brünnhilde ten months earlier. He devoted the second half of the programme to a 'run on' of three great episodes from *The Twilight of the Gods*—Siegfried's Rhine Journey, the Funeral March and (which was where Miss Lawrence came in) Brünnhilde's Immolation, the standard excerpts being linked by additional material from the score in such a way as to provide forty minutes of continuous music—'a Wagner symphony,' as somebody called it. This was Barbirolli's own idea and doing. The concert had begun with Beethoven: Symphony No. 2 and Miss Lawrence in 'Abscheulicher!' (*Fidelio*). Gilman did not think much of Miss

Lawrence that night. Barbirolli, on the other hand, moved him to a flight that fittingly closes this chapter:

For an indication of the real Beethoven . . . we had to depend on Barbirolli and the magnificent orchestra. And they did not disappoint us. Mr. Barbirolli's version of the Beethoven of the Second Symphony is, like all that we have heard thus far from him, vital, clear, distinctly felt and perceived—perceived with the eye on the object: on, that is to say, the music. This conducting has unassailable integrity. It is never phoney, insincere, external. It is the product of a musician who seems to have but one concern, the highest possible to an interpreter: the unobstructed and unadorned conveyance of the master's thought.

The result of this attitude, this honourable preoccupation with reality and inner truth, was most profoundly moving in Mr. Barbirolli's conducting of the *Götterdämmerung* excerpts. . . . Here, to the amazement and delight of incredulous Wagnerians, emerged the veritable, authentic Wagner. Here was the requisite breadth of pace, so that the great phrases once again found time to speak, to breathe and unfold and culminate, while the grandeur and tenderness of Wagner's mighty song made its overwhelming registration on the spirit. . . . Let us say in a necessarily brief notation that this newly recovered Wagner is in the great tradition— unhurried, unminimised, uncompressed; large in span and implication, uttering that noble and exalted beauty without which Wagner does not live.

CHAPTER TEN

TOSCANINI'S SHOES

THINGS were going well for Barbirolli and the Society alike: 'You only have to look at our Sundays to see that.' The orchestra's Sunday afternoons at Carnegie Hall, or important parts of them, were broadcast and listened to throughout the country. People had plenty of inducement to stay away from them, therefore, and that is what they had been doing in grievous numbers for some time. Under Barbirolli the process stopped and the situation improved. By the end of November things had looked up to such an extent that commentators were saying Barbirolli had 'caught on' and was bringing new people in; or that it was all due to heavier pay packets and better times; or that clever persons behind the Philharmonic were up to tricks of high-pressure salesmanship, as yet undisclosed, which were paying off. There was one Sunday afternoon in particular when the crush for Tchaikovsky's No. 5 and the pianist Casadesus in concerted pieces by Weber and César Franck had the management beaming and preening. Except for the odd Toscanini gala occasion, no crush like it had been seen on a Sunday afternoon for years.

Soon after this a deputation from the orchestra went to the directors and said how happy they would be to have Barbirolli as their chief. During his fifth trial week, with five more weeks to go, the directors had a meeting about which he knew nothing beforehand or even on the day. That meeting gave the orchestra what they were after. The directors invited Barbirolli to become musical director and permanent conductor of the New York Philharmonic Society's concerts for a contractual term of three years as from the opening of the 1937–38 season the following October.

Here was the third vital challenge of his career. He was

becoming used to vital challenges. This one he accepted with rather less trepidation than the two previous ones: Judson's initial trial offer and his chance with the London Symphony Orchestra when Beecham stood down from the 'Elgar No. 2' concert eight years earlier. The 1937–38 season was to run for twenty-eight weeks; he would be in active charge for all but five mid-winter holiday weeks, when a guest, Georges Enesco, would take over. Out of 108 Carnegie Hall concerts he would be conducting nearly ninety. He had just passed his thirty-seventh birthday. With no antecedents to speak of on the international scene, essentially a man from the British provinces —which, in those times especially, enjoyed little musical prestige abroad as compared with the great regional cities of Germany and Italy—he had acquired one of the world's most coveted sceptres ten or twenty years earlier than men usually qualify for such things. What added to the lustre of the appointment was the reversal of policy which it denoted. John Barbirolli was to be the orchestra's first permanent conductor since Stransky who, as has been said, was 'permanent' for one season only, that of 1920–21.

For sixteen years the orchestra had been in the hands, season after season, of groups or small processions of principal conductors and guest conductors. In a single winter the baton would change hands as often as nine times. Toscanini had short or long terms with the orchestra during ten successive seasons, Mengelberg during six. Other great names that came and went, sandwiched between less resounding ones, were Bruno Walter, Furtwängler, Thomas Beecham, Otto Klemperer, Erich Kleiber. It was universally allowed that under Toscanini's welding baton the Philharmonic became as much an instrument (singular number) of Toscanini's unique mind and will as a concert grand under the hands of Horowitz. Few other visitors, whatever their spell or cleverness, brought off anything quite like this. With Toscanini gone it was feared that a continuing regime of 'part-time kitchenette conductors', as some wit called it, would rob the orchestra of thumbprint and profile. The directors explained the appointment in a statement signed by Mackay and the rest on the day of Barbirolli's nineteenth concert. (That night he conducted among other things the Bacchanale from *Tannhäuser*, flinging himself into the music with such gusto and youthful enthusiasm that Olin Downes was moved to declare that the performance had 'more authority and swing than any previous one this writer recalls'.) Barbirolli's engagement, said the directors:

... marks a new era in the Society's history. It is the solution, the board feels, of several major issues which have confronted the Philharmonic for some time: the need for a young conductor of artistic integrity who could build towards the orchestra's future as well as enhance its present; for a director whose talents are recognised in such specific terms as increased audiences; for a man strong enough and vital enough to mould the orchestra into a consistent personality and technical unity.

In Mr. Barbirolli the Society believes that this threefold problem can be solved. . . . Particularly encouraging has been the public's enthusiasm, evident in an amazing growth in attendance, especially at the Sunday afternoon concerts. A proportion of the augmented ticket sale could be accounted for by the general improvement in business conditions, but a large part of it is obviously due to the hold Mr. Barbirolli has gained on the music-lovers of this city since his début on November 5.

His ten-weeks trial, which had turned into triumph, ended on a Sunday afternoon in mid-January. Again he conducted the Bacchanale music; also the *Enigma* Variations, and his friends Bartlett and Robertson in Mozart's two-piano concerto K. 365, and standard excerpts from *The Mastersingers*—so much a programme after his heart that he might have compiled it primarily for his own pleasure. The scene at the finish was radiant and rowdy. People were on their feet and cheering. His players, too, were on their feet and looked happy. He shook hands with all the front-desk men of the strings, eight handshakes in all and an extra one for his concertmaster (i.e., leader and principal violin) Mishel Piastro. Then, with a backward step, he made a sweeping gesture that took in the entire orchestra. Recall followed recall. At last he made the hoped-for speech and seemed nervous about it. His hands were tightly clasped, his fingers working. There were thanks to his players—'these gentlemen, these artists, these devoted friends, who make it easy for me to give you listeners all I have'. Then a solemn note: 'I accept my task as permanent conductor for the next three years as a sacred musical trust.' He was called back for two more bows. Afterwards people went backstage to take individual leave of him with smiles and handclasps and fervent words.

Thanks mainly to the Sunday broadcasts he had found an incalculably bigger—and more communicative—audience than could ever have been his at home. At Essex House he already had a trunkful of letters from new-found admirers in remote and wild places as well as throughout urban America. Many listened in Canada. One listener in the Far North told how he had had to wait for the ink to thaw before he could write. At the peak of his season letters had been coming in at the rate of two hundred a day. Two secretaries helped him to deal with them.

Two days later he sailed for Southampton in the United States liner *Washington*. He carried an inscribed gold watch which had been given to him by his players. More than that: a telegram awaited him on board. It read:

THE MEMBERS OF YOUR ORCHESTRA WISH YOU BON VOYAGE AND GOOD HEALTH LOOK FORWARD TO PLAYING THE FINEST MUSIC IN NEXT THREE YEARS WITH A SERIOUS MUSICIAN FOR WHOM WE HAVE GREAT RESPECT AND AFFECTION.

Nothing had ever given him such professional pride as the possessive pronoun in '*Your* Orchestra'. On the day of arrival in London he caught the night train to Glasgow and, one week after leaving New York, was greeted on the platform at Central Station by a double row of wind players from the Scottish Orchestra who genially barred his way with 'See the Conquering Hero comes'. They had not seen him for a year. It was clear from his smile that he was essentially the same John. Plumper, perhaps. The trappings, too, were grander: greatcoat with wide astrakhan collar, for example, and very pointed, American-looking brown shoes. But these things were not of the essence. For his round-off concerts with the Scottish Orchestra he was billed as The Great Conductor. There were newspaper advertisements rubbing in New York and Toscanini's Successor. In Glasgow and Edinburgh he was to conduct thirteen concerts; in ten other Scottish towns nineteen. After these Scotland would see no more of him save as a guest conductor in an unpredictable future. In a letter which thanked the parent Society in Glasgow for releasing Barbirolli, Judson had praised him unambiguously and with emphasis. His concerts at Carnegie had achieved a success 'seldom equalled and rarely surpassed', a phrase which appeared to give Toscanini rather a run for his uniqueness. Recognition of Barbirolli in America had been 'outstanding and immediate', it was added.

An hour or so after 'See the Conquering Hero comes' and 'For he's a jolly good fellow', which was sung to an accompaniment of guards' whistles and exhaust steam, he was in the thick of rehearsal at St. Andrew's Hall. Brahms's No. 2 and Florence Austral singing in the Liebestod from *Tristan* were the crux of the morning. His first St. Andrew's concert was a 'Saturday', the house full and, in a way that Liebestods do not usually invite, festal. The noise of welcome when he came on amounted to a sort of community hug. That night everybody was delighted but Percy Gordon. Barbirolli *might* be world-famous. That did not mean you had to bow before his Brahms. Of the performance of the Second Symphony Gordon wrote: 'Mr. Barbirolli suggested, as he has done before in Brahms, that the classically ordered drama of the big Brahms score does not arouse his full sympathy. He is apt to do less than justice to the quieter periods by giving too much warmth of expression to the tender, lyrical ideas and to find in moments of climax a temptation to grow almost too excited.' Whether, being apt to do less than justice, Barbirolli in fact *did* it; whether, finding a temptation to over-excitement, he actually ceded to it—these were matters that Gordon exasperatingly left open. Barbirolli, if he paid any attention, was left not knowing quite where he was: not the most comfortable of situations.

Three nights later Miss Austral reappeared, singing the Immolation Scene from *The Twilight of the Gods* at the end of the 'Wagner symphony' as Barbirolli had produced it in New York. The 'real' symphony on this occasion was to have been that of William Walton, one of the season's long-promised 'novelties'. The audience found themselves hearing or re-hearing Brahms's No. 4 instead. This had been sneaked as a substitute line into a late advance programme, no explanation offered, although it was put about that there hadn't been time enough after Barbirolli's return for the orchestra to get-up the Walton. People apathetic towards post-Brahms symphonies or rootedly adverse to them bore the substitution with calm. The 'discreetly adventurous' minority fumed. Some S.O. supporters, they claimed, had put up, or might have put up, guarantee money on the supposition that works originally listed in heavy type (the Walton was one of them) would really come to pass. That they should have been fobbed off with the Brahms Four did nobody credit. Worse was to follow. In the annual poll for the 1937 plebiscite concert Dvořák's 'New World' symphony came first in the symphony class. On the night the 'New World' was dropped without explanation. Barbirolli conducted instead Tchaikovsky's No. 5, which had forty fewer votes. Another wail in the newspapers. Another excuse about too little time. The orchestra's spokesman wrung his hands over the orchestra's 'superhuman' task: nine concerts and attendant rehearsals covering Beethoven's 'Choral' symphony, among other matters, had been crammed by Barbirolli and his men into six days. Time simply could not be found, between Thursday morning and Saturday evening, for adequate rehearsal.

'But,' it was objected, 'the "New World" is a standard symphony and in every orchestra's repertory. If a symphony was to be done at all, the "New World" should have been as feasible as any.'

'Not so,' returned the spokesman. 'Mr. Szell, who has been taking over from Mr. Barbirolli, did the "New World" earlier this season, impressing on the orchestra his own interpretation of it. Mr. Barbirolli could not be expected—and rightly refused—to conduct the work without equal preparation.'

To which the objectors: 'Quite. Mr. Barbirolli opted for Tchaikovsky's Fifth instead. But Mr. Szell conducted that, too, earlier in the season, impressing his own interpretation of it on the orchestra. If there wasn't time to rehearse the "New World" there wasn't time to rehearse the Tchaikovsky's Number Five, so we're back where we were to begin with.'

The last word was with Percy Gordon: 'If the committee intend the patrons to take the plebiscite seriously they must take it seriously themselves.'

New York had left Barbirolli in a state of high jubilation, not the easiest of states to cope with. Soon he would be at work on programme-building for his first full season with the Philharmonic: thickets of detail to hack his way through, a mountain of scores to assimilate, box-office facts of life to balance against his duty and the Philharmonic's duty to high art, the spirit of the age, America's cultural destiny and other imponderables. With all this on the threshold of his mind, he still brought the old Barbirolli coolness and edged concentration to bear as soon as he picked up the baton. In his Scottish concerts he revelled. But the jubilation kept breaking through. It did so infallibly when he spoke to reporters.

Thus: 'Carnegie Hall was packed out for my first concert. Next day I knew I had definitely captured them. Seats for the concerts that came after were sold at once.' 'I was unable to buy tickets for my own concerts!' 'The enthusiasm for music is tremendous. For some weeks both the Boston and Philadelphia Orchestras were in New York as well as my own. The halls would be sold out for six nights running.' 'Carnegie Hall holds three thousand. We packed it out fourteen times a month. I managed to fill it even for Sunday afternoon broadcast concerts.' 'After my final concert . . . crowds filed past me shaking hands for an hour and a half. Some of them were in tears as they said "Au revoir".' An account in the *Observer* (January 24th, 1937) shows him at his most ebullient:

'Yes', said Mr. Barbirolli, 'it is really a modern fairy tale. I started conducting only ten years ago, and here I am today Musical Director of the New York Philharmonic Symphony Orchestra, one of the greatest honours the musical world can offer. I can truthfully say I have attained my greatest ambition. Remember, I am not only conductor of the New York Philharmonic but its musical director—virtual dictator of its musical policy.'

'You were really impressed by the orchestra itself?' he was asked.

'Oh, it is superb! My first and only nervousness concerned

how its members would feel about me, but I knew I had them with me after the first rehearsal.'

Mr. Barbirolli explained that the musical supremacy of the Phil was due to 'money, I suppose. You see, the organisation is backed by such rich guarantors. They can pay you so well for the six months season that you can afford to do nothing for the other six months of the year. I don't mean laze. I mean that during these six months one has the opportunity for serious musical study.

'There seems to be no limit to what the committee will pay for any first-class man. A chief player in the woodwind gets £50 a week. Also they are willing to give youth a chance. They don't feel they must wait till you have a long white beard. They want artists who still have long musical careers ahead of them, not artists whose careers are reaching their end.'

As to British compositions: 'Seriously, I do think my appointment to the New York Phil is good for English music. I mean, it surely enhances its prestige that an English conductor has been chosen for such a post. And I think I have gone the right way about increasing American interest in our music. In my future seasons I intend to play more of it, but that is at American request. I did not want New York to feel that I was too definitely a missionary for English music, so I went slowly at first. I played the *Enigma* variations, and my interpretation of Elgar seemed new to American audiences. They have now asked me to play the Elgar symphonies.'

'Was Elgar the favourite English composer?'

'No. I should say Vaughan Williams is their favourite. This is rather surprising. I had thought he would not be electric enough to appeal to them, but it is probably the essentially pastoral quality in his music that does appeal to them. Deep down they are fond of all things English.'

Three weeks later the *Observer* interview was reprinted almost as it stood in the *New York Times*'s main week-end music page. Some editorial hand noted that Barbirolli or the reporter had twice used 'Phil' for 'Philharmonic'. Otherwise the reprint carried no comment. This gave and gives it to this day an almost sardonic air. Who can read it without feeling almost afraid for him?

On the same page and immediately above, Olin Downes spread himself apropos Toscanini's prospective return to the New York scene and the flutter of anxiety the news had given rise to among the Philharmonic Orchestra's well-wishers and those of Barbirolli. While Barbirolli was Southampton-bound, Toscanini had signed a contract with the National Broadcasting Company of America to take over the N.B.C. Symphony Orchestra, after it had been reauditioned and reconstituted to his liking, for ten concerts, the first at the end of 1937, which he would conduct before invited, non-paying audiences in Studio 8H, Radio City. N.B.C. spokesmen were profuse in assurances that everything possible would be done to avoid clashes with the Philharmonic Society in the matter of programme content and radio time. Above all they had no intention, they reiterated, of putting on Toscanini and his orchestra in Carnegie Hall or any other public auditorium used by the Philharmonic or any other orchestra under the sun. The well-wishers of the Philharmonic and of Barbirolli were not placated. Fears went on being voiced that, even if confined to Radio City, Toscanini with a first-rate orchestra at his service—and mouths were watering at the thought of a first-violin section alone with six concertmasters or ex-concertmasters from other orchestras in it already—must in one way or another threaten the Philharmonic's supremacy and undermine Barbirolli's newly won sway in New York City.

Of these fears Olin Downes made light. What the future had in store for the Philharmonic, he intoned, 'will depend partly on John Barbirolli and the manner in which his interpretations compare, through the seasons, [not with Toscanini's broadcasts but] with those of the great visiting orchestras and certain distinguished leaders. No one conductor, however distinguished, makes the fortunes of the Philharmonic-Symphony.' Considering that the fortunes of the Philharmonic had been committed to one conductor, that conductor being Barbirolli, Downes's note was ominous.

The notion that Toscanini could be contractually barred or would lightly bar himself from Carnegie Hall, one of the historic hearths of orchestral music, was so unlikely as to be against nature. While the Philharmonic faction were still tremulous the N.B.C. lifted another corner of the curtain,

making them more tremulous still. In agreeing the terms of
the contract, Toscanini, it seemed, had stipulated for two
public concerts in Carnegie Hall apart from the ten broadcast
ones, the proceeds to go to some educational charity. Carnegie
Hall did not have to wait long for the Maestro's return. He
was back there during Barbirolli's first full season, in February
1938, his new N.B.C. Orchestra having then been before the
public for five weeks. His programme coupled Beethoven's
First and 'Choral' symphonies. It was his fifteenth 'Choral'
in New York since 1913. The hall sold out weeks ahead, the
'take' going to an Italian welfare fund.

All of which, Barbirolli said, was splendid. But, asked
someone, was the Toscanini 'invasion' going to be splendid for
the Philharmonic? Barbirolli's reply had a splendour and a
sturdiness of its own: 'Wherever Toscanini goes he raises
orchestral standards. His "invasion" will be an unmixed
blessing for American music.' It has been said that when
Toscanini heard of Barbirolli's three-years contract with the
Philharmonic Society he remarked, being querulously disposed towards the Philharmonic at the time, that they had
never offered *him* anything of the kind. The board answered
that he could have had a contract for life if he had asked.
Towards Barbirolli in person he was always amiable.

After the last of Barbirolli's Scottish concerts—which
brought him among other things a laurel wreath shaped like a
horseshoe and a farewell night which so crammed St. Andrew's
Hall that the front row of extra platform seats almost touched
the back row of the orchestra—he travelled south for the
glittering Coronation Season which Beecham had confected
for the Royal Opera House. He conducted an *Aida;* two
Turandots, these latter with Eva Turner and Martinelli, who
was singing Calaf for the first time; and two *Toscas* (Martinelli
again, Gina Cigna and Lawrence Tibbett). At one of his
Toscas the Maestro was in the audience.

That season Toscanini conducted concerts in London with
the B.B.C. Symphony Orchestra which were to shine down the
years like a beacon. He invited Barbirolli to his rehearsals.
Barbirolli went, all ears and awe. He said: 'That summer
Toscanini gave only a few concerts in London. But they gave
a new vitality to the English musical scene.' After this they

G

met at odd times in New York and also, until the war, during shuttlings by liner across the Atlantic. Sometimes they ate together on shipboard. In s.s. *Normandie* Barbirolli came to table one day with a score under his arm, Béla Bartók's latest: Music for Strings, Percussion and Celesta. Toscanini asked what he had there. This was his first sight of it. A detail that amused him was Bartók's bold time signatures which straddled two staves at a time and, he said, made the pages look like 'cartelline della tombola'—raffle tickets. Excluding Bartók he said of some other living composers, including a Russian émigré who had recently been granted a 'one man' concert with orchestra in Paris: 'They are making fun of people.' Barbirolli agreed. His comment on looking back was, 'I don't like to see young men praised beyond their deserts.' Another score they talked over was the Tchaikovsky Serenade in C for Strings. Toscanini isolated 'terribly difficult things in it, one especially for the 'cellos in the first movement. Problematical, nasty. It doesn't look anything on paper: one of those little passages that you only hear if they're badly played. Technically the passage is hard but not impossible. You have to work and work at it.'

Toscanini came to one of Barbirolli's Carnegie concerts. His verdict: 'John, my orchestra is just as I left it.' There were flatterers who called him 'Toscanini the Second'. The violinist Adolf Busch was by when somebody came out with this. 'No,' he corrected, '—Barbirolli the First!'

Much of the recess before his 1937–38 season was spent in preparing programmes. Whatever the length of his recess—and during imminent years he was to whittle it down to as little as a fortnight—the preparation of a full season spread over five fairly concentrated or wholly concentrated months and preoccupied him constantly all the year round. To what extent should he aim at unities of style, to what extent at contrasts, on the same night? Where did piquancy stop and bad taste start? There were composers who, in some moods, made bad bedfellows. By mere propinquity they brought out the worst in each other. 'Has it ever been thought', he asked, 'that one can assemble four of the best pieces of music and make an abominable programme?' His hearers (they were members of a Philharmonic-Symphony lecture group) had never thought anything of the kind. Before getting down to individual programmes he swallowed his mountain of scores. That summer he got through three hundred in two months; or so the newspapers said. They were all new or newish scores. For even then—or then especially—concert promoters tried to keep abreast of the times, dragging reluctant audiences with them into the twilight of neo-classicism and the delayed dawn of dodecaphonics lest the lot of them be lashed before posterity as stick-in-the-muds.

The music he gobbled through came from many nations. He was reported as taking a high attitude to nearly all of it. He believed he had seen all the French music that had been played recently and could find nothing in it worth playing himself. The Germans? Among the many scores which German publishers had submitted to him there wasn't one he'd care to produce. The Italians? Same story. Recently a new symphony by an Italian composer of some celebrity had been discussed 'with ardour' in Italy: 'If the work had been played to me and I hadn't been told who the author was, I should have guessed it was by some talented pupil of Vaughan Williams.' Much of the new music had ingenuity, first-rate craftsmanship. 'But works of real talent, music that has something to say in its own right and says it with distinction and individuality? No! How much easier it was to order long symphonic seasons two or three decades ago! What an influx of exciting new music then! I often ponder with envy the lot of some of my colleagues who were making programmes from 1900 onward and who were able to introduce to their audiences new works by Richard Strauss, Debussy, Sibelius, Ravel, Stravinsky, Delius and so on—works that became acknowledged masterpieces. Yes, in our time we have had great works. We are spoiled. We expect a masterpiece to be born every day. It happens that we have reached a pause, so to speak, in the development of great composers. But they will appear again.'*

For the coming twenty-eight weeks (Enesco's five included)

* Collated from *New York Times* interview, 17th October 1937 and letter quoted by William G. King (*New York Sun*). At this time Mahler and Bruckner did not figure as they were to from the 1950s on in his favoured roll of late-Romantics.

he schemed 445 performances of 183 works by seventy-five composers of five countries. The ratio of composer-nationalities suggested an effort towards fair shares and an even keel. There were eleven German composers, ten Americans, ten French, ten Russians and eight English. Wagner came top with sixty performances of twenty-two works, Beethoven second with thirty-nine performances of sixteen works. Runners-up: Mozart, Brahms, Berlioz, Richard Strauss, Weber and Mendelssohn. Where came Tchaikovsky? Not among the runners-up. Among the also-rans, rather. A relatively small number of Tchaikovsky performances went a longer way than some, however. That nearly as many American composers, all living ones, had been picked as any greatly pleased the forward-lookers and the patriots. Not all Carnegie-goers were as gratified. The plain music-lover, concerned to get solid satisfaction for his seventy-five cents or three dollars at the box office, who gave not a fig for the latest 'isms' and 'phonics', was healthily immune from musical chauvinism.

Barbirolli was the first to admit that there was a substantial repertory which American audiences wanted to hear over and over again: 'They want the classics—Mozart and Haydn, to name only the two greatest. They want Bach, Beethoven, Brahms. They want Wagner. They want the great Romanticists—Schumann, Schubert, Tchaikovsky, to name only three. . . . They want contemporary music whose genuine and lasting worth has been tested and established—for example, Debussy, Stravinsky and Sibelius.' Thus Barbirolli in an early radio diagnosis. Among the hundreds of scores which he had read through, fifty were by Americans. The ten chosen for performance* undoubtedly had merit in and among them. This may sound tame. People were greedy for masterpieces, not for mere merit. But did not Barbirolli warn against a whole and sole diet of masterpieces? Would not such a diet mean that 'quite worthy works' were sometimes valued at 'less than their actual worth'? Little the plain man cared. As associate manager of the Philharmonic concerts, Bruno

---

* Their composers were Daniel Gregory Mason, Joseph Deems Taylor, Abram Chasins, Samuel Barber, Arkady Dubensky, Charles Wakefield Cadman, Quinto Maganini, Walter Piston, Gardner Read and Quincy Porter.

Zirato knew as much as anybody about the plain man's likings. He made what struck Barbirolli as a brutal revelation. Whenever they announced first performances of new American works, said Zirato, many subscribers asked to have their tickets changed to the next concerts in which these works were not listed. Barbirolli admitted to being shocked by this and argued that it could mean only one thing: that such supporters were 'prepared to damn a new work before hearing it. . . . If a person hears such a work and doesn't like it, he is entitled to his opinion. But just to stay away when one is programmed certainly does not help the Society or the conductor in their efforts to give new music its proper chance.'

A prior duty was involved, of course, that of the Philharmonic Society to help the customer to music he could be pretty sure, on previous samplings, of enjoying. In any case, because many people picked, say, five sorts of music to spend their money on, it did not follow that they 'damned' a sixth sort 'sight unseen'. The programme builder's dilemma is perpetual. Barbirolli busily tried to dodge its horns. He said more than once that over 90 per cent of the new scores he went through had finally to be rejected, 'not because they are all unworthy of performance but because I have never believed, nor shall I ever believe, that the Philharmonic concerts should become an experimental forum'. Yet the hope and the hunt for new music good enough to coexist against what time has winnowed from the old are almost as is the hope for life against death. The thought of fixed repertories going stale, of a great art working itself out as the last lode will be worked out of the world's last gold mine: such a thought has always been too macabre for even extremists among the musically conservative. Weighing vogues against longer-term verities, public appetites against public revulsions, tactics of promotion against that element of awe, almost of worship, which lay at the root of his being and gave it purpose in more than a merely professional sense, he built his programmes as best he could, without fixed rules, depending on his own judgment as much as upon data about audience preferences. One thing was sure. He could not please everybody: 'Trying to please everybody is the quickest way to insanity for any conductor, as it is for people in any walk of public life.'

The job was unremitting. It ate away his holidays. By this time, indeed, he had lost appetite for what most people or, if it came to that, anybody, would call holiday. 'The conductor's so-called holiday', he understated, 'can hardly be called a rest-cure. I personally find that after months spent in programme research and study the actual period of conducting comes as a blessed relief.'

The rest of this chapter and some of the next deals in summary fashion with his first two full seasons in New York and takes us into the first months of Hitler's war. The musical aspect of these years (1937 to 1940), which will come up for survey in its place, is telescoped meantime so that something may be said of controversial incidents and important happenings in Barbirolli's personal life.

Coming ashore from the Cunard-White Star liner *Britannica*, he was met at the pier this time (October 1937) by his concert-master Mishel Piastro, the faithful Ethel Bartlett and Rae Robertson and a boy pianist, aged six, whom he had heard play the previous season on an East End 'settlement' platform. This was not the only prodigy in the offing. Soon he would be rehearsing Mozart's D minor piano concerto K. 466 with a plump, bushy-haired eleven-year-old. When the time came at Carnegie Hall, this newcomer played with 'an ease and musicianship' which, belying his bare knees and open-necked shirt, 'astonished those who remembered, or said they did, that début of another boy prodigy, Josef Hofmann, fifty years earlier'. At this time Hofmann was sixty and played concertos for Barbirolli with unflawed art. Julius Katchen was the new prodigy's name. Barbirolli did much to launch a massive career which death cut tragically short thirty years later.

That autumn he rehearsed in an auditorium with new carpeting and fresh paint on the orchestral 'background', with its two porticos near either wing for all the world like temple entrances in *The Magic Flute*. All this sprucing up was to mark the new era and welcome the new man. Even the hall staff had been reuniformed, none looking grander than Gus Wade, doorman on Fifty-Sixth Street since nobody knew when,

and once a regimental bugler in the Grenadier Guards:
service in Egypt under Garnet Wolseley, as anybody could
tell from his cheery gruffness and grey moustache: military
band flautist in his day: and English as an orchard of pippins.
He and Barbirolli were born on the same date. The publicity
people made a lot of this. On one of their birthday nights the
cameras clustered around as a cake was brought in with
one hundred and twenty-two candles on it, the sum of their
years. As they posed on either side of it, former Private 52537
Barbirolli, John, Suffolk Regiment, said: 'The title of this
picture shall be: The Empire Still Stands.' A pleasantry: but
the Nazi menace, by this time rarely off front pages and wave-
lengths, gave it a sombre undertone.

His opening night had as much social glitter as could have
been wished. The glitter was reinforced by $18,000 worth of
new subscriptions turned in by a committee of 'pushers' who
had been hard at it since the previous season ended. New York
was spontaneously glad to see him back. Gilman wrote: 'The
second oldest orchestra in the world was conducted by one of
the youngest leaders ever to have full and permanent charge of a
great symphony orchestra in America: John Barbirolli, who is
thirty-seven. The large audience greeted him as a friend
whose ways they have approved and whose ministrations
evidently gave them pleasure, for the young Englishman—
slight, alert, dynamic, was exuberantly greeted and heartily
applauded. . . .[He] again revealed the qualities that made
him so well liked last year—innate and vivid sense of rhythm
as the essential life and pulse of music; the concentration; the
unmistakable integrity of purpose; the unawareness of the
audience; the use of the podium as a stand from which to
control the orchestra rather than as a pedestal for himself. . . .'

After the concert his players had him along to a beer party
in their clubroom. The party had been arranged at short
notice. There was no other guest. The players were as glad to
see him back as anybody. The new broom had swept nobody
off his feet or beat. Clearly the general policy was going to be:
new players when old players retired, not (as a rule) before.
He had said admiring things in public about their quality and
spirit and was to say more: '. . . men whose conscientiousness
and devotion to duty are beyond all praise. The principals

and players train like athletes. They dare not eat before concerts. They turn pale before an important solo.' Again: 'I am the worst of nuisances to rehearse with. Long experience as a string player has made me particularly demanding on that section. But the orchestra co-operate with me perfectly. So perfectly that the other day I became frightened. . . . I made a slip. The orchestra slipped with me. This was a high tribute to myself. But the responsibility of it frightened me. I cannot afford to make mistakes.'

Everything sounded cosy and seems to have been as cosy as it sounded. Already, however, there were murmurs that only one thing is worse for music than an orchestra that gets on badly with its conductor, namely, one that gets on famously with him.

'Mr. Barbirolli', wrote an observer of the Philharmonic scene, 'would do well to realise that the Philharmonic *can* play as well as any orchestra there is but will only do so if it is made to. Its performances under his baton too often seem well intentioned rather than completely realised. Rehearsals and performances had perhaps too much the atmosphere of an informal evening of chamber music at home instead of a concentrated effort by professionals to perform music as perfectly as possible. Relaxed informality is one way of being popular with the men of the orchestra; but I doubt whether he will get the best playing out of them thus.'*

A similar thought was insinuated rather than expressed outright by Olin Downes after a memorable Lotus Club dinner. The occasion was the close of Barbirolli's first season as the Philharmonic's musical director. He was the guest of honour. They put up Joseph Deems Taylor to propose the complimentary toast. Now Taylor was a writer, a radio commentator—and a composer. A week or two earlier Barbirolli had conducted excerpts from a comic opera of his, *Peter Ibbetson*, and the following season Taylor was to give inter-mission talks about Barbirolli's programmes over the air on a coast-to-coast network. 'No enemy', wrote Swift, 'matches a friend.' Taylor's speech to the Lotus Club, heard on a nation-wide radio hook-up, included an unlucky sentence to this

* Arthur Mendl in an article from New York, *Musical Times* (London), April 1937.

effect: 'The extraordinary thing about Mr. Barbirolli's tenure of office is that people have begun to realise that the Philharmonic is a *great* orchestra.'

Rare meat, this, for the indignation of Olin Downes.

Come! Come! [he wrote]. Was the arrival of the fêted Mr. Barbirolli really necessary for that? We thought the fame of the Philharmonic-Symphony was long acknowledged —even before the eleven years of Mr. Toscanini's leadership of that body, and it was proclaimed in no measured terms when Mr. Toscanini took the Philharmonic-Symphony to Europe in 1930. Did the New York public have to wait until Mr. Barbirolli arrived to find out about it?

'No more stomach-aches' is a reported remark of an orchestral player when Mr. Toscanini departed from the Philharmonic-Symphony post. It is a dangerous standard by which to measure an artist—as dangerous as the assumption that a leader who does not ask too much of his men, while encouraging them to play according to comfort and individual genius, is a builder of the future.

The test, however, was whether New Yorkers were coming to the concerts in good numbers and enjoying themselves to ovation point when they got there. His season ended with repeats of a standard Wagner programme: the concluding scene from the first Act of *The Valkyrie* and the vastly popular 'Wagner symphony' from *The Twilight of the Gods*, sung by Miss Lawrence and Mr. Kullmann of the Metropolitan Opera. In his speech at the end Barbirolli exulted in the splendid audiences he had had even though the Depression—'or should I say Recession?'—was not absolutely over. More young people were coming to the concerts. A great thing that. At this point he became almost ponderous, a rare thing with him: 'The youth of this great city is aware of its heavy responsibility. The interest of youth in these concerts shows us that the heritage of the great masters will be handed down intact by this great organisation for many years to come.' Most young people, like their elders, came to hear music for joy, even for that humbler thing pleasure. Yet his last thought had the right ring. Austria lay newly raped. Outrages of the same kind

G*

were preparing beyond other frontiers. 'In moments such as these, of strife and insane hatred', he said, 'music becomes more than an entertainment. It becomes necessary to us as a means of keeping our sanity.'

Then to Europe. Part of the recess he spent in France, taking with him the usual half hundredweight of scores, few of them palatable. The 1938–39 season was to follow on the lines of the previous one: twenty-eight weeks of subscription concerts including a fortnight's mid-winter break when Enesco would again be the guest. (The same arrangement was made for a later season. Enesco was taken ill. The break was reduced to a week.) In effect he would have no leisure. He throve on that. Once more nothing had been swept away by the new broom. Seven new players came into the orchestra, replacing seven who had died or retired on pension. Of the seven newcomers five were American-born, two from Italy, and four were still in their twenties.

When he was asked whether he had any special memories of the 1938–39 seasons and contiguous ones, he singled out two productions. One was Act II, *Tristan and Isolde,* which he conducted without cuts—'a thing which had never happened in New York before, although it sounds incredible. Up to this, apparently, it had always been cut, even at the Metropolitan.' Kirsten Flagstad was his Isolde, Eyvind Laholm his Tristan. A Marke and a Brangäne, a Kurwenal and a Melot: all were on the platform. The other programme he remembered was the first American account of Rossini's 'Petite messe solennelle' —'Rossini's little joke, for it takes all of two hours.' This just about filled Carnegie Hall three times in a week and had the critics purring. The choir who sang in it were so grateful for the privilege of doing so that they gave him a parchment scroll commemorating the event; all their names (215) were written on it. Odd that in addition to these two adventures Barbirolli did not name a third: his production of orchestral music from *Pelléas et Mélisande.* From Debussy's opera he took three act-preludes and nine entr'actes or act-finales. He used no singers, for practically all his material was non-vocal. A few vocal phrases which could not well be taken out were transferred to instruments. Mélisande's 'Oh! pourquoi parlez vous?' was given to the oboe, Arkel's 'Si j'étais Dieu' to the trombones, and so forth. There was no textual change or addition except one horn note linking the first prelude with the first entr'acte. 'I had always wanted to turn the *Pelléas* interludes and preludes into a concert suite,' he said. 'In the theatre, as soon as the curtain goes down for these interludes people start talking, and you hear the scene-shifters at work. It struck me that it would be a good thing if people *heard* the music for once in a way.'

Subject, of course, to the proviso that in music one man's good is apt to make another man grimace. So it was in this case. Downes's attitude could have been predicted merely from what we have learned of him already. He wrote: 'This music, lacking the tapestried harmonics of Debussy's stage, becomes a thing adrift, helpless, a succession of beautiful sounds, sometimes monotonous and of none too vertebrate a nature. The *Pelléas* music is not sufficient in itself and contrasted unfavourably with the *Eroica* Symphony [which neighboured it]. Nothing could have been more calculated to put Debussy's music at a disadvantage.'

For Gilman the performance meant that Debussy had truly come into his own. There had been impressive performances of *Pelléas et Mélisande* in American opera houses, he wrote; yet it was safe to say that Debussy's 'uncompanioned score' had never been played by a pit orchestra capable of giving what the music held. He went on:

Pelléas is music for a virtuoso orchestra, for a body of expert instrumentalists with whom sensitive and beautiful playing has become a habit—a habit of which they can be reminded by a conductor who knows what he wants from them. Opera-house orchestras are not usually of this order. The ideal performance of *Pelléas* requires in the pit an orchestra of symphonic rank; and to ask that is, no doubt, to ask too much.

It is evident that Mr. Barbirolli cares deeply for this work, and he had communicated his affection to his players. It was an enriching experience to hear the great orchestra discourse this infinitely sensitive music, which is often so evanescent that it seems as though the breath of human utterance would dispel it. They played it as though each

individual virtuoso had felt intensely the quality of the
score, with an ear for its sorrowful, grave voices, its lingering
cadences, twilight moods; knowing, perhaps, that they
confronted some rare, unprobed existence of the spirit.

Another season ended, this one with a students' Saturday
night of Wagner (*Rienzi* Overture, the *Tannhäuser* Bacchanale,
the *Tristan* Prelude and Liebestod, the Ride of the Valkyries,
four *Mastersingers* excerpts) and a Sunday afternoon mainly of
Mendelssohn (G minor piano concerto with Rudolf Serkin)
and the Brahms Symphony No. 1. It could not be said that
New York and Glasgow were alike as two peas. What could be
said was that Barbirolli treated them as if they were. He
could not have done other without being untrue to himself.

The Sunday afternoon concert over, he and the orchestra
drove to the New York World's Fair, a pleasance with a
concert hall; here they were to open an international music
festival. Before the concert proper Barbirolli waited in the
wings for another baton to say its say, that of Fiorello La
Guardia, Mayor of New York City. On the strength of an
hour or two's coaching the previous day, the mayor mounted
the rostrum, put his glasses on and, with 'forceful, accurate
beat', led the orchestra through a specially composed fanfare
into 'The Star Spangled Banner'. He did it all from memory,
pushing his glasses up on to his forehead when the music
mounted in excitement, and rounded off his final beat in the
Toscanini manner, with arms upflung in triumph. After which
Barbirolli and his players attended to the *Roman Carnival*
Overture, a new American piece, *The Pleasure Dome of Kubla
Khan* and Beethoven's Fifth Symphony. All that remained then
was three concerts at weekly intervals which he was to conduct
in a Detroit radio studio under the sponsorship of Ford Motors.

After the last of these he sailed for four months in Europe.
They were to be among the four most momentous months of
his life.

CHAPTER ELEVEN

EVELYN

Towards the end of his time in Scotland, on the Monday journeys by train from Glasgow to Edinburgh and in odd corners here and there away from platforms, coaching rooms and the like, Barbirolli often sat with Evelyn Rothwell, his principal oboe, some instrumental score open before them, their eyes intent upon it, now her finger tracing some thematic line, now his. They would discuss what laymen respectfully call 'the finer points', praise, pick holes and, in nine cases out of ten, find themselves in quick agreement. In so far as they had time for scholarship both were scholars. They burrowed happily in collections of antique music and new.

Evelyn's researches from student days onwards in the music library of the British Museum and elsewhere had practical ends in view. She was a busy editor and arranger of music written for the oboe or adaptable to it, and soon became a teacher of international note. Outside specialist circles nobody would have guessed she was an *authority* on anything. Few important persons have been so little capable of self-important airs. The world at large knew she was a leading orchestral oboist and that she gave recitals and played in chamber music and concertos. But she was given to laughter and seemed genuinely unburdened as well as light-hearted by nature, the last person on earth, or so it seemed, to have compiled (as she was doing already) and edited for the printer *990 Difficult Passages from the Symphonic Repertory for Oboe and Cor-Anglais.** Barbirolli, too, was a frequenter

---

* '. . . by Evelyn Rothwell, Hawkes and Son, London, 1951.' Her other listed publications as editor and arranger include: *105 Difficult Passages Selected from the Works of J. S. Bach*, 1951; *A Book of Scales for the Oboe*, 1953; editions and/or arrangements of Trio No. 1 in C major for oboe, violin and 'cello, Charles Suck; Concerto for Oboe and Strings by E. Eichner (1740–1777); Haydn's Concerto in C for Oboe and Orchestra (listed in the B.M. catalogue among doubtful or spurious works); Four Sicilian Miniatures for oboe and piano by Alfonso Gibilaro (Barbirolli's brother-in-law) and pieces for the same instruments by Franz Holford and Michael Head.

of libraries; indeed, he had libraries in his blood. They developed a touch of recluse in him which admirably tempered the man of ovations and the enchanter of multitudes. The concertos for oboe which he derived from Corelli and Pergolesi were produced with Evelyn Rothwell in mind and, as has been mentioned, he often conducted her in them.

They were by no means his first essays as an 'arranger'. As early as 1928 he had brought out Six Airs by Henry Purcell and others, arranged for 'cello *or* violin and piano. One of his reviewers was pleased to be severe. Why, asked the *Musical Times* (November 1928), include the *Tambourin* of Rameau in the set? Nobody could call *Le tambourin* an *air*. 'More questionable', the reviewer went on, 'is the rough and ready method by which the 'cello part has been made accessible to the violinist. To retain the key and transpose an octave higher is to ignore one of the most important problems of adaption. The A string is the most brilliant of the four strings of the 'cello and it is the weakest string in the violin. In all these Airs the most effective violin strings—E and G—are neglected. The G string is used once only and in one piece only . . . The fingering also is more careful in the 'cello than in the violin part.' In 1928, perhaps, he had yet to find his touch.

Burying himself in Handel, he emerged with two 'arranged' concertos, one for viola, the other for the B flat clarinet, both with string orchestra. New York listened with respect and some relish to his *Elizabethan Suite* for strings and four horns arranged from the keyboard pieces of Byrd, Bull and Farnaby; his transcription for lower strings, horns and trumpets of the Bach chorale 'Vor deinen Thron tret' ich'; and another derivation from Purcell, the Suite for strings with optional woodwind (four horns, two flutes and English horn). This last includes Dido's lament from Purcell's opera. Barbirolli gave it (inevitably) to the English horn. At his second performance of it in New York the hall brimmed with enthusiasm. He had the English horn come to the front of the platform and take a bow. Gilman swore that a lovely, perfumed person with a spray of orchids on the row in front took a kindly look at the hornist and said to her companion, 'That must be Mr. Purcell'.

In New York as everywhere, true music-lovers were ardent and, once the music began, single-minded. The minds of others,

capable of bizarre division, could attend at one and the same
time to the winged tranquillity of Mendelssohn's Andante and
to such matters as who was sitting with whom, tiara and all, in
the box next to Clarence Hungerford Mackay's. Again, such
feats of dual focus happen the world over. The degree to which
they happened in New York, just how the sublimities of classical
music were intervolved with limousines and lustre chandeliers,
column-long guest lists in the women's pages and what an
important thing it was to read (and be known to read) the
French *Vogue* as well as the American edition of it: such niceties
had been taken in at a glance by Barbirolli during his first week
with the Philharmonic. Soon they were to be taken in by Evelyn
Rothwell. Not only as musicians but also as judges of the social
scene he and she were likeminded and (as close friends had come
to realise during the Edinburgh days) well on the way to
becoming each other's *alter ego*.

What follows surprised nobody in the Barbirolli circle.

The radio concerts in Detroit had kept him until 4th June.
He landed at Southampton nine days later. As it happened,
the decree which dissolved his marriage became absolute on the
same day. He and Evelyn married on 5th July 1939 at the
register office in Holborn. The baker's shop in Southampton
Row was a minute or two away. No getting away from his origins.
He was a son of Bloomsbury still. The wedding reception was at
Pagani's, Great Portland Street, in the big room where plate
glass protected signatures scribbled on the wall by famous or
dimly remembered or now forgotten singers and fiddlers, conductors, pianists and impresarios and even a composer or two.
Everybody knew that war was imminent, not least those who
said there wasn't going to be one. Would the bombs be as
bad as everybody imagined? Or worse? Both the Holborn
register office and Pagani's were to suffer, the latter especially;
the room with the wall signatures was shattered during the
'Blitz'.

For the moment people were going about their affairs as
though this was a summer like any other. The Barbirollis honey-
mooned in Normandy and Brittany and were back in London
late in August. The sands had all but run out. A cablegram from
New York welcomed them. It was from the Philharmonic

management and required Barbirolli to report there without delay. New York knew as well as he that war involving Britain was extremely likely. If he did not sail at once and if Britain *did* enter the war, he would probably be pinned down in Britain until heaven knew when; in which case how could the Philharmonic contrive to salvage its 1939-40 season, now only five or six weeks away? Strong family ties and citizenly instincts alike made the idea of leaving repugnant. But his New York contract had an indemnity clause which left him with no choice. The situation was this. If he broke his contract by refusing to return while peace obtained and the shipping lanes were still open, the Philharmonic management, suing if necessary, would mulct him in 'thousands of dollars.' This he could not afford, partly because of heavy professional expenses and partly because of private commitments, including provision for his widowed mother. These outgoings substantially offset a salary that was lordly by English standards—equivalent, it was put about somewhat later, to 'hundreds of pounds a week'. There was nothing for it but to report back as demanded.

He secured a passage in the French liner *Champlain* and applied for one on Evelyn's behalf, for she was resolved to be with him. That autumn people were queuing and clamouring for passages to America in numbers without precedent. At the United States Embassy the backlog of permit and visa applications was formidable. They told Evelyn she must wait for a later boat. Barbirolli sailed alone. He could do no other. *Champlain* left Le Havre on 29th August with many musicians, theatre people and film actors on board; so crowded that sixty passengers had to bed down in the playrooms. Barbirolli thus passed the Third of September, 1939, the day of Britain's entry into the war against Hitler, at sea, behind portholes and stateroom windows fitted with newfangled blackout covers. Passengers with portable radio receivers had them impounded, and throughout the voyage radio news bulletins were curtailed. For listeners ashore horror did not delay. On that first day of war the British liner *Athenia*, outward bound, was torpedoed without warning two hundred miles off the Hebrides. Over a hundred passengers went down with her. *Champlain* docked on the scheduled date, 5th September. The directors of the Philharmonic Society were among thousands who sighed relief. As a security measure a news blackout had been imposed on the movements of all ships wearing the flags of belligerent nations. Judson couldn't be certain that Barbirolli had arrived or would arrive until he set eyes on him.

The season's opening night at Carnegie Hall was as bejewelled and befurred as any within memory. Barbirolli discoursed Mozart in C major, K. 338—the last of the 'Salzburg' symphonies; César Franck's in D minor; and a set of variations with fugue on *Underneath the Spreading Chestnut Tree* by Jaromir Weinberger. Weinberger was an exiled Czech. Much had been heard in Glasgow and Edinburgh, thanks to Barbirolli, of a backslapping polka and fugue from an opera of his, *Schwanda the Bagpiper*. He had dedicated his new score to Barbirolli and had given some of his variations subtitles that could be taken as a compliment to Barbirolli's native land: 'Mr. Weller, Senr., Discusses Widows', 'The Highlanders', 'Her Majesty's Virginal', 'The Dark Lady' [of the Sonnets] and so on. The audience liked the piece very much. At the end they thundered their gratitude. Weinberger bowed from a box, then came to the platform and, joining Barbirolli, bowed to renewed thunder. Against the grisly perspectives of history that opening night has an almost hallucinatory sheen.

A week later Barbirolli coupled Beethoven's Seventh with what amounted to a novelty: *both* concert suites from Ravel's *Daphnis et Chloë* ballet. The first suite, the one oftenest performed, was too short for the programme balance which Barbirolli had in mind. As to the second and longer suite, he had never been satisfied with its sudden yet casual opening. He therefore extracted a brief linking passage from the ballet and ran the two suites together with imposing effect. The climax of the second suite, reported Howard Taubman in the *New York Times*, was 'perhaps the maximum tonal volume Carnegie Hall would hold.' Not that Taubman minded. On the contrary he was pleased; in his view the double *Daphnis* came off well. There were already signs, however, of dissent from some of Barbirolli's extremer dynamics. Did he not at times throw the orchestra's weight about too exuberantly a thought too abruptly? Apropos Beethoven's Seventh even Gilman broke off a characteristic eulogy to warn him that Carnegie Hall was an extremely resonant auditorium where an orchestra needed no forcing to achieve a rich and powerful *fortissimo*. In Berlioz's *Benvenuto Cellini* and Beethoven's Seventh alike, he went on, there were times when 'the sound of the magnificent orchestra passed beyond the point at which puissant beauty becomes unmusical noise'. From the Seventh Barbirolli turned a day or two afterwards to *La Mer* and William Walton's *Portsmouth Point*. He spent the morning of October 25th rehearsing these scores, then went on to the Biltmore Hotel for a Philharmonic League luncheon in his honour.

'This', he told 500 fellow guests, 'is a happy day for me, because today my wife sails from London to join me here next week.'

Evelyn's voyage was uneventful. She was with him in time for a Schubert night that ended majestically with the 'Great' C major Symphony.

In the following account of her settling-in the quoted phrases are from conversations with Evelyn Barbirolli, Lady Barbirolli as she had become in the meantime, ten years later or more.

When she first sighted New York she was still young and, about clothes, 'terribly green'. She had been given to understand that it was much easier to buy clothes in America than at home and therefore took out nothing but her honeymoon things—'I might have done better'. She took out her oboe as well. 'But I dropped oboe playing altogether so that I could concentrate on the social side of John's job.' Their home was a furnished suite high up in an apartment block in Central Park South, a fashionable quarter, 'because that was necessary'. It was fascinating at dusk during that first winter to look from the sitting-room window and watch hundreds of other windows light up sporadically in skyscraper after skyscraper. 'We did no "splash" entertaining. We hated that and hate it still. We have never wanted to live in a "splash" way. We entertained quietly, as we do now—personal friends and family (when the family don't happen to be thousands of miles away!)'. Her social duties were constant as well as onerous. 'There was something every day. We were always being invited to tea parties. I always went with John. The "ladies of the committee", you know. Wearing the right sort of clothes was important. And saying the right sort of thing. Over there music is tied up with the social round.

It isn't my way or my idea of music at all. But that's the way it is, and you have to fit in.'

Occasionally she practised the oboe to keep herself 'in touch', but concert work was shelved for the time being. 'I will never play in public unless I can be sure of preparing properly and giving of my best.' She went to all John's concerts and to most of his rehearsals. 'I would sit towards the back of the auditorium, and he would consult me about balance—whether the violas were coming through, let us say, or whether there was too much trombone. That sort of thing. I became his second pair of ears.' She went on being that to the end. The players knew what was going on and did not jib, for as some of them confirmed thirty years later, Evelyn Barbirolli was a charmer—*and* a musician to the finger tips. As time went on she played oboe with groups of Philharmonic string players, her husband sometimes bringing out his 'cello, at private chamber music parties on traditional Barbirolli lines.

That winter she went with Barbirolli and the orchestra on a fourteen-days' tour of fourteen cities. This was the Philharmonic's longest trip since 1928-29. It involved 103 players, all men, and two young women, the second being the orchestra's press liaison officer. They took with them a repertory based on what they had played since mid-October in New York: such things (in addition to pieces mentioned already) as Schubert's Symphony No. 2 in B flat, the second and fourth symphonies of Brahms, the usual helpings from *Götterdämmerung* and *The Mastersingers*, Debussy's rarely heard Rhapsody for Saxophone and Orchestra, Elgar's Introduction and Allegro for Strings, two preludes from *La Traviata* and Tchaikovsky's *Romeo and Juliet* fantasy. Starting at Scranton, Pa., they went on to Washington, where the diplomats and their wives scintillated in force, played to 3,600 in Chicago and crossed the border for three concerts in Canada, the most important of these being in Ottawa where, the Governor General and party having installed themselves in the ceremonial box and stood for the National Anthem, Barbirolli, his baton at the ready for Berlioz's *Roman Carnival*, became aware of a disturbance behind him. Latecomers were loquaciously sorting themselves out in the aisles. He turned and looked daggers at them laid his baton down and made tart comments to his principal violin. Noise stopped. Those near their seats crept into them guiltily. Others tiptoed to the nearest wall and froze themselves against it.

At audience-taming and audience-quelling he was a practised hand. One of his early feats had been on a *Bohème* night at the Theatre Royal, Glasgow, in 1936. Before the beginning of the last act, he reminded his audience that at the end of the previous acts some of them had started clapping before the last note had sounded from the orchestra; and would they please do better next time? He was heeded. The eight bars of postlude after Rodolfo's anguished 'Mimi!' on upper G were heard in reverent silence; which does not happen often. Four nights earlier Beecham had been in the same pit for the same opera. He, too, had asked the house to hold its applause at the end. The house did nothing of the sort. Beecham shouted 'Shut up!', then flinging down his baton, told the audience they were a pack of savages and strode off. A further memory is from the 1950s. Touring with the Hallé Orchestra Barbirolli reached the Theatre Royal, Dublin, a notoriously restive house when symphonic music is afoot. On its rostrum a few weeks earlier a noted German conductor, exasperated by audience chatter, ostentatiously looked at his watch and made off into the wings— a sure way of getting quiet but a drastic one. Barbirolli, too, had chatter to contend with but stayed on the rostrum, lolling against the rail in the manner of one disillusioned to exhaustion point. After a few moments he turned round and gave the audience a slow look-over with such disdain on his face that even the innocent felt they had been up to something discreditable. Thus did he clear the way for *Fingal's Cave* and Berlioz's *Fantastic* Symphony.

He and the orchestra were back in New York a day or two after his fortieth birthday. They plunged into rehearsals for concerts with Fritz Kreisler, who was down for the Tchaikovsky violin concerto in an edition of his own. Wearing a black alpaca jacket which buttoned up to the neck in the Toscanini manner, he toiled away until dishevelled, fagged and thoroughly happy. As always, the presence of Fritz Kreisler buoyed him high. The great man rehearsed in his shirtsleeves, waistcoat unbuttoned, watchchain looped across his diaphragm. He conceded that the Tchaikovsky concerto was lovely as it stood. What a fount of melody! But, more than with any other great Tchaikovsky piece, its 'workmanship' left much to be desired. So he was quoted as saying in a programme note. It turned out that to put the 'workmanship' right he had made cuts in all three movements, elaborated the cadenza and touched up the instrumentation here and there in such a way as to thin and refine the music's texture and, as some thought, rob it of Slavonic 'devil'.

A week later came a concert for the Finns, on whom the Russians were making war. The afternoon opened with the *Finlandia* Overture of Sibelius, a work which because of current pangs and stresses had never sounded quite the same before that winter and has never sounded quite the same since. As soon as Barbirolli lifted his baton several in Carnegie Hall rose to their feet and remained standing. When the full brass joined in the final patriotic paean the entire audience rose spontaneously. The applause had a fever in it which went much beyond music considered as music. Barbirolli responded with a gesture towards Box 57. There sat Herbert Hoover, the previous President of the United States. With him sat Evelyn, hostess of the afternoon. It was at Hoover's instigation that this Sunday had been proclaimed as Finland Day by the Governor of New York State. At Barbirolli's gesture the applause turned to cheering. When Hoover stood to acknowledge it the cheering redoubled. Barbirolli made a discreet master of ceremonies for demonstrations of this kind, always shrewd in his timing. A year later came Sibelius's seventy-fifth birthday. He cabled him thus: DEAR FRIEND AND MASTER WE ARE PROUD TO HONOUR YOU AND OURSELVES PLEASE ACCEPT AFFECTIONATE SALUTATIONS AND WISHES OF YOUR DEVOTED BARBIROLLI. After which, at Carnegie Hall, he conducted *Finlandia* again, the First Symphony and the tonepoem *The Return of Lemminkainen*, which were transmitted by short wave to Finland for the Master to hear. Another attention was a gramophone recording which Barbirolli and the Philharmonic had made of the Second Symphony. A copy went out via the Finnish Legation, New York, and drew a letter from 'your devoted admirer Jan Sibelius', who affirmed that he always felt more than happy when he knew his works were in 'your masterful hands'.

Another visitor that season was a young introvert from England with a beaky profile and crinkly hair, of whom more was to be heard on both sides of the Atlantic. The name was Benjamin Britten. He had recently composed a concerto for violin and orchestra which ended with a passacaglia. He was to make rather a habit of passacaglias. In those days the form was so archaic as to be almost insurrectionary. The score of the concerto found its way to Barbirolli's desk, one in the unremitting procession of scores to be weighed up and, for the most part, found wanting, He put it into a programme in March 1940. Rossini (the *Semiramide* overture) went before, Beethoven's Fifth Symphony came after. The audience did not quite know what to make of the concerto but applauded liberally because the solo part, as any eye could see, was very difficult, and Antonio Brosa, the soloist, had come through it stylishly and with confidence. Britten had another work on the stocks, the *Sinfonia da Requiem*. This he was composing in memory of his mother. Through the British Council he and other representative composers (among them Richard Strauss for Germany and Darius Milhaud for France) were asked by some Japanese government agency to write pieces for the official commemoration of the 2600th anniversary of the founding of the Mikado's dynasty. The *Sinfonia* happened to be of a type and scale suitable for festival performance. Having obtained an assurance that there would be nothing jingoistic about the commemoration (there were strong feelings in the West about Japan's continued subjugation of Manchuria), he cabled Tokyo with a description of the score, including its sub-titles—'Lacrymosa', 'Dies Irae' and 'Requiem Aeternam'—'all of which struck me as compatible with a creed which involves ancestor worship.' The Japanese accepted the work. He completed the orchestration, posted the score to the Japanese Embassy in Washington, who saw it off to Tokyo.

Then, says Britten, 'all hell was let loose. I was summoned to the Japanese consulate in New York and had an absolutely furious letter read out to me from someone in Tokyo. The writer said I must have known it was an insult to Japan to submit a work of Christian character. I replied by letter that, since I was a Christian, it was only to be expected that I should have submitted a work of such character.' Inevitably the score joined the procession to Barbirolli's desk. He put it into another programme (29th and 30th March 1941) topped by Rossini (*l'Italiana in Algeri* overture) and tailed by Beethoven (the violin

concerto, with Erika Morini). The *Sinfonia* has a finale of
widely undulating harps below and tranquil flutes above whose
drooping yet consolatory theme is the symbol of many home-
comings, one haven. Although they may not have been fully
taken in and assessed at the time, these pages made a luminous
mark in music: not a blaze, to be sure, but something to outlive
as well as console its day. Into Barbirolli's work seasoned
observers read tenacity and warmth; they were struck by the way
he watched over the *Sinfonia*, by the solicitude as well as micro-
scopic accounting he gave to it. Once more he had Britten with
him on the platform, a self-effacing, almost self-deprecating
figure.

His first wartime season ended on a Sunday afternoon early
in May with a mild orgy of Wagner: *Tristan* Prelude and
'Liebestod,' the 'Waldweben' from *Siegfried* and the *Tannhäuser*
overture. He had been re-engaged for two seasons more. The
season immediately ahead, 1940-41, would be a little longer:
thirty weeks instead of twenty-eight, and he would be in active
charge for twenty-two weeks, a reduction of four weeks on
1939-40. This curtailment was rational. Even Barbirolli's lust
for work could not have been expected to survive another winter
with a mere fortnight's break—or less if his substitute went sick.
During his eight weeks' absence two guests of outstanding gifts
and prestige were to be in charge: Bruno Walter and Dimitri
Mitropoulos, each down for fourteen concerts. It was too early
as yet to say much about the next season but one. Already,
however, people were thinking about it busily, for 1941-42
would take the Philharmonic, whose first concert had been on
December 7th 1842, into its centenary year, with all that
centenaries imply in the way of gala nights and bouquets and
choice oratory and grander pedestals than usual for whatever
musical gods were on offer. Would the grandest of the pedestals
be reserved for Barbirolli? Would he take the inaugural concerts and the end ones and all the big ones in the middle? Friends
speculated; so did people who were not so friendly. Like all men
who have risen high and quickly from nowhere, he had his
enviers. To rivals who consider they have been done out of a
plum appointment, the man who gets it commits something
more than an indiscretion; he is guilty of a serious offence,

success. Barbirolli had offended greatly, and it was hard to
forgive him.

It wasn't in New York only that he succeeded. The exasperating little man was in demand far and wide. For five spring and
summer months in 1940 he was supposed to be out of mind and
out of sight, recuperating and score-grubbing. But no sooner
had he laid down his baton at Carnegie Hall than he turned up
at a music festival in Vancouver, British Columbia, dispensing
Beethoven's Fifth to a Saturday-night crowd of six thousand in
a concert arena under the stars. Thence to California. In the
Hollywood Bowl twelve thousand, the season's biggest Friday
night turn-up, heard him in Sibelius's No. 2 with the Los Angeles
Symphony Orchestra. In a third musical pleasance, Ravinia
Park, Chicago, looking trim and singularly cool on a night of
sweltering heat, he took the Chicago Symphony Orchestra
through the Fourth Symphony of Brahms wearing an admired
tail coat, white waistcoat and white tie. He made eighteen guest
appearances in all that summer. Everywhere he conducted
masses of people were curious to see him. That was because they
had already heard him much. Ever since 1936 the Columbia
Broadcasting System had been putting out his Sunday afternoon Carnegie Hall concerts on a coast-to-coast network of over
a hundred stations. They had made a national figure out of him
without his lifting a finger. He never had anything against radio
audiences. The reverse, in fact. More than once he said that
when it came to 'adventurous' programmes radio listeners
tended to be gamer than indoor audiences.

He conducted the last of his eighteen 'holiday' concerts in
Vancouver after returning there with Evelyn in September—
'an enormous affair in a huge cinema in aid of the Canadian
Red Cross. I played an oboe concerto with John [her first
professional appearance outside Britain]. People were curious.
We were a huge draw.' For the rest of the month they stayed
on in British Columbia. 'We had a house in the mountains six
or seven miles outside Vancouver, overlooking lovely country.
We wore slacks and windbreakers and walking shoes and walked
in the woods, crossed fjords by boat.' Such idylls were snatched
from the usual stacks of scores and programme drafts. These
were with him everywhere, in woodland shacks, railway trains,
automobiles, at his bedside wherever his bed happened to be.

'We spent three summers in Vancouver. We had another little house in Beverly Hills for our California trips and John's concerts with the Los Angeles Orchestra. I used to play oboe occasionally at private parties in Hollywood. We saw a lot of the Horowitzes. [Horowitz always charmed—and could be unaccountable. Coming on at one of Barbirolli's concerts for Rachmaninov's third concerto, he picked up the piano stool and minutely scrutinised one of the legs before playing.] I remember a night when Horowitz and Iturbi played piano duets for hours on end. A lot of film people came to the parties: René Clair and Walter Pidgeon and Eddy Robinson. Also Chaplin. When the bombings began he questioned me and John about letters from our families. He remembered the scenes of his childhood and asked us: "Are the Lambeth Baths still standing?"'

Before returning with the Barbirollis to New York let us look again at Gilman, whose writing in the *New York Herald Tribune* remains the most heartwarming record of a phase in Barbirolli's career which was not without its chills and glooms.

From Barbirolli's production of Delius's *Appalachia* variations he emerged in an ecstatic dream; from his performance of Walton's *Façade*, including six pert numbers which Philharmonic subscribers had not heard before,* with a chuckling pen, America's oldest, gravest and most reverend orchestra (he wrote) having been transformed by Barbirolli's wand into a super jazz ensemble that made Paul Whiteman's band [one of the most obsessively popular outfits of the day] seem by comparison 'very staid, old-fashioned and conservative gentlemen indeed'. Even Benny Goodman and his virtuosi had better watch out. With a little practice Barbirolli and his men could probably make them sound like the village band of Frogville. Vaughan Williams moved him in a way that will seem excessive to a generation that has turned its back on most of the things that 'R.V.W.' stood for. In 1940, however, his was 'keynote' music. Of the suite from *Job*: 'Mr. Barbirolli's insight into this rarefied and subtle music was searching. . . . He set it before us with an affection and solicitude that matched the justice of his conception . . ., [directing] the score as he only can who cares

* Fanfare, Scotch Rhapsody, Country Dance, Noche espagnole, Popular Song, Tango-pasadoble.

for it and cherishes it and has felt to the end of its intensities.'
In Barbirolli's Wagner he went on delighting; exclaimed over
' . . . the golden processional of the *Meistersinger* overture. Of
this Mr. Barbirolli secured a performance that will scarcely be
matched for beauty and translucence and integrity until he and
his magnificent orchestra play it again.' His *Götterdämmerung*
excerpts left the audience not merely moved but, he said, *shaken*
by the music's greatness. In the same programme he did ' . . .
the noble [Prague] Symphony of Mozart', a performance which
brought out 'the deep and seasoned beauty of the Philharmonic
strings and the lucid clarity of its solo woodwind. Certain
chromatic passages for the violins and the woodwind at the
beginning of the slow movement still haunt the ear, as though
they had captured some of the living essence of Mozartian
loveliness and fervour.' Barbirolli's *Enigma* was remarkable for
'a breadth and feeling that were conveyed with especially
moving power in the noble "Nimrod" variation. Here the tonal
richness and grandiose power of the Philharmonic's magnificent
strings encompassed Elgar's purpose to the full. His Sibelius
No. 1 was large-moulded and dramatic, his Sibelius No. 3
attuned to the exceptional structure and textures of that score;
his *Iberia* (Debussy) a performance of scintillating light and
magical evocation.'

As we have seen, there was one concert, a Beethoven-Berlioz
occasion, when Barbirolli's 'louds' were not altogether agreeable
in Gilman's ear. This, however, is the only adverse note which
the present writer has turned up in Gilman's relevant writing.
In New York he was foremost among Barbirolli's champions.
And his championship was to be tragically cut off. Three days
after Barbirolli came ashore from *Champlain*, Gilman died of a
heart attack. His death was lamented by men of very different
temper and outlook from his own. 'When he pleased,' said Olin
Downes, 'no colleague on either side of the water could rival
the music of his prose.' Barbirolli had not met him personally
but they exchanged letters occasionally about Philharmonic
programme-notes which Gilman wrote. One of these concerned
the *Pelléas et Mélisande* concert suite, dear to both of them.

An obituary tribute by Barbirolli spoke of ' . . . that
great critic and artist in words . . . Particularly do I treasure
the notes he wrote for my arrangement of [the *Pelléas*] preludes

and entr'actes. The exquisite beauty and sensitiveness of his mind were never more lovingly revealed [than here], and perhaps it was fitting that it should be so, for surely in this music there was something of his own remote yet fragrant spirit.'

One of Gilman's last music pages carried substantial extracts from a lecture by Barbirolli to the Philharmonic supporters' league. *A Conductor on Conducting*, he headed it. The final quotation was this:

I would like to urge any young musician who contemplates this most arduous and responsible of careers to make his watchwords INTEGRITY and SINCERITY (to yourself) and LOYALTY (to the man whose music you are seeking to interpret). Never think, 'What can I *make* of this piece?' but try to discover what the composer meant to say . . . Performances that are made merely a vehicle for indulging the vanity of a personality, however talented that personality, can only lead us away from that which should be the goal of all true musicians: Service to that great art which it is our privilege to serve.

The qualities which Barbirolli commended to others had been discerned by Gilman in Barbirolli himself. Without knowing it, Gilman had taken leave of Barbirolli with a thought of some profundity on which they were at one. Critics and artists rarely part in such amity.

CHAPTER TWELVE

'CRITICAL TORRENT'

THERE had been a change of wind in the Carnegie precincts. A nip was in the air. At the end of the 1939–40 season Arthur Judson had talked disquietingly about takings. No need to worry about 'average' music lovers, he said; they had done their duty by filling the average-priced seats. The real problem, he advised his subscriptions committee, was how to fill the higher-priced ones, boxes especially, on Thursdays and Fridays. The rest of the house would take care of itself—'we hope'. A week later he spoke to reporters in the same strain. The need was for larger audiences at lower prices, he said. Then, as if by way of afterthought: 'The musical world is starting on a new epoch of building conductors. No one knows as yet who will be the future Koussevitsky or Stokowski.' Reading this, Philharmonic subscribers must have concluded—and perhaps were intended to conclude— that some sort of a race was on and that, even if Barbirolli was in the running, the race was open. During a concert at which Barbirolli conducted Bartlett and Robertson in two double piano concertos—a new English work, that of Arthur Bliss (future knight and Master of the Queen's Music) and a Liszt rarity, the *Concerto Pathétique* ('bad Liszt, poorly constructed . . . banal and bombastic . . . all posturing and pseudo drama,' judged Olin Downes), Mayor La Guardia made an appeal for money which was heard on a C.B.S. 'hook-up'. He said that money from ticket sales wasn't enough for the orchestra's upkeep.

What of the 'amazing' rise in attendances that Judson had saluted during Barbirolli's 1936–37 term? 'Curiosity accounted for that', writes a historian of the Carnegie scene. 'Naturally there was [at first] a certain enthusiasm for Barbirolli. He was by no means a bad conductor. The trouble was that he did not wear very well . . .; he was just not in the Old Maestros' league.'* Barbirolli's own diagnosis had to do with the new economic pressures. He was reported as saying that, with taxation rising, the rich man 'is either going to be poor, or he is going to think he is poor'. Sooner or later American music would have to be subsidised by the American State. Four years earlier he had euphorically depicted the Philharmonic as an orchestra privately subsidised to the limit of its needs and with a lavishness that no English orchestra would dare even to dream about. Since 1937 the situation had changed to the hurt of many and to the detriment of his own interests more, perhaps, than he was quick to realise.

Meantime even the tax-burdened rich went on taking their wives to hear concerto gods. With Artur Rubinstein in any Beethoven piano concerto followed by the 'New World' Symphony, Barbirolli could fill the hall at two concerts on successive days and venture at one of them on something supposedly unpalatable—say, Eugene Goossens' Concertina for double string orchestra. Other concerto occasions that made a mark, taking the fancy of the crowd or the critics or both, were inspired cooperation between Barbirolli and Sergei Rachmaninov in Beethoven's first piano concerto on a night marred, for the rest, by a substantial walk-out of anti-Brucknerites after the second movement of Bruckner's Seventh Symphony; and (something of a scandal to prim minds) the jazzman Benny Goodman in Mozart's clarinet concerto K. 622, which he played blamelessly, even beautifully, To sublime, solid and expected stuff—Beethoven, Schubert, Brahms, Tchaikovsky and Sibelius—he added the first Philharmonic production of Bizet's youthful and 'redis-covered' C major Symphony; Debussy's *Sommeil de Lear*, intended as incidental music (but never used) for a famous production of Shakespeare's play at the Odeon, Paris; and amiable things, usually for strings alone, by Purcell-Barbirolli and Bach-Barbirolli. One night Vitali-Gibilaro made their bow *in absentia*. The family circle, now centred upon Streatham and still under Mamma's ubiquitous surveillance, was never far from Barbirolli's mind. Finding he hadn't time enough to

* *The World of the Carnegie Hall* by Richard Schickel, Julian Messner Inc., New York, 1960.

transcribe a certain Vitali chaconne for full orchestral strings, he passed the job on to his brother-in-law, Alfonso Gibilaro, whom we have already met. From Streatham Gibilaro sent a transcription which was much to the taste of Carnegie subscribers. It built up through a set of delicately scored variations to a resounding finale in which the strings were joined by full organ. Even Olin Downes said nice things. Occasionally there were excursions to hotel ballrooms where hundreds of Philharmonic leaguers would sit down to an evening of what Barbirolli likened to music-making among friends, intimate and informal. If the ballroom happened to be the grand ballroom of the Plaza hotel, the leaguers sat on little gilded chairs among red velvet hangings, cream-and-gold walls and crystal chandeliers. Thirty or so picked strings from the Philharmonic would bow and phrase fetchingly in Vivaldi, Marcello-Barbirolli, Johann Strauss's 'Wine, Women and Song' and perhaps (it certainly happened once) Holst's *St. Paul's* Suite. Sometimes the concerts of the Philharmonic League were in the afternoon. For these Barbirolli would wear striped trousers and spats and a superbly moulded morningcoat with satin lapels.

The season unfolded more or less as it had been planned. For three weeks astride November and December he took the orchestra to sixteen cities,* conducting seventeen concerts outside New York, then handed it over to Mitropoulos, Bruno Walter and Damrosch for his mid-winter break.

Soon after returning to New York he gave an interview to the *New York Times* (2nd March 1941) mainly about problems which arose in planning programmes intended to be heard by 'live' audiences and radio listeners at the same time. In the course of it he permitted himself an aside: 'Guest conductors in moderation . . . can only benefit an orchestra; but for the development and maturity of an orchestra one man must be in charge.' A fortnight later, Marshall Field, successor to Mackay as president-cum-chairman of the Philharmonic, announced the Society's scheme for 1941–42, the first of two successive seasons in celebration of the orchestra's centennial.

---

* Ann Arbor, Baltimore, Boston, Chicago, Cincinnati, Columbus, Fort Wayne, Lansing, Milwaukee, Pittsburgh, Providence, Saginaw, Springfield, Toledo, Washington and York (Pa.).

The upshot of this announcement and hard arrangements which followed upon minor modifications of it was a parcelling out of the forthcoming winter among ten conductors—some of them men before whom mankind at large was in the way of falling on its face as soon as they lifted a baton. Barbirolli was inevitably to be overshadowed. Leopold Stokowski was among the ten. Eleven years earlier he had conducted the Philharmonic Orchestra, one 'guest' among a total for that season (1930–31) of five conductors. The Philharmonic had seen nothing of him in the interim. To Stokowski was accorded the honour of opening the anniversary season and conducting its first fortnight. Toscanini was to bring up the rear, conducting as a sort of coda to the main jubilations a Beethoven festival of six concerts that would start with the Missa Solemnis and take in all the symphonies and all the big concertos. After an absence of seven years he would be returning to an orchestra from which his spirit had never been exorcised. Between Stokowski and Toscanini the rostrum was to be taken for a fortnight at a time or even for three weeks or a month by eight others: Barbirolli (second after Stokowski in the order of appearance), Bruno Walter, Mitropoulos, Fritz Busch, Koussevitsky, Rodzinsky, Eugene Goossens and Damrosch. All except Koussevitsky, Busch and Goossens had conducted the orchestra before. In the share-out of concerts Barbirolli undoubtedly came off best. He was down for six during the season's third and fourth weeks and another fourteen at what was called the end of 'the season proper', although, bearing in mind Toscanini's 'coda', it was only penultimate.

In a situation of this kind the number of rostrum dates a man has been allocated may be impressive or even flattering. It does not, however, commit the allocators to like liberality in the future. In Schickel's view the intentions of the Philharmonic board were quite other. He says they used the centenary celebrations as an opportunity to ease Barbirolli out of his post. 'The trouble', he writes,* 'was that Barbirolli did not wear very well. . . . It is doubtful if anybody could have successfully followed Toscanini to the Philharmonic podium, and there was bound to be a let-down, on the part of the

* Op. cit. (See p. 203.)

audience and orchestra alike, once the goodwill of the new
man's welcome had worn off. So, although the first half of his
[1936–37] season went extremely well, it was not long before
the first droplets of criticism fell, droplets that were to swell to
a torrent by the time the Philharmonic celebrated its 100th
birthday and simultaneously let Barbirolli go as sole conductor.' The inference is clear. The board demoted Barbirolli
because, with his champion Gilman gone, the critics were, in
the main, against him. What Schickel describes as a critical
torrent is described by another American writer and contemporary witness, David Ewen,* as 'a rain of critical
denunciation.'

Undoubtedly the New York critics had truculent pens.
Their opinions were apt to be contagious. They halted many a
vogue, dispersed many a following. It may therefore be well to
take a look at what the two most eminent among them,
Downes and Virgil Thomson, were saying about Barbirolli's
merits, demerits and achievements. Of Downes (*New York
Times*) we have had samples already and shall return to him.
Thomson, his opposite number on New York's other great
daily, the *Herald Tribune*, came from Kansas City, spent much
time in Europe (preferably Paris; he was a devoted South-
Banker) and composed in many forms and media: symphonies,
sonatas, chamber music, choral music, operas, orchestral
suites, film scores, ballet scores. At the time we are discussing
he was in his middle forties but younger looking, an exuberant
gnome. Recently returned from France, where he had witnessed
the first phase of the German occupation, he had been
appointed Gilman's successor on the strength of earlier
critical writing. It was not his music that made a critic of him
but the sting in his nib and the fact that his prose, while
talking down to nobody, was easy for anybody to take in.
His first assignment was Barbirolli's opening concert of 1940–41.
This being the 99th season of the Philharmonic and the
concert anything but festive in his view, he headed his piece
AGE WITHOUT HONOUR and, in his own word,†
'snubbed' John Barbirolli by publishing with it a photograph

* In *Dictators of the Baton*, New York, 1943.
† *Virgil Thomson* by Virgil Thomson, Weidenfeld and Nicolson, London,
1967.

Photo: Radio Times-Hulton Picture Library

Speaking at a reception after conducting the first London performance of Vaughan Williams's *Antartica* Symphony, 1953.

At supper with Amaryllis Fleming, the 'cellist, and Augustus John, after conducting the Hallé Orchestra at a London Promenade concert, 1953.

Photo: Radio Times–Hulton Picture Library

not of the conductor, a frequent first-night courtesy, but of his concertmaster, Mishel Piastro. This, in part, is what he wrote:

Beethoven's Overture to *Egmont* is a classic hors d'oeuvre. Nobody's digestion was ever spoiled by it, and no latecomer has ever lost much by missing it. It was preceded, as is the custom nowadays, by our National Anthem, [a performance with] more weight than brilliance. It had the sombre and spiritless sonority of the German military bands one hears in France these days. That sombreness is due, I think, to an attempt to express authority through mere weighty blowing and sawing in the middle and lower ranges of the various instruments rather than by the more classic method of placing every instrument in its most graceful and brilliant register to achieve the maximum of carrying power and richness . . .

Elgar's *Enigma* variations are an academic effort not at all lacking in musical charm. I call them academic because the composer's interest in the musical devices he was employing was greater than his effort towards a direct and forceful expression of anything in particular. Like most English composers, Elgar orchestrates accurately and competently. Now, when a man can do anything accurately and competently, he is always on the look-out for occasions to do that thing . . . Mr. Elgar's variations are mostly a pretext for orchestration, a pretty pretext and a graceful one, not without charm and a modicum of sincerity but a pretext for fancy work all the same, for that massively frivolous patchwork in pastel shades of which one sees such quantities in any intellectual British suburban dwelling.

One of Barbirolli's gods was thus sent sprawling. Then came the turn of another, Sibelius. Of the Second Symphony: 'I found it vulgar, self-indulgent and provincial beyond description. I realize that there are many sincere Sibelius lovers in the world, though I must say I've never met one among educated professional musicians. . . . I realise that this work has a populace-pleasing power . . . not unlike the power of a Hollywood Class A picture. Sibelius is in no sense a naïf; he is

H

merely provincial. . . . Perhaps if I have to hear much more of
him I'll sit down one day with the scores and really find out
what's in them. Last night's experience of one was not much
of a temptation to sit through many more.

'The concert as a whole, both as to programme and as to
playing, was anything but a memorable experience. The music
itself was soggy, the playing dull and brutal. As a friend
remarked who had never been to one of these concerts before:
"I understand now why the Philharmonic is not a part of
New York's intellectual life." '

After his copy had gone to the printer, Thomson, doing the
statutory thing, went with his new colleagues to John Bleeck's
restaurant next door and waited for freshly printed copies of
the first edition to come in. The company at Bleeck's admired
its 'hard hitting'. In his autobiography Thomson says the piece
clearly read as a strong one, although 'it contained, I knew,
any number of faults, including seventeen appearances of the
first personal pronoun.' In a later passage he calls it 'brutal
with overstatement'. There had been one cut in proof. Thomson
had disapproved of the audience. 'Undistinguished' was his
word for it. On the advice of the paper's cultural overseer this
came out. The notice drew a 'stream of protest mail', but
Thomson went on writing in much the same vein for fourteen
years. For the rest of Barbirolli's term in New York he paid
little attention to him, most of Barbirolli's concerts being
covered by 'second strings'. Of a Brahms No. 2 he complained
that it was 'routine Barbirolli, displaying a tendency to
alternate soft passages with tons-of-bricks *fortissimi*—a vice
which has spread around in America. His tendency to whip up
these same passages into a positive fury is an imitation, I
should say, of Mr. Toscanini's most serious fault as a musician.
. . . The futility of it was measurable by the restlessness of the
audience and by the number of quiet sleepers visible.' One
Eastertide he went to an afternoon concert of sacred and
other solemn music including *Parsifal* excerpts. 'The real
trouble with Mr. Barbirolli's conducting', he diagnosed, 'is
his lack of a firm rhythm. His soft passages drag and his loud
ones hurry. There is no rhythmic sureness anywhere. When he
busies himself with detail the music fails to progress; and when
he whips it to a climax the details fall out of proportion.

Either they get lost or they become over-assertive. Last night's readings were all on the detailed side, and so the music never seemed to be getting anywhere. . . . *Parsifal* must have a beat, and it must return to the beat after each departure. If it does not do this it fails to hold the attention. Last night the basic pulsation was wholly vague, and the audience in consequence got restless.'

Coming now to Olin Downes and the *New York Times*. In a city where much else was going on he could not be expected to attend all concerts conducted by its sole resident concert conductor. Often he would opt for the Metropolitan Opera or keep his space and hyperboles for such visitors as Koussevitsky and the Boston Orchestra, Stokowski and his Philadelphians, Toscanini and the C.B.S. orchestra in Studio 8H or Beecham and the New York City Symphony, an orchestra recently assembled from the ranks of otherwise unemployed musicians with the blessing and backing of Mayor La Guardia and W.P.A. (Works Progress Administration), one of the instruments of Roosevelt's second New Deal. When left to second, third and fourth strings, Barbirolli received a modicum of pats on the head as well as curt reproofs or wiggings. Downes himself was capable of pats, even of strokings. On Barbirolli's first night in 1936 he shook his head over a tendency now and then to drag a tempo here and sugar a phrase there (this of Mozart's Symphony in C, K. 425) and dawdle sentimentally elsewhere; but in the Fourth Symphony of Brahms he discerned 'exceptional virility, grip, lyrical opulence and, on occasion, the impact of the bear's paw. . . . In general a red-blooded, dramatic and grandly constructed reading.' And (later) of Brahms's No. 2: 'On the whole a warm, honest, healthy reading—and more than that in the slow movement; the score was treated with true breadth and discoursed with a noble passion.' The pace and 'retards' of the Finale might not have been safe for the orchestra or agreeable to the listener. Yet 'exhilarating spirit and sunny splendour' were in evidence. He was almost as greatly taken by Barbirolli's *Mastersingers* overture as Gilman had been, extolling its 'fine proportions, admirably chosen *tempi* and the stirring enthusiasm of a young conductor on firm ground and in love with his task'. There was an early Haydn symphony that 'sparkled and sang'; a Beethoven's Eighth which had brilliance and 'a contagious gusto'; a 'Jupiter' Symphony (Mozart) of 'easy flow and felicity of statement'; a splendid night with Horowitz (Tchaikovsky's B flat minor concerto) when Barbirolli truly shared the glory and wild applause at the end; and a *Bourgeois gentilhomme* suite (R. Strauss) that was all 'lightness, dexterity, delight and humour. Seldom has this music appeared so felicitous in idea and in execution, so warm in colour.' Also a Schubert 'Great' C major with the *tempi* 'just right, the music sounding from the orchestra as if liberated and speaking in the most natural way, the young conductor beside himself with the excitement and joy of music. . . . An admirably straightforward, full-blooded and lyrical conception.' (A later performance of the 'Great' got the lash: 'There were many shortcomings. Mr. Barbirolli has yielded to the bad habit of those conductors who have made it fashionable to hurry the slow movement. This music used to be dragged. Last night it almost always inclined to hurry. The Scherzo needed less coarse and heavy tone. Its flight was a sprint.')

Then Sibelius, a touchstone. Downes had begun popularising Sibelius nearly thirty years earlier. In recognition of his service to Finnish music he was made a Commander of the White Rose of Finland by the Finnish Government during Barbirolli's second year with the Philharmonic, that is to say, a quarter of a century before Barbirolli was similarly honoured. Of Barbirolli's Sibelius performances that of the little-heard Symphony No. 3 was the only one that got an unqualified pat on the head from Downes, a man skilled at patting a head and tweaking an ear in the same sentence. 'One of his best performances. . . .' he pronounced. 'The slow movement can become monotonous. Mr. Barbirolli brought to it a freshness of feeling and a rhythmic vitality that sustained the interest; . . . he interpreted the whole work with breadth, a strength that was not feverish, and a genuine simplicity which . . . said much more than ranting. The Third Symphony has rarely been so convincing.'

The First and Second symphonies were a different matter. Downes reviewed two Barbirolli readings of each. The summarised phrases that follow are collated from his four notices.

Of Sibelius No. 1.—More in the score than Mr. B got out of it. Places in slow movement where he was episodic. Result: loss of cohesion and form. Some of the wind overblew and were out of tune. Strings had fine fullness and sonority. Other instruments lacked quality and proper balance. . . . Hard to agree with Mr. B's conception of the work. Reading had exterior effectiveness but proportions and accents forced. Orchestra constantly whipped to frenzy. Anticlimactic turmoil. Exaggerated retards and pauses. Trombones were shifted from usual position and directly faced audience. This did not help. Brass so heavy in places that nothing else could be heard.

Sibelius No. 2.—Marred by some over-rapid *tempi* and exaggerated *tempo* changes. However, vitality, primitive power, the berserker spirit and breadth of climax were there. Epic style, in fact. 'This should grow into one of Mr. Barbirolli's best interpretations.' [For Downes, at any rate, it didn't altogether do that. Of a second performance:] Thoughtful reading in bardic vein. Breadth and sweep of line, real sense of form, sensitive detail. But, in places, *tempo* too suddenly whipped up or slowed down. Hence the sudden and disproportionate breadth of the peroration. A too calculated performance which, had the music been given its head, would have been a completed instead of a conditional success. . . .

What has been set forth already includes the entire residue of compliment that can be sifted from the seven-year bulk of Downes's relevant writings. The prevalent note is animosity. Bach's sixth Brandenburg concerto? Muddy. Slow movement didn't hang together. *Don Quixote* (Strauss)? Tame, inadequate, unrevealing, trivialised. 'Not a task for one with such a limited grasp of its contents as Mr. Barbirolli.' (Two years later *Don Quixote* came up again. The second performance was 'markedly superior to the first but not up to what Strauss had in mind'.) The *Flying Dutchman* overture? Weber's *Euryanthe* overture? The overture to *A Midsummer Night's Dream*? The *Lohengrin* prelude? Noisy and exaggerated. Forced climaxes. Artificially whipped-up excitement. Coarse-fibred tone. Imperfect attack. So slow that climax didn't come off. Good bits, yes. But pretty bad woodwind intonation. And sometimes enthusiasm got the better of him, to the detriment of tone and style.

In Schönberg's *Verklärte Nacht* he tore passion to tatters, confusing external intensity with hurry and excessive demonstration. In the César Franck Symphony his touch was theatrical, insensitive, short on stability, apt to be wrong in speed and, in most ways, unFranckian. In the *Nocturnes* of Debussy his approach was heavy. Not enough mood and sensitivity. In Debussy's *Iberia* he showed 'a fine disregard ever and anon' for the subtler details, obscuring them with faulty tonal balances. Schumann's Fourth Symphony he slowed and sentimentalised in part, indulged in mannered phrasings and fell far short of the score's potential. Impossible to speak well of his *Rhapsodie espagnole* (Ravel); owing to technical imprecision, faulty balance and superficiality of approach, 'much wasn't heard that is in the score, while some things were so curiously balanced that it was surprising to find them there at all.' The *Bourgeois gentilhomme* suite whose performance he praised so roundly came last in an all-Strauss programme of which he wrote as to the earlier part: 'We had not heard the Philharmonic-Symphony Orchestra play so badly and inaccurately, with as many accidents, with such poor intonation and such scramblings as in *Till Eulenspiegel*. Nor was the playing of *Don Juan* anything to write a letter—or an article— about. In fact, it could be imagined that the second half of the programme (which included an operatic soprano in the closing scene from *Salome*) had been thoroughly rehearsed while the first had not.'

About Barbirolli's concerto accompaniments Downes wrote civil things from time to time in the same key as most other critics. But even on concerto nights he kept a rod to hand. Presumably as compensation against another piece in the same programme, Arnold Bax's Fourth Symphony ('much ado about nothing' futile, forced, longwinded... conventional, repetitious), Heifetz played in the Tchaikovsky violin concerto, a performance found grossly wanting. The concerto's last movement, said Downes, was for the greater part 'taken at such a breathless speed that often the violinist could not give the necessary weight and fullness of tone to brilliant passages, and the orchestra was hard put to scramble after him.' About his concert version of the uncut second Act of *Tristan and Isolde* Downes was ruthless. He began with an understatement. Barbirolli's reading, he suggested, could hardly have helped the principals. Then: 'He drove the orchestra wherever there was a shadow of excuse, [not only] covering the voices but also . . . effectively concealing elements of Wagner's counterpoint.' He conceded that from the beginning of 'O sink' herniede' the performance was more subdued and had beauty. But tonal imbalance robbed the Act of much of its logic. Also, apparently, of some of the words. Wagner, he reminded his readers, anathematised 'those who forget the importance of the singing voice and the significance of a text clearly conveyed by the ideal singer, who would have little chance, for the greater part of the time, against Mr. Barbirolli's dynamics'.

Sometimes he turned from what he judged to be Barbirolli's shortcomings as a conductor and stormed against what he chose to conduct. Many an English composer came in for a scorching. It must be said that, unlike Thomson, he occasionally dropped an approving phrase about the *Enigma* variations and Barbirolli's treatment of it. The rest of Elgar he burnt at the stake. Heifetz played in the violin concerto, a collaboration which gave Barbirolli especial joy and was acknowledged by Downes to have engrossed their audience. That, wrote Downes, was Heifetz's doing, however, not Elgar's; and he let himself go about what he took to be the deficiencies of a piece that 'got worse and worse' as it went on—'the bad, involved style of the pompous beginning'; the 'commonplace, bourgeois, Belgravian' slow movement; and a Finale that built up 'pretentiously, having neither tension nor cohesion'. Two months later Barbirolli brought the E flat Symphony to the Carnegie Hall platform as one might carry some reliquary into a chancel. (The metaphor may seem far fetched. But consider. Twenty years later in Edinburgh, after conducting the other Elgar symphony, the one in A flat, he picked up the score and, turning to an ebullient audience, solemnly kissed it. The E flat always meant at least as much to him as the A flat. Before both his mind and heart genuflected.) In 1938 the E flat was no more a repertory piece for the Philharmonic than for any orchestra in the world. The Philharmonic players, indeed, were, perhaps, farther removed from its emotional fabric than many. But something of Barbirolli's awe and passion lodged with them; they succeeded in 'incarnating' the score. The performance moved Downes to this:

> The depressing character of the Second Symphony . . . is neither its workmanship nor its manifest sincerity but its evident fatigue. Hearing it gives the sensation of a worn-out culture which died at the roots a long time ago. You listen and you murmur respectfully. You pray for the end. Not that the work is one of fiendish dissonance. Quite the contrary. The playing can be little more than suave and meaningless and tired. It seems to come from an over-exploited source, and it is difficult not to associate this spiritual lassitude with a culture that has lived its day and must perhaps suffer collapse before there comes fresh strength and creative inspiration.
>
> One thinks of Europe, exhausted in her art and hopes of the future. Sterile experiment is left. The symphony tries this and that device, always used skilfully, not sufficing to produce any real impulse which would result in creation. The best part is the slow movement. But after all, it is paper. . . . The feeling back of the music is 'ersatz'.

Two months before it was known how many and which hands were to conduct the Centennial concerts, Downes devoted a weighty music-page article to what he thought wrong with the Philharmonic Orchestra and what should be done to put it right. It was a woeful survey. In it he cited Barbirolli without naming him.

Looking back to the crucial 1936–37 season, he exclaimed over the directors' decision in mid-stream to give a three-year contract to one out of five guest conductors before he had been extensively heard and before the other guests had even shown their faces. The directors, he went on, had had reason to repent their haste. During recent seasons playing standards in general had 'gradually slipped in tone quality, technical cleanness and accuracy of intonation, as well as in broadly interpretative directions. It has been shown clearly that a conductor who is only industrious and routine will not fill the bill where this orchestra and its conductor are concerned. The conductor must be an orchestra-builder . . . and a musician of unquestioned authority and communicative power.'

Since 1927 the Philharmonic had enjoyed a resident monopoly: which meant that the orchestra could pursue any policy it liked on the assumption that the public must take it or leave it. 'In fact', he continued, 'this never works with the public, as the history of the earlier weeks of this season [1940–41] and of preceding Philharmonic-Symphony winters has demonstrated. You cannot make people come who do not choose to do so. Audiences just stay away. The great majority of New York's symphonic audiences of late seasons have patronised first the Boston Symphony and second the Philadelphia Orchestra.' For remedy the directors must bring in Stokowski, who was unsurpassed as a builder of orchestras, and invite Toscanini to return, if only for gala performances.*

This is what, in effect, came to pass. But with these two eight others who have already been enumerated came to the 'kitchenette'. On the assumption that the broth was as bad as Downes made out, it was hard to see how it would improve if stirred by a succession of ten batons, even if the ten included two or three so-called magic ones. Virgil Thomson had a thought or two on this aspect:

'A string of guest conductors, although obviously the first thing the Philharmonic management would think of, is the last thing the Philharmonic musicians need. They have been so thoroughly guest-conducted for thirty years [Thomson either forgot or chose to ignore Barbirolli's four permanent seasons] that they have become temperamental, erratic and difficult as only first-class musicians can become when subjected to every known variety of brow-beating and wheedling. The best birthday present the Philharmonic could offer itself and us would be a good, permanent, full-time conductor, somebody worthy of the job and capable of assuming all its musical responsibilities. . . .' At this point he conferred gender upon the orchestra as if it were a yacht or a racing car: 'What the Philharmonic needs is a lord and master who will take some of the jumpiness out of her and put her to work [beneficiently] for a city that loves her and supports her and complains about her.'†

* *New York Times*, 12th January 1941.
† Quoted by Schickel, op. cit.

H*

For the first Centennial concert (10th October 1941) the platform was flanked by American flags. The biggest audience seen at a Philharmonic opening in over a decade, exulted Downes, waited a-quiver with excitement for the entry of Leopold Stokowski, 'the glamorous, the unpredictable'. Stokowski began with his best-selling transcription of Bach's D minor toccata and fugue. Then on to Beethoven's Fifth. Carnegie Hall had rarely known a more quivering night or, indeed, a more quivering fortnight. Stokowski departed in a cloud of glory. Barbirolli followed. His six concerts had a core of standard symphonies: Brahms, Beethoven, Mozart, Dvořák, and took in a 'required' native novelty, William Grant Still's *Plain Chant for America*; also, on the same night, a Philharmonic patroness having died, Henry Wood's orchestral transcription of the Chopin funeral march, a surpassingly bad one, thought Downes. Somewhere along the line the Polka and Fugue from *Schwanda* recurred and made many people happy. It may have been on this occasion that Weinberger, again spotted in a box, was wafted down and gave the conductor a euphoric hug and kiss. On the last of his six nights, Barbirolli conducted Casedesus in the Ravel piano concerto for the left hand only, an uncommonly elegant half-hour. Then he and Evelyn packed for a long recess-tour, with conducting dates in Vancouver, which by this time had made a habit of him; Seattle, Cincinnati, where he relieved the resident conductor, Eugene Goossens, for *his* fortnight's contribution to the Philharmonic season; and, more memorably, Los Angeles.

Although their country was neutral as yet, Americans in general were articulate and active in their sympathies towards Britain and her allies. Soviet Russia's entry into the war started off fresh waves of enthusiasm. 'Drives' for Mrs. Winston Churchill's medical-aid-to-Russia fund became the fashionable thing. For this cause, at the Shrine auditorium, Los Angeles, in the presence of 7,000, Barbirolli conducted Horowitz, Heifetz and the L.A. Symphony Orchestra in an all-Tchaikovsky programme. He started with *Romeo and Juliet*. Then came the violin concerto and the B flat minor piano concerto, separated by the Waltz and Elegy from that Serenade for strings, Op. 48, which he had scrutinised on shipboard with Toscanini. Far from being shadowed or shrivelled by the night's Heifetz - Horowitz fever, the Serenade fragments bloomed and went well:

'Indeed, we had to repeat the Waltz. The point is, the orchestra were very good. I took tremendous pains to play all the dynamics. That lovely, quiet ending, for example.' At rehearsal some of the players had asked him what 'arrangement' they were playing:

Barbirolli: What d'you mean?
A player: Well, it sounds quite different. It *is* an arrangement, isn't it?
Barbirolli: Yes, Tchaikovsky's.

In telling of this he added: 'The Serenade is a more difficult work than people think, because it gets a lot of ramshackle performances. When you come to make a recording of a thing like that you find it takes the finest players all their time. There are people who disparage the Serenade, I know. That's due to all the slovenly performances. As a rule Tchaikovsky concerts are given to rake in a bit of money. Nobody rehearses. Nobody takes the job seriously. I don't conduct Tchaikovsky often in London nowadays [1964] because I treat him with the same respect as I treat Brahms at his best. Not everybody else does. He was a great composer. He was one of the greatest craftsmen of music.'

The first week of March (1942) saw him on the New York rostrum again. A newspaper headline said: BARBIROLLI BACK, ABSENT FIVE MONTHS as if to rub something in. He had two ballroom concerts and seventeen Carnegie nights or afternoons ahead of him. As he worked sedulously on, a glowing notice or two came his way. One of Thomson's assistants, Jerome Bohm, wrote after a performance of the *Firebird* suite that he had never thought him capable of getting such ravishing, just and delicate sounds from his orchestra. He made a deep impression, no easy thing in that place and at that time, with Vaughan Williams's *Five Variants on 'Dives and Lazarus'*. A programme note said these were being done for the first time by the Philharmonic. Not so. Adrian Boult had conducted their première as a Philharmonic concert in June 1939 as part of Britain's contribution to the New York World

Fair. At one of his Thursday nights a sturdy apparition from a past which, in the 1940s, was popularly and, for that matter, authoritatively supposed to be much deader than it had ever been, listened from a Carnegie box to the first performance of Alexander Gretchaninov's Symphony No. 4, namely Gretchaninov himself, Russian expatriate, a pupil (fifty years earlier) of Rimsky-Korsakov, seventy-seven years old and with another fourteen years to go. Barbirolli had originally intended to produce the symphony three weeks earlier in a programme that included the Vitali-Gibilaro Chaconne, but there hadn't been time to copy the band parts. At the end the old man came on to the platform and made his bows to the sort of applause which at that time came the way of all Russians whatever their age, calling, school or anterior allegiance. Then he went back to his box and listened to another Fourth symphony, that of Tchaikovsky, whose career had briefly overlapped his.

There was a fantastic, elbow-rubbing Sunday when Beecham reappeared with the New York City Symphony Orchestra at 5.30 p.m. Earlier that afternoon Barbirolli had taken the Philharmonic through Brahms's No. 4, a Mozart violin concerto and Lalo's *Symphonie espagnole* and a new overture, *King John*, which had been dedicated to him by its composer, the Italian expatriate Mario Castelnuovo-Tedesco. A new audience trooped in as soon as Barbirolli's trooped out. Beecham's players took over the platform after the shortest feasible interval. They, too, were working by stop-watch. When Beecham had finished there was to be another 'out-and-in', for a 'cello recital was billed to start at eight-thirty. Having bounced his men through *The Star Spangled Banner* at record speed, Beecham did a symphony by a young Englishman, Richard Arnell, Dvořák's No. 4 and Berlioz's *Royal Hunt and Storm*. An audience which had paid as little as twenty-eight cents a seat relished all. Unhappily there was something else, a piano concerto, Mozart's in G, K. 453: and the pianist was Beecham's second-wife-to-be, Betty Humby, whose performances were not always matter for ecstasy. She looked pretty 'but seemed to have no aptitude for the piano' or, to particularise, for a piano which happened to be out of tune not only with the orchestra but also with itself. To make the situation more interesting, Beecham conducted from between the audience and the piano instead of from the far side of it, as is more prudent in concertos; some of the players could not see his beat for the propped-up piano lid. This account is based on a *Herald Tribune* review by Robert Lawrence. With the concerto, wrote Lawrence, the proceedings took a nose-dive. Miss Humby was applauded none the less. The applause had a polite ring.

From this infelicity as from various others in a sonorous career, Beecham emerged with his aura undimmed. He appeared with the New York City Symphony at pairs of concerts during three successive wartime seasons while Barbirolli was in America, attracting big and distinctive audiences, relatively classless and with more young people among them than were usually seen at Carnegie Hall. Between concerts he talked in a lordly and arbitrary way to luncheon clubs and interviewers. Of his 'New Deal' orchestra, made up in part of talent which only a Beecham could ignite to much purpose, he said: 'I like conducting any orchestra that can play the notes. I am interested in what may be called the genus orchestral player. I don't say they are all musical. That would be going a bit far. . . .' Drawling dicta in this vein delighted everybody within earshot. Even orchestral players grinned and exchanged winks.

In private he talked on many themes and, not always fulsomely, of many people. Fellow musicians came under rallying or patronising or scathing scrutiny. Word spread of his surprise that the Philharmonic directors had made so much of John Barbirolli. With the New York City Symphony he seems to have worked minor wonders. But the Philharmonic remained illustrious. It had the dominant name, the best players and a mellowing tradition. Almost all the world's great batons from Beecham's boyhood up had served it. During three seasons— 1927–28, 1931–32 and 1935–36—he had been among the Philharmonic's guest conductors. That he had not been included in the Centennial scheme occasioned surprise and grumbles in some quarters. It was all very well giving a show to the younger end of the English school, said the grumblers. But when matched against the Toscaninis and the Koussevitskis, the Walters and the Stokowskis, Barbirolli and Goossens were surely a bit underweight? On Beecham's part a touch of

pique is traceable, perhaps. Talking of the English orchestras
he had formed or salvaged in thirty or forty years, he said of
one of them, presumably the London Symphony Orchestra:
'When I took it over it was almost as bad as the New York
Philharmonic is today.' He said this at a time when Barbirolli
was still 'guesting' at Carnegie Hall. Not long afterwards he
was offered a summer series with the Philharmonic at the
Lewisohn Stadium, New York, accepted promptly, all aversions
swallowed, and drew open-air crowds whose size depended
beyond a certain point on who was billed for the night's
concerto. With Artur Rubinstein he drew 18,000, with
Kreisler 16,500 and with Betty Humby-Beecham, as she now
was, 6,000. By this time, however, Beecham's thoughts were
bent on home.

So, in good time, were those of Barbirolli. He meant to see
something of Britain as soon as he was through with his
scheduled commitments at Carnegie Hall for March and April;
even sooner if the exigencies of wartime Atlantic crossings
dictated an earlier passage. A creeping worry had become
fixed anxiety. As soon as he put his baton down or a score
aside he fell into a state of mild torment about Mamma, his
sister, his brother and his nephews, all of them in what
amounted still to a rear battle-zone. That spring was to see the
heaviest air-raid casualties in Britain since the last month of
the 1940–41 'Blitz'.* There were the letters from home. There
were the newspapers. There were the radio news bulletins.
These served only a limited purpose, because: 'I didn't *really*
know what was going on. I was terribly unhappy. By 1942 I
felt so badly about it that I said to Evelyn, "I don't know
what's going to happen to me if I don't get to England and see
what's happening for myself." '

About one happening at home he was pretty clear. An
under-supply of popular amusement and a greater need for it
than in peacetime, combined with more money in many more
pockets, had fortuitously produced an orchestral boom which,
if forecast in peacetime, would have been scoffed out of court.
Many a music-hall 'regular' paying his shilling for the gallery

* In April 1942 there were so-called Baedeker raids on Bath, York,
Exeter and Norwich. In these raids and sporadic ones elsewhere 938 people
were killed and 998 injured.

without looking at the bill, his mind set on equilibrists, quick-change comics, songs in the Harry Lauder or Vesta Tilley vein and so forth, found himself listening to the Grieg piano concerto, Jarnefelt's Praeludium, Schubert's 'Unfinished' Symphony and even more out-of-the-way matters. He would return for more, perhaps because there was little else to return for, perhaps because classical music frightened him less than he had supposed it would. Barbirolli had heard about the boom from the Labour politician, A. V. Alexander, among others. Alexander, who sat in the House of Commons for the Hillsborough division of Sheffield, was one among several friends of his in that city, where he conducted much and was to conduct much more, who, although fond of music, happened to be prominent in other callings. At this time he was First Lord of the Admiralty in Churchill's wartime inter-party government and set on a course that led from Co-operative Wholesale Society politics to a viscountcy, leadership of the Labour peers and an earldom. In a letter to 'My dear John' he described how music was flourishing. There had never been anything like it before. How wonderful it would be if John could be in the thick of it all! Here, to use Barbirolli's image, was a straw. He clutched at it.

'I have ten weeks to spare this summer', he wrote back in effect. 'I would be delighted to spend those ten weeks con-ducting English orchestras at my own expense, without fee, solely for the orchestras' benefit—if only you can get me home.'

No private citizen could get *himself* home. The days were gone when a man wishing to cross the Atlantic telephoned a travel agency and booked a passage for the date of his choice or whim. Alexander promised to do what he could.

'Apparently', adds Barbirolli, 'he went to Churchill, who said: 'Well, if he's fool enough to want to come, let him come.' On the strength of Alexander's encouragement he offered his services to the London Symphony and London Philharmonic orchestras. Both accepted gratefully and scheduled him for what snowballed to a total of thirty concerts during May and June, most of them in English provincial cities. In accordance with the undertaking to Alexander there were to be no fees. He would meet his expenses out of his own pocket. Profits were to go to the orchestras or to specified charities. One of his

London dates was to be the last night of an international
music festival at the Cambridge Theatre got up by the meteoric
Jay Pomeroy, whose operatic and other enterprises during the
war and for a few years after it made agreeable commotions
in the musical world. His Cambridge Theatre programme was
to be all-Beethoven: *Leonora* No. 3, the Seventh Symphony and
the fourth piano concerto with Louis Kentner playing in it, the
proceeds to be earmarked for Mrs. Churchill's aid-to-Russia
fund. Four other conductors were in the festival—Adrian
Boult, Malcolm Sargent, Anatole Fistoulari and Charles
Hambourg. For all the smattering of foreign artists and
foreign names—Borgioli, Pouishnoff, Daria Bayan, Novak-
owsky, Kiriloff—the affair smacked comfortably of old English
concert routines.

Having rounded-off his arrangements with London, Barbirolli, while getting on with his Carnegie concerts, mentally sat
back and waited to hear, through the British Consulate and
British Information Services, New York, news of the
passage which Alexander had promised. By this time America
was in the war, Pearl Harbor a weeping wound in millions
of American hearts. But war had put no mute on symphonic
music. Carnegie audiences began to be dotted with khaki.
Occasionally there would be a uniformed soloist. It was a
great time for Tchaikovsky. There was a Saturday night and
a following Sunday afternoon when he had the hall full and
overflowing with the same programme: the *Nutcracker* music,
Romeo and Juliet, two movements from one of the orchestral
suites, the *Pathétique* symphony—and no concerto. To him
fell the honour of conducting on the afternoon of the Philharmonic Society's anniversary day, 2nd April 1942. Anniversary day brought no music of a special or celebratory kind.
It did not even get a programme of its own. What Barbirolli
conducted that afternoon was, in fact, a repeat of what he had
conducted the night before. It included a new Barbirolli
transcription for strings, 'Wenn wir in höchsten Nöthen seyn'
('When we are in sorest need'), the chorale which Bach
dictated to his son-in-law a few days before he died, music
with salves of its own for a world under stresses of a scale and
kind that Bach never imagined. The Westminster Choir were
on hand for the 'Stabat Mater' of Pergolesi and for the Grail

Scene from *Parsifal* preceded by the Prelude and Transformation Music. The *Parsifal* excerpts drew a disobliging note from Virgil Thomson which has been quoted already. During the same week he conducted Yehudi Menuhin twice in the Beethoven violin concerto, one of the performances being at a Red Cross benefit concert that ended with helpings of Johann Strauss and Sousa's *Stars and Stripes For Ever*. As guest of honour among hundreds at a party given by Theodore E. Steinway, third piano-maker of his line, and Mrs. Steinway, he cut a hundredth-birthday cake, Mrs. Steinway clinging to his free arm in excited glee. The cake was a huge disc, a sort of sweet millstone set with miniatures of orchestral players in concert position.

At last news of his passage came through. He was to sail in mid-April. The sailing date preceded his three terminal Carnegie dates at the end of the Philharmonic's season proper. Nothing for it but to free himself by exchanging these dates with two earlier ones for which Bruno Walter was billed.

On 12th April 1942 he did another Tchaikovsky programme: *Francesca da Rimini*, Fourth Symphony, etc. Even when offered Tchaikovsky audiences could be fickle; there were five or six hundred empty seats. A programme note said he was to leave *soon* for guest appearances in England. 'Soon' was hardly the word for it. He had, in fact, just time to turn round, do a bit of light packing and board s.s. *California Express*, 3,000 tons, a Norwegian freighter built for the fruit trade but now carrying less perishable foods: 'I literally came home with the bacon.' He was one of six passengers. They gathered they would make Liverpool in ten or twelve days.

While the convoy that included *California Express* was eluding U-boat packs, Marshall Field made a first announcement about the 1942–43 season. Again there would be a string of guests, Toscanini and Bruno Walter among them. Barbirolli was to conduct for a month towards the end of the season. His portion was to be eighteen concerts. The easing-out process was now obvious to everybody.

CHAPTER THIRTEEN

WARTIME FORAY

THE passage took not twelve days but twenty-three. Evelyn, who had not been allowed to accompany him, worried somewhat towards the end: 'By the time we docked at Liverpool she thought I had been buried at sea with the honours that are accorded on such occasions.' He was to be away, crossings included, for about three and a half months, returning at the end of July. Deciding to fill in the time with secretarial training, she learned 'mild book-keeping', how to type, set up a letter, keep files and so on: 'I thought all this might come in useful. Owing to the war there were staff shortages everywhere. And we were getting near the time when John's contract would expire. We might need a secretary and not be able to get one. I'd be the secretary.'

S.S. *California Express* reached Liverpool early in May. Down the years Barbirolli often described that day, almost always in the same language: 'Coming ashore after America was wonderful. I haven't a drop of English blood in me. It was marvellous all the same. The first thing I did was to walk into the refreshment buffet'—as such places were called then—'at Lime Street Station and have a glass of *warm* bitter beer and buy a packet of Player's cigarettes: which made me feel I was really home again. One of the most wonderful days of my life.'

Then London. Paint peeling from stucco. Fruit shops with nothing in them but potatoes, old carrots and turnips. Searchlights at swordplay in the night sky. Shopmen snipping off clothing coupons and food points. Streets aswarm with men and women and uniforms of many nations. Drabness everywhere. Cheerful faces nearly everywhere. And gaiety. The homecomer exclaimed at 'the wonderful spirit that is abroad'. There were the acres of bomb rubble. And sliced houses with high wallpaper bared to the sky and fireplaces clinging where rooms had been

blasted away. One acre of ruin gave him a sharper pang than
the rest. Queen's Hall was a calcined shell, the inside a heap of
debris. The place where, as a boy, he had given his first concerto
concert and where as a young man he conducted his first Elgar
No. 2 and his first *La Mer* of note had been hit by incendiaries
two years earlier to the month. A friend who met him coming
away noted the drawn face, the shake in his voice. 'We went for
a drink, and he needed it.'*

In advertisements up and down the country he was THE
WORLD-FAMOUS CONDUCTOR and THE MAESTRO OF THE NEW YORK
PHILHARMONIC ORCHESTRA. The People (for it is hard to think of
mid-war audiences just as audiences) rose to him thunderously.
That he was conducting for the L.P.O. and the L.S.O. and for
certain war or musical charities was pretty well known, but
there had been no trumpeting of the fact. When told, in idioms
alien to those among which he had lived for most of seven years,
that he was doing a rather splendid thing or that his concerts
were absolutely tophole, he would reply that they were 'just a
little offering'; that his object was to show his admiration of (*a*)
'the national spirit' and (*b*) the L.S.O.'s pluck (or the L.P.O.'s,
as the case might be) in touring on through Blitz, blackout and
schedules of one-night 'stands' which, because of erratic and
comfortless transport, taxed players' stamina unprecedentedly.
The welcome he got for his Beethoven programme from a jam-
packed Cambridge Theatre on the last night of Pomeroy's music
festival made him feel more than ever how worth while it had
been to come over—'even if I never get back'. This last phrase
was no rhetorical one. He was to return, as he had come, by sea
during a recrudescence of U-boat warfare which, for some
months, made Atlantic crossings a deadlier business than at any
other time during the war.† First with the L.S.O., then with
the L.P.O., he criss-crossed the country in overcrowded trains
which had a way of sitting unaccountably in deep countryside
or a few hundred yards outside stations where everybody wanted
to get off. The welcome the Cambridge Theatre had given him
was repeated by warm-hearted thousands all along the route in

* *One Hundred Years of the Hallé*, C. B. Rees, Macgibbon and Kee, 1957.
† During his absence from the U.S., including a total of six weeks or
so on shipboard, 370 merchant ships of nearly 2,000,000 tons gross tonnage
were sunk by U-boats in the Atlantic.

concert halls which, even if they didn't look much, were nos-
talgically remembered and loved. With its comradely wartime
crowd, less attentively dressed and younger on the average than
those of other days, even the City Hall of Sheffield had an
endearing look, and that was saying much; for, as he was to say
later, he knew of no more ridiculous place for music-making in
the world: 'Two stone lions sit in the middle of the platform, one
on each side of the artists' entrance. It's like coming up out of
Trafalgar Square underground station. Because of those con-
founded lions* one half of the orchestra can't see the other half.
The place is as bad for speaking as for music. I once made a
speech there. A very good speech. I ought to know. I had the
pleasure of hearing it three times. At the end of every sentence
I had to wait until it had bounced back twice.'

Such was the spirit of summer, 1942; the sentiments to which
it moved him were such that the old deficiencies did not oppress;
he was delighted to encounter them again. In Sheffield he did
Elgar's Introduction and Allegro, the *Firebird* Suite and
Tchaikovsky's Fifth. Other symphonies he toured were
Beethoven's No. 7, Schubert's No. 5 and Brahms's No. 2. At
home as in America, Tchaikovsky rode high; long the butt of
rabid Brahmsians and the 'good taste' zealots, he had found a new
if unpretentious public for whom (as for Barbirolli) his scores
were caves of enchantment. To Tchaikovsky's Fifth symphony
he added *Francesca da Rimini* and *Romeo and Juliet*. For the rest
there were the usual orchestral helpings from *Tristan*, *Die
Walküre* and *Tannhäuser*, the *Enigma* variations, bits of Delius
(including *A Song of Summer*), some mild Debussy (the *Petite
Suite*, for instance), a Bach-Barbirolli piece or two and the usual
fringe of Rossini and Johann Strauss overtures. Towards the end
of his round with the L.P.O. he did a pair of concerts at Walsall,
smaller than most of the places they served (population just over
100,000) and, perhaps for that reason, enthusiastic to the point of
frenzy. It was a Black Country borough, small sister of Coventry
which lay to the south-east, its core torn out by Hitler's bombers.
The steel works, iron works and engineering plants of Walsall
were at it night and day. So were the great collieries on the rim
of the borough. Even so, Barbirolli's first concert nearly filled

* Some years after the war the lions were removed and other improvements made to the platform.

the town hall. His second was a sell-out at two shillings a seat to six shillings. All you could buy at the doors were standing places. These went as quickly as the box office could take the money. Many were turned away. From the *Thieving Magpie* overture to the *Enigma* everything brought joy and din that were reminiscent of cup-tie Soccer when a goal is scored. It was as though all had been famished and were appeased at last after long waiting. At the end he was called back six times, exhausted, serious of expression and blissful. He lifted a hand to still the tumult and said: 'I have come a long way to be with you. It has been well worth while. Only *the best* is good enough for an audience such as you have shown yourself to be.' It is doubtful whether he ever said anything so straight from the heart to any Royal Philharmonic Society audience or to his Carnegie faithful.

People were waiting backstage to shake him by the hand. There was one who overtopped the rest by head and shoulders, a tousle-headed giant with a schoolboy's smile: Frank Mullings, visitant from a past that reverberated still, 'one of the finest Tristans I ever heard' the one English actor-singer of his time whose diction ennobled every syllable he sang, however silly the text might be. When the crowd thinned they sat down and talked joyously.

On all his tours he was accompanied by Nonna, black-haired, bright and hardy. Who could have thought she was turned seventy? She bore the skimpy food, the dawdling trains, the occasional wail of sirens denoting a 'lone raider' overhead and a score other small tribulations with tough composure, as a Biscayan peasant might have borne them. Although essentially impervious to music, as has been said, she was tenaciously and tenderly proud of her son. Returning south for a round-off concert with the L.P.O. at the Royal Albert Hall in aid of King George's Fund for sailors, he stayed with Nonna at Streatham. Ever since he left for New York she had kept a room ready against his, or his and Evelyn's, return. When in or near London he would never have dreamed of staying anywhere else: and so it continued until the end. This time, as on earlier occasions, he went up on rehearsal mornings by No. 8 electric tram from Streatham to Victoria and from Victoria to the Albert Hall by bus; the Maestro of the New York Philharmonic Orchestra would get off at the Kensington Gore stop with a swarm of players carrying fiddle cases. 'You ought to take a taxi,' admonished Nonna. He did not heed her. In any other conductor this would have been demagogic, a failing of which he was entirely free; it just happened that such simplicities were part of his nature and rides on tram tops and bus tops among life's abiding pleasures. During that last London week-end, 1942, he was heard by a full Albert Hall, that is to say, by over 6,000, in Berlioz's *Roman Carnival* overture, *A Song of Summer*, the *Firebird* Suite and Tchaikovsky's Symphony No. 4; and found time for a talk to 'cello students at the Walenn school. He told the students that despite the recognition that New York had given him he had been unable to resist coming back to England in her hour of trial. Because he had a contract to finish, he was obliged to return. 'But I will come back year by year until Europe is liberated.' That was not quite how things fell out. He was to be better than his word.

He returned in a Fyffe 'banana boat', 5,000 tons, which gave the handful of passengers a little more elbow room than had been his case on the way out. The convoy ran into submarine packs and, during one of these encounters, lost three ships in an hour and a half, one of the three being next in line to the Fyffe boat. They made New York in twenty-two days. 'On the two trips, there and back, we were attacked by subs seven times.' He made straight for Los Angeles, where guest engagements were to spread over three months. Committee women welcomed him back with awe. He told them of the privations which Britain was bearing with a grin and had something to say about the way American civilians whimpered over slight wartime inconveniences. Evelyn and he had musical friends to their villa in Beverly Hills. He played 'cello to Horowitz's piano and to Francescatti's violin. There was a summer night that remained with him ever afterwards: Hollywood Bowl under the stars; warmth in the air; a multitude listening to Delius's *First Cuckoo* in unflawed silence; everything just right; glossy, almost, in its perfection. There were 15,000 in the Bowl that night.

At Carnegie Hall he took over the Philharmonic Orchestra in mid-February from Bruno Walter, who had taken over from

Fritz Reiner, who had taken over from another chain of stars.
In the wings Fritz Reiner (again) and a newcomer called Efrem
Kurtz were waiting to take over from him. Bruno Walter would
be back to end the season with a fortnight in April. More
than ever Philharmonic arrangements had the look of a banana
layer cake. The orchestra did not always sound as good as a
banana layer cake tastes. Which surprised nobody who knew
much about orchestras. He reopened with a Thursday-night-
Friday-afternoon programme that was topped by the *Italiana
in Algeri* overture and tailed by Beethoven's Seventh. In between
came a suite by Villa-Lobos and a set of variations by Deems
Taylor promisingly entitled *Marco Takes a Walk*. It was not for
these latter that G.I.s stood two deep at the back of the hall.
Both audiences made a fuss of Barbirolli, giving him several
recalls. They were glad to have him back. It sounded as if they
had missed him. And so his eighteen-concert schedule unwound:
as to symphonies the César Franck, the Brahms second, Mozart's
G minor (No. 40), Vaughan Williams's *Pastoral* and, as might
have been expected, Tchaikovsky's Fifth twice in one week-end.
Beethoven's Seventh he took out to Fort Monmouth, Red Bank,
New Jersey, on a night which ended up with *Tales from the
Vienna Woods* and *The Stars and Stripes for Ever*. His repertory
around this time has a dusty, weary look. Not everything was
exactly hackneyed. But by 1943 Respighi's *Fountains of Rome* had
little true refreshment to offer; curiosity had been quenched.
Even with a nice-looking girl pianist playing the piano part in
it, Scriabin's *Prometheus* tonepoem was an ember from yesterday
rather than fire from heaven. Once more he yoked the *Daphnis
and Chloë* suites and brought out *Mother Goose*; in the Carnegie
context of that time, the opulence of the one and the smartness
and quaintness of the other sounded over-rich and awry. Why
no *Rite of Spring*? Running through these bland valedictory
programmes one misses a peppercorn or two, the touch of rock
salt. A little post-1911 Stravinsky would have been just the
thing. In this matter, Stravinsky was in transition. During his
early days with the Scottish Orchestra he told a columnist that
ever since *The Rite* Stravinsky had been 'on the downgrade'.
Who could have foreseen his devotion, when the time came, to
the Concerto in D for string orchestra or the zest to which *Le
baiser de la fée* would move him?

So far as concert-goers could observe from in front he was the same fiery, intently scrupulous Barbirolli as they had known since the autumn of 1936. On the rostrum his gestures of stimulus and curb, the left-hand caress which gave silk to a melody, the composure and gravity with which he walked on and off and made acknowledging bows: these things were exactly as before. Outwardly there was no change. Inside him much was going on.

A blow had fallen, or at any rate had become public property, a few days after Christmas. At the end of an afternoon meeting the Philharmonic board let it be known through Marshall Field that the post of musical director and regular conductor, vacant since the Centennial and Barbirolli's demotion, in effect, to the status of guest, had been revived and that Artur Rodzinsky was to take over in that capacity at the beginning of the 1943-44 season. Seven years earlier Rodzinsky had been brought in from Cleveland to conduct the last eight concerts of a season whose first ten had been Barbirolli's proud charge. From the start his ambitions had been fixed on the Philharmonic baton; after Toscanini left he considered himself as qualified for the reversion as anybody. Apart from artistic aptitudes, he was said to have 'pull' with radio promotion interests which might profit the Philharmonic Society in the matter of broadcast concerts. Five or six years older than Barbirolli, bearer of a Vienna law degree, which was why he was called Doctor Rodzinsky, contentious by nature and a great quarreller with musical boards of governors, he had qualified as a conductor in Poland, whence—on the strength of a *Meistersinger* which he heard Rodzinsky conduct in Warsaw—Leopold Stokowski had summoned him to Philadelphia, where he became his assistant, in the late 1920s. It was Rodzinsky who, by Toscanini's commission, 'reconstituted' the N.B.C. Symphony Orchestra after auditions in 1937 preparatory to the Maestro's taking it over. Because of this and other orchestral operations he was regarded among Philharmonic players as a man with a taste for drastic measures and the ability to see them through. Fear that the Philharmonic rostrum might go to Rodzinsky was one of the things that had made them welcome Barbirolli's initial contract. That contract, it will be remembered, was for three years. That, as some of the players saw it, meant three years of protection from arbitrary

weedings out and plantings in. In the event their immunity
lasted twice as long. And now the thing they greatly feared had
come to pass. Rodzinsky struck months before the date named
for his take-over. One day in February the orchestra were
toiling away at a programme that might have been considered
chastening enough in itself. There were to be three 'novelties':
an *Epic March* by John Ireland, Ernst Toch's *Big Ben* (a 'variation fantasy' on the Westminster Chimes) and a concerto for
violin, string orchestra and organ 'in the style of Antonio
Vivaldi'. As might be supposed, the last-mentioned was by
Fritz Kreisler who, restored to the concert platform, was up to
pasticcio tricks again. While Barbirolli was in mid-rehearsal
the Philharmonic board had a pregnant surprise meeting and
issued another ukase over Marshall Field's signature. Seventeen players were to be dropped from the Philharmonic rota,
including Mishel Piastro, the leader, and six other first-desk
players. Piastro had led the Philharmonic ever since Toscanini
invited him to the post in 1931, tantamount to a laying-on of
hands. Field's statement said the dismissals had been recommended by Rodzinsky.* No such sweep had been known in
America since 1924, when Koussevitsky changed twenty-four
players in the Boston Symphony Orchestra. There was an
important difference between the two cases, however. The
Koussevitsky sackings came after his first season. It might have
been supposed that Rodzinsky, too, would stay his hand. It was
true he had had limited experience with the Philharmonic as a
guest. Did this warrant his leaping in with a cleaver before the
season had ended and while his predecessor was in the saddle?
Pained feelings and partisanship were not confined to the band-
rooms. On the night of the first of the two Kreisler concerts,
Piastro made his entry after the other players were seated, as
leaders invariably do, and got the customary round of applause.
There were some in the audience who kept up the clapping
after he had taken his seat and went on when Barbirolli entered.

* According to an editorial in *Musical America*, 10th March 1943, the
unfortunate timing and manner of the board's statement were forced upon
it by a New York newspaper which, having come into possession of some or
most of the information, forced the issuance of a general press release 'to
avoid publication in this one paper of an unauthorized and possibly
incorrect news story'.

Barbirolli joined in the applause as he stepped up to the rostrum. What it sounded like was a pro-Piastro demonstration and, perhaps, an anti-Rodzinsky one.

His last pair of concerts fell on Saturday night and Sunday afternoon 6th and 7th March. He was saddled with two more first performances 'in New York' or 'by the Society': a fantasia and fugue on *O Susanna* (Lucien Cailliet) and Paul Creston's *Threnody*. A U.S. Army corporal played in Liszt's first piano concerto. Then Tchaikovsky's No. 5, always welcome and always immense but, given Barbirolli's long term in New York and his Englishness, inept as a last word on leavetaking. After the Sunday afternoon repeat and the ovation it drew, he put down his baton and said, 'There has come to an end my seven years with the Philharmonic Orchestra.' Then everybody stood up, the players like those in front, and sang 'Auld lang syne'. It might have been Glasgow at the end of a 'plebiscite' night.

Two American writers already cited in these chapters must be quoted for their summings up a decade and a half later. 'To be catapulted into such a position—successor to Toscanini and substitute for Furtwängler—was a fate not to be wished on one's worst enemy', wrote Robert H. Mueller. ' . . .The task proved an insuperable one, and Barbirolli ultimately returned to England with a few voices still proclaiming that he had been the victim of a raw deal.' And Richard Schickel: 'He was not a colorful or imaginative conductor and . . . not a very forceful one. He tended in the opinion of more than one critic to give readings rather than performances, and he never gave the impression of completely possessing the work. He was workman-like, however, and deformed a piece less than some of his more flamboyant competitors. Probably the most damning thing about him was boredom with the necessity of trying to project an interesting and engaging public personality. No legends real or imagined surrounded the Barbirolli personality, and the public did like to make legends of its conductors.'

During the last seasons, when mutual euphoria between rostrum and public had worn off and his assignments were being drastically cut down, John Barbirolli went through much and ultimately came out the stronger for it, his character annealed. With friends in New York, Beverly Hills, Vancouver, he talked blithely and volubly, maintained a tranquil front, burrowed through the usual piles of scores, busied himself endlessly with dynamics, bowing nuances and the like. At rehearsals, however, his mien was disquieting. There, towards the end, he was a different man. The lines of his face, his gait as he came on and went off, the set of his shoulders: all told of unhappiness. So, at all events, this writer gathers from players who at that time had served the Philharmonic for a decade or two and were to serve it as long again. 'A very unhappy man', 'broken hearted', 'a broken man', 'completely demoralised'. Such are phrases used by one or other of these observers. One writes: 'Poor Sir John! Taking over from Toscanini when young and relatively inexperienced was like stepping into the lion's den—as, come to that, it would have been for almost anybody. It didn't take long for him to endear himself to us. . . . Unfortunately, his stature as a conductor did not grow fast enough to satisfy our fickle and uninformed New York audiences, not to mention some of our critics, whose caustic remarks and evaluations were certainly ill-founded.' Another: 'One of the main reasons why the orchestra deteriorated was that the memory of Toscanini stayed fresh during the whole of his stay with us, and as time went on that memory had a more vivid impact. Toscanini's shoes were too big for John Barbirolli or anybody else. It was a terrible situation for him towards the end. He was on the chopping block. I remember how sad he looked. He no longer rehearsed with the old thoroughness and care for detail. I felt very sorry for him. No conductor ever underwent the ordeal he endured as a young man and survived as he did. Not only survived but *grew*. It shows what a remarkable person he is.'

While his association with the Philharmonic was petering out he ran into trouble of a more immediate and searching kind: 'The all-powerful musicians' union decreed around this time that everybody—even the great soloists like Heifetz and Horowitz—would have to be members of the union to play with union orchestras. I remember Heifetz and Horowitz consulting me. They were very annoyed. I said, "Well, it means you can't earn anything if you don't join." The union wanted to apply the rule to me. The snag was that to be a member of the union you had to be an American citizen. That was something I boggled at. Much as I love the Americans, grateful though I was for their kindness, changing nationality in the middle of a war is not the sort of thing any decent person does. I'm sure no American would do it. And I wasn't going to do it. That is what finally decided me to break with America. I knew I must get out.'

One fairly certain way of getting out, sooner or later, was to get into uniform. Early in 1943 there was some prospect of his being drafted on grounds of residential status into the U.S. Army. 'Fine,' he commented ' . . . I shall be seeing England again.' Things have never happened to Barbirolli in any such routine way. His career thus far had been the product of beneficent bolts from the blue. Another of these was on the way. One night towards the end of February he came off the Carnegie platform after conducting Tchaikovsky, Ravel and Vaughan Williams's *Pastoral* Symphony to find a cablegram awaiting him. It was from Robert J. Forbes, Manchester, England, and asked: WOULD YOU BE INTERESTED PERMANENT CONDUCTORSHIP HALLÉ ORCHES-TRA IMPORTANT DEVELOPMENTS PENDING. Principal of the Royal Manchester College of Music, Forbes was an old acquaintance of Barbirolli's and a solid many-sided musician—the only principal, ran the common-room pun, whose musical interest was compound. As a young pianist raised and newly trained in the North, he had served Ysaÿe, Kreisler and Casals as accompanist on long Continental tours. As a concerto soloist he took with impartial gameness Tchaikovsky's B flat minor and the one by Delius, at a time when Delius's music was still looked on by the Germanophil majority as peculiar and debilitating. As a conductor he gave hundreds of operatic performances, mainly with the O'Mara company and the B.N.O.C. It was mainly through the B.N.O.C. that he and Barbirolli came to know each other. An influential committee man of the Hallé Concerts Society, Forbes had been put up to telegraphing Barbirolli by his chairman, Philip Godlee, of whom more in the next chapter. Founded by a companion of Berlioz and given further lustre by one of Wagner's henchmen, Hans Richter, the Hallé, Britain's oldest orchestra, had been going since 1857 and, when Godlee took over during the war, seemed unlikely to go on much longer. To prevent its being squeezed to extinction by visiting orchestras and, above all, by the Northern Orchestra of the B.B.C.—which had claims of its own on the services of a majority of Hallé players—Godlee decided to call in some conductor of fame and mettle and rebuild from the ground up. The new Hallé was to be a truly permanent orchestra instead of a hibernator which, as with the Scottish Orchestra, wakened up for winter only. The players were to be on fifty-two week contracts. And there was to be no 'sharing'. If a man played for the Hallé he played for the Hallé only.

Godlee had heard Barbirolli conduct and knew something of the authority and address with which he had overhauled the Scottish National. Another thing he knew about was Barbirolli's relative freedom and the anxieties incidental to the status of wandering guest on a vast continent with conducting dates a thousand or two thousand miles apart. Other great English conductors were pre-empt. Neither Henry Wood nor Malcolm Sargent could see his way to settling in Manchester, for that was what the remaking and relaunching of the Hallé imposed. Beecham, who had long associations with the orchestra and retained his presidency of the Hallé Society, lingered on in America and would not be home for another year and a half. Clearly, Barbirolli was the man for the job. Hence Forbes's cablegram. It made a joyous day for Barbirolli. He noted the phrase about 'important developments pending'. What might that mean? For the moment he was incurious. On reading the message he said at once to Evelyn: 'This is it. We are going home.' Details could be dealt with later.

In a situation of this kind it does not do to let the other side know right away that one's mind is made up. His reply, cabled three days later, was a masterly compound of reticence and non-committal cordiality. He was always interested, he said, to consider the permanent conductorship of an orchestra with as great traditions as the Hallé Orchestra. Soon after his last Carnegie Hall concert a lengthy letter from Forbes gave him the meat of the project. They were prepared to pay a salary which would make the Hallé conductorship the most lucrative musical appointment in the country. (It came out later that, largely because of Godlee's drive and audacity, for on English standards it was nothing less than that, the Hallé committee were prepared to go to £5000 a year.) Musical policy would be placed entirely in his hands. Already advertisements were running in London newspapers and those of four great provincial cities inviting instrumentalists to apply for membership of a reconstituted Hallé Orchestra on the basis of yearly contract, pay to be union minimum 'at least'. There were to be two hundred concerts a year. The idea was that Barbirolli should conduct one hundred and fifty of them. Godlee confirmed all this in a formal offer on behalf of the Society on 5th April. By the middle of the month Barbirolli had formally accepted Godlee's offer. He booked passages in a neutral ship (Portuguese). The Battle of the Atlantic was still on, but they saw little or nothing of it. Lady Barbirolli remembers that 'John had his head in scores all the time, and I read books. We were both very tired after a strenuous season.' The ship docked at Lisbon. They were lucky enough to book seats in a plane that took off for London two days later. Originally they had been booked for a subsequent flight, the regular commercial one from Lisbon to Ireland. On 2nd June he was met by Godlee and Forbes at London Road Station, Manchester. On the same day it became known that the aircraft for which they were previously booked had been shot down by a German fighter on the strength of a Nazi intelligence report that Mr. Churchill was on board. There were no survivors. The actor Leslie Howard was among those lost.

Since much of this chapter sounds a wry, even melancholy note, it is well to skip chronology and end upon a cheerful one. All came right in the end.

The New York Philharmonic Orchestra saw nothing of him for sixteen years. He was back with them in 1959 for ten concerts spread over four weeks, the first being on New Year's Day. With him he brought Vaughan Williams's newest symphony, the Eighth in D minor, the one whose autograph full score bore a dedication in the composer's hand: 'For Glorious John with love and admiration from Ralph.' Rehearsals at Carnegie Hall fell between Christmas and New Year's Eve. When he entered for the first one the Philharmonic players rose from their seats and applauded for a minute or two. Thirty-three of his old players were still on the rota. Some who had been pensioned off had come along. So did the widows of some who had died. 'There was a good deal of weeping. It was one of the most touching moments of my life.' The rehearsal over, he mixed with old friends. Saul Goodman, the timpanist, came over with a snapshot of Barbirolli which he had taken in 1937 and asked him to

autograph it. Barbirolli threw his arms about him. They talked
of excitements years before; among other matters of Goodman's
drumming in two new and formidable virtuoso pieces by Bartók:
Music for String Orchestra, Percussion and Celesta and the
Sonata for Two Pianos and Percussion (orchestral version,
1940). A thing that startled Goodman, as it startled many others,
was Barbirolli's thinness. They remembered him as a plump
young man. The loss of weight was readily explained: 'I've had
an operation. A fearful operation. They practically lifted out
my inside, cleaned it and put it back again.' Another change.
While giving as much time and thoroughness to rehearsal as ever
before, he was technically quicker and more decisive. Vis-à-vis
orchestral players he was judged to have acquired new psychological insights; he could make a page sound as he wanted it to
sound without taking it to bits so assiduously. His entrance on
the night touched off 'one of the greatest ovations I ever
received, one of the greatest ever heard in Carnegie Hall. That
shows I hadn't been forgotten.' Downes was no more. The concert was covered for the *New York Times* by Howard Taubman,
whose memory went back to Toscanini and covered the entire
Barbirolli interim. As well as the Vaughan Williams symphony
there were Elgar's Introduction and Allegro and the second piano
concerto of Brahms with Gina Bachauer playing in it. Taubman's
weighing up amounted to this: Barbirolli had acquired poise,
address, breadth of view; he had become an artist in his own
right; was purposeful and sure-handed; his conducting had
'grown a spine'. Shipshape procedures. Command of style. Co-
herency, consistency. Approach mellow rather than 'bardic'.
Broad, flowing *tempi*.

The note was warmly respectful. Not so that of the audience.
The audience was rapturous. After the final ovation Barbiroll
spoke of his emotion 'at returning to . . . . this great concert hall
of yours and this great orchestra of yours—and mine. They were
mine for seven years. . . . You [indicating in turn the audience
and the players] have made me a happy man indeed.' Some
nights afterwards, two late-comers having entered when he was
on the point of starting the *Dream of Gerontius* prelude, he
paused and focused the most withering glare on them that
Carnegie Hall had seen for a long time. New York loved him,
and it was comforting to be loved. But New York must watch it.

CHAPTER FOURTEEN

HALLÉ HERITOR

THE time has come to pick up the threads of June 1943. One of the Barbirollis' immediate problems was where to live. Evelyn says: 'We had no house. John's place in London had been blitzed. So we had no furniture, no pots, no pans.' During odd hours snatched from secretarial work for John which kept her busy sometimes until two in the morning and entailed typing up to forty letters a day, some of them long letters, she followed up 'to let' and 'for sale' advertisements and such private tips as came her way. For the time being they stayed outside Manchester at Alderley Edge with the Godlees, practised and cordial hosts.

Certain things which Philip Godlee disclosed when he met him off the train that first day made Barbirolli stare in consternation. It appeared that at Godlee's direction Barbirolli and the new Hallé Orchestra had been booked for concerts galore, including an inaugural festival in Bradford little more than a month ahead. One little difficulty. There wasn't any new Hallé Orchestra. There wasn't, indeed, any old Hallé Orchestra to speak of. 'When I arrived from America,' he used to say, 'I found that instead of the Hallé Orchestra which had been promised me I had only twenty-three players.* I had been expecting at least seventy. To all intents and purposes the Hallé had ceased to exist as an independent entity.'

The old Hallé had, in effect, been killed a month before he agreed to take it over. He had been called in not to head a going concern but, in words which he used later, to revive a corpse. Until the last moment the corpse had flourished passably. Like every other orchestra in the land the Hallé had done well out of the orchestral boom. Latterly it had been giving concerts up and down the country, London included, at the rate of nearly a hundred and fifty a year and was making a modest profit. The

* Sometimes he put the number at twenty-six.

Photo: Erich Auerbach

Cooking was one of Sir John's lifelong hobbies.
In his Manchester kitchen, 1949.

With Lady Barbirolli (professionally known as Evelyn Roth-well, solo oboist in concerto and chamber music) at London Airport, 1955, after Scandinavian conducting tour.

boom was expanding. By increasing its concert schedule from
about three a week to five a week—as its doorstep rival the
Liverpool Philharmonic Orchestra was in process of doing
under magnetic Malcolm Sargent—the Hallé might turn a
modest profit into a comforting one and regain some of its
prestige. Uncertainties and subordination were quickly under-
mining it, however. 'Subordination' is a grave word. No lighter
one will meet the case. The directors of the Hallé had become
less than masters in their own house. They could not benefit
to the full from the wartime boom by taking on more work
because there were circumstances that ruled it out.

For long there had been problems in Manchester as to which
players might play for whom and when. The city had a second
orchestra, the B.B.C. Northern, with a regular strength of thirty-
five. These thirty-five served in both camps. For the Hallé they
played during specified parts of the year on a concert-to-concert
basis. During the remaining parts of the year they were under
contract with the B.B.C. for studio concerts mainly. Godlee, who
had been an increasingly influential Hallé committee man for
six years, realised in good time that the orchestra was sick.
The only way to save it from dissolution through rivalry and
encroachment was to re-form it on a permanent basis, much as
the Liverpool Philharmonic had been re-formed by Sargent,
with fifty-two-week contracts for all its players, who thus would
be at nobody else's beck and call. The corollary of a permanent
orchestra would, of course, be a permanent full-time conductor;
there could be no return to the gaggle of guest conductors who
had recurred annually since Hamilton Harty's resignation ten
years earlier.

Such was Godlee's idea. Not his alone, perhaps. But he was
the only person in higher Hallé circles with the will and the skill
to see it carried out in short order. A maimed giant of a man
with an artificial leg and an artificial eye, toll of the first world
war, during which he had served as major with the 3rd City
('Pals') Battalion of the Manchester Regiment, Godlee ran a
family weaving mill and calico printing plant and had a finger
as committee-man, governor, chairman or leading spirit in
many laudable pies from boys' clubs and homes for old people
to Manchester University and the Manchester bench of magistrates. Among scattered or intermittent interests there was one

I

constant: music. He founded and ran an amateur orchestra; with his children (four) and sometimes with professional musicians he played viola or violin in chamber music (Mozart-Haydn onwards) in his own and friends' houses: and may be said to have known what was what in most musical matters within the range of an orchestra which, in his younger days, had been saluted by good judges as the best in the country.* At the end of 1942 he was made chairman of the Hallé Concerts Society. Six or seven weeks later two disturbing pieces of information came his way. One was that the B.B.C. had decided to extend its option on the services of the thirty-five 'joint' players. The second was that outside orchestras had greater incursions in mind against Manchester. The time had come to act.

The first step was to pick a permanent conductor. Godlee turned over in his mind various 'probables' and 'possibles' and settled upon Barbirolli. As has been said it was he who put Forbes up to the cablegram which Barbirolli had received in New York on February 25th. In a little over a week he carried his scheme through the Hallé committee and put out his advertisements for players .To this bait, for the advertisements were nothing less, the B.B.C. Northern Orchestra quickly retorted by guaranteeing their thirty-five nearly twice as much work as under preceding contracts and, in consequence, nearly twice as much pay. Henceforth a player on either side must choose. He could opt for the B.B.C. Northern. Or he could opt for the Hallé. No longer could he play for both.

What did the choice entail? A job with the B.B.C. Northern Orchestra carried a fair degree of professional prestige; as well as being stable and secure it was 'resident' in the sense that most of the concerts were studio concerts and within handy distance of the players' homes. Members of a reconstituted, all-the-year-round Hallé would fare less snugly; they would be called on for many more concerts in ever remoter towns, travelling thousands more miles a year in chock-a-block trains that were ever more erratic. Players who entered the service of the new Hallé would sacrifice what little remained of their home life to cash in (if the rank-and-filer's eight pounds a week amounted to that) on a piano-concerto-cum-Tchaikovsky craze which might peter out

* For an extended account of a forceful and out-of-the-way character see Appendix 3.

any month as quickly as it had come. Even in boom conditions an orchestra prospers according to the prestige of its conductor. If a conductor has no prestige or too little his orchestra runs aground. At the time the B.B.C. Northern players were required to make up their minds which side to chose, Barbirolli's name had not been publicly circulated. Not surprisingly, most of them turned Godlee down and stayed where they were. Of the thirty-five only four came over to the Hallé. They were players whose quality was some consolation against their fewness—Laurance Turner, who was to be Barbirolli's principal violin and orchestral leader, Pat Ryan (his first clarinet), Philip Hecht (principal of his second-violin section) and Arthur Shaw (his principal double-bass).

All this happened while the negotiations with Barbirolli were afoot. Three weeks before his appointment as its permanent conductor, the Hallé Orchestra, as it nominally stood, had been sliced down the middle. On one side stood the B.B.C's thirty-five. On the other side was the rump of twenty-three cited above, that is to say, men unconnected with the B.B.C. Northern Orchestra who, aside from Hallé concerts, freelanced in several northern cities. If interested they would have to be auditioned like anybody else. If all proved up to scratch, the total playing strength at Barbirolli's disposal, taking into account the four seceders headed by Laurance Turner, would be twenty-seven. He needed seventy players at least. Where was he to find the other forty odd?

Wartime call-up for the Forces and the munitions factories had already taken toll of orchestral talent throughout the country and gave no sign of abating. The newspaper advertisements for players had brought in about two hundred replies. Few of the applicants had had full time orchestral experience. Many were elderly. Many were in their 'teens. And, as appeared later, some were mothers with growing families. Barbirolli was faced with the most daunting job of his career; in its way a more daunting job, perhaps, than had faced any conductor before or has happened since. The début concerts of the Hallé-to-be were to open at the Princes Theatre, Bradford, on July 5th. That left him with a fraction over three weeks in which to sift the two hundred applications, scheme and conduct auditions in several cities, assemble the orchestra and give it a

week's drilling. Clearly, the thing could not be done. He set to
and did it. Two days after his preliminary talk with Forbes and
Godlee, while on a quick visit to London, he ran into an administrator of the London Symphony Orchestra and told him what
he was about.

'But, John, it's hopeless', said the L.S.O. man. 'It just can't
be done. It's impossible.'

He answered: 'I like to be given impossible things to do. It
suits me.'

Not for the first time the impossible moved him to bizarre
over-confidence. He is reported as having said during that first
week: 'The New York Philharmonic Orchestra is the greatest
orchestra in the world. I mean to make the Hallé Orchestra an
even greater orchestra than that. . . . I hope eventually to make
Manchester the Vienna of England, with a great symphony
orchestra playing for opera as well as in the concert hall.'* A
permanent opera house for Manchester with the Hallé Orchestra
serving it had been Beecham's vision thirty years earlier and
has been dreamed of ever since.

Evelyn eventually found a smallish flat in the suburb of
Rusholme. For furniture and household things which were
unobtainable in the stores or impossible to get at short notice,
she went to a Government 'blitz' repository where a New York
friend, formerly at British Ministry of Information headquarters, had dumped salvage from his blitzed London home. Armed
with the friend's authority, she sorted out such remnants as
were usable (they were thick with grime) and shipped them
north: 'Those were hectic days. No charwoman. I had to clean
the flat and try to find things to eat. Down to Manchester with
the shopping bag; picking up oddments of furniture; carrying
packhorse loads.' Then back to her typewriter. Since concerts
were being planned for camps and war factories as well as for
the usual concert halls, and since the Hallé Orchestra-to-be was
recognised as part of the war effort, she was officially defined as
in a 'reserved' occupation; otherwise she would have been in
uniform or factory slacks.

Auditions began. She was with John at all of them. He had

* *The Star*, London, 5th June 1943.

talked of auditioning six hours a day; often he put in seven or eight. Many whom he listened to were in the market only because physically unfit; they had been rejected by Army and other medical boards. 'Nothing wrong about that', he said. 'People with flat feet might very well have straight fingers. In those days of national call-up flat feet were a positive godsend. We didn't dare bar anybody. . . . Sometimes it was very depressing. We'd go a whole day and find nothing'. Occasionally there was comic relief of a wry kind. An old man came along with his double-bass. Given a standard test-piece, namely the fugato tune from the Scherzo of Beethoven's Fifth Symphony, he played it all on one note, keeping his finger at the same point on the string. Out of curiosity Barbirolli handed him something even harder: the passage in Verdi where the double-basses, pacing the murderous Otello, climb from deep E flat to high C flat. 'Have a go at that', he suggested. The old man did as he was bid. After plodding up-scale he paused. 'It's further up than that,' he was advised. He went up a bit further. 'No—higher still'. The old man looked blank. Barbirolli took the instrument and showed him how it should be done, hitting the high C flat dead centre. 'Up there?' said the old man wonderingly. 'Nay, I've never been up as high as that!' A tactful way was found of telling him he wouldn't do.

Dud days, humdrum days and middling ones were leavened by days of discovery that are affectionately talked about still. A trombone from a Manchester variety pit 'who had never heard of symphonies, still less played in any' was given something from a Brahms finale including a high A that troubles even seasoned players. His A came out firm and sweet: 'For him it was an A like any other A. He had played it for George Robey, so he played it for Brahms. It didn't make any difference.' In a room above Forsyth's shop in Deansgate—for long the address from which Hallé affairs, or some of them, were administered— he heard a seventeen-year-old flautist who had put in a year at the Royal Manchester College of Music and had played a little with a scratch symphony orchestra based on the south. Name: Oliver Bannister. He brought with him a book of flute and piccolo studies. Barbirolli chose a nineteenth-century Italian piece, then two others. He listened with contentment and surprise. 'Would you like to play for me?' he asked without further ado. 'I'd like to very much.' 'Right, I'm going to make you my second flute.'

At that stage, admittedly, a third flute wasn't on the cards, partly because there weren't enough players on the market and partly because there wouldn't have been money enough to pay them. A season or two later Bannister became the orchestra's admired first flute and, many years later, the equally admired 'first' of the Royal Opera House Orchestra, where he remains at this writing. Barbirolli always spoke of him as 'one of the great flute players of our time'. Sometimes he would add: 'He was pinched from me by Covent Garden.' When they lose players of merit conductors often speak of pinching and poaching. As will be seen, Barbirolli—or, to put it more exactly, the Hallé concert-goer—was to suffer a great deal of this after the re-formed orchestra got under way and newfound talents began to look around them. It is well to remember, however, that orchestras are not houses of bondage; that, in music as elsewhere, free men cannot be appropriated; and that those with exceptional gifts are entitled to accept such better bids as the market may offer.

For string players he drew largely on Lancashire and Yorkshire. Twelve days before rehearsals were due to start he had found principals for all five string departments but still wanted a dozen rear desk players. From his earliest Hallé days he made much of Northern string tone. He maintained, among other things, that there was more of it: 'Quality is more important than numbers. In the Hallé there are no passengers. All my string players produce big tone: bigger tone than you get from the London orchestras, even though we play with fewer numbers. Big tone has always been a characteristic of Northern orchestras.' Half or more of his brass and woodwind leaders he found in and about Manchester. The rest came from the Scottish Orchestra, Sadler's Wells Opera and the London Symphony Orchestra. One of his L.S.O. acquisitions got him out of a fix. Four days before the start of rehearsals he was still stumped for a principal horn. On that day he was telephoned by young Livia Gollancz,* who had heard of the vacancy by

---

* Daughter of the late Sir Victor Gollancz, founder of the publishing firm that bears his name, of which she is now the head, having concluded her career as a professional musician.

chance. Miss Gollancz had been the L.S.O.'s fourth horn since coming out of the Royal College of Music in 1940. Barbirolli knew something of her work, having, during his 1942 'foray', conducted her in the *Eroica* and other Beethoven symphonies. The job was promptly hers; she put in for thirty shillings a week more than the standard rate and was as promptly conceded it. Nobody had ever heard before of a young woman—or even, for that matter, a mature one—leading the horn quartet of a historic orchestra; there are few more exposed or exacting roles in music.

There were plenty of her own sex to keep Miss Gollancz company. Third horn was a young woman ex-school teacher who, at audition, had played stretches of Strauss and Mozart horn concerto. Second oboe likewise was a young woman. So, more startlingly, were one of the double-basses and, from a rather later date, the kettledrummer, Joyce Aldous, a redoubtable player. In all twenty women, mostly young, were among the seventy players who reported on the afternoon of June 28th at the Houldsworth Hall, Manchester (noted throughout the North then as now for its midday concert series) for the first of a week's rehearsals. The proportion went up later to twenty-three and ultimately included a woman trombonist. Such a ratio, although dictated by wartime circumstances, would have provoked nudges and raised eyebrows anywhere. It might have been expected that Manchester's eyebrows would rise higher and stay up longer than most. It was not, by tradition, a noticeably feminist town musically considered. When Hamilton Harty took over the Hallé in 1920 he got rid of all the women players and barred the sex rigorously for the rest of his term. He did this not because he thought little of women as artists but because of his notion that mixing the sexes in an orchestra militated against 'unity of style' as well as raising awkward problems of accommodation when the orchestra was on tour. As things turned out, Manchester, like other cities regularly served by the Hallé took the infiltration with cheerful equanimity. It accorded with the spirit of the times, if that mattered. What certainly did matter, as emerged during the coming season or two, was that Barbirolli genuinely fused the talents of all genders, just as he fused those of hardbitten veterans and of youngsters straight from music college. Under his impulsion artists of the rarer sort, their minds bent on, say, baroque chamber music or pandiatonicism, found themselves playing 'eye to eye' with men from palm courts and bandstands. No other conductor in the land—or, perhaps, anywhere—could have made a true and resonating whole out of so heterogeneous a lot.

In that first line-up at Houldsworth Hall there were twenty young women, as has been said, twenty-three old Hallé players, a dozen men over military age, another dozen (many of them young) who were medically unfit and three who had been discharged from the Services on medical grounds. Barbirolli's rehearsal rota, then and for many years, gave him a third more work to do than his players. There would be three hours for strings only in the morning, three hours for wind and percussion only in the afternoon (or the other way about) and three hours for everybody in the evening. After the evening rehearsal he would go home and sit up bowing master copies into the small hours. He said: 'I rehearse nine hours a day and always feel fine at the end of it—if things have gone well.' As had been the case in Glasgow and at Carnegie Hall, he was full of bounce and tenacity at ten in the morning. If there was something wrong with the phrasing of two bars in an eight-bar subject, as likely as not he would have the offending section repeat all eight bars until the flaw had gone. The older hands took to counting repetitions sotto-voce: 'Seventeen . . . twenty . . . twenty-three.' For the younger hands everything was adventurous and revealing except the music they were rehearsing. The only unusual thing about the seven programmes* in preparation for Bradford—admittedly neither the place nor occasion for ambitious flights—was that they included only one piano concerto and no other concerto of any kind. About this there had been what was known in the North as a great to-do. One of the first things he had learned on getting off the train

---

* Which included: Symphonies—Beethoven Nos. 5 and 7, Schubert No. 8, Mendelssohn No. 4, Brahms No. 2, Tchaikovsky No. 5. Overtures—*Mastersingers, Thieving Magpie, Tannhäuser, Merry Wives of Windsor, Oberon, Irmelin.* Miscellaneous—*Romeo and Juliet* (Tchaikovsky), *l'Après midi d'un faune, l'Arlésienne* suite, *Epic March* (Ireland), *Enigma* variations, Intro. and Allegro for Strings, *Eine kleine Nachtmusik, Capriccio Espagnol,* Scherzo from Octet (Mendelssohn), *Valse triste,* 'Sheep may safely graze' (Bach-Barbirolli).

in Manchester was that the Bradford concert society, in conjunction with the theatre where the concerts were to be given, had booked five concerto pianists for the week: Irene Kohler, Moiseiwitsch, Eileen Joyce, Cyril Smith and Clifford Curzon. That, said one and all, was a sure way of packing 'em in and selling the theatre out. There is no doubt that on this point one and all were right. Barbirolli would have none of it. He told Godlee and Forbes that he hadn't come all the way from America to conduct a parcel of piano concertos. Without more ado he telephoned the concert agents concerned cancelling four out of the five pianists whose names had been pencilled in, retaining only Curzon. Afterwards, at a press conference, he expatiated upon what he held to be an inimical vogue: 'I have been horrified since my arrival in this country to find that it is practically impossible to give an orchestral concert which does not include a piano concerto, preferably *the* Tchaikovsky [B flat minor]. I want to do away with that. Not that we intend to dispense with soloists. We shall include them in our programmes from time to time, so that the great concertos may be heard in their proper proportion.' To this Godlee added a characteristic flourish: 'The piano concerto racket is finished. The pianists are worn out, the pianos are worn out.' It was long before Barbirolli let the subject drop. 'There's no need for this piano concerto craze', ran one of his later pronouncements. 'In many places people go to see such and such a soloist with his double octaves and his bangings. . . . But you can fill a hall without Rachmaninov. I have proved it. . . .'

Was there not something over-censorious, perhaps, in this? Under the mysterious stimuli and social reshufflings of wartime, symphony orchestras had been blessed—or saddled—for three years with an engrossed new public which was finding its way about the standard repertory bit by bit and sorting out its likes from its indifferences. If they relished the sporting sense which a tune-packed piano concerto was apt to give, that of the loner at a keyboard in combat with the blowings and scrapings of seventy (or, better still, a hundred), if they went on listening to Tchaikovsky's first, Rachmaninov's second, Grieg's Op. 16 and even Schumann's Op. 54 as avidly as Barbirolli once listened to the '1812' Overture, what harm was there in it—what harm (if it came to that) in 'double octaves and bangings'—for

I*

themselves or anybody else? The truth is that piano concertos and concertos generally—media which, thanks to his work in the recording studio, had cemented his early reputation outside it—were no longer his main line of conducting business (he had moved on and up from the role of 'orchestral accompanist' par excellence a dozen years earlier); nor were they by tradition any special business of the Hallé Orchestra. Those of the public who expected one concerto with every meal or, better still, two would have to seek elsewhere.

There were long faces in Bradford. The local organisers went over to Manchester in deputation and pleaded with Barbirolli to restore some, at least, of the discarded pianists. He wouldn't hear of it. From Bradford presently came reports of sluggish bookings. A week or so before the opening concert the César Franck Symphony, Sibelius's No. 2 and the *Firebird* suite were taken out and replaced by Beethoven's No. 7, Schubert's 'Unfinished' and Mendelssohn's 'Italian'. Curzon's piano concerto was to have been Rachmaninov's C minor. It was replaced by the Grieg. Most of these changes could fairly be regarded as a move from popular towards hyperpopular. Officially they were put down to the want of certain instrumental 'extras', among them bass clarinet and double bassoon, whom it had not been possible to engage and rehearse in time for *Firebird* and the César Franck. Nothing could have illustrated more strikingly the technical penury Barbirolli was up against.

The opening programme (*Mastersingers* Overture, Tchaikovsky's *Romeo and Juliet*, Delius's *A Song of Summer* and the Brahms No. 2) played to a sprinkling of empty seats and jubilation from all the full ones. Next morning everybody who wanted to know what was what looked to the *Manchester Guardian*. Cardus was away in Australia, his chair given over to Granville Hill: a scholarly pen which limpidly reflected its owner's nature and gentle temper. Throughout the North he was affectionately known not as Granville but as 'Grannie' Hill, a benign critic and well schooled. At this time he was in his middle sixties. He had made his first mark as an organist almost half a century earlier; around the turn of the century had given recitals on the Crystal Palace (London) organ among others; as a pianist had accompanied noted singers on many platforms, some of them rigged up for concert parties that toured devastated areas behind the French battlefronts during the first war. He had lectured on music and taught it and, for the *Manchester Guardian*, written about it from the 1920s on, most of the time as Cardus's second string. As Barbirolli's chief and constant judge during the next eight years, he wrote many cordial and even marvelling things about the Hallé's second birth and blooming under Barbirolli. On the new Hallé's first night, however, he made it clear that, largely because of the youth and inexperience of many of its members who, he said, were given 'no easy time', the orchestra had still some way to go:

> John Barbirolli conducted with the utmost intensity of style and called for a similar concentrated expression from his players. . . . The *Mastersingers* Overture had notable rigour, needing a little more rhythmic ease and a more flowing line. . . . In *Romeo and Juliet* the conductor made still heavier demands on the players . . .; there were occasional inequalities in balance between strings and woodwind, the unkind acoustics of the theatre emphasising them. . . . Much of the playing betrayed that points made during rehearsal were being observed with such extreme carefulness that the effect as a whole became rigid. In the D major Symphony of Brahms . . . the playing had many virtues; it was, indeed, often brilliant; the excessive anxiety to make every point caused the music sometimes to lose its flow and sound laboured. Such faults as we have mentioned can, of course, be quickly overcome, and in a little while the new Hallé ensemble should show a splendid unity and eloquence.

From Hill's notice and later writings by other hands that summer and autumn the picture is clear. The new Hallé was superbly drilled, quiveringly proud of its conductor and ambitious to make a name for itself. Its members were so anxious to do, bar by bar, what they had been told to do that they played most of the time with clenched teeth and white knuckles, so to say. Their keenness went far beyond the strict line of duty. Finding more comfort in the relatively poky Princes Theatre—exceptional in that it stood on top of another with different owners and doors on to a different street—than in the theatrical lodgings which had been found for most of them, they made a point of meeting, outside scheduled rehearsal hours, in the larger dressing rooms for a bit of supplementary practice. Barbirolli was proud of this and made much of it to reporters. Occasionally he sounded the defensive note. Thus: 'There are some who exclaim at the high proportion of women players. They think women can't produce as much tone as men. As if physical strength had anything to do with it! It's a personal gift. Sometimes you get small men with big voices, small brass players who'll bring the roof down. The same thing can apply to women musicians. Don't forget, you're hearing this orchestra boxed in on a theatre stage. You're getting only half the tone they really have. In the concert-hall they'll be as powerful as a 100 per cent male orchestra.' Then the clinching point: 'Remember, the B.B.C. Symphony Orchestra, the first English orchestra that Toscanini conducted, was forty per cent women.' In musical arguments Toscanini's name silenced everybody. Whoever cited it won the day.

By the middle of its début week the new Hallé had, as the locals put it, caught on in Bradford, another armaments town (weaving an enormous mileage of uniform cloth) which toiled in triple shifts and, as to throngs of its people, spent such wartime holidays as came their way at home. Queues for the gallery were lined up two hours and a half before the doors opened. Hundreds were turned away by House Full notices. By the end of the week Barbirolli knew that his new orchestra was going to be good. Then back to Manchester for another six days' rehearsal slog. During those six days they prepared or made a start on five more symphonies—Schubert's No. 5, Dvořák's No. 5, Brahms's No. 4, Mozart's No. 34 (K. 338) and his G minor (No. 40); half a dozen tonepoems, suites and 'miscellaneous'— Sibelius's *Swan of Tuonela*, the *Waldweben* of Wagner, Tchaikovsky's *Francesca da Rimini*, Ravel's *Mother Goose* suite, the third Slavonic Suite of Dvořák and 'On Hearing the First Cuckoo'; and a short string of piano concertos (including a pair of Beethovens, Nos. 3 and 5), indispensable after all. The following Sunday they packed for Scotland. Some inner need impelled him to cities where he knew he was loved and was known to be loved. Edinburgh and Glasgow had been put at the top of the Hallé touring schedule accordingly.

Almost by his own spell, the orchestra helping somewhat, he

filled the Usher Hall with six concerts in a row, one of them
on a midweek afternoon ('and in midsummer, too!' underlined
the box-office manager), and did almost as prodigiously with
another six the following week at St. Andrew's Hall, where some
of his appearances had the crammed, exuberant quality of his
old 'plebiscite' nights there. As sheer business, impresarios
agreed, nothing like it had been known in the history of orchestral touring either north or south of the Border. The programme
which, in Edinburgh and Glasgow, drew the longest queues and
quickest sell-outs took in Debussy (*l'Après-midi*) and Tchaikovsky
(*Romeo and Juliet*) or Schubert (Symphony No. 5) and the
Enigma but were topped and tailed alike by the *Merry Wives of
Windsor* Overture, the *Fledermaus* Overture and *Tales from the
Vienna Woods*. Of the *Tales* Percy Gordon, at it still, wrote in
the *Herald* that they were almost too artfully told. Gordon's
notices were compounded as before: one penn'orth of praise,
almost always in general terms, to three penn'orth of particular
blame. Barbirolli, he complained, had been over-impassioned
and inaptly dramatic in Delius. He had over-vitalised the
'Dorabella' variation in the Elgar. He had got his speeds wrong
in Schubert's 'Unfinished'. In one way or another he had fumbled
climaxes in Brahms's No. 2 and No. 4. And twice, betraying 'a
former fondness', he had let rip inordinately with the kettledrums
which, it seemed, contrived to be assertive or aggressive (even,
it was hinted, dictatorial) and dull-toned into the bargain.

None of this troubled Barbirolli's public. It was so much
water off a duck's back. At a dozen concerts he got ovations
from audiences that numbered such old friends as were not away
at the war and a army of young new ones who were as much
taken by the springcoil and quiver of Barbirolli's musical passion
as the audiences of ten years earlier had been. His last night in
each hall ended in a hullabaloo of recalls. Concert subscribers
are usually a staid lot. In Edinburgh, especially, it was remarked
that they shouted, stamped and beamed as though after a goal
at a football match. If not sung, 'Will ye no' come back again'
sounded in some thousands of heads. It was hard to let
Barbirolli go. Edinburgh and Glasgow did the next best thing.
Each booked him for another week's concerts in the early
summer of the following year.

At least one observer during the Bradford week had thought

he looked subdued when mixing off platform, as briefly happened once or twice, with non-musicians. Whatever there was in this, Scotland dispelled it and toned him up. Henceforth he would be able to put New York behind him for the time being. It is remembered that for a long time he never talked of his own accord about the Carnegie Hall and his Philharmonic years. He was committed now to a very different battle. Part of the battle would be wide-ranging competition. As a touring conductor he would be up against many rival orchestras. Among these, intermittently, would be his old charge and 'child', the Scottish Orchestra. In Scotland he was pestered into making two last-night speeches. He might have been expected to plug his new Hallé. He did nothing of the kind. The Scottish Orchestra was his theme. He wished it well and appealed to Scots of all communities to cherish it with their money and their ears. This was professional chivalry, in music no common thing.

His regard for Scotland had one quality. His regard for 'the North' had another. By the North he meant that welter of manufacturing and trading communities which spread to two coasts and are bounded otherwise by Tyneside and the Potteries, a terrain overhung by the smoke of kilns and steelmaking and clothmaking, clangorous here with shipyards, humped elsewhere by the spoil of coalmines. For Barbirolli, Northerners were not as other Britons are. As is often the way with imaginative Southerners, he romanticised them a bit. He found them hard and true: 'The fascination of the North! You feel that if you've achieved anything here you've *really* achieved it.' He delighted in a happening at Hanley, the 'Hanwell' of Arnold Bennett's 'Five Towns'. There was a night when he treated Hanley to the *Freischütz* Overture, the *Irmelin* Prelude, Mendelssohn's 'Italian' Symphony and, in the second half, Sibelius's No. 2. A message came to him during the interval that somebody was after his autograph. Couldn't the person, whoever he was, come round (he asked) at the end of the concert? Well, said the messenger, the person was a soldier who couldn't stay to the end because he had to get back to his unit. 'Oh, that's different. Bring him in.' In came the soldier. His grip was of iron. He said: 'A wonderful concert, sir—so far.' In other words, the first half had been all right. But he wasn't going to commit himself further: 'I've never forgotten that. He didn't give a damn about my coming from New York or Covent Garden or anywhere else. I was now "Manchester", and that was that! The respect I have won from these people is a thing I greatly prize.' Manchester itself—'which nobody, by the wildest stretch of imagination, could call a beautiful city'—was none the worse for its uncomeliness when you came to think about it. Very much the reverse: 'A strange thing. . . . I generally find that nerve centres of the highest activity are to be found in rather drab cities. Their very drabness lends itself to concentration and achievement. . . . The nerve centre of music in Italy is Milan, you see: not Venice or Florence. Sometimes places of extreme beauty have a little of decadence and debility about them.'

There could be no doubt as to Manchester's rating as the musical nerve centre of the North. Manchester above all was the place where, as the fifth permanent conductor of the Hallé after Charles Hallé, Hans Richter, Michael Balling (1912–1914) and Hamilton Harty, he had to rule and be revered. Let us look at the problems that faced him there; how he coped in Manchester and forty other towns on the Hallé touring beat; and how quickly reverence set in—and set firm.

CHAPTER FIFTEEN

RINGMASTER'S ROUND

FIRST, the touring. At a glance his rounds of Britain and those of his players, who did even more than he, seem too fatiguing to be true. In twelve months to the end of June 1944, they put in two trips to Scotland and between them scoured successively the North West as far up as Carlisle; the North East out to Newcastle and Middlesbrough and as far down as Hull; the Midlands, taking in Birmingham, Nottingham, Coventry, Leicester; and the South and South West, including four bookings in or around London. The London concert gave them their first prestige plume and signalled Barbirolli's acceptance as a national figure, his orchestra as on the way to becoming a national asset. Some account of it is given later in this chapter. There were certain week-ends that became an established treadmill, persisting for years, as appears from this managerial account:

We play Middlesbrough Saturday, Newcastle Sunday. That's routine. We leave at ten-thirty on Saturday morning, two coaches and instrument van, from Windmill Street behind the Free Trade Hall, with HALLÉ ORCHESTRA on the direction indicators. Barbirolli is in the first coach, up in front with Laurance Turner, the leader. Always he has a score on his knee. Ten or so of the players travel in their own cars. The coaches carry seventy. At Middlesbrough we have an hour's seating rehearsal to get the 'feel' of the platform. Then tea. Then concert from seven to nine. On to Newcastle, an hour's journey. Morning rehearsal in Newcastle, ten till one. Concert is from three till five. Then tea and back to the coaches. We're home between eleven and half past. . . . Sheffield is no picnic, either. We leave Windmill Street at ten and reach Sheffield for lunch. Three thousand school kids troop into the hall: school concert lasting an hour-and-a-half. After this an hour-and-a-half's rehearsal. After that the grown-ups' concert, half-past seven to half-past nine. With a bit of luck we're back in Manchester by eleven, in time for late buses to outlying parts. . . . And so it goes on. A heavy week runs to seventy-two hours. Half of this time is spent on the road. An average week is fifty-five hours.

Especially in the South an occasional air-raid warning sounded. With the coming of the V1, known as the 'flying bomb' or 'doodlebug', these warnings multiplied: 'On our way back from an engagement', Barbirolli remembered, 'the sirens would sound, so the trains would stop, and we'd have to wait. At that time there were all-night buses in Manchester that ran every hour. Sometimes we'd get into Manchester at, say, five minutes to four in the morning, get off the coaches carrying our luggage (there was nobody to carry it for us), just miss the four o'clock bus and wait until five. Rehearsals were at 10 a.m.—and everybody turned up. We were all sustained and exalted in some way by our successes and by the conditions of the time. I don't think anybody ever spoke of it as hard work.'

Concerts and their equivalents (i.e., recording sessions at which he did Bax's Symphony No. 3 and Vaughan Williams's No. 5) totalled 271 for the year. Of these Barbirolli conducted 191. His tally would have come to 195 but for days off for sickness, when substitute batons were brought in. He was still robust and an obdurate worker, though not physically foolproof. With the distinguished Albert Sammons he toured the Elgar violin concerto. In Yorkshire he conducted it twice through first-stage influenza and a third time with a temperature of 102, after which he went to bed, handing his baton at the interval to Laurance Turner, his leader, for Mozart's 34th Symphony and *The Walk to Paradise Garden*. Eighty of that first season's concerts were conducted by other hands, among them Sargent, Basil Cameron, Julius Harrison, R. J. Forbes, Clarence Raybould and George Weldon, who was to become his associate conductor with the Hallé.

It did not follow that when somebody else took a Hallé rostrum Barbirolli was idling. He did not know how to idle. The thought of sitting down or strolling about or standing and staring instead of submitting to such compulsions as score-study, bowing parts, programme planning, coaching sessions and the like filled him with something like dread. Once he tried to explain: 'I like to take time off from conducting and stay at home working and studying without having to answer the telephone and without going out at all except for a drive to some place I want to see or for a little picnic, if we're staying in the country. I call that heaven. I don't call it holiday. I've never been on holiday in my life. The thought of holiday disturbs me.'

'You have something against holidays?' he was asked.

'I find them disturbing, depressing. I was like that, or nearly like it, as a child. We used to go for our fortnight to Brighton. I used to beg to be allowed to take my 'cello with me.'

'And they let you take it?'

'Oh yes, because they knew of my fear, a kind of fear, of being idle. . . . I have that fear still. Between concerts I *must* study and rehearse. If I have one rehearsal in a day I can enjoy the rest of it. Evelyn says that with one rehearsal a day I'm "bearable". . . . This is something I don't boast about. I think it's reprehensible. But there you are.'

Rehearsals must, of course, be added to the toll of his and the orchestra's public engagements. Sometimes he brought the orchestra back to Manchester for the odd week or day or half-week and put them through the usual split sessions and, in the evening, a joint one: the routine nine hours for him, six hours for the others. Otherwise they rehearsed on the road. Two hours' rehearsal for every hour of public playing was said to be the average somewhat later on. During the first year it may have been more than that. From rehearsal-base they went now and then to faraway concert-halls that meant a double journey of twelve hours. Seven-day weeks were not unknown. Most of the days were long and comfortless. They were made up for at night by thronging, warmhearted and jubilating audiences and sometimes by the new-found dash and sweetness of their own playing. Some of the jubilatings happened in halls where symphony orchestras of note rarely trod. How often had Wigan heard such a conductor and such a 'band' in anything like *The Fountains of Rome, Firebird, Mother Goose,* the Brahms No. 2 and the Schubert No. 5? To Stockport he brought the Brahms No. 4, Beethoven's No. 8, the César Franck, Tchaikovsky's *Romeo and Juliet,* the *Waldweben* and much fine Mozart, Elgar, Delius. Nor was Walsall or Tooting, Salford or Sale overlooked. As he began, so he went on (helped later by junior batons, of course) for the best part of twenty years.

It may be said that, especially in the beginning, a virtually unsubsidised orchestra was obliged for revenue's sake to fit in a multitude of small-town 'stands' while deriving its essential prestige from great cities, especially those with pretensions and universities. At the same time it is hard to think of any other conductor who would have kept it up as hard and as selflessly as Barbirolli. 'Selflessly' is not a word to use lightly. What it conveys here is that for Barbirolli music was more important than Barbirolli. Therefore it didn't matter much to him where he made it. There was a certain happy imperviousness about the man. In twelve months, at the behest of E.N.S.A.,* he took the Hallé to thirty or more military camps, giant factory canteens and (once) to a cathedral (Chester) and dispensed from the standard Hallé repertory to soldiers and airmen and makers of shells and guns and battle-planes. Most of his hearers were as innocent of symphonic music as of Milton, James Joyce or Homer. Their ears were unspoilt and, on that account, perhaps (said the hopeful) all the better for so genuine an initiation. Invariably the surroundings on these occasions were bleak or banal. He did not seem to notice them. His first concert in a Royal Air Force camp was not quickly forgotten.

There were two hours of rehearsal in Manchester, 1.30 to 3.30 p.m. Then everybody piled into a train. A removal van went ahead with the 'heavies'—kettledrums, harp, double-basses. High tea (spam sandwiches) was served in a camp canteen for everybody but Barbirolli, who peeled off into a corner for half-an-hour with his latest study piece. The concert was held in a hangar big enough to hide a village in, church and all. At least, that was how it struck civilians who peered

* Meaning Entertainments National Service Association.

through its draughty gloom. Outside it airmen of many grades
were queuing in the dusk to pay their threepences and sixpences for Johann Strauss, Schubert, Delius and Tchaikovsky.
The women of the orchestra had travelled in slacks and
sweaters. They trooped into W.A.A.F. quarters and came back
wearing the same long black dresses they put on for 'splash'
concerts in the Royal Albert Hall for the Royal Philharmonic
Society. Barbirolli began with the *Fledermaus* Overture.
Beyond the range of the platform lights the hangar was
gloomier than ever. A man from E.N.S.A. counted the threepences and sixpences at a table with a pencil torch held
between his teeth. He made a lot of noise. The first part of
Fledermaus was almost ruined for many. Barbirolli must have
noticed. By this time, however, Johann Strauss had him air-
borne, as somebody put it. He was much beyond minding
what in any case could not be remedied.

The players, too, had their immunities. The incessant
touring that first year would have killed half of them, or at any
rate scared them off the payroll, if they had not been buoyed
up by three things. First, the indomitable streak in Barbirolli
and his highmindedness. Second, the knowledge that in
refloating the Hallé against crushing odds they were making
musical history. Third, the 'wartime spirit' which, after four
years, still (surprisingly) had much kick in it.

During much of the year, however far the touring trail
happened to take them, Barbirolli came dutifully home and
gave at least one concert a week (later at least two) in Manchester, their hub, soul and springboard.

Barbirolli had conducted his first Hallé concert (the César
Franck symphony, Mozart's No. 40, the Purcell-Barbirolli
suite, etc.) ten years earlier when thirty-three and little known
outside the opera house. Since then the city had grown into,
or had been forced into, new ways of looking at music economically and even into new ways of listening to it. A residue of
veterans with the new Hallé had been with the old one as far
back in some cases as Richter's day. Before the Kaiser's war
and until as late as 1930, although the Hallé season was con-
stricted, averaging two and a half concerts a week in and out
of Manchester during the winter only, good rank-and-filers

bumped their earnings up to five pounds a week ('good money then,' as Barbirolli testified from his own days in theatre pits) by getting orchestral dates 'up the line', as it was known: that is to say, with local orchestral and choral societies elsewhere in the North: Sheffield, Leeds, Bradford, Hanley, Bolton and the like. The Hallé then had a hundred players. Thirty of them had a regular job every other week with the Liverpool Philharmonic Orchestra, whose Tuesday and Wednesday concerts slotted into the Hallé's blank Manchester dates. Every sizeable café put on at least a three-piece band (piano, viola, 'cello) which played the *Merchant of Venice* suite and *Madame Butterfly* pot-pourris while calico merchants ate beans on toast. Cinemas offered work for flutes, clarinets, cornets and trombones as well. Nine central theatres had orchestras of twenty or more. Forsyths of Deansgate were constantly sending out refined string-and-woodwind outfits to garden parties, hunt balls, 'at-homes' and such. Every other parent in the region wanted one of his youngsters to learn the fiddle—or even the bassoon or French horn. You taught these mysteries in your front parlour at five shillings a lesson if you were moderately self-confident, at seven-and-six if you thought a lot of yourself. A snug and busy scene. It could not last for ever.

In the early 1930s an east wind swept musical Lancashire. Café orchestras and cinema outfits dissolved. Parents began to be chary of putting their children to a profession whose bottom seemed to be falling out. By the time Barbirolli returned or during the late 1940s only two of the nine central theatres were running orchestras; most of the other seven had become cinemas. That meant an end to front parlour fiddle lessons. Some of the musical societies 'up the line' had been killed by the Kaiser's war. Others were killed by the cotton slump. True, the Hallé remained; but a reduced average of two concerts a week (winter only) at a guinea-and-a-half per concert (and morning rehearsal) for the rank-and-filer kept the wolf from nobody's door. By the outbreak of Hitler's war many men had turned to other jobs, becoming clerks and shopkeepers. Most of those who stayed on did so by the skin of their teeth.

Then the wartime concert boom—and boon. The veterans

buckled to as thankfully as could be expected from members
of an orchestra which, to quote a phrase which is written into
official Hallé records, was 'thirty per cent. under strength and
forty per cent. underpaid'. Nobody ventured to hazard by
what percentage they were overworked. That reckoning,
not in percentage terms, came two or three seasons later,
when the management acknowledged that Barbirolli and his
players, as well as the Society's sick-pay resources, were
under excessive strain. It was acknowledged further that if,
to pay its way, the Hallé went on touring and giving concerts at the current lunatic rate it would be burnt out within
five years.

Barbirolli had conducted his 1933 Hallé début in the
orchestra's cradle and home, the old Free Trade Hall in
Deansgate, a venerable and promiscuous property. As usually
happens with hallowed public halls of this kind, many who
went there regularly for music vaguely concluded that music
went on there all the time. They were wrong. During the day
there were busy ins and outs and stock deliveries at offices and
small warehouses in the basement that were let to cloth
dealers and other brokers at ten shillings a week. The main
hall was often given over to business efficiency exhibitions,
Christian Science lectures, Communist rallies at which, it was
put about, pound notes were often seen in the collection
plates and Fascist ones at which blackshirts pummelled
hecklers in the aisles. On Monday nights a 1,000-watt flood-
light was lowered from the ceiling for boxing or all-in wrestling
and a ring put up alongside the platform which itself was set
with ringside seats for these occasions at half-a-guinea. Welter-
weights and star wrestlers with such names as The Angel,
The Tiger and Carver Doone dressed in artists' rooms
backstage and came on to the platform through the same
doors as had been used a few nights before by Rachmaninov,
perhaps, or Kreisler, Beecham or Henry Wood, Bruno
Walter or Igor Stravinsky. Monday nights sold out infallibly;
it sometimes happened that nearly as many were turned
away as got in. Hallé nights did nothing like as well. When
Stravinsky conducted his violin concerto with Samuel Dush-
kin there were many empty seats. When Wood did the Verdi

Requiem the place was half empty. Even *Messiah* had fallen off; the traditional Christmas repeat performance of it had to be dropped because the turn-up was thin. Manchester had gone into a musical decline which, it was feared, would resume and quicken once the precarious stimuli of wartime passed. All of which showed what Barbirolli was up against implicitly.

The Free Trade Hall will come into our story again. For the time being it was out of action, its handsome early Victorian walls (intact to this day) an enclave of blitz rubble, following a heavy incendiary raid, the first of two on successive nights, three days before Christmas 1940. The last music heard there, an hour or two before the raid began, had been *Messiah*, conducted by Sargent.

For his and the new Hallé's first Manchester concert, on a Sunday afternoon in mid-August 1943, Barbirolli chose a place on the outskirts, King's Hall, a timber stadium within the Belle Vue 'funpark', neighboured by monkey houses, express roundabouts, a scenic railway and a vast stand for firework displays. There were rings of seats for 6,000 and a central arena that was used, or came to be used, indifferently for mammoth oratorios, boxing, political rallies and circuses: particularly circuses. Concert programmes carried schedules and plans of train, tram and bus times and routes so that sober thousands who had never ridden an express roundabout in their lives could find their way there from other parts. The day before that first Manchester concert Barbirolli came in for rehearsal. The previous night he had conducted in Sheffield (Tchaikovsky, Wagner, Debussy, Elgar and Schubert), where he had had a full and joyous house. A functionary showed him to the conductor's room. The door had a notice: Ringmaster's Office. There were jokes about whether he would need a whip and silk hat. He either became genuinely fond of King's Hall or made the best of a dubious job. More than once he praised its acoustics: 'Plenty of nice, soft wood around. Wooden floor, wooden walls, wooden roof. That gives much better results than your modern builder's rubbish.'

The size of the place was disquieting. How pull in 6,000? Qualms were unwarranted. Long before starting time queues ringed the vast fireworks stand, hoping for unreserved seats at one-and-six. Not a reserved seat left. Ingesting six thousand was no easy job. Barbirolli began the *Mastersingers* Overture twenty minutes late. After this and the second piece (*l'Après-midi*) people were still struggling to get in. Hundreds had to stay outside. The wooden walls were almost creaking. Not until the third item, the *Enigma* variations, was the crowd settled and tranquil. The afternoon ended with Tchaikovsky's No. 5 and a storm of joy, the little man bowing with hand over heart, heels together, impassive of mien. The Tchaikovsky had overwhelmed. When had it been known to fail? To be sure, there had been other things which didn't come off quite as well. There had, indeed, been wincings. In *l'Après-midi*, reported Granville Hill, much of Debussy's delicate tone shading was 'sadly marred by sounds of merriment in the gardens'. A 'funpark' was no sealed-off sylvan pleasance of the Glyndebourne sort. The people who ran it could not be expected to stop switchbacks for the sake of symphonies. Or so the realists argued. Grumbles recurred nevertheless.

Later that season House Full notices went up again for an all-Beethoven afternoon (Symphony No. 8, the *Eroica* Symphony and the third piano concerto, with Denis Matthews) and for an all-Tchaikovsky one ('1812' Overture, movements from the Serenade for Strings, a *Swan Lake* suite and Symphony No. 4), the latter selling out in competition with an imminent pair of all-Tchaikovsky programmes by the London Philharmonic Orchestra at the Manchester Opera House. After the Beethoven concert Hill complained that the amusement machines outside the hall had set up 'a perpetual pedal base' inside it; on top of which the hall's acoustics gave too much prominence to the brass. Another writer deplored 'whoops and howls' of switchback riders during the pianissimos of the *Eroica*'s slow movement. Seven all-Beethoven concerts later, all vastly attended, whoops and howls having percolated at most, one devotee decided that he had had more than enough. After the second *Leonora* overture and the 'Emperor' concerto (Denis Matthews again) there was an interval. *Egmont* and the Seventh were to come. The devotee leaped on to the platform and adjured members of the audience to write complainingly about the noises to the Belle Vue management.

He got small thanks from the management of the Hallé who put out a chilly statement. The Belle Vue people, they said, did what they could to remedy noise nuisance as quickly as possible. If objections were pressed to their logical conclusions there could be only one outcome at week-ends: a homeless Hallé.

By the time this statement was put out the orchestra had found a new home for 'week-night' concerts in the Albert Hall, a little way down Deansgate from the shell of the Free Trade Hall. Of the Albert Hall more in a moment. Meantime the orchestra made do with three 'super cinemas' on the outskirts, at Didsbury, Stretford and Prestwich. These were available on Sundays only. 'Cinema Sundays' alternated with the big Sundays at Belle Vue. For the time being there were no week-night concerts at all. Acoustically and in other ways the cinemas had their limitations. During an all-Russian night at Prestwich (*Pathetic* Symphony, *Golden Cockerel* suite and the Arensky variations on a theme by Tchaikovsky), Barbirolli put his baton down and the concert was held up for a few minutes by a noisy electric fan 'whose merry note', wrote Hill, 'could not at first be silenced.' At Didsbury he took the quick movements of Mendelssohn's 'Italian' Symphony so very quickly that 'the ear could hardly catch the repeated notes, though doubtless they were well and truly played.' That is Hill again. 'Doubtless' denoted doubt, as it often does, and Barbirolli was given the benefit of it. Only a crystalline acoustic such as that of the future Royal Festival Hall could have expounded what was really happening that night in Mendelssohn's Vivace and Presto. With the orchestra boxed in or on summarily adapted stages, the cinemas were anything but crystalline in effect. Yet in the Longford Theatre, Stretford, Barbirolli brought off a *Fantastic* Symphony that Hill judged to be probably the most vivid performance of it ever heard at a Hallé concert. This was more than a compliment. Accolade is the fitter word. For decades the Hallé had been credited by competent judges with a better understanding of Berlioz and a sounder technique for him than any other orchestra in the land. The *Fantastic* was, in fact, almost a Hallé property. Charles Hallé had given the first performance of it in England at the Free Trade Hall in 1879. On the same platform and others in the North during the 1920s, Harty had won for it a huge, rapt following.

Especially when we bear in mind the Hallé's preoccupation with box office (its choice lay between a fairly high ratio of 'popular' symphonic programmes, on the one hand; and, on the other, the bailiffs and bankruptcy), Manchester in the middle 1940s was not much of a place for musical trail-blazing, even if Barbirolli had been inclined that way: which he wasn't. Yet in the cinemas and even, occasionally, at Belle Vue, he put on many works from the outer rim of his repertory: for example, d'Indy's *Symphonie sur un chant montagnard*, Fauré's incidental music to *Pelléas et Mélisande*, Bizet's Symphony in C, the occasional 'Brandenburg' concerto, *La Mer* (of course), Delius's double concerto (first Manchester performance, two of his leading players, Laurance Turner and Haydn Rogerson, playing the solo violin and 'cello parts), Bax's Symphony No. 3, Vaughan Williams's No. 5 and his *Dives and Lazarus* variants, and, loftiest of all, perhaps, a piece which he had pored over in facsimile manuscript years earlier: Mozart's Adagio and Fugue for Strings in C minor (K. 546) which began as a piece for two pianos and ended for strings—either string orchestra or, according to some scholars, string quartet, an alternative which, to Barbirolli's way of thinking, wouldn't do at all. Once in a while a venture would fall flat. When he put on a modern English tonepoem, J. B. Moeran's *In the Mountain Country* and followed it up with Mozart's 'Linz' symphony and Sibelius's No. 5 (whose finale was still strong meat for many), the result was 'too many empty seats—especially the high-priced ones'. The moral was clear. Without a best-selling soloist and helpings of Tchaikovsky, Rachmaninov and Beethoven (the No. 5 or the No. 7) or Grieg and Johann Strauss, one couldn't really be sure of filling the house and making it roar. Another thing that couldn't be taken for granted was a feeling for musical humour, if such a thing exists. As we have seen, he had had Carnegie Hall overtly chuckling at Walton's *Façade* music. When he put on selections from the *Façade* suites at Prestwich the audience sat them out with straight faces, some looking positively glum. At the end 'he reproved us from his desk for not emitting even a snigger', reported the *Manchester Guardian*. He repeated two of the movements in the hope that his hearers would relent and hold their sides. They were straight-faced as before. Walton was to their liking for all that.

At a time when, owing in part to the U.S.S.R.'s military successes, Soviet music and most other Soviet manifestations were commanding an excited deference everywhere, he was much nagged to put a bit of new or newish Russian music into his programmes.

'I do not', he replied, 'believe in playing works simply because they are by Allies. However, in view of requests that have been made, I have been going through the scores of some of the Russian works that are available in this country, and if I can find enough suitable ones I shall play them next season.'

He did rather better than that. Three weeks after giving this promise he took the *Freischütz* overture out of a Didsbury programme and put in a *Festival Overture* by Nikolai Budashkin. He repeated Mr. Budashkin's piece a few times that season. Then it sank without a ripple. The promise of more Soviet pieces to come was kept. The 1944–45 lists included two symphonies by living composers: Prokoviev's *Classical* symphony and Shostakovitch's No. 5. Both were played on the same night and conducted by Albert Coates, for long chief among this country's musical Russophils. It is odd that during these years Barbirolli did not try his hand at Shostakovitch's No. 1, another symphony lodged in the Hallé tradition. The first English performance of it had been under Harty during the orchestra's 1931–32 season. For revival under Barbirolli's regime it had to wait until 1947, when not he but Nikolai Malko conducted it.

By that time the orchestra had found in central Manchester 'temporary' quarters of a less temporary kind. The cinemas served until the early spring of 1944. Jumping ahead of strict chronology, we take leave of them here. From the autumn of 1944 onward and until the restored Free Trade Hall opened its doors (1951), the Hallé supplemented its Belle Vue series with mid-week concerts at a place which has already been mentioned, the Albert Hall in Deansgate, the home of a Methodist mission. It had (and has) mild stained-glass windows with a red-rose-of-Lancashire motif worked into

them. On the day before a concert the janitor would take out
the communion rail and put in two extra rows of tip-up chairs.*
Up went two platform extensions on props, one for the harp,
the other for viola desks. On very crowded nights avid latecomers paid a shilling a head for seats under these platform
flaps. They couldn't see what was going on, and what they
heard was odd. Uncanny to encounter the libertine strains of
Richard Strauss's *Don Juan* or a brace of Johann Strauss
waltzes in this prim home of prayer. Barbirolli's retiring-room
was the minister's vestry: portrait of a departed divine over
the gasfire, high-backed chairs, green-painted safe in the
corner.

At a pinch the Albert Hall held 1,800. This proved to be
little more than half enough. So, from the third season onwards,
the Society duplicated its concerts, Tuesday night's programmes
being repeated on Wednesday nights. Thus was Manchester's
musical appetite slaked. Barbirolli sometimes called the
Albert Hall concerts his cognoscenti concerts. When more
himself he spoke of 'my posh concerts'. The Belle Vue affairs
were officially styled 'Popular'. But were they as 'popular' as
all that? During his second season he risked Elgar's E flat
Symphony there. In the prospectus, resorting to capital
letters, he had asked for a 'FULL HOUSE WHEN WE PLAY
THE SECOND SYMPHONY OF ELGAR AT BELLE
VUE'. He got what he wanted: a house of six thousand.
Clifford Curzon played Tchaikovsky's B flat minor piano
concerto in the same programme. Perhaps that had something
to do with the multitude. The fact remains that the E flat had
long been not a draw but something of a box-office damper.
It is to be concluded that Manchester turned up for the E flat
because Barbirolli had bidden it to turn up. Already, then, he
was a voice in the land. So far as the E flat was concerned,
his writ was not limited to Manchester. Soon afterwards he
took the symphony to four other northern towns and got
capacity audiences in all of them. In the mid-1950s he was to
draw good and engrossed houses in Newcastle, Middlesbrough,

---

* In another Nonconformist church on the orchestra's Lancashire
circuit the communion rail was immovable and divided the orchestra to
the detriment of ensemble, especially in the case of the second-violin
section, whose players sat on either side of it.

Nottingham and Hanley as well as Manchester with an all-Elgar programme: E flat Symphony, the Introduction and Allegro and the 'cello concerto.

Like any permanent orchestra the Hallé craved for a place of its own to rehearse in. Luckier than most, it found what it was after: a disused Sunday school up a flight of steps in a mean-looking street (Hewitt Street) in crammed, humming central Manchester where theoretically there wasn't room enough for a man to hang his hat up. All around were cotton offices, warehouses, little engineering shops. Although the rear wall had a vestigial rose window in cheap stained glass, the atmosphere of the place toned well with its surroundings. It had a bleak, anti-musical air. The players quickly found a name for it: The Factory. Here, during odd weeks or half-weeks or on odd days snatched from comings and goings to towns and cities in most parts of Britain, Aberdeen at one extreme, Bournemouth at the other. Barbirolli rehearsed at the rate of two hours for every single hour of public playing. He exhorted, railed, ridiculed now and then, and sometimes pretended to lose his temper. On cold days he wore a check lumber jacket, relic of his tramps with Evelyn in the hills above Vancouver. Sharp memories come back of the early Factory days. Again the baton's peremptory rap. 'Three bars before 270. Let's have a real staccato, oboes. And I don't hear enough viola tone. I want to hear you *sing.*' The violas have another try and are told that that's better. At their second go the oboes positively spit their notes and get an endorsing nod. His eyes are everywhere. They never miss a thing. In something by Brahms a rear-desk 'cellist plays the first phrase of a melody, properly, on the G string. For the following phrase, a higher one, he sticks to G instead of transferring to the D string, involving himself for some obscure reason, probably bravado, in the hazards of seventh and eighth positions. Barbirolli spots his misdemeanour at once and points a condemning finger: 'Hey, you at the back there, you're on the wrong string. You should be on D man, D! I want tone, tone, *tone!*'

Often he wanted not *tone* but a whisper. The whisper had to be of quality. As usual there were dissertations on the point of the bow and its meaningful use. After a crowded Tchaikovsky night at Belle Vue a newspaper notice was passed from hand to hand in the bandroom. The critic said: 'Sometimes one felt that Mr. Barbirolli pushed his love of a delicate pianissimo too far for so vast a hall.' Somebody said what a pity Tchaikovsky hadn't scored for whispering baritones (muted). There was no bitterness in this. The players 'belonged' to him from first desks to back. And he 'belonged' to the players.

There were others in whom Barbirolli aroused a possessive itch: his friends of the London Symphony Orchestra, for example. The L.S.O. were now the Royal Philharmonic Society's chosen orchestra. This did not bring in a great deal of money but meant a bit of glory. Barbirolli had not been back in England four months before he was conducting them at a R.P.S. concert in one of those 'J.B.' programmes at which the reader must be yawning by this time: Mozart's Symphony No. 34, the *Dives and Lazarus* variants, the *Firebird* suite and the second symphony of Brahms. In January 1944 he was with them again, conducting his *Elizabethan* suite, the Elgar violin concerto (with Sammons), the *Mother Goose* suite and Beethoven's No. 7, another mixture as before. His success with the R.P.S.-L.S.O. public, the response of the players and the eager cordiality of the orchestra's directors strengthened his hand for an imminent tussle with those who were running the Hallé.

For weeks he had been on the simmer about the orchestra's sketchy administration and vague budgeting. Nine days after his second R.P.S. concert he had a showdown with Godlee and others of the committee. What follows derives mainly from Barbirolli's recollections some years later. The orchestra, he pointed out, were playing at the rate of well over 200 concerts a year (he should have said well over 250) on no subsidy and very limited resources. So far they had been very successful. But he was beginning to wonder. In their original letter the Society had assured him there were sufficient funds 'available in the form of guarantees' to make the venture a sound one. Turning to the treasurer he asked: 'Those resources you talked about. What do they amount to? How long would they keep us going if public support fell off and we couldn't pay our way?' It appeared from the treasurer's answer and Godlee's admission that there was only enough money to keep them going for a fortnight. The disclosure, seven months after the event, that he had been summoned from New York on so precarious a basis made Barbirolli stare and exclaim.

'Ah!' replied Godlee, 'we were taking a great risk.'

Barbirolli: 'Well, maybe you *were* taking a great risk. But you committee men are all heads of firms and things. You are wealthy businessmen. Music is something you devote your spare time to. You are all right. My situation's a bit different. I was taking a great risk, too'—a greater risk, he might have added, than he had ever bargained for—'and so were my players.'

For him the crux was that the Hallé's wealthy businessmen were not being businesslike enough. 'I have given you', he said, 'a first-class orchestra despite a tenth-class management.'* He then brought out his shotgun, in a manner of speaking. The committee, he said, must make up their minds on management reform within a week and present a business schedule in two months' time. If the reform and the schedule were to his liking he would stay on with the Hallé. Otherwise he would go. By this time the directors of the London Symphony Orchestra were making competitive approaches. Ultimately they offered him their permanent conductorship at £6,000 a year (£1,000 up on what had come to be known as the British conductor's trade-union rate), the playing strength to be ninety. (The Hallé strength stayed at seventy for another two years, then went up to eighty: not much to boast about, since that had been the orchestra's size as early as 1865.) The committee came to heel. They presented their business schedule on the dot; it estimated what the orchestra was going to cost and how much money it could expect to earn. At the same time they found a secretary-cum-general manager of parts in T. Ernest Bean, a musical amateur with business experience (*Manchester Guardian* circulation department) and a cool, lucid mind. To considerable desk talents he added an uncommon capacity for talking business with musicians of imponderable temperament. Into the bargain he had a ready

* Quoted by Michael Kennedy, *The Hallé Tradition, a Century of Music*, Manchester University Press, 1960.

and impish pen. Later on, as the first administrator of the
Royal Festival Hall, he compiled a regular programme squib,
Point Counterpoint, which quoted leading critics against each
other to diverting effect, a liberty which some of the critics
resented.

In view of the business schedule and Bean's appointment
Barbirolli put away his shotgun. Courteously declining the
L.S.O. invitation, he reapplied himself to his mission in the
North. For the first time he had found himself professionally
at a road fork. The good things of his earlier career—the
recording contracts, the Covent Garden touring directorship,
the Scottish Orchestra, the New York Philharmonic—had
come to him on platters or had dropped from the clouds. This
time it was a matter of choice; and the choice was gruelling.
It would have been a harder choice if his Hallé work had been
easier. That work, he said, was, during those first years, 'of a
toughness that in normal times I don't think anybody could
have endured. . . . The stimulation of the thing, the thought of
what the orchestra were doing for me in those days: these were
in themselves reason enough for my decision. I couldn't bear
the idea of leaving them.' The idea went on being unbearable
to the end. In the 1960s he said: 'The question is always being
asked, "Why do you stay in Manchester?" In reply I start by
asking: "Why did Richter leave Vienna and come to Manchester?" Richter would never take an appointment in London.
When he conducted at Covent Garden he went there as a
guest and took a lot of his Manchester players with him. And
he always came back. So it is with me. I shall be with the
Hallé to the end of my days.'

Thus he was committed for good. He regarded this as
licence to grumble more openly. His decision, in 1944, to stay
on roughly coincided with his first concert for the Hallé
Pension Fund. Once more the Belle Vue Hall creaked at the
joists for infallible richness: the *Cockaigne* overture, Rachmaninov's second piano concerto (with Colin Horsley), two
Lohengrin preludes and the Ride and closing scene from *The
Valkyrie*. For this night he had an orchestra of one hundred and
twelve players: half again more than the usual strength. Most
of the additional players were from the B.B.C. Northern
Orchestra who, as ex-Hallé men and members of the pension

fund, were free to play for him under its auspices once a year
and at no other time. Pretending that he was still uncommitted
professionally, he said to an interviewer that night: 'If Manchester will give me an orchestra like this for good I will
remain here. I am forty-four. I have sixteen years of active
career left [he had twenty-six, as it turned out]. I should like
to spend those years in Manchester. But Manchester will have
to wake up.' If 'wakening up' meant enabling Barbirolli to
take on more players, Manchester was slow about it. It was not
until 1951 that he was able to increase playing strength to
eighty-eight. By this time the Hallé was back in the Free Trade
Hall and on a relatively roomy platform. Admittedly he would
have found it hard to seat eighty-eight in the Albert Hall.
'Wakening up' could, however, be taken alternatively as
applying to immediate money matters. In a few months he
had won a massive public following in Manchester and was to
maintain and even increase it down the years. On 'official'
Manchester he and Godlee did not make anything like as
much impression. Something will be said later about his
wrangles with a grudging corporation over subsidies and
guarantees. During those early and needy months he lost no
opportunity of preaching to public authority about their duty
to pay up and look pleasant.

One of his pronouncements followed a couple of monumental days at Belle Vue. On the first day he conducted
Tchaikovsky (*Romeo and Juliet*), Mozart (the *Nachtmusik*), the
'New World' symphony, *On Hearing the First Cuckoo* and *The
Bartered Bride* overture before seven thousand young people in
the morning and another seven thousand at night. His hearers
were school-leavers, boy scouts, girl guides and members of
'pre-service' organisations generally. They had paid a shilling
a head. Hundreds of them made do with standing-places in
passageways. Again it took such a time to squeeze them in that
the concerts started twenty minutes late, and intervals had to
be scrapped. He filled the hall again the following night, this
time with an audience of adults. At the end he said: 'In two
days I have played to 20,000 at three concerts. This orchestra,
starting with every disadvantage, has gathered The People
around it. [That he was speaking, as it were, in initial capitals
is clear.] I feel I must bring music within the reach of The

K

People. Because the Hallé Orchestra rehearses constantly and because good music costs thousands of pounds to produce, the importance of subsidies becomes increasingly evident.' Again, responding to the principal toast at a public luncheon to the orchestra and its conductor:

> And now as to money. Unlike Oliver I would not ask for more. I would ask for a lot more. In twelve months the Hallé has spent seventy thousand pounds on concerts and has paid its way. I cannot possibly ask the orchestra to repeat such an arduous undertaking if the highest standards are not to be maintained. The late Sir Henry Wood was right when he said: 'Music must *not* be asked to pay its way.' When a number of concerts have to be given at an 'uneconomic' rate, who is to bridge the gap if we are not to slip back and make fine music the prerogative of a privileged class—who don't seem to want it anyway—rather than the natural right of the masses, those masses who, time and time again, at E.N.S.A. concerts and concerts for the Forces, have proved to me that they are hungry for the very best that can be given them? . . . You must see to it that we, the Hallé Orchestra, visit Canada, Australia, South Africa, America. We shall be ambassadors of trade as well as of art. . . .

Why trade should have been dragged in is hard to see. Yet the radical note and the imperative mood ('You *must* . . .!') were unmistakable. They denoted a confidence that had not been bred of his Manchester achievement alone or of anything that befell him anywhere else in the provinces. Clearly, it came of the new Hallé's London début. This happened during their second summer. The Hallé had been shortly preceded in London by the resuscitated Liverpool Philharmonic Orchestra, which gave concerts in and around the capital under Sargent and other batons. Then came Boult's turn with the B.B.C. Symphony Orchestra: four concerts at the Royal Albert Hall in matters ranging from Wagner's *Venusberg* music to Beethoven's 'Choral' Symphony. Barbirolli and his orchestra followed close upon the heels of Boult. The occasion was momentous. Again the promoters were the Royal Philharmonic

Society. Their season was long over, but the second anniversary of the signing of the Anglo-Soviet Treaty was at hand; they had decided to put on an additional concert in honour of it. From the Baltic to the Black Sea, Soviet arms were piling victory upon victory. More than ever, the English, like other Allied peoples, were rather wrong in the head about the U.S.S.R. That night the Royal Albert Hall was crammed. That is to say, there were nearly as many people in it as at a Belle Vue overflow night. More than that, it was put out that applications for tickets had been six times in excess of the seating. There were quite a number of people who had come for the music. Barbirolli gave Budashkin's *Festival* overture another airing. For the rest: Liadov's *Enchanted Lake*, the *Pathetic* Symphony and Prokoviev's third piano concerto (with Kendall Taylor).

'In an incredibly short space of time', found the *Observer*, 'Barbirolli has welded his team into an orchestra which, by general consent, can even now take its place among the leading orchestras of the world.' The *Musical Times* had a feeling that now and then he was sacrificing logic and balance for effects of a questionable kind: 'In the opening of the *Pathétique*, for instance, the melody of the bassoon should be more prominent than the harmony of the basses. But in Mr. Barbirolli's reading the bassoon obliterated every trace of the harmony, as the roar of an elephant obliterates the twitter of a sparrow.' The writer allowed, however, that, between them, the new Hallé and the Liverpool Philharmonic, coming south to challenge the London orchestras, had established 'once more' the orchestral supremacy of the North.

Barbirolli never went so far as to assert the North's supremacy. It would have been tactless, to say the least, in one of the London Symphony Orchestra's guest conductors to do so. What he did, in reviewing his and the Hallé's first season, was to proclaim a legend:

Our beginning in Bradford was rather inauspicious. Within a few months we were being quoted as an example to other orchestras. What is now known as the Legend of the Hallé was established. Sometimes things start on top and gradually decline. We started at the bottom. Our ascent was rapid. . . .

CHAPTER SIXTEEN

BATTLE FRONTS

AFTER their second fortnight in Edinburgh and Glasgow and five concerts in and about London, rounding off at Watford, the Hallé players put aside their instruments and took a month off on part-pay, the month being July 1944. Nobody expected Barbirolli to sit back, even if he had been capable of it. It had been his idea and, at one stage, E.N.S.A.'s, to take the orchestra to Italy, which swarmed with Allied troops and was dotted with army camps as far north as recently-liberated Rome. For want of air transport the idea had to be dropped. It was arranged instead that he should fly out and conduct symphony concerts mainly for the Forces and incidentally for Italian civilians with such native orchestras as had survived upheaval.

He was allowed to take half a hundredweight of band parts. He took only a few conducting scores, having been given to understand that for the rest he would find what he wanted in orchestral libraries on the spot. In this he was disappointed. He was to open with four concerts in the San Carlo opera house, Naples. The library there had included a symphonic section. Its shelves were almost bare. No Tchaikovsky, no Brahms. It was said that a score of Brahms's second symphony had been presented in token of goodwill by an American woman who loved both Italy and the German classics. It had been stolen almost as soon as received. He needed scores not to conduct from (this he could have done from memory) but to rehearse from. Making a quick dash to Rome, he rooted about for an hour and returned with the *Mastersingers* Overture, the *Enigma* variations, *On hearing the first cuckoo*, the 'New World' symphony and a few other pieces: enough for two programmes; enough, bearing in mind the extraordinary musical hunger of the times, for four concerts, since hearing a fine thing twice is no surfeit for starved ears.

274

It could not be said that the San Carlo orchestra was in good shape at rehearsal. He subjected it to the Barbirolli drill. At first the players had not known what to make of a conductor born and bred in London who talked the Venetian dialect and had been in charge of the New York Philharmonic Orchestra for seven whole seasons, as they generally understood. His feeling for Italian music was what mollified them. He put them through two *Traviata* preludes: 'At the end', he was to write, 'they rose spontaneously and shouted "Bravo, Maestro, bravo!" . . . The first violin added, "Maestro, why don't you *stay* here?"' It could not be said that their form offered much inducement.

At prices from sixpence to a florin, five tiers of boxes and other parts of the house were pretty well filled on the opening night; two generals attended—an English one, Maitland Wilson, and an American one, Mark Clark; there was no drift-out or overt walk-out between items, as occasionally happened on E.N.S.A.'s more ambitious 'culture nights'; and the genuineness of his recalls at the end warmed Barbirolli's heart. The orchestra had not satisfied him. 'Still, I got something out of it.' On the third and fourth nights the doors had to be closed half an hour before the announced starting time; already the theatre was packed to suffocation. From Naples he went on to other cities and other ripe old theatres, conducting revived or rescued orchestras beneath ornate ceilings and festive chandeliers, amid the red plush, gold leaf and white paint of a dead epoch in a land sundered by want and squalor as well as seared by war.

From Rome, Bari, Taranto, he wrote home of continuing triumphs, as happy in his achievements as a child and no more inclined to understate them than any child would be. Of Bari, for example: 'By some magical means the theatre was made to hold fifty per cent more than it should.' It was during E.N.S.A. missions that he put on khaki again. During the day he went about in uniform of the sort commissioned officers wore, and very natty he looked with his gloves and swagger stick. At night he reverted to the uniform of his vocation: tails and white tie which, as happens everywhere and at all times, made the music seem more important to many ears. During his Italian trip there were no reserved seats for anybody except the occasional general or some other notable whose presence offered example and lent prestige. It rejoiced Barbirolli, an earnest adherent of the Plain Man, to see colonels queueing outside theatres with privates long before concerts began. He found this a grand sight, 'indicative of the great natural discipline of our race even in these days of growing democracy'.*

However much democracy was growing or appeared to be growing elsewhere, it did not take conspicuous root in music, where vogues were determined and power still exercised, less through majority votes than by the genius and passion or insight and resolution of individuals. Such individuals were not dictators, to be sure. 'Leaders' was a safer word. Barbirolli was a musical leader in the making, almost made. Beecham had been one for over thirty years. Their followings did not coincide but overlapped.

Long before Hitler's war—during the Kaiser's war, in fact—Beecham had been an open-handed friend of the Hallé, enabling the Society to put on twice as many concerts as in peacetime, paying the orchestra's bills, conducting it for nothing and feeing substitute conductors† when he had to stand down. All in all, as the Society publicly acknowledged, he got the Hallé out of a hole; without his help the orchestra could not have survived. The Society being for a while without a permanent conductor, Beecham became its 'musical adviser' and, on Elgar's death in 1934, its President, an office that might mean little or much according to its holder. In the spring of 1940 he left England and spent four years in the United States, or based on the U.S., guest-conducting, haranguing, putting people in their place and making as brilliant a boon and nuisance of himself in his middle sixties as the world could wish. It never occurred to him to renounce his presidency of the Hallé Society. That he should be relieved of it occurred to others. Sooner or later he would be coming home. (He did this sooner than most people expected, although Godlee had early wind of his return, landing at Liverpool a few days before Barbirolli opened his 1944–45 season.)

* 'Colonels and Privates Queued Together', by John Barbirolli, *Radio Times*, 22nd September 1944.

† In some cases the fee was nothing more than a modest expenses allowance. Often the substitutes were newcomers so grateful for Beecham's patronage that they would have been happy to conduct for nothing or even pay for the chance.

In four years the musical scene had, especially to homecoming eyes, changed drastically. From 1909 onwards it had been Beecham's way when he founded an orchestra to put a proprietorial ring-fence round it. That, roughly, was the case with the splendid London Philharmonic Orchestra, after his launching of it in 1932. When he sailed for New York in 1940 the L.P.O. in his eyes, at any rate, was not a thing on its own feet but a Beecham emanation. Left to fend for itself in an extremely insecure hour, the L.P.O. presently turned itself into a self-governing 'co-operative', which was little to Beecham's taste. What more likely than that sooner or later he should seek another orchestra to 'requisition' and rule? And, since he was its President, what handier choice than the reconstituted Hallé? Such a pounce was to be circumvented before it had a chance to happen.

To obviate a Hallé with two bosses, one of whom (Beecham) would assuredly consign the other (Barbirolli) to the role of acolyte, Godlee wrote Beecham a letter which, without advert-ing to these possibilities, regretted that, owing to the President's absence overseas and consequent inaccessibility, the presidency had been allowed to 'lapse'—a very wrong and reprehensible thing on the Society's part, admittedly—but was now to be revived not to Beecham's benefit but in favour of the sitting Lord Mayor of Manchester and his successors, through whom it was hoped to get financial backing for the orchestra from public funds.

On the face of it this was a blandly impudent performance. But for the true issues at stake it would have been inexcusable. Beecham reacted with choler and scorn, giving interviews, issuing public statements and writing letters to the press which taxed the Hallé Society with atrocious manners and made mince-meat of Godlee's ostensible case, not a difficult matter. On the merits of the dispute as presented by both sides to a perturbed public it did not appear that Barbirolli's rights and interests were or might be implicitly involved. It was Godlee who even-tually brought Barbirolli into the picture. In a circular to mem-bers of the Hallé Society he wrote: 'During these most difficult war years Mr. Barbirolli by his untiring devotion has created an orchestra which has already earned an international reputa-tion worthy of the best tradition of the Society. If, therefore, your committee *has to choose* [this author's italics] between an absentee President who refuses to co-operate with the Society and a conductor who has proved himself willing to devote his whole energies to the cause of music in Manchester, there is no doubt where its choice must lie. . . .' Thus it came to the general ear, bewilderingly, that persons and personalities were in some ways at loggerheads. Beecham, affecting a lordly ignorance of what had been happening to the orchestra during 'these most difficult war years', let it be known that he was sticking to the presidency and that he was putting 'President of the Hallé Society' on his visiting cards and business notepaper. He added what must have sounded to Barbirolli and Godlee like a threat: 'I have decided that forthwith . . . I shall take . . . a more personal interest in the affairs of the Society. It is only too obvious that they require . . . friendly guidance . . . I have been connected with the Society off and on in one or more of the following capacities: impresario, manager, creator and maintainer of orchestras . . ., and last but not least as an executive artist, for over thirty years, and it is not outside the range of possibilities that one day I may do so again.'

At one stage in the wrangle Barbirolli had hoped that a little goodwill on his part might ease the tensions. Accordingly he had written to Beecham in comradely vein. Beecham's continuing obduracy angered him. He unbosomed himself bitterly to those who stood close to him professionally. Had not Beecham talked him or tried to talk him out of New York? Had he not told directors of the New York Philharmonic or their intermediaries that in making Barbirolli permanent conductor they had exalted an upstart?

'If Beecham comes back as President', he told Godlee, 'I shall go.'

That Godlee publicly and semi-publicly 'took on' Beecham by pen and word of mouth, unavoidably using arguments that must have struck the outsider as flimsy and gratuitous, was a conspicuous act of loyalty that won Barbirolli's gratitude and did much to strengthen the bond between the two men and deepen their friendship. In the end Beecham's sound and fury signified nothing. Pouncing on the circumstance that the presidency was not provided for in the Society's old constitution, the committee held that the office therefore had no 'legal' validity and drew up

a new constitution (1946) which omitted it even more conspicuously. There, on the surface, the wrangle ended. By this
time Beecham, having founded his third English orchestra, the
Royal Philharmonic, was deflected and possessively busy.
During years to come, he and the R.P.O. could not always be
sure of doing well on Barbirolli's home ground.

His first (and only) concert with the R.P.O. at Belle Vue, in
December 1948, drew an audience of 2,000. Four thousand
empty seats is a lot of empty seats. He had been warned that
booking was sluggish. 'What, Sir Thomas,' he was asked by a
reporter on arriving in Manchester, 'are your immediate plans?'
'To get back to London as quickly as possible', he drawled.
The concert ended with a magnificent *Heldenleben*. The lonely
2,000 stamped and cheered. For his recalls he was obliged to
make a longish circuit of the arena. Next time, he said, if there
was to be a next time, he would put in for a motor-scooter or, if
it didn't run to that, roller skates. He discussed the auditorium
mockingly; supposed it was once for cock fighting; conceded
that it would make a splendid bear pit. On his way out through
a stage-door throng of admirers, mostly women, he paused and
held forth blisteringly: 'So far as I am concerned, Manchester is
the worst city in the world. And, incidentally, I am not coming
here again.'

'Oh, Sir Thomas,' pleaded one of the admirers, 'don't say
that!'

'No, madam,' he intoned, 'I am nearly seventy years of age,
and I'm tired of playing to savages.'

It is hard not to read into this performance some pique
against Barbirolli and his committee. For his part, Barbirolli
never spoke of Beecham the artist except with admiration and a
touch of wonder. But what he had heard in New York, followed
by what he took to be Beecham's predatory design on the Hallé
Orchestra, left a longish after-taste. Beecham's talent, he would
say, had been cosseted by the family 'pill millions'. His own had
enjoyed no such advantage. His portion had been uphill struggle.
And he had had some success. In a single year he had won a
public which came mainly from that lower middle class from
which he himself had sprung as, indeed, Beecham did. His
orchestra and his following might be the work of an 'upstart'.
But nobody was going to be allowed to make off with them.

K*

Halfway through a slightly less harried season than their first
(this time concerts were down to 258, Barbirolli conducting 146
of them), the players filed into a reserved coach on a train
journey between Newcastle and Bolton, Lancs. A doctor inoculated the lot of them. A week later, after taking part in a vast
Messiah on a Sunday night under Sargent at Belle Vue, they
were inoculated again. At half-past-eight next morning, a brisk
mid-December one, accompanied by Barbirolli, Evelyn and
Bean, they boarded a train at London Road Station for some
destination, presumably a seaport, in the south of England
about which everybody had been kept in the dark for reasons of
military security. What everybody did know was that they were
to sail from this unnamed port to another across the Channel
and give sixteen 'Forces' concerts in Northern France and the
Low Countries. Some of the concerts would be in towns within
a shortish march of the fighting line.

Two days earlier the Nazis had launched their last great
offensive in the West from the Ardennes. Antwerp, a major
Allied supply port, was one of their objectives. It was also on the
Hallé's itinerary. Hitler's directive was: take Antwerp, then roll
up the British-Canadian armies on the Belgian-Dutch border.
The Hallé's trip could not have been more piquantly timed. No
other orchestra had visited this battle zone. According to
Barbirolli's information certain other orchestras had undertaken
to go but in the end thought better of it.

The port of embarkation proved to be Folkestone. The ship
on which they were to have sailed wasn't there. They spent the
night in a requisitioned hotel. Next day Barbirolli, Evelyn and
the rest were taken down to the quay and queued up for lifebelts
and iron rations. Then they boarded s.s. *Canterbury*, remembered from the pre-war cross-Channel service, now a crammed
troopship. Whether because of fog, which was thick, or mines,
which had to be swept, *Canterbury* and all aboard her stayed
in harbour for two days. Shore permits were hard to come by.
Food ran short. Iron rations had to be broached. They lived on
tea and bully beef. Everybody slept in deck space on pallets, no
distinction made between conductor and private, colonel and
back-desker. To pass the time some of the players got together
as for a music-hall pit, put on performances as best they could of
'pop' numbers and got community songs going. Somebody

found a cloth cap and a choker and obliged with comic-songs and patter. Barbirolli did what he could to help. He was one of those who scribbled parts on backs of envelopes and, for want of music stands, held them up before the players. Some of these entertainments were in the 'saloon', where soldiers sprawled with their kit. 'We were so cramped', Barbirolli remembered, 'that the trombonists were in danger of knocking out soldiers' teeth.'

The party had left Manchester on a Monday morning. They disembarked at Ostend after dark the following Thursday, having steamed in convoy with destroyer escort, at about the time they should have been giving their first concert, which was billed for the Palais des Beaux Arts, Brussels. The Palais was packed with expectant khaki, the platform set with music stands. A noted pianist, Leff Pouishnoff, came on as substitute and gave a recital. He, too, had been having transport difficulties; theoretically he should have been on his way back to England. From Ostend the orchestra drove through the night in one motor coach and troop carriers, reaching Brussels at 2 a.m. That afternoon they rehearsed in a hall so dark that Evelyn, groping her way across the platform, fell over the edge, broke an arm and had to turn in an oboe concerto which she was to have played in several programmes. Two concert hampers went astray. One of them contained Barbirolli's dress suit, the other a set of nuts and bolts for the xylophone which features in *Marco Takes a Walk*. Barbirolli had resigned himself to conducting in slacks, gum boots and a tweed jacket when, minutes before the concert, his gear turned up, entailing the quickest quick-change of his career. The xylophone had already been put together with bits and pieces from a music shop.

There was an audience of 2,500 at the opening, all Service men and women; they wore the uniforms or insignia of half a dozen nations. Again Nazi tanks and motorised infantry were swarming towards the Meuse. The tails and white tie, the dinner jackets and the long black dresses on the platform were an incongruity and a comfort. Concerts listed for Antwerp had to be cancelled; the cinema where they were to have been given had been hit by a rocket bomb. Even so, the Hallé went one better than had been purposed, playing not sixteen concerts in all but seventeen, five of them in Brussels, the rest in Ghent, Lille,

Ostend and Eindhoven. In bitter weather they came and went
by truck and troop carrier through a countryside of calcined
walls, rubble mounds, charred woods, burnt-out tanks. In most
of the towns, theatres and halls survived in something like
working order. Some nights were incredibly crowded. On the
top level of a tiered opera house soldiers stood like carytids
behind the seating, heads bowed because of the low ceiling. In
another theatre listeners were massed backstage where, as Bean
put it, they could not see, and behind glass partitions at the back
of the stalls where they could not hear. Ghent was among
Barbirolli's salient memories. Here he conducted the young
Arthur Grumiaux in the Mendelssohn violin concerto—'the first
Jewish music [hitherto under Hitler's ban] to be heard in
liberated Holland'. During this performance buzz-bombs were
heard passing over the hall from launching sites back east.

Eindhoven, however, was the place most remembered. Here
they were to have played thrice. In the event they gave seven
concerts at the rate of two a day, or, in one case, three. Although
the town had been much knocked about by Nazi demolition
squads during the withdrawal, most of the players were found
civilian billets. There were forty of these. On the first day
Barbirolli, as ex-officio billet-master, went round the billets to
make sure his men (and girls) were reasonably comfortable.
One door at which he knocked was that of a girl violinist. 'Come
in,' she said. No sooner had he done so than the landlady
entered, hard and sceptical of eye. 'Are you married?' she asked.
This became one of the tour's embroidered jokes. There was
little else to joke about. On his way to the next billet Barbirolli
saw children tagging a laden coal cart. Dodging the driver's
repeated 'whip behind', they were snatching lumps of coal for
their mothers who followed with bags and baskets.

The Eindhoven concerts were in a theatre-cum-lecture hall
attached to a great factory where radio equipment was made.
It was without an audience ramp, seated a thousand on the flat
and was somehow stretched to take a hundred or two more. The
roof was holed. There was no heating. Often the players played
in greatcoats, a few of them wearing 'balaclavas'. Many also
went to bed in their greatcoats, fully clad underneath, and
thankful for the Army whisky ration which had been negotiated for them.

'The fighting line was twelve miles away', said Barbirolli. 'Soldiers used to come in from the front, laden with equipment and weapons, and listened in their dirt, dumping their stuff as near to hand as they could. We gave two concerts a day: full symphonic programmes including Sibelius No. 2 and *Eine kleine Nachtmusik*.* After the programme proper we'd play encores for two hours. We'd play until midnight. We'd play until Tommy Cheetham [librarian] ran out of music.'

The final encore was apt to be either a setting of *A Londonderry Air*, which began with a beautiful solo for the French horn; or that relic of Barbirolli's years in Glasgow, Gibilaro's *Fantasia on Scottish Airs*. With home far off and so much ruin and misery to hand, rather more soul was put into these pieces than they usually got in peacetime and perhaps more heart-strings were touched. During one sequence of encores, a few minutes after the concert was supposed to have ended, a Nazi fighter plane came over and harmlessly strafed the main street, which, in the ordinary way, would have been thronged with homing concert-goers. While playing the orchestra could hear the fighter's guns 'tattering away', as one of the girls put it. Twice while the orchestra was back in Brussels awaiting trucks for Lille or Ghent, the Luftwaffe made sweeps over the city. Once they were treated to a 'dog fight' almost immediately overhead. Christmas Day found them at the Palais des Beaux Arts again. Barbirolli conducted the English pianist Solomon in *the* Tchaikovsky piano concerto in the afternoon and again at night to crowded, happy tumult. Between these performances the E.N.S.A. hotel put on a brave attempt at Christmas dinner. The meat was tough, and there wasn't much of it. The players gathered round Barbirolli and drank his health. The concert that night, as on New Year's Eve, ended with *Auld Lang Syne*, stoutly sung, the orchestra leading—and a lot of emotion.

The voyage home began with their troopship running aground on a sandbank outside Ostend harbour. The tide soon floated

* Also in the Western Front repertory were Beethoven's No. 5, *The Walk to the Paradise Garden*, the Calinda from *Koanga*, *Romeo and Juliet* (Tchaikovsky), the *Mother Goose* suite, *l'Après-midi*, the transcription of *Sheep may safely graze*, the *Rienzi*, *Semiramide*, *Schöne Galatee* and *Thieving Magpie* overtures; the Mendelssohn violin concerto, already mentioned, and Tchaikovsky's B flat minor piano concerto.

them off. They were in Manchester within two days. Apart from the Nazi fighter over Eindhoven the only immediate physical risk they are known to have run was during a break in a cross-country journey when they were shooed and waved back to the road by a stentorian sergeant who said they had chosen a minefield to stretch their legs in. Hardship had been their lot if not danger. They had borne it with sprightliness, youngsters and veterans alike. (The veterans included one in his seventy-third year, Charles Collier, the harpist. Collier was one of those Manchester players whom Richter took to Covent Garden in 1908 for his cycles of *The Ring* in English. He survived to see the war out and see the first years of peace in while still serving Barbirolli.) The Hallé's seventeen concerts had been attended by 20,000 Servicemen and women. Later on Barbirolli paraphrased Churchill: 'This', he said, 'was the Hallé's finest hour.'

CHAPTER SEVENTEEN

EXCURSIONS & ALARUM

So far as his crowding commitments with the Hallé would permit he began to pursue with alacrity and relish the career of international guest conductor or musical privateersman, a side of his work which, for all his rostrum rounds in the United States, had until now been impeded and latent. At the same time he was bent on winning international recognition and 'take-up' for what he took to calling 'this great orchestra of Manchester's and mine'. At this point it may be expedient to consider some of the sallies which, during their first ten years together, he made either with the Hallé or on his own to concert halls overseas.

Their first really resounding excursion was in May–June 1948. They should have gone to Prague for an international festival. In February, however, Czechoslovakia came under the Soviet harrow; which disposed of the international festival and much else. With only a few weeks' leeway, the British Council, as sponsors and financial guarantors of the project, deftly switched it to Austria, arranging five concerts in Salzburg, Innsbruck, Graz and Vienna, transport between these cities and feeding arrangements to be provided by the military authorities in the British, French and American military zones.

Towards the end of May the orchestra took off from Blackbushe airfield, Surrey, soon after dawn, in two Wayfarers, followed by a Dakota carrying the heavy instruments. As always, Barbirolli travelled with the party but up in front. He was in R.A.F. 'issue' flying boots. A hair-raising flight. They should have been in Salzburg by midday. Forced down at Frankfurt by rainstorm, hailstorm and electrical storm, they did not take off again until four in the afternoon, when conditions were little improved. The radio transmitter went dead. Getting no reply to the endless stream of messages they were sending out, the control staff at Salzburg had an ambulance standing by. Hearts were in mouths, but all ended well. In the way of hardship the tour almost matched up at times to what they had been through in the Low Countries. Although on some journeys they could have travelled by private car, Barbirolli and Evelyn preferred, except when obliged to go ahead for press conferences or broadcast talks, to put up with unsprung, straightbacked seats on bumpy buses and to take their turns in open-sided troop-carriers. Rain poured. The cold numbed. Coming to flimsy bridges in mountain country everybody dismounted so that the buses could creak safely across. There were breakdowns and fickle relief transport which, on one journey, went far astray, then turned up inopportunely and wouldn't be denied when the beef stew was *au point* and everybody just sitting down to it at a wayside inn. It was late afternoon. They hadn't eaten since breakfast. They got into the relief bus ravenously hungry for another corkscrew crawl by mountain roads. At last habitations; uniforms, swagger sticks, welcoming faces; an hotel where tables were spread and they had their first bite for thirteen hours.

The place was Graz. It is remembered for another reason. Here the second oboe went down with tonsillitis. Evelyn deputised for him, which was not altogether as simple a matter as it sounds. At Salzburg the previous night she had played in the Mozart oboe concerto wearing silver lamé, the only evening dress she had with her. The girls of the orchestra wore 'regulation' long black dresses. To appear among them as second oboe in silver lamé would never do. Evelyn did it nevertheless—but with a black 'top' borrowed from one of the other girls. Feeling something like guilt, she crept rather than walked on to the platform and off it.

Mischances and, up to a point, privations were accepted as jokes, as part of a privileged adventure. The adventure and the privilege consisted, quite simply, in working for Barbirolli. This feeling came out strongly in Vienna. Here he was already known. The year before, in aid of funds for the rebuilding of the State Opera House, now a blitz shell, he had conducted two performances of Verdi's *Requiem* at the Theater an der Wien, which retained the backdrop used at the first performance of *The Magic Flute*; and, among other things, Beethoven's

Symphony No. 7 from the rostrum of the Gesellschaft der Musik-
freunde where Brahms had once reigned. He was never slow to
remind listeners and readers* of august associations and fore-
runners. His players gloried in them, as they gloried in the
chock-a-block auditoriums and in the dozen recalls and ten-
minute ovation which ended his second appearance in the
Grosser Musikvereinsaal. There had been like jubilations all
along their itinerary, starting with Innsbruck where, since the
public had hoped for two concerts and there was time for only
one, he admitted them free to the afternoon rehearsal. Every
time he pulled up the orchestra to correct a fault or make good
phrasing better the audience clapped. Some orchestras might
have resented this as over-officious. The Hallé men and girls
found it amiable in an odd sort of way. Each concert ended with
the *Enigma* variations, which is why the British Council organisers in Vienna called the tour Operation Enigma. The only
unobvious piece he took out was Roussel's *Bacchus and Ariadne*
suite. For the rest there were the usual Barbirolli things, a few
of them less familiar to Austrian ears than they are by now to
the reader's eye: Mozart's Symphony No. 34, Beethoven's No. 7,
Dvořák's No. 4, *A Song of Summer*, Vaughan Williams's Tallis
Fantasia and the Purcell-Barbirolli suite.

In letters written after the visit and by word of mouth,
Barbirolli told of prestige and triumph won 'note by note'; of
Anglo-American relations cemented; of magnificent playing,
even of orchestral mastery; of the tonic effect their own achievements had had upon his players' corporate spirit.

*   *   *

Later that summer a tonic came *his* way.

He took his orchestra to the Edinburgh Festival, an institution
of which, although it was only a year old, the world was
already taking reverent and excited note. There he was heard
by Ernest Newman, than whom, it is safe to say, no other music
critic in this country ever wielded sceptre with such wit and
prestige for so long a time. Newman's first notice of the 1948
Festival said disparaging things about the French conductor

* Readers he addressed from time to time in *HALLÉ*, the orchestra's
publicity magazine; he wrote an article about his Vienna visit in the issue
for December–January 1946–47.

Charles Munch and the Concertgebouw Orchestra from Amsterdam ('playing of . . . flatfooted mediocrity') and about Malcolm Sargent's and the Huddersfield Choir's attempt at Fauré's Requiem ('a loud-mouthed travesty'). He went on:

[We] had full compensation in the concert of the Hallé Orchestra under John Barbirolli on Monday. I had not heard Mr. Barbirolli for, I think some twenty years. He has developed into a conductor of the international front rank and has made the present Hallé Orchestra an instrument of exceptional sensitivity and polish. The whole programme— an Elizabethan suite, the 'Haffner' Symphony, Villa-Lobos's brilliantly coloured *Descobrimento do Brasil*, Stravinsky's neatly artificial concerto in D for strings and the Sibelius No. 5— was beautifully played. Of the Sibelius I do not hope ever to hear a more splendidly convincing performance. It was an inexpressible pleasure to see for once a great work gradually taking shape in performance as it must have done in the mind of its creator, developing steadily, logically, from acorn to mighty oak and treated respectfully as something existing in its own right, instead of being a mere vehicle for 'conductor's effects' and Flash-Harry trash of that sort.*

Everybody in music and many outside it knew that the 'Flash Harry' gibe must be aimed at Sargent, for this was the nickname by which he was becoming known. It is true that Newman had considerable praise for Sargent's conducting of Bach's B minor Mass and *Belshazzar's Feast* (Walton), the latter especially. But his notice certainly denoted a shift of some importance in musical vogue. The accolade had been reserved for Barbirolli. It was almost a laying-on of hands.

* * *

More tonics were administered. In the spring of 1949 he took the Hallé to Holland for three concerts in The Hague and one in Leiden; the following August to Belgium to give a pair of festival concerts at Knocke-le-Zoute. In 1950 it was Portugal's turn; they treated Lisbon and Aveixa, Oporto and Braga to nine

* *The Sunday Times*, September 5th 1948.

programmes compounded of Haydn, French 'impressionists', Elgar, Delius, Vaughan Williams. . . . By this time their ten pounds a week was being bumped up to thirteen pounds 'by increments according to service'.

Orchestral managements all over the country were fishing and bidding in Manchester. Barbirolli's line was that generally speaking his players preferred to reject outside offers and stay on because they liked to work with him 'and be the Hallé Orchestra'. He acknowledged that in such matters loyalty could go too far. Certainly there were some who knew when they had had enough. By the time of the Portuguese tour only twenty players remained of the original (1943) rota. Fifty had gone to other orchestras and the London freelance pool for better money. Replacements were continuous. After ten years survivors from 1943 were down to seventeen. During one sequence of four years he was to lose principals from the 'cello and viola sections, a principal flute, a principal trombone, a principal trumpet and three principal horns. Thus he held sway over perpetual flux, over a perpetual game of outs-and-ins. Yet he was credited by some and often credited himself with making flux sound always the same. In short, however many old faces went, however many new ones came, Hallé timbres never changed a particle except, perhaps, when the orchestra was off form. So it was claimed, at any rate. Hallé sound, the same thing as Barbirolli sound, became a Manchester dogma.

His guest roamings during these years were to Cannes, Florence, Rome, Berlin. . . . In the Titania Palace twice and in a radio studio once, Easter 1950, he conducted the same programme, Brahms's Symphony No. 4 being its hub, with the Berlin Philharmonic Orchestra. Since the Philharmonic had no music library left because of the bombings, he took with him his own orchestral parts. However far he travelled, a Barbirolli night meant Barbirolli bowing and phrasing. This was not his first meeting with the Berliners. He had conducted them at one of the early Edinburgh Festivals. Idiosyncrasies which had been evident at rehearsals then were evident now. He seemed to be asking for the point of the bow on every other page. They found a nickname for him: Herr Spitze. Berlin was to become a regular jubilation for him and the orchestra

and for a newly won and steadfast following whose delight in
Barbirolli and his programmes was the more striking in that
nothing quite to match it happened, or, at any rate, recurred,
in other great German cities. Year after year, at concert after
concert, 'recalls' continued long after the Philharmonic
orchestra had packed up and left for home. There were memorable Elgar nights: among them a double performance of the
'cello concerto. His soloist was the principal 'cello of the
Philharmonic, Ottomar Borowitsky. Not only did he rehearse
Borowitsky; before the rehearsals and during them he coached
him in a part and in a score of which he had unrivalled nook-
and-cranny knowledge. As we have seen, he had played at
one of the London Symphony Orchestra's 'cello desks in the
concerto's ill-starred première in 1919. Also he had played the
solo part in Bournemouth for Sir Dan Godfrey and his orchestra
in their enterprising Winter Gardens series. This Bournemouth
occasion was the concerto's second public performance anywhere. Another score which he took to Berlin from Manchester
(he brought it from the Hallé Society's archives, in fact) was
more in the nature of a homing bird: that of Bruckner's
Symphony No. 7, inscribed to the Society by Hans Richter.
Richter had conducted the first Viennese performance of the
Seventh in 1886. Eighteen years later he introduced it to
Manchester where, two more generations on, Barbirolli became
its devoted legatee. Another Bruckner that he conducted in
Berlin was the No. 9. This he coupled on three adjacent
nights with Mozart's No. 40 in a programme repeated twice
to mark what would, had he survived, have been the ninetieth
birthday (September 17th 1966) of a great Berliner, Bruno
Walter. It was his custom to conduct the Berlin orchestra
every season in several pairs of concerts. His autograph was
plain on most of his programmes, especially the symphonies
he chose. In a single month (January 1966), for example, he
did the *Eroica*, Vaughan Williams's No. 5 and Mahler's No. 6.
To the end the players called him Herr Spitze. Other pseudo-
nyms were more cumbrous. 'Der italo-englischen Gentleman
des Taktstocks' was one that got into print.

Rome, too, saw much of him in the 1950s as during the
last two decades. With the Santa Cecilia and Rome Radio
orchestras he did Vaughan Williams's Symphony in E minor

(No. 6), a newish work (first performance, April 1948) which had an immense vogue during the first post-war decades, especially among those who, without encouragement from the composer (the reverse, in fact), swore that it 'portrayed' war's desolating of flesh and spirit. For a while after its première Vaughan Williams felt uncertain about the Scherzo movement. While pleasing everybody else it did not quite come off for him. At the Sheldonian Theatre, Oxford, he heard Barbirolli conduct the Sixth twice in one day, first at rehearsal, then in public. On his own initiative Barbirolli took the Scherzo at a slightly slower tempo than the one marked in the score. At once the Scherzo made full sense to the man who had written it. Vaughan Williams thanked him for his act of elucidation and altered his metronome mark accordingly: a considerable compliment, as Barbirolli rightly claimed.

Henceforth the Sixth figured much in his programmes. The farthest he took it was to Sydney, New South Wales. Again, 'took' is used in the wide literal sense; he had with him his annotated full score and the players' parts as bowed and phrased after his master copies. For reasons of a non-musical sort, his first Australian date (Sydney Town Hall, 29th December 1950) is talked about there to this day. From their first meeting he got on agreeably with the Sydney Symphony Orchestra and lost no time in praising it publicly. Touching upon some cricketing topicality, he said there might be holes in the wicket at Melbourne—'but there are no holes in the orchestra at Sydney!' It was skilled. It was fine. It was splendid. Two mornings later he conducted the final rehearsal. Vaughan Williams's No. 6 and Brahms's No. 2 were to be preceded or interleaved by the *Thieving Magpie* overture and *The Swan of Tuonela*. The rehearsal ended at 1 p.m. Barbirolli seemed content with the way things had gone.

The concert was due to begin at eight o'clock. At 7 p.m. one of the viola players looked in at the Town Hall; he had it in mind to practise a passage or two before the others turned up. There was no music to practise from. His music-stand was bare. So were all the other music-stands. In accordance with the usual practice on concert days, band parts for the entire programme had been left out in readiness for 'the night'. Some party—or

more probably, bearing in mind their weight, some parties—
had made off with them. The violist gave the alarm. Janitors,
clerks, policemen, Town Hall officials, broadcasting officials
began a cranny-by-cranny search, leaving hardly a carpet
unturned. The search was in full swing when the public began
to trickle in. It was still on at 8 p.m. Two thousand bewildered
ticket-holders were in their seats by this time. They saw men
burrowing under the rostrum and clambering about the organ-
loft. Reporters were asking questions backstage.

'Can you suggest any motive for the theft, Sir John?'

'I'm at a loss.'

'Have you any enemies here?'

'Not that I know of. Certainly not in this fine orchestra.'

By 8.20 the audience were beginning to stir discontentedly.
A spokesman of the Australian Broadcasting Commission, who
were promoting Barbirolli's visit, came on and explained what
had happened. A search was being made for duplicate music,
he said. By this time Barbirolli and his old Queen's Hall colleague Eugene Goossens, who was the Sydney orchestra's
resident conductor, accompanied by three orchestral players
and an orchestral librarian, were driving to the Sydney Conservatorium. The place was locked up and in darkness.
Goossens, the director of the Conservatorium, had a key to the
back door. The back door was behind locked gates. Another of
the party, who happened to be a 'cellist and therefore one of
Barbirolli's professional blood brothers, took Goossens's key,
climbed the gates, entered through the back door and, opening
the front one from inside, let in the rest. In the Conservatorium
library the party turned up and checked band parts of the
Brahms No. 2. So far as the rest of the prearranged programme
was concerned they drew a blank. The *Mastersingers* and *Oberon*
overtures were chosen as substitute pieces. Barbirolli had not
rehearsed these in Sydney but was assured that the players
knew them backwards way as well as the right way round.

At 8.50 p.m. the A.B.C. official appeared on the platform
again and announced that there would be a concert after all.
At one minute to nine Barbirolli appeared and got the hero's
welcome which is invariably given, the world over, to conductors who, through no fault of their own, have almost been
made to look silly. No trace of jumpiness now. Composed of

manner, he gave a little speech in his best English drawl. He did not think the night's sensation could be blamed on the Thieving Magpie: 'If I'm wrong about that we might say, or Churchill might say, "Some magpie! Some thief!" ' Then he turned his attention to Weber.

A few minutes after the music began a telephone sounded in the Town Hall superintendent's office. A voice at the other end of the line asked to speak with Barbirolli. When asked who he was and what his business, the caller hung up. Twenty minutes later the same voice came back to ask whether the concert was on and if so what music was being played. He was told, misleadingly, that the orchestra was playing the programme as advertised. He made sounds of consternation and hung up again. Soon after 11 p.m. a third anonymous call was received by a Sydney newspaper. Again a male voice. Theme: the missing music. It would be found, if anybody cared to look, in the Health Department office adjoining the auditorium. He had put it there himself, working single-handed while three pals kept watch at the doors. Why had he done it? Well, he admired Barbirolli and wanted him to have something to remember Sydney by. . . .

The music was found where he said it would be found. It had been stacked on top of a cleaner's cupboard. None of the anonymous calls could be traced. Nobody was brought to book.

The audience that night numbered 2,200. Five of them did not wish to hear the changed programme and got their money back. The rest seemed pleased enough. Relief that fiasco had been avoided made the performances sound better, perhaps, than they were. Of the unrehearsed *Mastersingers* overture Barbirolli said it could not have gone better if they had been rehearsing it together for five years. Absolutely first-rate, he insisted. They had played superbly. They had played like angels.

From the start it had been arranged that there should be two concerts at the Town Hall, with the same programme on consecutive nights. So Sydney heard Vaughan Williams's Sixth after all. He took it to other Australian cities. Everywhere it was listened to attentively. 'They loved it', he said on returning to England. 'Australia is still a new country. It has not had time to develop the usual prejudices against new music.'

He was now Sir John. He had been knighted in the Birthday Honours of June 1948. The printed note of thanks and apology which he sent to congratulators whom he could not reply to personally mentioned that he was immersed in a Scottish tour with the Hallé and that this was to be followed at once by festivals at Cheltenham and Harrogate—'a particularly intensive period of concerts, rehearsal and travelling'. One got the impression of uncommon bustle over assignments of no great consequence.

Illustrious events followed close upon, however. Immediately before leaving for Australia, in mid-December 1950, he received the gold medal of the Royal Philharmonic Society. Thus he joined an august company, living or dead, of composers, executants and conductors: Brahms, Delius, Elgar, Rachmaninov, Sibelius, Richard Strauss, Walton; Paderewski, Kreisler, Cortot, Casals; Von Bülow, Henry Wood, Beecham, Harty, Weingartner, Bruno Walter, Toscanini. The medal was handed to him by another holder of it, Vaughan Williams, during the interval of a R.P.S. concert which Queen Elizabeth, the present Queen Mother, attended. That night the Royal Albert Hall was crowded as if for a Saturday night 'Prom'. Vaughan Williams's oration had rung with cordiality. He said in part:

An ancient prophet once told us of a valley of dry bones. These dry bones at a magic touch sprang to life and rose up and became an exceedingly great army. Tonight we are here to do honour to one who can take the dry bones of crotchets and quavers and breathe into them the breath of life. Now, what is the secret of Barbirolli's power? Wagner used to say it was the business of the conductor to find out where the melody lay, and I think part of Sir John's magic lies in the fact that he can always spot the melody—however unpromising sometimes. (Laughter*) Barbirolli, like another great conductor, started life as a violoncellist—playing what is to my mind the most melodic of all instruments—and I believe that, like his great colleague, his motto will always be *Cantare, cantare*.

Now, every artist has his own special instrument. The

---

* People laughed because Barbirolli had just conducted one of Vaughan Williams's symphonies (the Sixth, of course), and the composer's point about melody was interpreted as a dig at his own music.

conductor plays on the orchestra, and I know that Sir John
would be the first to admit that without this magnificent
instrument to play on much of his magic would be powerless.
And I know that the Hallé Orchestra for their part realise
that, proven metal though they all are, they would not be
able to ring true unless fashioned and moulded by their
conductor. So together they form a great and mighty army,
and together they march to victory. . . .

Among the thousands who heard this were Nonna and the
entire Barbirolli clan, a total of twelve according to one count,
in-laws and young included. After the concert they all went
back to Streatham, John and Evelyn with them, for supper at
Nonna's flat. One of the family had made a cake decorated with
the R.P.S. medal, a conductor's baton and the opening bars of
a Beethoven sonata in sugar icing. Barbirolli checked the Beethoven quotation and said the cake-maker had got it right.

There would not be many more R.P.S. nights at the Albert
Hall. On the South Bank of the Thames, near Waterloo Station,
a new auditorium was going up, the Royal Festival Hall, which
was expected to take much business away from the old one.
When the Festival Hall was finished Barbirolli took one look and
grimaced. Many a musician with tastes for the sister arts as well
as his own found in the hall's exterior the worst of every world.
It was utilitarian and pretentious, they said; humdrum yet
flashy. Barbirolli was with them entirely. At home little or
nothing was heard of his disapproval. It was not until his second
Australian tour (1955) that he touched off controversy on the
subject. In Sydney reporters asked him what sort of design he
would favour for the opera house which the State Cabinet of
New South Wales had decided to build at Benelong Point on the
Sydney waterfront. 'Personally,' he replied, 'I hope it will be
classical in design. A church should look like a church. An opera
house should look like an opera house. Nothing could be worse
than to have it look like the Festival Hall in London—a black
spot on the landscape if ever there was one.'
For days the aesthetes of Sydney boiled over, for and against,
into newspaper letters columns. There were musicians who said
how right it was that the outward appearance of an opera house
should bear some relation to what went on inside. A citizen just

back from the South Bank likened the Festival Hall to a cross between a hangar and an iron foundry. Much of a solemn sort was heard from 'progressives', several of them architects, about new materials, new knowledge and new needs. Why borrow porticos and pillars from the past? It was as silly to say an opera house should look like an opera house as it would be to say a knight should look like a knight. 'Who', asked a 'Sydney Design Group', 'could imagine Sir John conducting in gleaming armour? Possibly the thing could be managed, but surely the encumbrances would cramp his style?' In a last word Barbirolli hoped he might see the plans for the opera house when they were ready. At his most pessimistic he could not have foreseen what ultimately went up: less an opera-house, so far as could be judged from its outside, than a mammoth yacht, prefabricated sails all set.*

However, no conductor in his right mind was ever known to be put off either an opera house or an auditorium by the cut of its façades. On technical test the acoustics of the Festival Hall seemed reasonably good. When asked to conduct two of the inaugural concerts he accepted with alacrity. Going in with his orchestra for rehearsal on a Friday morning in May (1951), he sang from the rostrum a few bars of Italian opera to the empty seating and said cryptically that the resonance surprised him; which was taken as a compliment. As the rehearsal went on he paused now and then, handed the baton to his leader and moved from point to point in the stalls and elsewhere to judge how the famous Hallé timbres were coming over. That night he got many of his audience by the throat with an implacable account of Vaughan Williams's austere Symphony in F minor (No. 4: 1935) which, according to the fanciful, depicted the 'Fascist decade' and its tensions. The savagery of the piece was artfully set off by a Rossini overture, the intermezzo from Delius's *Fennimore and Gerda* and the Mozart Fantasia and Fugue for string orchestra. In good time next morning the Hallé Choir, who had been engaged for his second concert, set off for the South Bank from London Road Station. Their special train had room for a hundred or two non-singing 'supporters' as well.

* Or, in various aspects, 'a very large artichoke [or] the likeness of a vast dish of mussels [or] a stack of mitres discarded by half-a-dozen immense Australian bishops.'—James Cameron, *The Sunday Australian*, Feb. 28, 1971.

The women singers were to wear new concert dresses in maroon and cream. It was going to be a great day in more ways than one. Business in hand: the Verdi *Requiem*. The performance is remembered outstandingly for the thunderclap and brimstone of the 'Dies irae'. For this Barbirolli had brought in an outsize bass drum, whose boom had singular fulness and warmth. His first Festival Hall ovations were heady. They were followed by something headier still.

That week-end the semi-mythical Leopold Stokowski was in London, billed for *l'Après-midi*, Prokoviev's *Scythian* suite, a three-year-old symphony by an American and his own infallible transcription of Bach's C minor passacaglia and fugue. His Friday night was free. He spent it at Barbirolli's concert. Soon afterwards Barbirolli received this from him:

> I feel I must thank you for the great pleasure I had in listening to your superb concert recently in the Royal Festival Hall. I was thrilled by the power of the performance and delighted with its finesse. You and your associates in the orchestra have developed one of the rare, truly great orchestras of the world. It was such a pleasure to see how you differentiated between the styles of Rossini, Delius, Vaughan Williams and Mozart.... Please do me the favour of thanking everyone in the orchestra for their beautiful playing. Manchester is fortunate to have such a conductor and such an Orchestra.

He had entered his fifties. The preternatural boyishness was almost gone. At last he looked grown up. His persona had laurels and a niche. He was much courted, often deferred to. In the autumn of 1950 it had been officially put out that Karl Rankl, the first musical director of the State-subventioned Covent Garden Opera Company (founded in 1947) would be leaving in the summer of 1951 and that Barbirolli was to conduct as a guest during the following season. It would be the first the Royal Opera had seen of Barbirolli since 1937. It was a very different Royal Opera now. No more the brief glitter of international seasons. A resident company mostly of British artists— but laced from time to time with hypnotic names and some-times with hypnotic talents from afar—sang opera most of the year round except when their co-tenants, the Sadler's Wells

(later Royal) Ballet were dancing there. As musical ruler of the
new Covent Garden he would have been given scope and play
for a bent and abilities which, to the end, never had full exercise.
Inevitably, it was promptly and widely inferred that he had been
invited not merely to 'guest' but also to step into Rankl's shoes.
He let it be known that, while he had entered into arrangements
with the management of the Royal Opera to appear regularly
as their guest—'My conducting dates for future seasons are
now being negotiated; or had one better say discussed?'—his
commitments to the Hallé had first claim upon him still. 'I
have no plans', he added, 'for coming back permanently to
London.'

To begin with it looked, nevertheless, as though he—or the
Covent Garden board—might have some such thought in mind.
He conducted during three seasons. During the first of these,
1952–53, the company put on 147 performances. Of these
Barbirolli took the lion's share, conducting fifty of them. There
were four other conductors. Their shares were: John Pritchard
32, Reginald Gooddall 26, Peter Gellhorn 26, Erich Kleiber 13.
Barbirolli may not have been musical director but, in the sense
that he was the one who did the most work, he was certainly
conductor-in-chief. His first season brought him seventeen *Aidas*,
thirteen *Bohèmes*, eleven *Tristans*, seven *Turandots* and two
Orpheuses. (About the Orpheuses more in a later chapter. They
are a memorial to something in his life which transcended
music.) To the old rostrum he brought those sotto-voces, niceties and detonations of orchestral timbre which he had been
cultivating from his earliest days, whether in the concert hall
or the opera house. As exhibited in *Tristan* these were not to all
tastes. Even his 'Italians' came in for hard scrutiny.

A new critical voice was at large in the land. *Opera*, a magazine founded and edited (until 1953) by Lord Harewood,
cousin to the Queen, who, with admired aplomb, contrived to
be an active director of the Royal Opera at the same time, was
much attended to in Floral Street and, as time went on, further
afield. On his *Bohème* first night Barbirolli, according to wont,
gave a little speech before the last act. The performance up to
that point, he said, had been exquisite. (The *Opera* writer said
that in fact it had not been very good.) He asked the audience
not to spoil it, if they had any respect and affection for him, by

applauding before the orchestra had done playing. 'An unfortunately phrased' speech, commented the *Opera* writer, not without reason. About the audience's respect and affection there could be no doubt. As had happened in so many theatres during the Covent Garden touring days, they hugged and bussed Barbirolli, figuratively speaking. Even so a dissentient voice was literally heard now and then.

Some of his *Aidas* fell, like his last previous assignments there, during another Coronation season, that of Queen Elizabeth II. In this production he had three leading sopranos in turn, one of them Maria Callas, whose Norma had recently swept the town off its feet. There was a Thursday night in June when she acted, enounced and, as to much of the rôle, sang Aida with an eloquence and passion which, in the opinion of some discerners, failed to excuse a shrill and uncertain top register. Yet she and others on the stage were singers of such experience that Barbirolli might have been expected—or so the *Opera* critic argued— to give them their heads on tempo at certain points; instead of which 'he was out of time with them at the end of almost every cadence and often hurried on when they were still finishing a phrase'. It was a gala night. At the close: cheers and jubilant stampings of feet for everybody. In the half-second lull before the ovation for Barbirolli set in, however, a voice up in the amphitheatre got in with: 'It isn't very good, is it?' Thus ended an exciting, mixed sort of Thursday.

Friday brought another 'Coronation' occasion. Barbirolli was one of four knights—the others being Beecham (who was a baronet into the bargain), Boult and Sargent—who had been engaged to conduct between them eight celebratory concerts. His orchestra was the London Symphony, the 'meat' of his first programme—apart from Brahms's second piano concerto, with Clifford Curzon—being Vaughan Williams's Symphony No. 5 which, fancied *The Times*, he seemed to 'cherish' less than usual because just before starting upon it he had been disturbed by an influx of latecomers. His second concert, which came two days later, included a stunning *Fantastic* Symphony and a Haydn No. 88 in which 'the really soft string *pianissimi* proved particularly thrilling, perhaps because a true whisper is rarely and with difficulty to be obtained in [the Royal Festival Hall]'.

That summer brought a further 'royal' occasion. The Queen
was soon to proclaim and set up the short-lived Federation of
Southern Rhodesia, Northern Rhodesia and Nyasaland. The
wind of change was not yet evident, the Unilateral Declaration
of Independence twelve years away. In Southern Rhodesia,
destined to become an independent republic, a Cecil Rhodes
centenary festival was in the making with imported culture in
prospect: a Shakespearean troupe, ballet (Sadler's Wells), opera
(the Covent Garden company) and a symphony orchestra.
Which symphony orchestra? For a little while there was some
uncertainty. Then the titillating news broke in Manchester.
The Hallé had been picked.

Once more the orchestra took off from Blackbushe, nearly
a hundred players and their instruments in a York and a
Hermes, on a round trip of 13,000 miles. Watching their
departure on television, an interested party, the Queen Mother,
remarked how happy everybody looked. She and Princess
Margaret were to follow soon after to take part in official ceremonies and attend a Hallé-Barbirolli gala concert. Before the
gala night there were thirteen concerts, with changes rung on
five programmes. Symphonies were the backbone, one of them
a novelty, Vaughan Williams's No. 8 (the *Antarctica*), the rest
'old inevitables': Brahms's No. 2, Sibelius's No. 2, Haydn's No.
88, the *Fantastic*. . . . Also there were concertos: one of the
Beethovens for piano, a Mozart for violin and the Mozart for
oboe (with Evelyn as soloist); and a few inevitables from other
categories: the *Enigma*, *Till Eulenspiegel*, one of the *Daphnis and
Chloë* suites and the *Thieving Magpie* overture. . . .

The place where these things were heard and other culture
happened was built of corrugated iron, screened and camou-
flaged, and called The Theatre Royal. There were seats for
three thousand (although two hundred more were squeezed in
for the gala concert); and the acoustic was generally held to be
good, which was more than might have been expected, though
not proof against intrusive noise. A railway line ran close by
with ungated level crossing where, at seven past nine each night,
a train halted and sounded its whistle for a minute according to
regulations. During a performance of the *Enigma* variations the
whistle is said to have sounded all too audibly during Variation
XIII, with its quotation on the clarinet from Mendelssohn's

Calm Sea and a Prosperous Voyage overture. Afterwards one of the orchestra's wags said to Barbirolli, 'It must have been the boat train, sir.' The days were sweltering, the nights very cold. Many who came unprepared would have been glad of rugs and hot water bottles. At the end of the *Antarctica* symphony, for which he wore his greatcoat and many of his players pyjamas under their dress suits, Barbirolli turned to Laurance Turner and, in a double allusion that brought in the icebound summit of Everest, newly scaled by Colonel Hunt's expedition, said, 'I don't know whether you reached the top first or I did.'

When the festival was over Barbirolli claimed that on average every member of the (minority) White population of Bulawayo had attended one concert and that other Europeans had travelled thousands of miles to hear 'my great orchestra'. It could not be claimed that the theatre was full every night, however; round figures suggest that the concerts as a whole played to two-thirds capacity or a little less. Each night a block of seats was set apart for Africans. In some of the printed comment that followed a certain selectiveness is to be traced. The Africans, as many as a hundred at a time, would sit spellbound and unstirring through the music, too shy or too overwhelmed to clap and stamp as the Whites were doing so frantically all around them. One of them was quoted as typical of the rest: 'Sir, we didn't know there was anything so beautiful in the world.'* Some of the things attributed to Whites, many of them pioneer settlers ripely traditional in outlook, were not as poetic or apropos. For example: 'What are those large fiddles they're playing upside-down?' 'Do they *really* need a conductor?' And: 'You [the orchestra at large] must come out to the game reserve. Be sure to bring your instruments with you.'

Like the Africans, Barbirolli was spellbound when he had time to be. He revelled in everything that happened to and around him: in the cricket match he umpired on the Bulawayo Wanderers' ground; in the *braavleis* which followed the cricket— 'succulent meats cooked in deep embers, probably the most primitive form of cooking—and still the best, I would say'; in

---

* This and the three remarks that follow were quoted from a Rhodesian newspaper or directly reported by one who was present at the concerts, Sir Geoffrey Haworth, Bart., a future chairman of the Hallé Concerts Society, in *HALLÉ* (magazine), September 1953.

the convoy of private cars, driven by members of the Bulawayo
municipal orchestra which took them out to Cecil Rhodes's
tomb in the Matopo Hills; in being called upon to lay the
foundation stone for extensions to the Rhodesian Academy of
Music; and, not least, in a list of howlers committed (or invented)
by music students who either couldn't or pretended they couldn't
get his name right—Sir John Bradman (after the noted
Australian cricketer), Sir John Broccoli, Sir John Bismarck,
Sir John Barrymore, Sir Barber Olley. When the Theatre Royal
turned itself from a concert hall into an opera house he went
back and conducted Covent Garden casts in *La Bohème* and
Aida. After one of these performances he and Evelyn took David
Webster (now Sir David), administrator of the Royal Opera,
back to their hotel for dinner. Barbirolli had done the cooking
himself, of course. Almost impossible to get a meal served in
Bulawayo after eight. Partly for this reason and partly to
indulge his hobby, he had had a small refrigerator and a cooker
put in their suite.

For him, unashamedly, the gala night crowned all other
revels and solemnities. 'An enormous audience!' he exulted. Not
another soul could have got a toe into the theatre. And 'every
body, please note, in evening dress'. Thus he addressed *HALLÉ*
(magazine) readers. The royal box blazed with orders and flowers.
Altogether, he added, the scene suggested not a relatively newborn city but an occasion of State in some great and ancient
capital. That night, conducting among other matters, his
Elizabethan Suite, he used the same baton with which, ten
years earlier to the day, he had conducted his first concert with
the reconstituted Hallé in Bradford. He had not known the
baton was still about. Without saying a word to anybody, his
devoted librarian 'Tommy' Cheetham had put it by for a
suitable anniversary occasion. Barbirolli mentioned this circumstance when, at the interval, he and Evelyn were presented
to the Queen Mother and Princes Margaret, both of whom he
found 'extremely sensitive, knowledgeable and enthusiastic
listeners'. The Queen Mother wished him another happy ten
years with the Hallé.

When speaking of his 'active career' at that time, he did not,
as we know, give himself longer than that. From the late 1940s
onward he had a chequered health record. Ailments were for

Photo: Erich Auerbach

Sir John rehearsing with the Dowager Lady Fermoy (piano),
who often partnered him and oboist Evelyn Rothwell (Lady
Barbirolli) in chamber music.

Photo: E.M.I

During 1963-64 season Sir John conducted the Berlin Philharmonic Orchestra publicly and (as seen here) at recording sessions
in Mahler's Ninth Symphony.

ever laying him low. Invariably he bounced back more quickly than seemed natural. Why could he not, or why would he not, sleep more? Was he not burning himself out? Such questions nagged those who knew him best and cared for him most. They went unanswered. At Bulawayo he had conducted Denis Matthews in Beethoven's fourth piano concerto. The two of them were staying in the same hotel. On the last day Matthews chanced to be up and about at five in the morning. There was a light in Barbirolli's room. He entered. Barbirolli was walking back and forth in his dressing gown, 'talking, talking'. Kenneth Crickmore, who had succeeded Bean (now in charge of the Royal Festival Hall) as manager of the Hallé, was asprawl in an armchair in evening dress, fast asleep. At 4 a.m. the first of two home-bound aeroplanes had taken off with Hallé players. He had been at the airport to see them off. Ever since the previous night's concert ended he had been awake and bright and talkative.

How did he do it? 'Simple. Unlike other people who sleep very little, I never worry about it. I never think of the word *insomnia*.'

L

CHAPTER EIGHTEEN

KATIE & UNCLE RALPH

T HESE years brought a friendship that was brief and deep
and indelible.

Kathleen Ferrier's voice had beauty of a kind that seized
impartially the unschooled multitude and musicians of fastidious ear. A single phrase of hers—a single note, even—could
carry more meaning than the gamut and entire musical bag-
gage of many a voice that enjoyed noisier and longer fame. As
used here, *meaning* denotes more than beauty of the sensuous
order. It covers also an innate musicianship that leapt and
ripened on little or no academic training; and, more remarkably, emotional undertones which, conveying (as it seemed) a
sort of goodness from outside and beyond the singer, must be
described as ethical; there is no other word that fits. In a
movingly percipient memoir* which came out after her death
Barbirolli made the point that, having been out of the country
since 1936, he learned of her rise belatedly. This is innocently
misleading. As late as 1943, the year of his return, there was
little or nothing to learn about. 'In 1943', wrote the accompanist Gerald Moore, one of his five fellow memorialists,
'[Kathleen Ferrier] was unknown.' Moore does not mean
to be taken literally, of course. For eighteen months she had
been in much demand on recital platforms in the provinces
and was beginning to be heard in standard oratorios. That she
should not, at this stage, have come to the ears of so prepos-
terously busy a man as Barbirolli was in the natural order of
things.

* One of the six tributes by eminent musicians which comprise *Kathleen
Ferrier 1912–1953: A Memoir*, edited by Neville Cardus (Hamish Hamilton,
1954). In this account of her friendship with the Barbirollis *The Life of
Kathleen Ferrier* by her sister Winifred Ferrier (Hamish Hamilton, 1955)
has been helpful also.

Twice she sang under his nose, as it were, without his being any the wiser. In 1945 and 1946 she was Malcolm Sargent's contralto in vast *Messiahs* at Belle Vue with a choir drawn from three Northern cities. After the second of these performances she stayed on in Manchester for a Houldsworth Hall recital that made Granville Hill clasp ecstatic hands. Never had he heard a contralto voice of such beautiful quality; as an artist Miss Ferrier had few rivals anywhere in the concert world. Hill was only a critic, however. It was for others to open the vital doors. On the strength of a *Messiah* they chanced to hear her take part in towards the end of the war, she was taken up by Benjamin Britten and Peter Pears, who were carried away by 'the nobility and beauty of her presence' as well as by the warmth and deep range of her voice.'* Thus she was chosen to sing Lucretia in Britten's new opera *The Rape of Lucretia* at the first post-war Glyndebourne Festival. At Glyndebourne she sang also the lead in Gluck's *Orfeo ed Euridice*—for which she had coaching in Italian from Gibilaro, Barbirolli's brother-in-law—and, at the first Edinburgh Festival (1947), on Barbirolli's old Usher Hall platform, in Mahler's *Das Lied von der Erde* with the Vienna Philharmonic Orchestra under the revered Bruno Walter. All this happened in a little over twelve months. A voice which not long before had scurried endlessly from platform to platform on the C.E.M.A. and E.N.S.A. circuits was now pinnacled before the world.

Like most committed and impassioned artists, Barbirolli paid little attention to what the world was thinking. In some situations a preferred criterion for him was what people thought with whom he worked from day to day and upon whose professional judgment he knew he could rely. It chanced that certain of his players had accompanied Kathleen Ferrier in some radio programme of no great moment. Her voice had bowled them over; they were full of it. Knowing that *The Dream of Gerontius* was coming up at Belle Vue in March 1948, they pressed him to give her the Angel music. He provisionally agreed. But first, an assay. At Sheffield, while *Gerontius* was preparing, he had her sing another Elgar work, the song cycle known as *Sea Pictures*. It was not a happy occasion. At rehearsal the acoustics of the City Hall so worked on his nerves that, when

* Benjamin Britten in the Kathleen Ferrier *Memoir* (ibid.).

things went technically awry, he threw the score at some mis-
creant's head and narrowly missed Kathleen's. Perhaps because
of this incident but more probably because the *Sea Pictures* did
not mean much to her, she sang them with nothing more than
a chill competence. Barbirolli was dashed, even distressed.
Gerontius put things right, however. The warmth and breadth
and stately articulation of this her first Angel under his baton
gave him at last a rounded insight into her art as it then stood—
and as he imagined it might become.

A superb Angel, yes. He felt that she could sing an even
better. What she needed to bring out the finest in her, he
reasoned, was an exercise in some markedly different aesthetic
and idiom. He begged her to prepare for him the *Poème de l'amour
et de la mer* of Chausson: music of the 1880s with tinctures from
d'Indy, Franck and *Tristan* to words (by Bouchor) which,
lamenting the poet's lost mistress, beseech the sky and winds,
the brooks and little green paths to bring her back. For
Barbirolli the *Poème* was 'one of those minor masterpieces we
never hear. Chausson is a lovely artist. I say *artist* advisedly.
There's an analogy here. Consider these Impressionist painters
whose works are now fetching such fantastic sums. Even the
minor Impressionists are doing that. Now, the minor French
and Belgian composers are as much painters of their epoch as
the minor Impressionists were. Chausson is in this class. If
instead of putting his art on music paper he had put it on
canvas, he would be sought after at enormous prices.' At first
she did not see eye to eye with him on this. For *Orfeo* she had
been coached in Italian, for Mahler's *Das Lied* and other matters
in German. Now she was asked to take on French: on the whole
a stiffer phonetical challenge. Friends talked her into it.
Telegraphing acceptance while on a concert tour of the United
States, she bade her agent tell Barbirolli he'd have to play
loudly 'to cover up my Lancashire accent.'

Gradually she was won over by the task and, up to a point
by the work. She first sang it for him in Manchester on two
successive nights in February 1951. Later performances of the
Poème were to have greater fluency and feeling. Her French
would never be as good as her German. Yet already she had got
pretty well to the core of Chausson's and Bouchor's nostalgia.
'Le temps des lilas et des roses ne reviendra plus': this and the

rest were a very different world from her predestined one—
that of 'He was despised', 'Der Tod und das Mädchen', the
Four Serious Songs of Brahms, Bach's B minor Mass and so on.
To Barbirolli's way of thinking the venture had come off. He
was confident that Katie's general style and artistry would be
the suppler for it. (To him and to Evelyn from now on she was
always 'Katie' in token of a new-found friendship based not on
musical affinity alone but on a whole assortment of likenesses
and common likings.)

After Chausson, Gluck. Three concert performances were
imminent of *Orfeo ed Euridice* by the Hallé and other Northern
societies. Katie was to be his Orfeo at all three. He looked forward to this enterprise with passionate eagerness. On the
Chausson nights there had been something leonine about his
conducting. Both nights ended with a virtuoso account of
Schubert's 'Great' C major. Of the finale he made a stupendous
thing. That was generally agreed. He took people's breath away
and sent them home exalted and bemused. He had no business
to be on the rostrum at all. Ten days earlier he had been met in
at London Airport by Nonna, the Gibilaros and others of the
'clan' after a four-days flight from Australia. Since leaving
England two months earlier he had lost over two stone in weight.
He looked ill and was in pain. Enteritis, said the doctors. He
talked gaily and largely, leaning on a walking stick which had
belonged to Tsar Nicholas II of Russia. 'Where did you get
that?' asked Nonna. From an admirer in Adelaide, it seemed.
There was the usual family party that night at Streatham.
He was down for a Hallé rehearsal the following afternoon,
then concerts in Wolverhampton and Bradford, all within
five days. He rubbed his hands prospectively at these delights.
They were not to be. He got through the rehearsal, then
collapsed.

The doctors diagnosed an appendix condition as well as
enteritis. They put him to bed. Obviously, there would have to
be an operation. His mind was set none the less on *Orfeo*, billed
for Belle Vue, Hanley and Sheffield on March 4th, 7th and 10th
respectively, the last of these dates being three weeks ahead.
Could the doctors perhaps put the operation off for three weeks
and a bit? Could they not give him some interim treatment to
'keep him going'? The doctors thought it could be done. He

had gone to bed on a Monday. He stayed there for four days. On
Sunday the doctors put out a bulletin that he was over his
enteritis. Simultaneously he reappeared at Belle Vue, clamor-
ously received by a great audience who clearly loved Barbirolli
the man as much as they thrilled to Barbirolli the conductor.
There had been no time to rehearse the Mozart C minor
Fugue. He gave them *Eine kleine Natchtmusik* instead; also
Beethoven's Symphony No. 1 and a *Rosenkavalier* suite.

Everything went trimly, touched now with glucose, now with
pepper. Everybody had read about his illness. Everybody but
Evelyn, his surgeon and the general manager of the orchestra,
the only ones in the know, concluded that he was himself again.
They knew nothing of the twinges or of the surgeon friend who
examined him backstage before every rehearsal or performance
and during the intervals. The date of the operation had been
fixed; he was to go into the private patients' block of Manchester
Royal Infirmary two days after the last of his three *Orfeos*. A
complex production to prepare and travel. It kept him so busy
and happy that he forgot his appendix for hours on end. In
three cities *Orfeo* was sung by the same three principals, Katie
being chief among them—and by three different amateur
choirs. The business of having their singers coached in Italian
gave chorus masters and others much to sweat over and strive
for. The Orfeo of Katie was superb: all anguish and glory. Were
her Italian vowels all they might have been? Perhaps not. Did
Barbirolli try to unload pulsing Verdian passion on to the classical line of 'Che farò senza Euridice?' ? That, too, was imputed.
And could it be honestly said that Manchester was positively
panting for mythology laced copiously with recitatives in a foreign tongue, the whole intended not for the concert platform
but for stage production? The turn-up at Belle Vue was considerably less than for an average Hallé concert. There were
over 3,000 empty seats. From this time onward Barbirolli
yearned to conduct Katie's Orfeo where it belonged, in the
theatre. Her figure and the way she carried it, her tranquil and
finely moulded features, the serenity and the tensions of her
gaze: all cried out for the proscenium arch and everything that
goes with it.

On the day of the third *Orfeo*, a Saturday, he told her what
he had been concealing, namely, that on Monday he would be

going into hospital. He was cheerful and induced cheerfulness in others. With Evelyn and Katie and a few others of the *Orfeo* production or the Hallé organisation, he supped that night at a Sheffield hotel before motoring back to Manchester. It was one of the liveliest and happiest parties he ever knew. He had no intention of letting himself be operated on without one more concert. On the Sunday afternoon he was at Belle Vue again, coping urbanely and impeccably with the Brahms violin concerto and the César Franck symphony. His appendix was taken out two days later.

They warned him he must not do any conducting for at least six weeks. The main season was almost over. His remaining concerts were taken over by assistants or guests. He began score reading, as someone put it, 'almost before he was out of the anaesthetic'. His special study, long looked forward to, was *Messiah*. His collation of early autograph scores left him with a passion, not shared by all his colleagues, for Handel's original orchestration, or much of it. He found with delight that in the opening section of the chorus 'Glory to God' Handel had marked his trumpets parts 'Da lontano ed un poco piano' ('Rather soft and as from the distance'), the kind of direction one sees in opera scores or those of neo-Romantic symphonies. No other researcher seemed to have noticed this instruction; at all events, said Barbirolli, it did not appear in any printed edition that came his way. Elsewhere he restored what he held to be the original sub-divisions of string parts, making the main mass of players act as foil here and there to smaller groups (e.g., solo quartet and quintet) in accordance with concertino-and-ripieno tradition. Out went Mozart's additional woodwind parts to 'The people that walked in darkness.' Handel's bare string octaves, said Barbirolli, were more than enough, a stroke of high genius. 'To play "The people that walked" in any but its original form', he used to say, 'is a crime and should be made indictable.'

That same spring Katie, too, went to hospital. Because of nagging discomfort she had consulted a specialist. He diagnosed a growth in the breast which was to be removed without delay. Her operation followed Barbirolli's by less than a month. Soon she would be thirty-nine years old. She had been a professional singer for less than a decade; one of the world's elect for a little over five years. There were barely two more years to go. She came through the operation and convalesced with no shadow visible upon her. There may have been forebodings. If so, she kept them locked within and faced the world, as many remember from those times, with humour and composure. By summer she was travelling and singing and eating well and laughing irrepressibly. Her voice and art had if anything gained in span and beauty. They were to lose no particle of either until muted for ever.

For Barbirolli she sang the Chausson *Poème* at the Edinburgh Festival. A month or two later she was with him in Manchester at the ceremonial opening of the restored Free Trade Hall. The Queen was there; the Hallé brass went up to the roof and from its four corners sounded a magnified version of the *Fidelio* fanfare; after which and other matters Katie rose at the climax of the first *Pomp and Circumstance* March to sing—and lead the audience in singing—'Land of hope and glory' with a fervour and resolution that had everybody in patriotic goose pimples and many, Barbirolli included, in tears. During the pitiful residue of her life she sang for him in additional *Gerontiuses*, in *Messiahs*, in Mahler's *Kindertotenlieder* as well as *Das Lied*, indeed in almost all the big-scale works that she put most into and which brought the most out of her. There wasn't time for a great deal else, apart from the fun and affection of what quickly became in effect a family bond.

One of several things they had in common was a homeliness which, while deferring to solemnity and ceremonial in their right places, made mock of those who overdid such things: he with a dry sub-Cockney wit of Edwardian vintage, she with the raillery and realism proper to the North West, especially that stratum of the North West which, although a cut 'above' full-time dialect speech, made use of it at discretion to droll or tart or affable purpose. There was much of her parents in her. Her father had been a school-teacher, her mother a mill manager's daughter. Whenever she met the Barbirollis—in the foyer of the Royal Opera, say, or as fellow guests in a fashionable nave at the wedding of some musically inclined nobleman—she would greet them with 'Hello, luv!' in her broadest Blackburn accent. In Blackburn, during years when she was competing at amateur song festivals for gold medals, gold cups and silver rosebowls, she worked at the telephone exchange as a switch-board girl. Of these and other workaday matters she abounded in affectionate anecdote. She put on 'Lancashire' or standard English according to the mood or need of the moment. And so it was with Barbirolli. 'Isn't it a *grand* orchestra!' he would exclaim on stepping down from the Hallé rostrum, giving to 'grand' an aggressive vowel and a glow which the word rarely carries outside the industrial North. Katie would concur about the grandness of the orchestra and, praising his accent, tell him he was talking with clogs on.

It is said that most great artists, especially those for ever on the move from ovation to ovation across countries and con-tinents, lead isolated lives. In Kathleen Ferrier's case the feeling of being uncentred, of being cut off, must have weighed heavily at times. There had been a marriage. It turned out to be one of those which, as the saying is, do not work. On her initiative, though without discrediting either party, it was annulled after some years of separation. Her father had always been close to her; his last year or two overlapped her first fame. After his death and her mother's few close relatives were left. With her sister she lived in a tall block of flats near the top of Hampstead hill. Blackburn seemed immensely far off in space, time and human 'texture'. She remembered the family fireside from the 1920s on and the family jollities that went on there and the comfort of blood ties; and she sometimes wished that those times were back. Up to a point John and Evelyn and all the other Barbirollis—Nonna and John's sister and brother and their spouses and their growing or upgrown children—gave them back to her. Whenever she had engagements within practicable range in the North, she stayed with John and Evelyn in Manchester as a matter of course. They would not hear of her using a hotel, nor did she ever dream of going to one. At Nonna's parties in Streatham and other gatherings of Barbirollis in the South, she was adored and was gay, amiably teased and mimicked, told funny stories which had a Lancashire edge and occasionally sang comic songs, self accompanied. At least one of her songs was mildly 'blue'. More than one of her old inti-mates has spoken of her 'Rabelaisian' streak. This coexisted

L*

with a strict, almost puritanical personal code. So: among the
Barbirollis she was ex-officio daughter and sister-extraordinary.

In the New Year Honours of 1953 she was made Commander
of the British Empire. Barbirolli was one of the few who knew
of this in advance. It was he who, in large part, 'produced' the
family dinner party, attending to the menu and much of its
preparation, at which, on New Year's Eve 1952, the news was
imparted to a wider circle. Her sister Winifred was there and
her secretary-companion, Bernie, and a full rally of Barbirollis.
The clock struck midnight. Barbirolli rose, glass in hand, to
make a congratulatory speech. 'Dearest Commander', he
began . . . More than ever Katie belonged to the great, knee-
bending world: but not in the sense that she belonged to this
joyous midnight circle.

For some of John's and Evelyn's special tastes and hobbies
she discovered a natural flair. When Evelyn made some signal
addition to the Barbirolli collection of eighteenth-century
glass, she exulted perceptively. Whether at Nonna's table
or at John's and Evelyn's, she knew distinguished food when
she tasted it. He, in turn, acknowledged Katie's culinary
prowess, with especial praise for her fish and chips: not the
humble dish it is generally thought to be but one (he would
insist) that calls for the virtuoso touch. Her palate for wines
was another affinity. But pleasures had to be paid for. After
any meal with John and Evelyn she was apt to insist, in the
homely Blackburn way, on giving the staff a hand with the
washing up.

The Hampstead flat became another shared fireside. John
would climb the concreted approach and Katie's stair carrying
his 'cello, and sometimes Evelyn would bring her oboe. Spare
afternoons or evenings were given over to sonatas and trios, with
Katie at the piano; for in girlhood the piano had been her
ambition, and from early lessons she retained a keyboard technique that made Barbirolli's occasional attempts sound 'dubious'
(his word) by comparison. Not that he ever pretended to be a
pianist. (As a student he had acquired a rudimentary technique.
Marjorie Barbirolli remembers how, in the Glasgow days, with
the full score in front of him, he would pick his way through bits
of Beethoven's 'Choral' symphony, which he was then preparing for the first time, almost in the manner of a one-finger

typist. After that he had made a certain progress and sported a 'party piece', the Debussy prelude known as *Minstrels*, which he would play recklessly and with enormous dash, chuckling at his wrong notes as he went along. He played as amateurs often do, with a sort of flat-fingered touch; also with a fire and technical bravado that proclaimed the professional.) Jollity reigned. Behind it lay untold stoicism. No sooner was Katie well recovered from the breast operation than symptoms recurred that pointed to a grave cancerous condition. Again she was in the hands of the doctors for weekly or even more frequent treatments which, while they took nothing from her singing, encroached upon her public career. Barbirolli knew much of all this and divined more. With devotion and great delicacy, he took up his *Orfeo* dream and set about bringing it to pass. At Covent Garden, Katie should sing Orfeo for him as she had sung it for Ansermet at Glyndebourne. That was his resolve. She was all eagerness. He conferred with the Covent Garden people. They, too, were eager. There was to be a new production with new scenery, a moveless chorus on classical lines and much work for the ballet. Four performances were listed for February 1953. In the beginning there coaching sessions at Hampstead in Katie's big music room with its splendid grand piano (borrowed), at which Barbirolli contrived to accompany her in the recitatives. The age difference between them amounted to not more than half a generation. Even so, Katie's feeling for him was that of daughter as well as pupil. What commanded her loyalty and faith were his utter self-surrender to music and the patient scruple with which he pursued it. *Orfeo* had become *Orpheus*. They busied themselves as much with the English translation as with the music, practically retranslating the whole work.

Disease was beginning to rack her and hamper movement. Rehearsals began in the Covent Garden foyer. The weather was icy. She had to be helped down the concrete slope from her home and, at the other end, across the pavement to the stage door. Matters were so arranged that none, or exceedingly few save Barbirolli, saw anything of her comings and goings. There were days when she came straight to rehearsal from hospital treatments that could induce nausea. Yet, as soon as the music of Gluck struck up and her cue was imminent, she uncannily recovered her gait and tranquillity, moving, as Barbirolli testified, with electrifying grace and poetry. None with memories of it is likely to forget her *Orpheus* first night. Her opening invocation, 'Eurydice!' a simple octave drop, so brimmed the house with noble tone that more than one hearer questioned whether anything to touch those two notes had ever been heard within walls which had heard so much. On this night the conductor was not commander but servitor. It seemed as if even Gluck the immortal had found a mortal peer.

There was to be only one other *Orpheus* night. During the second act of this second performance something broke in her hip. Her leg gave way. She had to support herself on a balustrade. With fortitude and undimmed splendour of voice she sang through to 'Che farò' and a long thunder of applause. Afterwards people came to her dressing room with congratulations. She received them with smiles and said the right things. When the last of them had gone, her sister asked what she could do for her. She answered: 'Get me a stretcher, luv.' Two other performances were cancelled. There was no understudy, nor could there have been one, as Barbirolli pointed out. The rest of the tale is of sickness, pain and resignation. For callers she still put on a smiling and hopeful front. For weeks on end the only people she wanted at her bedside were her sister, Bernie Hammond and Barbirolli. Her birthday came round. She was out of hospital for it. The year before John and Evelyn had given her a birthday party. At a prearranged moment the lights had been doused and John had entered with a cake bearing four lighted candles, one for each decade of her life, and lyre and garland patterns and a bar or two from *Orfeo*. She had burst into tears, then smiled through them, explaining that she had never had a birthday cake before. Now she was forty-one. Again, delicious food, cooked by Nonna. Again a candled cake and adroitly chosen wines, including a 1912 port, as old as herself. A night of gaiety, solicitude, hope—and foreboding. Before autumn set in foreboding had the upper hand. Hope was gone. During the last anguishing weeks Barbirolli was often at her bedside. She told him that, when unable to sleep, she sometimes went through music in her mind, remembering all the notes, however complex the accompaniment, but now and then forgetting the words. She asked him to prompt her on the

Chausson and, when he did so, sang the opening phrases of the
Poème. No bloom had gone from her voice, no curve or caress
from her phrasing. At their last meeting she knew her time
had come. As he left she said 'Good-bye, luv.' She died on
October 8th 1953.

In his contribution to the 1954 Memoir he apostrophises her
as 'beloved Katie' and ends with these lines:

> Not without honour my days ran,
> Nor yet without a boast shall end.
> For I was Shakespeare's countryman
> And were you not my friend?*

In his study at Walton Lodge there were relics, one of them
a still-life in oils, for painting had been among Kathleen's
hobbies. It is signed 'Klever Kaff', the 'baby name' by which
she was known at home. That made him one of the old Ferrier
clan, just as she had been a coopted Barbirolli.

Something has been said of Katie's part in the inauguration
of the restored Free Trade Hall. This had happened in November 1951. In the Hallé's new home—for which they had to pay
a tidy rent every time they used it—he took the sort of pride
that a twelve-year-old takes in a fine new toy and several other
prides and satisfactions on top. The decorations were winsome
in a rectangular way. Barbirolli gave it to be understood that he
had had an advisory hand in some of them. If anybody to whom
he confided this did not seem pleased by the result he was
visibly damped, if only for a moment.

Memories died hard of the old interior, frumpish though it
had seemed. Along the walls that Hitler wrecked there used to
be pairs of engaged pillars. These sustained redundant arches
that were like eyebrows raised in astonishment not at, say, *The
Rite of Spring* but at the fact that *The Rite* had never been
played there. In the new Free Trade Hall, as in Glasgow and
New York and dozens of towns on the Hallé's touring beat,

* After (rather than by) Sir William Watson, whose first two lines,
which Barbirolli got wrong, read:

> 'And not uncrowned with honour ran
> My days, and not without a boast shall end!'

Barbirolli adhered passionately to the *Firebird* music. His staccato treatment of the brass chords at the end surprised customers who had been brought up on a statelier, sustained effect. When the point was raised with him he would explain that he had heard the chords 'staccatoed' by Stravinsky himself on American television. He had liked the effect and, since it was the composer's idea, had adopted it. The Concerto in D for strings (1946) and the suite from the *Baiser de la fée* (1928) have been touched upon in an earlier chapter. These were as far as he got in the Stravinsky canon. Here again he was swayed by the composer's example. During a tour of South America in the early 1960s he shared with Stravinsky a concert in Rio de Janeiro. When the time came for him to stand down he listened and watched from the wings, missing not a beat or a note, to *Le Baiser* as conducted by its maker. Stravinsky's uninhibited and emotional approach to the sweeter pages: 'amused me vastly,' he used to say. 'In some of the lovelier bits—for instance, in the movement where he quotes the Tchaikovsky song "None but the lonely heart"— he let go with the most wonderful dynamics and rubatos. It sounded like Duke Ellington almost. I must say it gave me enormous pleasure.'

Before leaving Rio he talked with Stravinsky at length. Not for the first time Stravinsky held forth on how important it was for the conductor to play exactly what he found in a score. 'You mustn't', he instructed, 'do anything to the music except what the composer says.' This applied impartially, it seemed, whether the composer was Stravinsky or Tchaikovsky or the two of them spatchcocked. As to what the composer had to 'say' in *The Rite*, Barbirolli remained incurious to the end for anything his public knew to the contrary. Manchester heard its own orchestra play this score, not under Barbirolli, to be sure, but under a guest conductor, for the first time in 1960. By then the old shocker was in the 'Pop' pantheon or on the threshold of it. (Not that its shifting metres [especially the 5/16, 3/16, 2/16 and 4/16 of the finale] were any easier to beat. It may have been these that put Barbirolli off.) Music was now presenting an entirely new set of inductions, perplexities, conundrums and, perhaps, delights. The age of Messiaen, Boulez, Luigi Nonno and Stockhausen had dawned, or erupted, upon a world which listened with worried concentration and often wondered what it was missing or whether there was much to miss. Barbirolli went to an early performance of Boulez's *Pli selon pli*. He was asked what he thought of it. Well, he mused, for him it had a French flavour. A sort of Gallic version of Anton Webern, one might say. Not everybody's music, perhaps. Not every orchestra's music, either. Few orchestras, he added, were equipped to tackle a score of such complexity. Also there was the question of rehearsal time. Had not the Hamburg orchestra spent thirty hours on it?

A follow-up question might have been put. Had *he* not spent fifty hours, with his orchestra, on Mahler's Symphony No. 9 before doing it for the first time in 1954? The answer would have been: 'Yes. And why not?' Certainly the Hallé was one of the 'equipped' orchestras. Its daily rehearsal schedule and general elbow room allowed for off-and-on preparation extending over weeks or even a couple of months when anything monumental was in the offing. In any case, for Barbirolli, Mahler was different, a case like no other, a *cause*, in fact. To Mahler we shall return.

At new British music he toiled away with dogged patriotism. In the late 1940s he and his orchestra had taken on the Cheltenham Festival of British Music, a newly devised 'show-case' for native talent and such native genius as, with luck, might show up. Every summer for eleven years they treated Cheltenham Spa to four orchestral concerts. So far as could be arranged, each programme carried a new or good-as-new piece by a Briton. When halfway through this venture he was asked how British music stood. He replied that in his own lifetime the prestige of the *best* British music—that, notably, of Elgar, Vaughan Williams, Delius, John Ireland, Walton and Britten—had increased greatly. There was a deal of 'quite good' new English music which had found its level. He did not see any of it being taken into the general repertory. The one composer who, he felt, had received less than his deserts was Arnold Bax. Of Bax's music he thought much. That the generality of concert-goers thought so little of it he found surprising. Perhaps Bax's bigger-scale works struck them as over-complex and overlong, he hazarded. He recalled Henry Wood's pioneering efforts at the Queen's Hall and those of Dan Godfrey at Bournemouth. At their hands stacks of new British pieces had received their first—and simultaneously their last—performances. Was it likely, he was asked, that much or any of the new stuff he had done at Cheltenham would mean anything to posterity? He doubted it. Much of the new music had been well-made, even talented. Posterity, he conveyed, needed rather more than that. Exception always made for Manchester, 'where I have so steadfast and loyal a following', it was always perilous from a box office point of view to put on elaborate British works, even the finest of them.

At Cheltenham he and his players worked hard and always seemed to enjoy themselves. What did the audiences get out of it? He found them 'receptive and patient'. The phrase hardly suggests corporate rapture. The new or unfamiliar pieces came in the first half of the programme. The second half was invariably given over, as Barbirolli had insisted it should be, to masterpieces that everybody knew or, if they didn't, could be depended to revel in at once. If audiences didn't get much fun out of the first half, the second half 'consoled' them, he said; in addition to which, Cheltenham was a gracious town with lovely flowers and a festival club that offered convivial pleasures, all of which induced 'a more charitable mood' in the concert-goer. That a charitable mood should be expected of concertgoers may seem surprising in more aspects than one. Some of the sponsored music they were invited to hear on various platforms was likelier to bring on yawning resentment. In later retrospects, which were not confined to Cheltenham, he claimed that he had conducted more 'first-and-last' performances than anybody.* 'Perhaps there is no great music being written nowadays', he went on ('nowadays' referring to the mid-1960s.) 'I am no pessimist. You can't expect geniuses to be born every day of the week. But there are people turning out symphonies and concertos today who have no business to be doing anything of the sort. And there's this mania for wanting to hear something new before you've digested half the fine music that already exists. . . .'

* Under his baton or those of assistant and guest conductors, the Hallé Orchestra was responsible up to the mid-1950s for seventy-one 'first Manchester, performances, twenty-one world premières, nineteen first performances in Britain and six first public performances anywhere, a total of 117.

The Cheltenham years, as has been said, were happy for all that, and they were happily remembered. For one thing, he could always be sure of meeting Ralph Vaughan Williams there.

There had been no falling off in the friendship that dated from his clarification of the Sixth symphony at the Sheldonian concert. Partly because of that comradeship and partly because the older he got the more curious he became about what the 'youngsters' of music were up to, Vaughan Williams made a point of attending the Cheltenham Festival throughout his last years: that is to say, until halfway through his ninth decade. Regularly at ten to ten in the morning he would turn up for the Hallé rehearsal and inquire what was coming up. Usually he had a droll or pungent phrase. 'Well, John', he would ask, 'who's the latest "wrong note" man?' His last Cheltenham Festival was that of 1958. He spent four days there, alert of mind and as active otherwise as his years would allow. There was something of immemorial timber in the man's character. This and his massive frame encouraged the fancy that he would never be laid low. At Cheltenham that year he had little more than a month to live. Barbirolli was to round off his four festival concerts with *A London Symphony*. After hearing it rehearsed, the composer said to him: 'Don't tell anybody, because it's not supposed to be so, but I think that's the best of the lot.'

By 'the lot' he meant eight other symphonies as well as the *London* (1913). Barbirolli was loyal to them all. When the total still stood at six, he conducted five of them seriatim in a single season at the Free Trade Hall. The one he stood down for was the first, *A Sea Symphony* (1909). Of this the composer had charge. From Manchester the production travelled two days later to Sheffield. Again Vaughan Williams conducted. At the afternoon rehearsal the orchestra was one 'cello short through some hazard. Barbirolli took the missing man's place. There was a musical job to do. He did it. What more natural? (Looked at in another light, that of musical demarcation lines and the traditional aloofness of conductors, what more singular?) It had not been his intention to take matters further. To play 'cello 'on the night' might look like a stunt, he thought. Vaughan Williams had a stunt of his own in mind, however, and he

talked about it to Barbirolli. Forty years earlier, while conducting the first performance of his *Five Mystical Songs* (settings
for baritone, chorus and orchestra of poems by George Herbert)
in Worcester Cathedral, he noticed, without being quite able
to believe his eyes, that Fritz Kreisler was playing among his
back desk violins. Again, what more natural? Kreisler was
down for the Elgar violin concerto immediately afterwards; he
had tagged on to the Vaughan Williams performance because it
was the only chance he had of warming up his instrument.

'So you see', said Vaughan Williams, 'I once conducted an
orchestra with Fritz Kreisler in it. I now want to be able to say
I conducted an orchestra with John Barbirolli in it.'

Barbirolli complied. That night he came on to the platform
with a knot of other players, carrying his 'cello by the neck, his
face set and serious. He had not got halfway across before the
audience spotted him. There was laughter and clapping. He
paid no attention. Taking the sub-principal's seat, he entered
into earnest conversation with the principal 'cellist, whose desk
he was sharing. Mimicking the disciplinary rôle of orchestral
leader, a farceur among the first violins rapped his music stand
with his bow as if calling Barbirolli to order. More laughter.
This time some of the players joined in. When Vaughan
Williams appeared Barbirolli stood in tribute with everybody
else while the old man slowly made his way to the rostrum. Of
his demotion that night Barbirolli was proud and told of it
joyously.

It was to Barbirolli and the Hallé that Vaughan Williams
gave the première of a symphony which has been glanced at in
an earlier chapter, his seventh, the *Antarctica* (1953), which
derives in part from his incidental music to a film, *Scott of the
Antarctic*. Although at most times pointedly articulate, he could
on occasion be shy to dumbness. When the *Antarctica* was finished
he wanted to show it to Barbirolli right away with a view to a
first performance by the Hallé but was so fearful of embarrass-
ing him in case he did not like the work that he found it hard
to explain what he was after. In the end he got it out. After
Vaughan Williams's death Barbirolli wrote of this as an adorable example of his friend's shy and sweet nature. Three years
later came Symphony No. 8 in D minor, formally dedicated to
Barbirolli. Like the *Antarctica*, this specifies a tingling, jangling

'kitchen' of peculiar variety and size. Among other things it calls for tuned gongs of the kind used by Puccini in *Turandot*, a vibraphone, a xylophone and tubular bells. These were no ordinary tubular bells. The last movement included 'yard upon yard' of glissandos for them. Whoever had heard of tubular-bell glissandos before? Barbirolli conducted most of the rehearsals in the Hewitt Street 'Factory'. The composer was at some of them. One rehearsal in particular is remembered. During a break he and Barbirolli leafed through publicity photographs taken at a previous session. There was one that showed the composer holding his nose with thumb and finger while reading the score. 'I must have detected a smell of Stravinsky,' he said. Everybody laughed. Hewitt Street was hardly Stravinsky country.

For the tubular bells Joyce Aldous forsook her timpani, which were taken over for the occasion by another player. At her first attempt on the glissandos she fouled the bells, bunching their lower ends and making a noise as if she had dropped the lot. Suddenly the knack came; or rather, she invented it. She worked with a hammer in either hand at different levels, using them as a child runs a stick over railings, 'glissing' up the scale with one hammer and down it with the other. On the night everybody seemed pleased with everything. When the composer came on to the platform at the end a few hundred in the audience stood up to clap. Then everybody else did the same. They were showing their affection for 'Uncle Ralph'. Mancunians' pride in their own conductor entered into it as well, however. Vaughan Williams made Barbirolli a present of the autograph score and, when Barbirolli put it at the orchestra's disposal so that all who had taken part in the première could write their names on the flyleaf, the composer wrote at the top: 'For Glorious John, with love and admiration from Ralph.' 'Glorious' is an epithet that was used of John Dryden. No publicity virtuoso could have thought of anything to rival it. 'Glorious John' became a household name of British music and is so still.

The glory that was Vaughan Williams's music did not persist so evidently. Soon after his death and a good decade before Barbirolli's the sway of his outstanding works—especially the fourth, fifth and sixth symphonies—began to slacken. Those symphonies were very much of their day, and in that day were attuned to certain Anglo-Saxon ways of looking at life and feeling it. Many surmise and some prophesy that time will restore them to something like their old favour. Barbirolli never wavered, either in heart or mind. He had coped and grappled with Vaughan Williams during years when much of his sound was far from axiomatic to many listeners and players. In his early thirties he had conducted the *Job* symphonic suite from the autograph score. The writing was exceedingly hard to read. Getting through it was something of a feat. But it was R.V.W.'s hand. If it had been Brahms's or Franck's he would not have revered it more.

CHAPTER NINETEEN

MAHLERITE

W HEN he was not riding in the front seat of the Hallé's leading motor coach or with his orchestral leader in a reserved train compartment, bowing parts, it could be assumed that Barbirolli had called upon his chauffeur. His chauffeur was Evelyn. She usually drove about 20,000 miles a year. John was usually with her over at least half that mileage. He would sit alongside the driver's seat, memorising a score as usual. In the ordinary way nobody travelled with them, because ordinarily there wasn't any room left over, the rear seats being characteristically littered—'John's mobile music library'. Study did not put a damper on conversation. He let Evelyn talk and talked back freely while pursuing the music with eyes and mind. As a practising musician she had never come upon such concentration elsewhere. Nor had anybody else. At home she would practise oboe scales by the hour with John in the next room—or even in the same room—mastering new music or rethinking old. He said: 'If I can't talk while reading music it means that really I'm incapable of getting it off by heart.' They did many Manchester-London trips, especially after his temporary return to the Covent Garden conducting strength. For each production there he had rehearsals that spread over a month and entailed a lot of shuttling.

Most of Evelyn's 'chauffeur' services fell during the summer, taking in his South coast tours with the Hallé and his festival work at Edinburgh, Cheltenham and Harrogate: 'We like to be together. After all, we've only been married since 1939.' This she said in 1952. In winter they saw less of each other, because Evelyn had her own professional career to look after. During a typical winter season she did seventy or eighty concerts: concerto work (not always with the Hallé) and much chamber music with one or other of two trios. That meant her being away from home three nights a week. Then there were pupils. In London and Manchester she would take ten or so hand-picked ones for advanced refresher courses, fitting them in as and when she could. She would have liked to teach beginners as well but had not the time for any but established players. Not only did she play the oboe, as she still does, with distinction; she was already an international authority on it. The first edition of her *Oboe Technique* (Oxford University Press) came out in 1953: an armoury for the embryo professional as well as engrossing for any musical amateur with a fairly well schooled ear.

For summer holidays (nominal in John's case), they usually rented a house near the sea in Sussex. They were especially partial to Seaford and Hove. Evelyn insisted on his taking time off from score reading and programme planning part, at least, of every day. They 'walked and walked; walking was our great pleasure' and, when it was warm enough, swam. Sleep was the only matter on which they disagreed. An early night for John, whether (supposedly) on holiday or at the peak of a season, was two in the morning. When two o'clock struck and anybody was within earshot, he was apt to say: 'I'm feeling on top form now. I always do at this hour. I'd like to start conducting *Tristan* now.' Since there never happened to be a *Tristan* cast on hand, he would vent his exuberance on the latest score, bowing master parts from scratch if they were new ones, restoring them if they were re-hired and his markings had been rubbed out (as often happened, to his indignation) by interim users. There was a night when he had been conducting the pianist Wilfrid Parry, an old friend as well as co-musician, in the Schumann concerto at a Manchester concert. Afterwards at Walton Lodge they sat up and talked. Evelyn went to bed before midnight. At two in the morning Parry found his eyes closing against his will. 'John', he said, 'I'm falling asleep. I've got to go to bed.' 'No', said John, 'you're all right. Have some tea.' As the hours went on he brewed additional pots of tea for his guest, saying 'I don't know how you can drink the stuff.' It was he who gave in first, however. Overtaken by a sudden yawn, he exclaimed, 'Heavens, Wilfie, do you know what time it is? It's half-past five!' And so it was. This appears to have been a record for Walton Lodge. Learning later in the day what had happened, Evelyn said John had never stayed up as late as that before. The less he slept and the less he ate the harder he worked. (Whisky helped; as much a food as a stimulant. For anybody else the equation would have been fatal. For Barbirolli it amounted to a condition of existence.)

It is doubtful whether music has ever known a 'permanent' conductor as permanent as he, whether in Britain or abroad. During his first ten years as their chief, he conducted three short of 1,500 concerts with the Hallé Orchestra. An average of 150 concerts a year involved something like as many additional days of rehearsal. Who else toiled so utterly and so happily? Nobody could say that Henry Wood and Thomas Beecham were idlers. Statistically considered, however, their schedules with the Queen's Hall Orchestra in Wood's case and, in Beecham's, with his first symphony orchestra or either of its successors (the London Philharmonic and the Royal Philharmonic) look trifling by comparison.

Or take one of music's most admired energumens of a later generation. Leonard Bernstein, Barbirolli's successor with the New York Philharmonic and one of the few ever to stay longer in that saddle than he, conducted the N.Y.P.O. as principal baton or principal-cum-musical director an average of seventy-five times a season between 1958–59 and 1968–69, most of his concerts being at Carnegie Hall. When Bernstein took his orchestra out of New York, it was usually on 'red carpet' tours which almost assumed the status of international missions. Very different the toilings and trudgings of the Hallé. Great cities abroad and at home had their turn, it is true. But when Barbirolli spoke of taking symphonic music to The People there was more in what he said than might be supposed. As we have seen, Wigan and Sale, Walsall and Stoke-on-Trent were accounted worthy. Not far from Wigan is Leigh, a mining town just big enough to have a mayor. Leigh listened to the Hallé one Sunday night in the Empire cinema. Afterwards there was a civic reception and dinner at which the mayor spoke. A slander was rife about miners. It was said that if miners got greyhounds and football they were well content with life. As a miner's son the mayor resented that very much.

Miners with an ear for classical music, in common with

Hallé customers of other kinds and condition, knew what they liked, another way (as Barbirolli often pointed out) of saying they liked what they knew. A glance will be useful here, independent of chronology, at his repertory as it persisted or developed to the end.

In a foreword to the Hallé's 1956–57 prospectus he conveyed that Manchester was perhaps less averse to orchestral 'novelties' than most other cities, especially London, with its 'endless repetitions' of Beethoven and Tchaikovsky. Neither of these composers was neglected by Barbirolli, however. They happened, by and large, to be the ones whom the customer liked most. And, as Schnabel said, the customer is never guilty. Beethoven's third, fifth and seventh symphonies he conducted oftener than anything else in his symphonic repertory; and at one period, the fourth and fifth piano concertos of Beethoven oftener than, for example, the *Enigma* variations, which is saying much. As to Tchaikovsky, a typical Barbirolli account of any of the last three symphonies or *Romeo and Juliet* or *Francesca da Rimini*, lived in the memory as something beyond a mere spell of music making; however like they may have been in tempi and dynamics, each performance differed from the next as an *event*; had a certain weight and colour of its own. Always when he came on to conduct, say, the Fifth, it was as though we were there for an unveiling. He had the knack of turning our fiftieth hearing of it into something as revelatory as our first. The Fifth he made peculiarly and paradoxically his own by handing over its last pages now and then to the orchestra. A point comes in the coda where the motto theme returns, spurring most conductors to fling and frenzy. At this point Barbirolli would, at times, stop beating; with arms at his sides he nodded the symphony to its close, as though the unveiling had also been an unleashing which left him with no more urging to do.*

To the concerted music and suites of Bach, Handel and a few eighteenth-century Italian masters he went on paying obeisance;

---

* One of the occasions when he did this was the night in 1963 when he received the Hallé Society's gold medal for twenty years' service with the orchestra. As an anonymous critic (*Daily Telegraph*, 30th September 1963) finely put it: '[He] conducted with nods of the head. It was as if he was listening to the achievements of two decades.'

and he never flagged in his duty to Haydn and Mozart. Above all things he remained, however, a man of the Romantic and late-Romantic schools. He never blushed for an established masterpiece because it *was* an established masterpiece. There were some who would have liked to see him do so. In New York a rabid innovationist once said how wonderful it would be to have a whole season of Philharmonic programmes without a single masterpiece in sight. Wonderful indeed, Barbirolli agreed. He added: 'Would you care to finance it?' The subject was allowed to drop. In a musical world of rising promotion costs and static or sluggish box-office receipts, nobody could forecast more shrewdly than he the loss that was likely to accrue from a specific 'modern' piece included in a programme otherwise tailored for the Plain Man. At the peak of his work with the Hallé, that is to say, before the late 1950s, when his commitments abroad began to multiply, Barbirolli and the Hallé played to an aggregate audience of between 400,000 and half a million a season. Within that total there were many who came to Hallé concerts twice a season or more. Half a million attendances means substantially less than half a million bodies. It was a massive following, nevertheless. And for most of his followers 'modern' was a word to pronounce with a grimace. If they knew what they liked, they also knew what they didn't like. Samplings from broadcasts by other batons and orchestras left most of them indifferent or hostile to anything later than Sibelius.

On Sibelius they were sound, even avid. In Manchester he would give paired performances in one season of all seven symphonies. He would go so far as to bracket in a single programme the third, fourth and fifth. People less bewitched by Sibelius than he thought this more than enough of a good thing for one night. As with much other music that went to his depths, Sibelius sometimes emerged rather as trees than as wood. On two occasions when he brought his orchestra up to the Royal Festival Hall, this was noted of Sibelius's No. 2 particularly.

After the first of these performances (6th April 1960), Cardus wrote in the *Manchester Guardian* that maybe Sir John was overmuch in love with music phrase by phrase. As a result he held up inner rhythmic urge and sought more variety of expression than the symphony needed. Cardus named two points, one

in the Andante, the other in the Finale, where specified pauses
were overdone to disconcerting effect. Of the second performance (5th April 1963) *The Times* said this: 'His super-sensi-
tiveness was more of a liability than an asset. Pursuit of detail
can make a structure of this size sound episodic rather than
expansive, and nearly all his changes of tempo were so exaggerated as to make this most sober of Northern composers
sound on the verge of emotional hysteria. Admittedly, it was a
performance of wonderful vitality and radiance, flawlessly
played by the orchestra. Stylistically it just was not true
Sibelius.' These judgments were in line with what critics had
been writing about Barbirolli's 'off' nights for thirty years and
more. Nobody paid much attention. Ernest Newman had seen
to that. Cited tirelessly down the years, Newman's emphatic
praise of his Sibelius No. 5 at the 1948 Edinburgh Festival (see
Chapter 17), automatically outweighed adverse assessments.
It crowned Barbirolli as the ripe and true Sibelius interpreter
of his day, authenticating for the general ear not only his
Fifth but also his disputed readings of No. 2 and everything
else in the Sibelius canon, tonepoems included. Manchester
had been on terms with Sibelius, if not as indoctrinated to him
as it was now, since Hamilton Harty's time. Sibelius was, in
short, a fairly familiar musical field; and, despite his ingrained
conservatism, Barbirolli acknowledged in his 1956–57 foreword that without incursions into unfamiliar ones no self-
respecting orchestra can make progress or even survive.

Certain fields new to his players were well remembered
stamping grounds for him. In the 1930s, when still little known
to English concertgoers, he was chosen—much as he had been
chosen by John Goss for the van Dieren opera some years
earlier—to recruit a small orchestra and conduct it at Wigmore
Hall in four 'contemporary' pieces, with Beethoven's first piano
concerto as bait or sweetener. The crux of the programme,
Alban Berg's Chamber Concerto for violin, piano and thirteen
wind instruments, was the sort of headbreaking stuff from which
conductors ran away in droves. Dorothy Manley was his
pianist, Frederick Grinke his violinist. There wasn't much
rehearsal money. Yet Barbirolli rehearsed cheerfully and endlessly—and induced everybody else to do the same. Before
playing the Berg he plumbed it. He did the whole thing, in

Grinke's phrase, for peanuts: an act of musical devotion that is remembered with marvel by those who saw it at close quarters. He revived the Chamber Concerto at Manchester during the early 1960s with Hallé wind players whom he inexorably drilled. Nostalgia played its part. Before the music began he told the audience that, however odd it might sound (and it sounded so still to three ears out of five), Berg's music was good music and rather easier to take in than when he and his friends first tackled it all those years ago.

His incursions or re-incursions into music of the New Vienna School culminated two years before his death in an exceedingly complex rarity, the *Pelleas und Melisande* tonepoem of Arnold Schönberg, a relatively early work (1911), which made enormous demands on his orchestra and comparable inroads on his study time. Quite a year before his first performance of it, he might be seen with the score on his knee, eye and mind wholly and anxiously riveted, aboard airliners and trains that were carrying him to remote orchestras and to programmes which, as likely as not, started with the *Gazza ladra* overture and ended with a parcel of Johann Strauss waltzes; the 'Unfinished' Symphony or the 'New World' or Beethoven's Fifth occurring somewhere between. Nostalgia entered into this enterprise, too. For him the *Pelléas* theme had extra-musical tincts and poignancies. These ran as a thread through musical contexts which had little in common or nothing at all. Before coming to the Schönberg tonepoem he had made much, as we know, of Debussy's *Pelléas* interludes as well as of Fauré's incidental music to the same play. Two of these scores and the Maeterlinckian provenance of all three evoked the Gallic side of him; also they stirred memories of eager exploratory days forty years earlier. Technically considered the Schönberg piece was one of the most exacting things ever undertaken by the Hallé. To some ears, indeed, the Hallé did not seem quite up to it.* The performance was listened to with a good deal of respect. A touch of rapture would have been preferred by all parties. Yet Barbirolli knew that if he did not extend his repertory he would go stale. Happily there were whole mountain ranges of late

* 'Much of its inspired and prodigious orchestration was lost in the obscurity caused by inaccurate ensemble and insufficient technique.'— Gerald Larner, *The Guardian*, 19th February 1968.

Romantic stuff for him to broach and conquer. He immersed and absorbed or reabsorbed himself in Anton Bruckner, Gustav Mahler and Carl Nielsen.

The second and third of this trio were great divisors at the time he took them up. In the case of Nielsen, musicians on one side of the fence dismissed the six symphonies and ancillary works as a retrading of 'Northern' bleaknesses and snugnesses of which the world had already had a surfeit from Sibelius. Nielsen was Danish, Sibelius was a Finn: which, in terms of a 'threadbare' musical ideology, amounted to much the same thing. That is what the 'antis' held. Those on the other side of the fence, Barbirolli fervently among them, claimed—with growing support—that Nielsen's aims and the savours of his music were individual; they asserted that the honest cordiality of his polyphonic writing in particular was a 'bread' of which the world stood much in need. He did Nielsen's Fifth mightily, winning a throng of friends for music which had been gathering library dust for two generations. Other conductors as well as he were working or went to work a little later in the Nielsen cause: which was also the cause of that sizeable public who like thematic stuff they can get their teeth into straight off and symphonic panoramas on the grand scale. He never claimed to have been a pioneer exhumer. His keenness was all the more striking, perhaps, for that. With Nielsen's No. 4, less accessible to most ears than No. 5, he wrestled wooingly and with mastery. He made a recording of it and listened to the playbacks with the contentment of one who sees justice done at last. 'A few years ago', he said, 'nobody had heard these symphonies—or even heard *of* them. We didn't know what we were missing.'

In the summer of 1963 he took the Hallé on an eighteen-day tour of Scandinavia. In the Tivoli Gardens, Copenhagen, they played No. 4 to an audience of Nielsen's fellow countrymen. It ended a programme otherwise as characteristic as his thumbprint of the old Barbirolli: *La Mer*, *In a Summer Garden* and a Mozart symphony (No. 29 in A). His rewards were a laurel wreath and deafening applause which resolved itself into complimentary slow clapping. The Copenhagen wreath was his second that trip. The first had been handed up after tumultuously successful performances of Sibelius's second and fifth symphonies at a Sibelius festival in Helsinki. At both of these concerts members of the Sibelius family were present. (The second one, which concluded the festival, was attended by President Kekkonen of Finland.) One thing he gathered was that those of the family and cognoscenti generally had been 'tremendously impressed' by the Hallé's string playing. On this theme he was fond of reading a small lecture. By playing all seven Sibelius symphonies in chronological sequence during one season, as they had done at home, the Hallé got a special, perhaps unique, insight, he said, into the technique and spirit of Sibelius's string writing. In playing No. 2 and No. 5 for the Finns they had crossed, as it were, a stylistic divide: 'No. 2, like the First, is very rhetorical. No. 3 I call the Transition Symphony. The technique and the spirit are changing. With the last four symphonies we come to a new Sibelius, an important thing to grasp. Stylistically you have to change. Actually you have to revise your methods of bowing almost. You have have to produce entirely different sounds. By doing the symphonies progressively from No. 1 to No. 7 you get into the way of this. That, I think, is what counted in Helsinki. It was obvious that my players had the Sibelius style, or rather styles, at their finger tips.'

Nielsen, Sibelius . . . 'The greatest is behind.' At least, that is how a massive faction views Gustav Mahler's place in the hierarchy. When Barbirolli embraced Mahler's music, what happened, or what developed, amounted to an act of adhesion, almost of fealty, as well as of implicit defiance. In a sporadic, sluggish way, English orchestras had been sampling Mahler, that is to say, picking him up and letting him drop, for decades. After the war, however, for reasons that were in part extraneous to the symphonic art, he was attended to in this country by more ears and sharper ones than ever before. Had he not emerged as music's perfect symbol of genius retrospectively spat upon and smothered in its homeland by racist fury?

Some of the sharper ears did not at all like what they heard. Not content with merely not liking, the more articulate among them damned Mahler with an abusive scorn and a wrinkling of noses never before incurred by a composer who was out of mischief and safely in the grave before most of his scorners were born. That Mahler was a Jew rarely or never entered into the case either overtly or, so far as one may judge, as an inner motivation. Anti-Mahlerites damned Mahler's symphonies not because of the composer's race but because they were in horrid taste; in a formal sense they sprawled and were all over the place; thematically they ranged from charm and prettiness (these were grudgingly granted) to orgiastic self pity, introspective whining, brashness and blare. To which Mahlerites usually replied that their man's philosophy, whether implicit or, as in his annotations, explicit, called for freer and wider symphonic structures than those of his Romantic predecessors, as well as for more diverse tune-material and, at certain points, rhythm of a more demagogic sort. They were symphonies that evoked yokel dances and, at times, more aristocratic measures; graveside grief and grazing herds; drillground blares; the gaiety of proletarian streets; and many grandeurs of full brass and much heart-warmth from the strings. Yes, yes, Barbirolli would agree, Mahler had his 'vulgarities'; but there was a way of taking these things which led to one's accepting them.

To many Mahlerites, No. 1 in D major is less than top-drawer Mahler. But this again was a score that Barbirolli could never touch without setting his seal upon the occasion and giving it a sort of immortality. The first half of the concert would be wholly un-Mahlerian—and short: say, the *Clemenza di Tito* overture, followed by Mozart's Serenade in C minor for two each of oboes, clarinets, horns and bassoons. The interval would be long. What followed invites the historical present. . . . The audience is waiting and, in a sense, primed. Mozart's woodwinds were heavenly. We are ready to forget them. He comes on with hand over heart in the way that has been his since the Chenil Gallery days. He adjusts his cuffs not because they need it but because *he* needs it. Cuff adjusting is one of his professional *tics*. With the thumb and forefinger of his left hand he delicately picks from the air something invisible and on the wing; a murmurous octave on the strings. From this octave five movements flow and flower on their way to a finale that propounds Inferno and Paradiso. The finale has a triumphant coda with chorale tune for seven horns and five trumpets. He motions up the horns. They play the tune standing. They give it full lung power. We are still in the 1950s. Mahler scholarship generally is only skin deep. Critics are apt to conclude that

having the horns stand up at this point is Barbirolli's patent.
Some critics are delighted. When he does it with the horns of
the New York Philharmonic on returning to Carnegie Hall,
one of them says the effect was stunning; at the end of it the
audience 'broke out into cheers and applause that moved Sir
John to tears'.*

The Times of London begs to differ, submitting that it isn't
'really necessary for Sir John to ask his horn players to stand up
like jazz players when playing the triumphant chorale at the
end'. Barbirolli writes a letter to the Editor putting matters
right. Far from being 'an unwarranted act of vulgarity on my
part [nobody had suggested it was], the upstanding of the
horn players is in accordance with a direction printed in
Mahler's score. . . .'†

When he had lived with Mahler symphonies for fifteen years
or so he lightly remarked that, like those of Bruckner, they were
not the sort of thing you could assimilate in five minutes. 'At
least', he added, '*I* can't. One interesting thing, though. The
more Mahler symphonies I learn the easier they get.' How much
easier? Something over a year later he estimated that to master
any big Mahler score (and three or four of the symphonies were
still outside his repertory) took between eighteen months and
two years. He never grudged a minute of such time. 'After all',
he would say, 'this is my life.' Another man would probably have
said that this was his job. But other men did not give as much
of themselves to music as Barbirolli did.

Mahler cost money as well as time. Accountants committed
to endless battle against concert deficits were alarmed by his
orchestral specifications. In the case of the bigger scores a
conductor bent on observing all Mahler's requirements, including the optional ones, has to find 120 players or more (as
well as a mixed choir and, perhaps, solo singers) and a platform
big enough to seat the lot except for small 'effects' groups
off-stage. Then there are the things needed for what once were

* *Musical America*, February 1959. With the New York orchestra he gave
four performances of Mahler's First on successive nights, January 8th–11th
1959. He received a telegram from the composer's widow: UNLIMITED
THANKS FOR YOUR PERFORMANCE OF THE FIRST SYM-
PHONY OF MY GREAT HUSBAND ALMA MAHLER.

† *The Times* critique in question (anonymous) appeared on 23rd
November, Barbirolli's letter on 29th November 1955.

out-of-the-way symphonic sounds: deep bells, cowbells, harness
bells, postilion's horn, rattle, mandolin, guitar and a sort of
birch besom for occasional use on the bass drum—or one of the
bass drums. Certain of the specifications are 'open-ended'.
The conductor is advised to use more of this or that instrument
'if possible'. In 1964 Barbirolli came to grips with No. 6. He had
a talk on the subject with his orchestral manager, Wallace
('Wally') H. Jones, who was also the Hallé's renowned tuba:

> Barbirolli: We may as well have a word about the 'extras'
> I shall be needing next season for Mahler's Sixth.
> Jones: Mahler's *Sixth?*
> Barbirolli: Yes, No. 6.
> Jones: Hey, wait a minute, I don't know anything about
> the Mahler Six.
> Barbirolli: Oh, it's just the usual Mahler—eight horns, six
> trumpets, five or six clarinets, two harps. . . . There's one
> place in the slow movement—and this is a typical Mahler
> touch—where he says: 'Many more harps'. So if you and the
> orchestral porter can walk on with eight or ten more, that
> will be all right.* But that's by the way. The great thing is
> the quality of the extra horns we shall be needing. I was very
> pleased with the ones you got me for the Mahler Two. They
> were really splendid. And, of course, it's economically better
> in view of the preliminary rehearsals if you can get me local
> extras.
> Jones: That's easy.

'Economically better' is to be noted. While never allowing
himself to be shooed off a big project by such considerations, costs often preoccupied him; he railed at niggard subsidies which drove him to money-saving expedients.† When he

---

* A jocular exaggeration. Mahler says nothing about 'many more'. His
direction is 'Harfen (mehrere)', which suggests discretionary additions to
the original two.

† There was an exceptional and lavish occasion in October 1960 when,
with the backing of the B.B.C., he marked the fiftieth anniversary year of
Mahler's death with two performances on consecutive nights of Mahler's
Symphony No. 7 coupled with Nielsen's No. 7, one of the programmes
going out on the B.B.C.'s Third Programme. For these concerts the
Hallé Orchestra was joined by the B.B.C. Northern Orchestra. He had
150 players at his disposal.

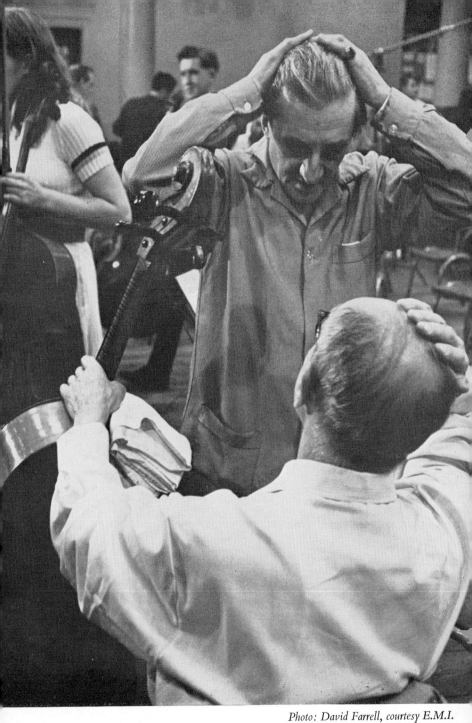

Photo: David Farrell, courtesy E.M.I.

A chat between sessions with an orchestral 'cellist while recording the Elgar 'cello concerto. Background left: Jacqueline
Du Pré (soloist).

On his 'home' rostrum, Free Trade Hall, Manchester, December 1964. Occasion: recording of Elgar's *Gerontius* with Hallé Orchestra and the cream of three choirs.

Photo: E.M.I.

brought Mahler's No. 1 to London it was noted with disfavour that off-stage trumpeters had on-stage duties as well which obliged them to troop back obtrusively. At that time the Hallé Society was losing money; strict application of the one-man-one-job rule was out of the question. Barbirolli was put off the much costlier No. 2 (the 'Resurrection' Symphony) for five years. Originally scheduled for the 1952–53 season, No. 2 had to be dropped partly on grounds of expense. In 1958, by trimming the orchestral list largely, if not wholly, in accordance with options authorised by the composer and by having brass players again double on-stage and back-stage duties, he made do with as few as 106 players. He had to find two solo singers and a mixed choir into the bargain. The Second rounded off a red-letter season (1957–58), that of the Hallé Orchestra's centenary. Two performances in one week cost £3,500 and incurred a scathing notice in the *Manchester Guardian* from Colin Mason, successor to Granville Hill (who had retired in 1952) and no promoter of the Mahler cult. It was not the quality of the playing and singing that displeased Mason but the quality of the music. The symphony ran for an hour and a half. Half an hour of it (namely, the middle movements or part of them) were charming enough; the rest rubbishy. Such was the effect of Mason's notice. A relatively young man for the *Guardian's* music chair, which he took over at thirty, Mason was from London and stirred new and sometimes nipping airs in and about the Free Trade Hall. Barbirolli was never deterred by anti-Mahler currents. He had known from the start that who-ever asserted Mahler and promoted him was giving battle. In the North and elsewhere, while confirming some in aversion to the symphonies, he made converts of thousands more.

(Reverting to Mason and, for a moment, looking ahead.—In a delayed London celebration of his seventieth birthday, Barbirolli conducted Mahler's No. 1, Britten's *da Requiem* and *Brigg Fair* at the Royal Festival Hall on December 11th 1969. Mason was there for the *Daily Telegraph*. His notice, while restating reservations about Mahler, had a cordial ring. 'As the eight horns stood up for the final pages of Mahler's First Symphony . . .', he wrote, 'the New Philharmonia Orchestra produced a volume and splendour of sound that drew cheers from the audience.' This was a parting note in a double sense.

M

Eight months later Barbirolli was dead. Colin Mason outlived
him by less than a year. His grievously early death, at forty-
seven, robbed journalism and musicology of a distinguished
mind and pen.)

In the summer of 1960 he took No. 2 to Tel Aviv for his début
with the Israel Philharmonic Orchestra. It filled the Mann
Auditorium. At the end there was a fifteen-minute ovation.
This was accounted for partly by Mahler's music and the fervour with which it had been performed and partly by a wholly
extraneous circumstance. The solo and choral texts, from the
Knaben Wunderhorn folk anthology and from Klopstock's *Aufer-
steh'n* (*Resurrection*) ode, were to have been sung in the original
German. On reaching Tel-Aviv, Barbirolli learned that survivors of Nazi oppression now settled in Israel had spoken by
telephone to the management of the Philharmonic and had
demanded that the text be sung in English. They threatened
demonstrations against Barbirolli and the performers if German
were used. 'To avoid unpleasant scenes' the management gave
way. The switching of texts presented no problem to either the
soprano soloist or the local choir who had been engaged; they
already knew both versions. The other soloist, Irma Kolassi,
from Greece, knew the German text only. She arrived in Tel
Aviv the day before the concert wholly unprepared. Barbirolli
spent some of that day and much of the next coaching her in the
English translation. He had been caught up in racist rancours
through no fault of his own. He had been under threat. He had
worked furious overtime. In the upshot he had made exalting
music. Tel Aviv's fifteen-minute ovation took into account all
these things. The Israelis rose to Mahler; and they liked
Barbirolli because, among other things, he was Barbirolli. He
acknowledged the compliment with a bit of plain speaking. That
a campaign against sung German should be launched in a city
of high ideals, a city where much German was spoken in the
streets, where films in German and newspapers in German were
shown and distributed and where German happened to be his
usual medium of communication with the orchestral players,
most of whom spoke it well: that such a thing could be not
only surprised him, he said, but seemed rather silly. Israel
prized him none the less, perhaps, indeed, the more, for his
outspokenness. In the Mann Auditorium that summer, he gave

five repeat performances of the 'Resurrection' Symphony to capacity houses of 8,000 people all told; then took the production to Jerusalem for one performance and to Haifa for two, all three being crammed. 'That', he said to an interviewer, 'wouldn't happen in many places. It certainly wouldn't happen in Vienna'—this being a dig at what may be regarded as the natural homeland of Mahler's symphonies. Milan was another city to which he took the 'Resurrection'. Mahler, he said, had been heard there before—'and disliked. The performance was so successful that it had to be given three times.'

The Mahler symphony to which he first dedicated himself publicly and with emphasis was the Ninth in D minor. From Manchester he and the Hallé bore it to the Edinburgh Festival and to other cities rather as a vast reliquary might be borne. At Carnegie Hall, with old friends and new of the New York Philharmonic, he did it on four consecutive nights, as he had done the First, winning a new crown. More signally, he took the Ninth to Berlin and had the Berlin Philharmonic Orchestra play it before an audience for whom Mahler, although not unknown to them or unregarded, blazed as a revelation. The ovation on this occasion went on for twenty minutes. Afterwards he went with the Berlin orchestra to a church in Dahlem which is also a recording studio. On the first day he ran his eye over the recording schedule. He said: 'I see you've got the last movement, the Adagio, down for a morning session. You can't expect people to perform that sort of music in the morning. It's too tense, too deep; there are shadows in it. Please rearrange the schedule so that we may do it in the afternoon or the evening. That will give the players a chance to get into the right mood.' His wish was carried out. The Adagio replaced a quick movement at one of the evening sessions.

Some months after this an old friend came to him with news of the English musicologist Deryck Cooke's 'realisation' of all five movements of Mahler's posthumous and supposedly fragmentary Symphony No. 10. Up to then the symphony had been publicly known only through occasional hearings of two extant movements only. These were in Barbirolli's repertory. Cooke's realisation had had a studio performance. The friend asked whether he would like to borrow a tape of it. The Tenth was obviously a work after Barbirolli's heart. Barbirolli sniffed

evasively and, as it were, folded up. He never addressed himself
in public to the Tenth as 'realised'. The first of the two Scherzo
movements has erratic rhythms and is not easy to 'beat'. It
may have been this that put him off. Some whom he converted
to Mahler or helped in that direction will always regret the omis-
sion. The Finale of the Tenth stands out in the Mahler canon
not only for its sovereign beauty but also because of the fashion
in which Mahler here reconciles antagonistic themes and war-
ring moods. It has been said that this movement is Mahler's
farewell to life. A Barbirolli recording of it would have been
treasured by many as his own valediction, too.

*　　*　　*

The reader will have noted by this stage that strict chronology
has gone by the board. How else cope with so crammed and
unquenchable a career? In the chapters that follow there will
be further leapfroggings in time, both back and forth.

CHAPTER TWENTY

FIRST CITIZEN

WHILE he was winning for the Hallé critical suffrages in London and other capitals of a sort which had not come the orchestra's way before, another power was tentacling through society, that Fifth Estate known as television. During television's first postwar phase in this country the B.B.C. had that Estate all to itself; it *was* the Fifth Estate, in fact. Within reason all tastes had to be catered for, whence it followed that cultural obligations weren't to be dodged. The musical wing of B.B.C. T.V. ran up a series called The Conductor Speaks. The idea was that conductors of note should be seen and heard with their own or other orchestras in reasonably accessible classics. They were to break off now and then and tell the switched-on millions about their careers and the pieces that were about to be heard. Nine conductors were picked for the first two seasons, which covered the winters of 1952–53 and 1953–54. Barbirolli, Beecham, Sargent, Rafael Kubelik and Nikolai Malko were among the nine.

Barbirolli's début was fixed for a night in November 1952. They put him down for three-quarters of an hour (9.45 to 10.30 p.m.). He was to be preceded by the Animal, Vegetable, Mineral 'quiz' and followed by the weather forecast. At that time his 'chauffeur' being otherwise occupied, he was using 'sleeper' trains between Manchester and London. After a night in the Covent Garden pit he would spent most of the return journey scribbling draft scripts. He dictated these to his secretary on reaching the Hallé offices in the morning. His first programme, transmitted from the Free Trade Hall, offered *Eine kleine Nachtmusik*, the two *Traviata* preludes and the *Barber of Seville* and *Roman Carnival* overtures. His personal anecdotes included the one about his father playing *Traviata* music in the

Leicester Square hotel lounge and how Lorenzo said the Act III prelude had been composed by God.

He did not make much of a hit with the television critics, an assertive and highly selective brotherhood. What of the millions? At that time the B.B.C. had a confidential 'rating' system, its scale running from nil for complete indifference to 100-plus for complete absorption. Barbirolli came out top on the first Conductor Speaks series. The runner-up was Beecham, five points behind. What accounted for his lead? 'Well', says one who was intimately concerned with the series, 'he was *human*. It was the human, homely touch that did it.' Some of the critics found him deficient technically; sometimes he would address unseen auditors to his right and left instead of talking 'to camera.' One writer, having praised the brilliance and fluency with which Malcolm Sargent had persuaded musically uneducated viewers to listen to unfamiliar music, complained that Barbirolli took the opposite course: 'He read from a script—and did not read well or easily. He seemed camera-shy. He needed rehearsal in how to speak well and easily.'* Yet again he got the highest popularity rating, with Sargent six points behind. One thing that marked him off from most televising conductors was the pride he took in his women players; he got the B.B.C. team to 'swing' their cameras on to the stars among them. The B.B.C. listed him for a third Conductor Speaks. When the time came he was ill and had to cancel it. Meantime other entrepreneurs had their eyes on him.

In 1954 the franchise for weekday commercial television in the London Area was granted by the newly-formed Independent Television Authority to a company called Associated Rediffusion, henceforth in this account A.-R. Six months before they were to go on the air, A.-R. appointed Barbirolli their musical adviser, promising him and the Hallé a fortnightly programme 'spot', each programme to run for an hour. The choice of music to be played was acknowledged to be Barbirolli's business. In the event, what he gave viewers, or what he had in mind for them, was roughly the sort of thing he had given his Saturday night following in Glasgow and at Belle Vue during the late 1940s on Sunday afternoons: that is to say, well-proved standard classics, Rossini-Johann Strauss-Suppé sweetmeats

* Robert Cannell, *Daily Express*, 6th November 1953.

and the occasional 'daring' bit—*La Mer*, for instance. It is remembered by A.-R.'s programme controller of the mid-1950s that he was willing to consider, and even try, any production device that was likely to disseminate good music, hitherto the joy of tens of thousands, or at best hundreds of thousands, but potentially, as Barbirolli saw the case, that of millions. He stated such visions, which were widely shared, in a reserved, businesslike manner: 'He might have been the chairman of the board of a particularly conservative firm of financial advisers in the City.' Yet, like everybody else in and around the A.-R. boardroom he was sanguine and inwardly excited.

The territory allocated to the new company by the I.T.A. had a population of nearly 15,000,000 and over four and a half million households. Before long four out of every five of those households would have television sets. Already myriad eyes were habitually glued to pipelined entertainment and occasional edifications. Also there were advertising interludes. From the advertisers vast revenues were expected. On behalf of good music Barbirolli nurtured expectations to match. An item appeared in Jordan's Daily Register almost on the morrow of his A.-R. appointment. It told of the setting up of a company to be known as Sir John Barbirolli Limited 'for the presentation of radio or television or other concerts and musical recitals'. He, Lady Barbirolli and the general manager of the Hallé were the directors; nominal capital £1,000 in pound shares. Not much more was to be heard of it.

On A.-R.'s opening night, which was also that of British commercial television generally, Barbirolli and the Hallé appeared amid inaugural pomps at Guildhall, London. They led 'God Save the Queen' and obliged with Elgar's *Cockaigne* on a night that offered also comic turns from the Wood Green Empire, scenes from Noel Coward comedies and professional boxing from the Shoreditch Empire. The world he had set foot in was bizarre and, as yet, unpredictable. Advertisers were proving coy and non-committal. For a time A.-R. looked like losing millions instead of raking them in. Two months after opening night Barbirolli and the Hallé were cut from one-hour to approximately half-hour 'slots' and transferred to off-peak viewing hours. The 'rating' compilers had a discouraging tale to tell. When the Hallé Orchestra came on thousands of viewers switched off, as they did for anything else of a grave or cultural kind.

'Although prepared to cater for minorities who appreciate more serious programmes, we have decided to put on such programmes outside peak viewing hours. Programmes like the Hallé Orchestra, documentaries and discussion features just aren't popular with the public. As a commercial organisation we have to give the public what it wants.' Thus a commercial television spokesman.

What the public wanted turned out to be 'jackpot' games (e.g., 'Beat the Clock'), 'Westerns' (e.g., the *Gunsmoke* series), sixty-minute helpings of variety from the London Palladium and a winsome American pianist called Liberace, whose ways with the pianoforte classics were not always those of the composer. Still, Barbirolli was granted his *La Mer*. Debussy-fanciers made mock of certain pictorial effects. Conductor and orchestra, they said, were submerged in seawater full fathom five. Could it be that somebody had confused *La Mer* with *La Cathédrale engloutie*?

There was a whole year, a year gapped and harried, as we shall see, by illness when he was off the 'box' altogether. During this time the advertisers had undergone a change of heart. Money began to pour in. A.-R.'s revenues presently topped £20,000,000. Three millions or so would be chipped off for the shareholders and rather more for the Inland Revenue. Once more culture and the fine arts were beckoned in. For them rather less was chipped off: between 1958 and mid-1961, for example, a total of £84,000, of which £17,000 went to 'orchestras and music societies.' Early on in his new A.-R. series Barbirolli was accorded a well-meant but debatable salute captioned 'Master of Music.' One of its messages seems to have been that men of rare zeal and talent are much the same as the rest of us. It was revealed that Barbirolli had celebrated his knighthood with a fish-and-chip supper. Some of the critics used cleavers. Here is a specimen:

The short review of A.-R. T.V.'s Master of Music programme is that it was vulgar without being funny. More and harder words, however, are needed to discuss this humiliating item. The production had Sir John Barbirolli and the Hallé

Orchestra playing in one studio while, in another, things were going on that I can hardly bring myself to describe.

After the first few bars of each piece the orchestra was faded out to make way for reconstructions of Sir John's career, sometimes narrated by nice, misguided Lady Barbirolli, sometimes dramatised by actors. . . .

The technique was that of an ill-written radio feature of 1935. One shot, of a supposed audience at Barbirolli's début with the New York Philharmonic went back further, to the era of the magic lantern.

The object of these fatuities was to present an hour of the Hallé Orchestra while preventing the audience from listening to it. This is what the I.T.A. calls balanced television.

It was an abject display of peak-time popularising, carried out by a company that despises its audience and at the same time is terrified of losing it. You would think it had made only £4,000,000 profit last year instead of £5,000,000.

In the fifty-four minutes we heard the Hallé Orchestra for perhaps ten minutes without once being allowed more than a few moments consecutively. Did Sir John know what was being done to him? A statement ascribed to the Hallé concerts manager next day said: 'Sir John knew what the programme was going to be like. He took part in the planning of it.'

He has said, or has been quoted by A.-R. T.V. as saying, that he will try any method of winning new audiences for music. Presumably these methods do not include forfeiting the music.

I am told that Sir John, for reasons I cannot imagine, feels under some sort of obligation to A.-R. T.V. He owes them nothing, but they will never be able to repay him for last night's debasing of his art.

It was a gruesome exhibition of the truth that you cannot touch pitch without being defiled.*

And another:

. . . Through the appalling script and [such] scrappy bits of music [as were] infuriatingly allowed to penetrate, a big

* Peter Black, *Daily Mail*, 12th November 1958.

M*

question loomed: Why does Sir John continually allow commercial television to desecrate his talents?

If his genius is to be wrapped up in such a cheap and patronising package, he must ask himself if he is really doing anything for the cause of music. I will give him the answer now. It is: Oh, no John, no John, no!*

If the Master of Music show was aesthetically a dead loss, was there ultimately no aesthetic gain? The contracts jointly signed by A.-R. and the Hallé Concerts Society in 1958 and in 1960 covered five years and provided backing for nearly a hundred and thirty sponsored concerts (i.e., concerts guaranteed against loss), most of them public performances in London and other parts of the South, the remainder televised from studios either in the evening, with adult audiences in mind, or in the afternoon for schools. There were limits to what even Barbirolli could undertake, of course. Many of the schools transmissions were taken by other batons. As musical adviser he kept an eye on the lot, however. 'This series', he said, 'will do an immense job towards building up an audience for the future. We shall reach more children than ever before . . . I am terribly excited about the whole prospect.'

The cream of the public concerts were twenty or so which he conducted at the Royal Festival Hall. Some of them began with 'God Save the Queen.' He used to conduct the first half of it facing the audience in the hope (not always realised) of getting everybody to sing the words. For the second half he turned to the orchestra. In concert halls throughout the land the National Anthem has always had its connoisseurs. The fire and zeal of Barbirolli's performances were highly considered. They brought out his most momentous frown. Of one of them a *Times* writer said that its *molto grandioso* quality smacked of challenge. 'Where', it seemed to be asking, 'is your Tommy Beecham now?'

For the rest, his A.-R. nights in London carried hour upon hour of music in which he had invested unsparingly of his nerve, blood and being. His first 1958 week-end, comprising two concerts, traversed Elgar (the Introduction and Allegro), Strauss (*Till*), Schubert (the 'Unfinished') and Beethoven (the

* Television Critic of *Daily Express*, 12th November 1958.

third piano concerto) to culminate in Bruckner's massive Symphony No. 4, the 'Romantic'. At that time the 'Romantic' was not much known in this country. Yet Barbirolli's performance of it happened to be the second performance of it on the same platform within a week. It had been the cornerstone of Franz Konwitschny's programme with the visiting Gewandhaus Orchestra, from Leipzig, four days earlier. An invidious conjunction. Barbirolli's performance had been schemed for nearly a year. As soon as it became known that the Leipzigers proposed to play it, Manchester asked if they would be so kind as to take it out of their programme and play something else. Leipzig stood its ground. Most who knew much about Bruckner or anything at all about how strings can and should sound in late-Romantic contexts feared, on hearing the Gewandhaus timbres, that the Hallé strings would find it hard to match up to them. When the Hallé's turn came their violins were judged by certain practised ears to be a shade less homogeneous than those of the Gewandhaus and therefore not altogether as ripe. And did not the Hallé's heavy brass, inquired the same ears, sound over-emphatic at times? Barbirolli always tended on certain types of climax to let fly with his trombones in a way that made for trouble in any hall whose acoustic had not become, so to speak, bone of his bone.

As to string ensemble, how could he hope, except on lucky nights, to bring off anything like the uncanny 'oneness' and sheen of relatively stable German orchestras when he had to cope with what one observer during these years called 'the money rot'? Some months earlier he and the Hallé Orchestra had rounded off their usual Edinburgh Festival assignment with a resounding Mozart-Mahler programme. At the end of it four young players went to his dressing room and made their farewells. He shook them by the hand and wished them luck. Many another man would have sulked and barred his door. They had been with him for two or three seasons. He had taught them the standard orchestral repertory; in fact, he had taught them just about everything they knew. They had been getting a basic wage of £13. 10s a week. Recording and broadcasting fees bumped this up to perhaps £17. Now they were off to the freelance pool in London. There they would soon be earning twice as much or more. As has been brought out earlier,

such defections had been going on since 1943. They were to
continue. Nor could it be taken for granted that as many good
fish were in the sea as came out of it. In one season alone, 1961,
the Hallé lost twenty players to orchestras that were increasing
their strength and putting up their pay. In the hope of replacements Barbirolli auditioned eighty aspirants, many of them
newly out of music colleges. The first fifty he heard were no
good. In the end he took on seven out of the eighty. For the
remaining thirteen he had to 'scratch around.'

The shortcomings in string ensemble especially that stemmed
from this problem were reflected at the Royal Festival Hall, a
highly competitive arena, in several Hallé performances besides
Bruckner's No. 4. What nevertheless gave the Hallé's Bruckner
and so much else nobility and legendary glow was something
that has been touched on earlier: Barbirolli's knack of turning
any one performance into an unrivalled and unrepeatable event.
He did the Fourth on a Sunday. Konwitschny had done it
superbly the previous Wednesday. Yet the old spell worked.
Those who heard both had the illusion on Sunday of attending
an unveiling. So it was with other big-scale scores which he
conducted at the Festival Hall under A.-R. auspices: the *Faust*
Symphony of Liszt, for example; Nielsen's No. 4 (two performances of it four years apart), Berlioz's *Fantastic* (another
'double': two impassioned and momentous nights even if, after
one of them, *The Times* did jib at his 'unnecessarily shattering'
fortissimos in the finale); three Schubert symphonies on one
night—the 'Unfinished', No. 5 and the 'Great' C major; an
unusual all-Beethoven scheme in which a 'cello and harp duo
from the *Prometheus* music preceded two symphonies—the
'Pastoral' and the Seventh; and something even more out of
the way: Tchaikovsky's *Romeo and Juliet* tonepoem with inserted
love duet, words after Shakespeare, sung by a soprano and
tenor from the opera house. (There was no great clamour to
hear this again.) Two splendid Mahler nights were added to
the tally. When he did the Seventh symphony its blazing
brass peroration brought the audience to its feet with spontaneous 'Bravos!' Two years later a like ovation crowned his
conducting of the 'Resurrection' symphony.

This was in the spring of 1964. The 'party' was nearing its
end. In came the Government's television levy. Revenues were

further and drastically milked. A.-R.'s grants to the arts and to science were cut at a stroke from £28,000 to £10,000 a year. In the wholesale realignments that followed Barbirolli and the Hallé passed, as 'regulars', from the television screen. Between 1958–59 and 1963–64 A.-R. had paid the orchestra nearly £35,000 to meet box office deficits on the concerts they backed. On top of this Barbirolli had a retainer and fees for the many sponsored concerts he conducted. One other orchestra had enjoyed the company's favour, the London Symphony. The L.S.O. was not made as much of, however. The Hallé differed from any other orchestra in the land and most other orchestras anywhere. They and their conductor were as one. After a fashion, each had made the other.

When he returned to the television screen in the autumn of 1957 after a longish absence, viewers with longish memories of him were disturbed by his wasted and, at times, haggard look. Here was a different Barbirolli. He had had a brush with death and come out of it well. Such encounters leave a lasting mark. From the age of fifty on he had been dogged unremittingly by ailments. At most of them he scoffed. He loved the medical profession. Several doctors were among his acquaintances. One or two were close friends. Whether near or close made little difference. When ill he tended to argue back at them and go his own way.

His second illness in 1949 (the first had been a bout of gastro-enteritis) was a classic case of the patient knowing 'better'. Returning that summer from a conducting tour in Belgium, he submitted to what he supposed to be a routine medical check. The day was a Friday. He was scheduled for concerts the following Monday and Tuesday with the Berlin Philharmonic Orchestra at the Edinburgh Festival. Two doctors saw him. Both were shocked by the condition to which overwork had reduced him. They ordered three months' complete rest and, after that, a lighter schedule 'to avoid serious complications'. For six years he had been conducting the Hallé Orchestra and guest-conducting other orchestras at home and abroad at the rate of two hundred concerts a year, with rehearsals on top—up to eight of them a week. All things considered it was astonishing that he was still on his feet.

He made it clear that he meant to stay on them.

Three months' complete rest smacked of three months' holiday; as we know, the bare idea of such a thing gave him a sort of anguish. For three hours he expostulated and argued back at the doctors; then, with Evelyn, took the road for Edinburgh and rehearsals with the Berliners, these and his festival concerts to be followed by a week's Irish tour with the Hallé. He had not been altogether as defiant as it seemed. Actually there had been mutual concessions. The doctors had withdrawn their stipulation of three months' rest. He for his part had agreed to confine himself to Hallé work, dropping all overseas and guest engagements elsewhere (Edinburgh and Ireland excepted) until further notice. Later that year and into the spring of the following one, he was to have made guest appearances in Basle, Zürich, Paris, Vienna, a Scandinavian city or two and, with the Berlin Philharmonic, in Berlin. All these engagements were nominally dropped. (Which did not prevent him when the time came [Easter 1950] from keeping the Berlin ones.)

The two concerts in Edinburgh at the 1949 Festival were the beginning of a long and prospering association with the Berliners which we glanced at in Chapter 17. Into each programme he introduced an Elgar piece, the first being the Introduction and Allegro, the second the *Enigma* variations, as well as something French, the *Bacchus and Ariadne* suite of Roussel: 'bold' excursions into styles and flavours which German players, argued certain strong reasoners of the day, must have found alien and perhaps inhibiting. Yet 'Barbirolli shone —particularly in a tremendous performance of the Sibelius No. 2'.* This was Ernest Newman's encomium—his second in twelve months apropos Barbirolli's aptitude for Sibelius. The Usher Hall was moved to grateful frenzy. In acknowledging it, Barbirolli accidentally and all unconsciously made a hand

---

* *The Sunday Times*, September 4th 1949. Barbirolli opened his second programme, as he had opened innumerable others, with a Rossini overture, his choice on this occasion being *Semiramide*. 'No really musical person—by which I mean primarily, of course, the music critics—would leave his comfortable home any evening in the year specifically to hear this', commented Newman; 'and if it chanced to be a bit of filling up in a programme of greater things the critics would assuredly, in their own expressive

sign identical with one which the Berliners had been trained
to regard as a signal of dismissal. Accordingly they rose
from their seats and left the platform in mid-ovation,
greatly to Barbirolli's embarrassment, skilfully though he concealed it.

As has already been told, he resumed guesting in the spring,
only to be brought down a year later by recurring enteritis and
appendicitis. After recovering from the 1951 operation he
battled obdurately against minor ills, including a debilitating
attack of influenza, until the beginning of 1956, when there
was a danger signal. Shortly before due to start a half-hour of
television music, he collapsed, came to after a few minutes,
took the rostrum as if his usual self and continued so until his
half-hour was up. Six months later, overstrain having again
been diagnosed, he conceded his doctor a whole day's rest.

The month after that, August, found him in Brighton,
ostensibly on holiday but, as usual, buried in scores, master
parts and programme plans. Two days after his and Evelyn's
return to Manchester he had another collapse, a more alarming
one. Again he was taken to the private patients' block at the
Manchester Royal Infirmary. The surgeon diagnosed an
intestinal obstruction of a non-malignant sort. The day was a
Monday. It was decided that he should be operated on the
following Friday. He spent much of the intervening days
thinking, talking and dictating notes about the forthcoming
Hallé centenary observation. Study scores were stacked near
his bedside. He looked forward with relish to sitting up after
the operation with Mahler's 'Resurrection' symphony in front
of him or, better still, Bach's St. Matthew Passion music. The
operation went well. The daily bulletins read soothingly to
outsiders. Sir John had passed a 'fairly comfortable day' . . .
Sir John was 'quite cheerful' . . . Sir John was 'resting quietly'.

idiom, give it a miss. But bring, at great expense, a German orchestra all
the way from Berlin to play this negligible bit of Italian music in the capital
of Scotland and an English conductor all the way from Manchester to
conduct it and apparently it becomes, by some magical transformation
which I am unable to comprehend, a 'festival' work, and we trudge all
the way to Edinburgh to hear it. Even I, doubtful as I am about the sanity
of the human race, had no idea it was as lunatic as this.'

. . . He had cancelled thirty-two summer and autumn engagements with the Hallé in and outside Manchester. Substitute
conductors were called in. Rehearsals resumed in the 'Factory'
at Hewitt Street. Players came and went busily. If a man got
on a bus carrying an encased fiddle or anything else that
looked like a musical instrument, the conductor—who, as
likely as not, knew nothing at all about classical music—would
ask, 'How's the Governor?' Incidents of this kind quickly came
to Barbirolli's ear. They delighted him. 'So', he would observe,
'I've become part of the city!'

His first post-operational phase was hardly as smooth as the
bulletins suggested. His progress was slow. It was also painful.
For the first time in his life since infancy, his ear went without
music. He could have had records played but chose not to.
Listening to music was, he said, pointless unless one listened
with complete concentration. That is how he listened to music
all his life. But the act of concentration now would take too
much out of him. All he could do for the time being was 'lie
back and think'. The hours were weary none the less.

When he began to feel himself again, it was not to sound that
he turned but to creative scholarship. He had a music stand
rigged over his bed. On it he set the full score of the St. Matthew
Passion music in the Bach Gesellschaft edition. The copy he
used had been given him by the Hallé Choir to mark his
knighthood and his fiftieth birthday. He had long had it in
mind to prepare his own performing edition of what he described
as 'one of the most sublime masterpieces ever penned'. Hitherto
he had never been able to set aside any time for it. Another
thing: the size and quality of the task both summoned and
inhibited him. He confessed himself almost terrified, indeed.
But now he had leisure; also something that resembled an
upsurge of confidence. At least he could make a start. The task
before him he defined thus: 'Bach left just the bare notes. In
289 pages of full score there are, I think, only one tempo
indication and six or seven dynamic markings. Obviously the
music must go either slow or fast according to the situations
that the music represents. The St. Matthew Passion text is
almost a series of tableaux. If you were allowed to put it on
the stage you could make a scenario of it. Your fasts and slows,
your louds and softs must be based on your feelings and your

instincts about these tableaux and the meaning of the words.'
He left the Infirmary seventeen days after the operation with a
first sheaf of annotations. He joked about his studies saying:
'It was a useful way of employing my time. After my last big
operation I studied *Messiah*. I don't know whether I'll do any
more new editions, because there's not much left of me they
can cut out.'

He had got his teeth into the St. Matthew task, hardly more.
Whenever he had a relatively free spell he would put in ten
hours a day at his desk. Three years later he had got as far as
the master-copy stage, involving parts for two choirs, a supplementary choir, two orchestras, six solo singers and three solo
instruments. Second thoughts led to a certain amount of
scrapping and re-writing. He put in another eighteen months'
sparetime work on the score. Then his edition was ready. It
had taken him four and a half years to perfect. The St. Matthew
Passion music is a lengthy work. He had edited the whole of it
and meant to perform it without cuts. His original idea was to
divide the performance, giving the first half on the afternoon
of Holy Thursday, the second half on Good Friday. There were
practical difficulties in the way of this. Barbirolli's edition of
'The Passion of Our Lord According to St. Matthew, set to
Music by John Sebastian Bach' reached the Free Trade Hall
on Palm Sunday 1961.

The place was packed, the audience solemn and intent in a
twofold way. This was *great* Bach. Everybody knew that. It
was also something on which Sir John had set his heart and
mind. That was hardly less important. The Hallé Choir, all
amateurs, as well as six professional soloists, sang the original
German text, enouncing it to admiration. And there were no
cuts. 'A complete performance down to the last *da capo*',
certified *The Times*. It needed ample elbow room. The first
half started in mid-afternoon and was followed by a two-hour
break. The second half ended at 9 p.m. Experts in the antique
spotted this and that. Flutes played where recorders had been
hoped for. Cor anglais stood in for oboi da caccia. On the other
hand there were oboi d'amore and a viola da gamba; also a
harpsichord as well as organ. Speaking of which, was it fact or
fancy that once during *pianissimo* singing the organ bellows could

be heard puffing away? . . . These matters were not of great account. What people carried away with them that Sunday were immense beauties of line and texture and, beyond these, an unfolded tale as burningly momentous as any that a theatre could tell.

Later in the 1960s he conducted several more performances on the same lines. All were deeply fervent occasions. They did not invariably fill the hall. For Barbirolli the need to ingest this score and give it forth again had been profound and imperious. Of what moment a scattering of empty seats?

He convalesced during the autumn of 1956 in Italy. He and Evelyn spent part of the time with John's cousins in Rovigo. They saw much of Verona, Vincenza, Venice and Padua also. Having been forewarned of the Barbirollis' visit, the director of the Rovigo opera house did some research in his archives. This was the theatre where, it will be remembered, Toscanini and Lorenzo Barbirolli had served in their youth as principal 'cello and principal second violin respectively. The director turned up pay receipts signed by both of them. They got seven lire per performance, it seemed, equivalent to six shillings in English money at that time.

On 9th December 1956 he reappeared at Belle Vue for *Messiah*. The place was crowded. Manchester had seen nothing of him for seven months. As he made his circuit to the rostrum the thousands rose to their feet and made a vast noise of jubilation and affection. No prince or homing conqueror could have been welcomed more patently from the heart. That day *Messiah* was sung by the traditional big choir: the choirs of Manchester and Sheffield combined, and there were solo singers who knew how to touch human heartstrings. As the music ended many in the audience were wiping their eyes. What had moved them? The music? Or Barbirolli's return? Probably their tears had something to do with both. In the Ringmaster's Office afterwards he said how glad he was to be back. He added: 'It was almost worth while being ill for.'

He was become First Citizen of Manchester—a title publicly if unofficially conferred upon him by one of Manchester's Lord Mayors, who thus stepped down gracefully from his own traditional pre-eminence. Recognition of an official sort, the

greatest in the city's gift, came in March 1958, when his name
was incribed upon Manchester's roll of Honorary Freemen.
There were cordial speeches and afterwards a banquet with a
lot of flowers including some in the shape of a 'cello. When it
was over the small boy in him came to the surface. He said of
the Honorary Freedom: 'It's not a thing they throw about,
you know. If you look at the list of Honorary Freemen you'll
see it has Clemenceau, Haig, President Wilson, Churchill and
Montgomery on it.' There were fifty-six other names on the
roll, not all of them as easy to remember.

The honour had its ironical, even rueful side, however. It
marked a sort of armistice in a running battle which he waged
on and off for nearly twenty years with the Manchester
Corporation over money support for his orchestra. In the course
of this battle he used guile, bluff and indignation, returning
hard words with soft answers or words harder still. We have
seen how, in 1944, when invited to take over the London
Symphony Orchestra, he had used the offer as a bargaining
counter against the Hallé executive. In 1948 he and Philip
Godlee used another offer, this time from the B.B.C., in
precisely the same way against the City Fathers. The B.B.C.
wanted Barbirolli to take over their Symphony Orchestra as
prospective successor—for part of each season, at least—to Sir
Adrian Boult, now nearing sixty, whose retirement was in prospect
because of an age-limit rule or practice. It was an offer to make
the mouth water, though not in any pecuniary sense, since
there would not have been appreciably more money in it for
Barbirolli; the attraction was that a better paid and therefore
more stable orchestra of one hundred players would enable
him to get better artistic results than a relatively unstable
orchestra of only eighty players, that being the strength at
which the Hallé was still pegged. From one public source or
another (i.e., the Arts Council, Manchester Corporation and
other municipalities in the North) the Hallé got grants amount-
ing to £18,000—much less, complained Barbirolli in a public
statement, than 'other world famous orchestras' were getting.
Much less, he might have added, than certain orchestras were
getting whose fame was less than worldwide. The Yorkshire
Symphony Orchestra, for example, received about two and a
half times as much from public funds as the Hallé.

At the end of 1949, Barbirolli added, he would be entering upon his sixth decade—'the last of my career'. Those would be the best ten years of his life. What to do with them was a tremendous decision to take. Using words which nine readers out of ten probably construed as positive assertion, Godlee hinted in various skilfully dovetailed pronouncements that, unless the orchestra was restored to its prewar strength, Barbirolli would shake the dust of Manchester off his feet. Consternation broke out. Shoals of letters came to the Hallé offices begging him not to go. No attempt was made to stay the starting tear. Barbirolli told a reporter that the letters were 'really touching, really beautiful, some of them written by seven-year-olds. . . . I have always been interested in the young people in Hallé audiences.' How many as young as seven turned up for the Hallé, even when school concerts were taken into account, did not appear.

It is not to be denied that the Town Hall harboured recalcitrants. One councillor gave a speech in which he thought the Hallé Orchestra wasn't as popular as some people 'cracked it up' to be. Another taxed Barbirolli with extravagance. Like Beecham, he said, Barbirolli had come back from America with big ideas. Manchester, he would remind him, wasn't America. Manchester hadn't as much money. To which Barbirolli replied: 'On the question of having big ideas for Manchester, I would like to know how one can establish an orchestra worthy of the city we serve on little ideas. . . . If Manchester wants a little orchestra, run by little men with little ideas, I agree that I and my colleagues of the Hallé Society are not the men for the job.'

Meantime, the Hallé committee, wondering where the money was to come from, put up the players' 'basic' wage by three pounds a week (a fact noted in an earlier chapter) and promised Barbirolli a playing strength of ninety-six as soon as they had a platform (notably, that of the restored Free Trade Hall) big enough to seat that number. On the strength of these concessions he announced that he was turning down the B.B.C. offer. It is doubtful whether he had ever intended to accept. ('I used it as a lever', he avowed some years later.) Two more years of dickering and bickering followed. Then the City Council came to heel. The orchestra had asked for a direct grant in place of guarantees against deficits. This the Council conceded, promising £9,000 a year for three years: ludicrously less than comparable orchestral subsidies at home and abroad but mollifying for the moment.

The moment was brief. No sooner was it ensconced in the restored Free Trade Hall than the orchestra found that, although the new auditorium had rather more seats than the old one, not enough money was coming in; admission prices had been set too low. But for drastic emergency measures the Hallé would have piled up a lethal deficit. The emergency measures included rather more work (Summer 'Proms', block-booked 'industrial concerts' and so forth) and less orchestral pay. The players' newly-won 'basic' of thirteen pounds a week was docked to eleven-pounds-ten and stayed so until 1957. Much had been said by Godlee and others publicly and privately about Barbirolli's sacrifices in the cause of Manchester —and music. They spoke truly, and might have said more. What did not come out at the time was that for solidarity's sake he voluntarily accepted a ten per cent cut in his own salary: this at a time when his fees for such guest engagements as he chose to accept with other orchestras in this country were three times higher and with orchestras abroad four times higher than his average fee-per-concert with the Hallé.

'Not', he privately commented, 'that money has ever mattered to me. As a touring guest conductor I could triple my income with ease. But I prefer to conduct an orchestra of my own in unhackneyed programmes most of the year. And there's another aspect. People often talk about the big salaries paid to conductors. The salary may be big, but with taxation as it is you don't see much of it. At the same time, we have to keep our fees high for two reasons—(a) prestige, (b) to give the youngsters a chance. I could say to myself: "What's the use of charging musical societies up and down the country so much? I don't pocket the money myself. I give more and more of it to the Government. It might be more profitable to charge a smaller fee." But if I did that the youngsters wouldn't get a look in. As it is, musical societies often find they can't afford my fee and have to turn elsewhere. Which is where the youngsters come in. In present conditions, big fees are not greed but a professional and moral obligation.'

True to their word, the Corporation made a direct grant of £9,000 a year for three years. Then they turned the tap off, pleading financial stringency. Battle was joined again. Godlee had died in 1952. This put a heavier dialectical burden on Barbirolli. Most of the verbal infighting was now left to him.

In 1956 he broke off his convalescence to give the Corporation a dressing down by tongue and pen. From figures which he put in that autumn it appeared that four other provincial orchestras—the Royal Liverpool Philharmonic, the Birmingham Symphony, the Scottish National and the Bournemouth Symphony—averaged but 183 concerts in 1954–55 as against the Hallé's total of 238 for that season; and that for this they got municipal subsidies averaging £24,750 as against *nil* in the case of the Hallé. In reply to the last point it might, he said, be argued that in a roundabout way—i.e., through contributions to a joint aid scheme set up by a number of Northern municipal authorities—Manchester Corporation had in two years paid the Hallé some £6,000. Not so, he contended. In rent for use of the Free Trade Hall and other charges, the Hallé had paid more than £6,000 back: whence it followed that the orchestra was 'no burden on the city at all.' The orchestra, he went on, had been straight. It had been honest. It had worked prodigiously hard. Its playing schedules were unparalleled in orchestral history. 'Why', he asked, '. . . do we have to be punished in this way?' Had not the time come for the City Fathers to examine their consciences? He put that question 'in all humility and friendliness.'

The City Fathers pondered with what contrition they could muster and, for the centenary season (1957–58) made a 'special grant' of £5,298; which, bearing in mind that the four other big provincial orchestras were getting twice or five times or even six times as much from municipal funds, merely confirmed the Manchester Corporation's parsimony. However, the players' basic was upped to £13.10s, leaving them ten shillings a week better off than in 1951, the year of the pay cut.

Another lull ensued. It lasted uneasily until the spring of 1960, when food for thought was given by the following figures which summarised the Arts Council's grants to provincial orchestras and those of local authorities during 1958–59:

Scottish National Orchestra (70 players):

Arts Council	£24,500
Municipalities	38,628
	£63,128

Royal Liverpool Philharmonic Orchestra (74 players):

Arts Council	£20,000
Municipalities	£38,931*
	£58,931

City of Birmingham Orchestra (75 players):

Arts Council	£17,000
Municipality	£31,297
	£48,297

Bournemouth Symphony Orchestra (65 players):

Arts Council	£20,000
Municipality	£16,230
	£36,230

Hallé Orchestra (90 players):

Arts Council	£12,000
Municipalities	£19,359
	£31,359

* Including £10,000 in respect of free use of the Liverpool Philharmonic Hall and offices, Corporation property.

The figures had almost a derisive air. They seemed to confirm the Hallé Orchestra in her rôle of symphonic Cinderella. It is true that, looked at from one side of the balance sheet, she appeared to be a well-found Cinderella. Hallé revenues were far greater than those of any one of her provincial rivals. That was because, in the hope (not always realised) of making ends meet and compiling a prudent reserve fund, the orchestra toured far more widely and gave far more concerts than any other orchestra in the world. Why, asked certain scrutineers, should keepers of public funds be open-handed towards so flourishing a box office? Because (it was answered) the box office, however flourishing, could never of itself sustain the morale of overworked orchestral players or even pay them enough to meet without anxiety their food and rent and clothing bills. Or, as Barbirolli stated the case privately:

> They [the Arts Council] do it as if it were a Welfare State means test. If you go down the drain and can't get engagements you get a lot of money. If you earn 81 per cent of your income, as we do, you get penalised for it.*

The 1960 storm blew up at a time when Barbirolli was preparing for concerts in Budapest and Prague and for his début with the Israel Philharmonic Orchestra. He paused and laid about him with acerbity. In a statement released to the newspapers he touched upon the depression and 'grave discontent' that prevailed among Hallé players. What else was to be expected? While receiving the same basic pay as members of other permanent orchestras, the Hallé players had to do far more work for that pay. Not surprisingly there had been defections. As a result the orchestra was now seriously under strength. Yet he was always being praised as Manchester's 'musical ambassador'; he was for ever being told what prestige the Hallé won for the city in foreign parts. Such compliments made him sick. They assorted ill with Manchester Corporation's

---

* The Arts Council put the Hallé's earnings for 1958–59 at 78 p.c. of 'total trading revenue'. The Scottish National Orchestra, which received over twice as much public money, earned only 44 per cent and gave but 151 concerts as against the Hallé's 238. Corresponding discrepancies in the case of the other provincial orchestras, although not as wide, made a sufficiently disturbing contrast.

contribution to the Hallé, a paltry sum when compared with what other cities granted to *their* permanent orchestras.

He ended on a minatory note. Unless an inquiry were instituted into the subsidising of British symphony orchestras or some system developed approximating to equal grants and lending sanity to Britain's orchestral system, he would end his term as chief conductor of the Hallé Orchestra at the end of the year.

This was his fourth threat of resignation in fifteen years. Having made it he set off furiously for Budapest, Prague and Tel Aviv in a Russian jet liner. On the same day an Arts Council spokesman made a defensive yet placatory reply to the following effect: The Arts Council did not *manage* the Hallé Orchestra. If the orchestra was overworked, it was up to the Hallé Society to decide what was the right number of concerts to give. As to money, the Hallé's estimates for the coming year showed a deficit of just over £22,000. The Arts Council offered to cover the whole of this in grants and guarantees, short of about £30.

On the face of it, the Arts Council had taken some of the wind out of Barbirolli's sails. Five months later, soon after the Hallé's 1960–61 season had begun, Barbirolli and his players being deep in preparation for their giant Mahler-Nielsen night, a further Arts Council report came out which, while scouting the idea of equal grants for the 'Big Five' provincial orchestras, hoped that in the near future those who subsidised them might come together to examine 'the implications and assumptions of the situation.' A non-committal formula. It went part of the way, however, towards meeting Barbirolli's demand. He let it be known, therefore, that his threat of resignation was withdrawn. He was not to make another such. Four having been revoked already, a fifth might not have been taken seriously. In any case, a corner had been turned. That season the players' 'basic' went up to fifteen pounds. A couple of seasons later the scale was adjusted to fifteen pounds for players newly out of college, increasing to twenty pounds a week at the end of their fourth season. These were the fruits of substantial increases in Arts Council and local authority grants.

Insofar as it concerned him, the battle was over. Something else had come to an end: his own overwork for the Hallé.

Back in 1958 he had stepped down from the post of conductor-in-chief and director of music to become chief conductor and musical adviser. At the same time he had reduced his 'hard' commitments with the orchestra to seventy concerts a year, leaving a balance of at least one hundred and fifty concerts in the hands of assistant conductors and guests. By the mid-1960s the Hallé was being conducted by an average of twelve conductors a season. It is true that Barbirolli often opted for more than his 'ration' of seventy engagements. Sometimes he would take a hundred or more, recording sessions included. In any case, he had not cut down his Hallé work for the sake of an easier life. His object was to take on more work with leading foreign orchestras. How he achieved that object will presently appear. In short, he was still doing two men's work —and travelling enough for three.

However far he travelled and however long he stayed away, his heart remained in Manchester. In conversation one year after his fourth and last threat of resignation he said this: 'I shall never leave the Hallé. I have a marvellous orchestra. It is wonderful to have built up something unique. It is a great family affair. I would be a very unhappy person without it. When you have made an orchestra as I have made the Hallé they know you very well and all your requirements; and that enables you to conduct very relaxedly. You don't have to push for effects. I expect I shall stay with the Hallé until I die.'

CHAPTER TWENTY-ONE

CULTURE TRAIL, TEX

AMERICA wooed him for years. American audiences had
long been vulnerable to English conductors, especially
those with inescapably English diction and what were
seen or fancied to be inescapable English traits. If, into the
bargain, the conductors were knights, so much the better.
That had been amply proved by Beecham and Sargent.
Barbirolli's turn (or rather, return) was long overdue. Of this
he had frequent reminders from Arthur Judson whom he had
known as administrator of the New York Philharmonic. Judson
was become an independent impresario of high influence.
He cabled Barbirolli as often (so it was said in Hallé
circles) as once a fortnight offering three-month guesting bouts
with crack American orchestras. Barbirolli always replied in
effect: 'Nothing doing. I shall not return to America until I
can bring the Hallé Orchestra with me.' To which Judson
regularly replied that this was a splendid idea and to bring the
Hallé by all means. Several European orchestras, English ones
among them, had found or were to find their way to the United
States. Not so the Hallé. There was a simple reason for this.
The Hallé could never raise the airline fare, put at about
£15,000 in the mid-1950s. Potential guarantors and subsidisers
in Manchester and London always looked the other way when
the possibility was broached.

Judson began to tire of staring at a stone wall. At last he
delivered what Barbirolli described as an ultimatum. His long-
standing invitation to the Hallé would be withdrawn for good
unless Barbirolli undertook to guest with American orchestras
during the forthcoming season (1958–59). This time Barbirolli
signed up. He made it known he was contracted for America
the day before becoming Manchester's sixty-second Honorary
Freeman. In his speech of thanks to the Mayor and Corporation

he mentioned the 'ever increasing number of invitations' he was receiving—and responding to—from the great European and American orchestras. 'I can assure you', he went on, 'that if the means can be found I would much prefer to undertake these tours with my own orchestra, and I still pray that the comparatively modest guarantee required for the Hallé to tour the United States may be found.'

The unpretentious, almost wistful note of this is memorable. It did not serve, then or ever.

The first fruits of his dealings with Judson were a three-months tour of North America in the winter of 1958–59 and a somewhat shorter tour at the beginning of 1960. On these trips he covered over 30,000 miles and visited a score cities as widely flung as Vancouver and New Orleans, San Francisco and Washington. With the New York Philharmonic, Philadelphia, Boston, Chicago, Cincinnati and Los Angeles orchestras, as well as others of lesser note, he conducted nearly sixty concerts, giving himself hardly a day's breather in an aggregate of twenty-four weeks. The programmes he toured were of a sort that had come to be accepted at home as standard Barbirolli. Several cities were given first hearings of Vaughan Williams's eighth and ninth symphonies and of Walton's *Partita*.* The last named piece, then relatively new, had been conducted by its composer at a Hallé concert nine months earlier following rehearsals at Hewitt Street, an hour's journey or less from the industrial town where Walton was born. Barbirolli attended the rehearsals, of which Walton had charge, following them from score. Of the *Partita* and of Walton's art generally he said: 'Never before did such beauty come out of Oldham.'†

During the first tour he spent a whole month at Carnegie Hall, the occasion (as described in an earlier chapter) of his radiant return after sixteen years to the New York Philharmonic

* His schedule included: Symphonies—Mozart No. 34, Haydn No. 88, Beethoven No. 5, Schubert No. 9, Brahms Nos. 2 and 4, Bruckner No. 4, Tchaikovsky No. 5, Dvorak No. 4, Elgar No. 2, Mahler Nos. 1 and 9. Miscellaneous—*La Mer*, *Enigma* variations, Introduction and Allegro, *Pelléas et Mélisande* suite (Fauré), *The Walk to the Paradise Garden*, intermezzo from *Fennimore and Gerda*, *The Planets* suite, *Romeo and Juliet* (Tchaikovsky), the *Capriccio Espagnol*, *Tam o'Shanter* Overture (Malcolm Arnold), *Elizabethan Suite* (Barbirolli).

† After Malcolm Tillis, op. cit.

Orchestra. That month culminated in four performances on consecutive nights, Thursday to Sunday, of *The Dream of Gerontius*. 'For each performance', he said, 'beloved Carnegie Hall, which holds three thousand, was absolutely full. It's a great tribute to the New York audience—and it was a great thing for me—that they should come to *The Dream* like that: twelve thousand of them in four days. You see, once people hear this music they cannot withstand the fascination and beauty of it.' The second tour took in nine cities. The fourth on his list was Houston, Texas. With the Houston Symphony, in the city's Music Hall, he did his *Elizabethan* Suite, Vaughan Williams's No. 8, Fauré's *Pelléas et Mélisande* music and *La Mer* at a Monday-Tuesday pair of concerts.

For six years or so Houston had enjoyed the services of Stokowski as conductor-in-chief. That tenure had ended. The people who ran the orchestra were looking out for a new man. It struck them at once that Barbirolli would do nicely. Approaches were made. In the autumn they announced that Barbirolli was to be the Houston Symphony's chief conductor and musical adviser. Beginning in October 1961, they said, he would put in three months with the orchestra, conducting six pairs of Monday-Tuesday concerts that month and November; and another six pairs in February and March. This arrangement involved no material encroachment (so it was contended) upon his Hallé work, which had already been much reduced by 'guesting'; it would simply be a matter of shuttling each winter between Manchester and Texas by jet-liner. There was a year of preparation. At the first opportunity he and Evelyn looked for living quarters in Houston. They hired a unit in an apartment hotel 'complete with our own kitchen. Evelyn will be with me. I shall cook. So will she.' The place was a little way out of town and beautifully situated. Six months before his debut season began he started sending out from England master copies to the Houston orchestral library. Sixty pieces of music were involved. Well before rehearsals started his bowings and fingerings had been transferred to stack upon stack of players' copies there. His twelfth and final pair of concerts, schemed to round off the season in March 1962, was given over to Mahler's 'Resurrection' symphony. He set

great store by this. It would be Houston's first hearing of the
work. For the Klopstock finale he had what he rated as a fine
choir, the Houston Chorale. In conversation shortly before
leaving Manchester for his new rostrum he said to this writer
that if he returned to Houston for a second season he meant
to do *Gerontius* as well. The 'if' seemed to imply that the appointment was not a permanent one.

'That's right', he said. 'This is just a test season. I'm conducting this time to see how I like it. Then we'll reconsider.'
Clearly, however, he was vibrant at the prospect. He could
hardly help this. Houston, as he saw it, was an infectiously
vibrant place—

'. . . one of the wealthiest cities in America. It's oil, you
know. And cotton. A progressive place. They have a
tremendous keenness to produce something absolutely first-
class in their theatre and their music and their medical schools.
I'm attracted by the fact that it's all *young* yet. It's a city that
hasn't had time to get bored. Tremendous development is
going on.'

'So money', it was put to him, 'is not necessarily inimical to
music and the other arts?'

'I don't see how it can be when you have all this enthusiasm
to produce something first-rate. I have a completely free hand
as to programmes. If wisely used Mammon is the chap. You
can't do anything without money. The last Edinburgh Festival
lost more money than ever before and has been voted a great
success. Doesn't that show? Take the Hallé. In the early days
the merchants dipped into their pockets to make the orchestra
go. Some people in this country don't like the idea of subsidies.
It's time they learned that the day of Maecenas is over. There
are no rich people left. The Houston orchestra, I gather, has
got the people of the city to put up a kind of guarantee. Rosalind
[the name of his secretary at that time] will give you an idea of
how it works. They put up a tremendous amount of money,
The People themselves, I mean. This is a splendid atmosphere
to walk into.'

When he called Houston one of the wealthiest cities in
America he was not overstating. During the 1950s and much
of the following decade, riches rained upon Houston steadily,
almost frighteningly. 'Downtown' Houston was a startling

example of what had come to be known as the growth pheno-
menon, pulling itself down and putting itself up again, thus
keeping abreast of the times (it hoped), at the rate of millions
of square feet of office space a year. In plum enclaves of the
business section during Barbirolli's tenure, buildings changed
hands at £700 per frontage-inch. The population was on the
way up from under 600,000 to 1,200,000, a process that took a
mere six years. During the same period banks multiplied from
thirty-five to sixty-four. Thousands of millions of dollars washed
in and out of them yearly, a vast tidal movement of spending
and earning. There were poodles with mink jackets and
diamond-studded collars. There were three universities. There
were three television stations. Also there was a Museum of Fine
Arts with, so people said, fine things in it. But the talk at art
parties ran rather upon Houston's private art collections and
the cash value of certain Impressionists and Post Impressionists
that were their pride: here a Gauguin worth $200,000, there a
Picasso that had fetched $185,000, elsewhere a Cezanne insured
for $600,000. For years Barbirolli had been reluctant to
wander at leisure in London because so little was left of the
city he had known and loved from boyhood up. (Looking at
the newest 'high rises' of steel, glass and concrete and reflecting
on what they had replaced, he would say: 'Hitler's bombers
were not the only destroyers.') Houston he judged by different
criteria. Here the writ of nostalgia did not run. He was amused
and spurred by all the briskness and newness. He got on
amiably with the people who ran the Houston Symphony. In
return they made a great deal of him. Their advance publicity
would have it that it was Toscanini in person who, in 1936,
chose him for the New York Philharmonic conductorship.

Back in the summer of 1913, when Houston was a smallish
town, Houston Symphony, or its embryo, had been a theatre-
pit orchestra. One summer afternoon, at the end of a vaudeville
matinee, the players went up on to their own stage to play a
Mozart symphony and excerpts from Bizet and Tchaikovsky.
The right sort of people came to that first concert of the
Houston Symphony. One of its historians writes: 'Although
born in a vaudeville house [it] was a dressy affair from the
start.' Conducted in its maturity by Koussevitsky as well as
Stokowski and by a guest list that included Sargent and

Beecham, the orchestra fielded ninety players or more and was ardently pushed by a cloud of senior patrons, junior patrons, committee men, ubiquitous committee women and board members of whom it listed one hundred and sixty or more. At the head of all sat General Maurice Hirsch, the President, defined by thumbnail biographies as successful attorney, world traveller, connoisseur, art collector, gracious host and music lover. During the second world war he had run a Price Adjustment Board. Monday nights during the season found him and his wife Winifred in the presidential box at all Barbirolli's concerts. They were well turned out and had smiles of a kind at which a man could warm his hands. The General cultivated a sonorous and improving turn of phrase. He thought highly of Houston and sometimes put his thoughts into print. Here are cullings:*

The Orchestra has not only kept step with the commercial, industrial and educational advances of our community but in substantial measure has influenced their growth. Its influence has changed the cultural world's opinion of Houston, which is now recognised as being on a high and fertile plateau of cultural growth. It is our problem, our challenge and our wholehearted determination to maintain and enhance the stimulating service the Symphony Society provides in our community ... Houston has come of age in its cultural life without losing the vigor and inspired objectives of youth. The time has passed for Houston to be culturally on the defensive and apologetic. ... Our cultural accomplishments are great but our aspirations are even greater. Houston has provided for [us] and for those who will come after us not only the physical surroundings of cultural opportunity but a pervading spirit which breathes into that environment the beauty of gracious and exalted living ... Houston can now proudly claim [to be] a city of commerce in its broadest meaning—and, in its finest aspect, a city of culture.

From this it might be supposed that for the Houston

* From *The Course of Greatness*, Houston Symphony's Maintenance Fund Campaign, 1962-63; and as quoted in *HOUSTON* Magazine, June 1961.

Photo: David Farrell, courtesy E.M.I.

Conducting Elgar's *Sea Pictures*, London, 1965. Soloist, Janet Baker. Orchestra: London Symphony.

Consults with the harpist Renata Scheffel-Stein during a *Sea Pictures* session.

Photo: *David Farrell, courtesy E.M.I.*

Symphony, as for other culture providers, to ask was to have—if, indeed, the asking was necessary. It rarely happens, however, that symphonic music lives off the fat of the land, even when the land is so inordinately fat as Texas. On strict scrutiny the 'tremendous amount' of guarantee money spoken of by Barbirolli did not seem to be there. Money had to be asked for and waited for. Always the orchestra could have done with more of it. A typical budget for one main (winter) season of thirty-two concerts (made up of sixteen repeat programmes), with additional dates for students and summer park audiences, worked out at $700,000. Of this General Hirsch could rely on getting $400,000 through the box office. The remaining $300,000, apart from a fraction from the city general fund, came haltingly from some 4,000 Houston folk who made yearly gifts of five dollars or more to the orchestra's maintenance chest. Houston's population was well over a million. In an age and country where numbers often denoted success or lack of it, 4,000 had a forlorn look. Even General Hirsch felt the number should have been 40,000.

On the English standards of a decade ago the Houston players were lavishly paid, or so it seemed at first glance. For a single programme, which they played twice on contiguous nights, and rehearsals that occupied the rest of the week, average rank-and-filers got £43 to £46, or more than twice as much as a Hallé player in his fourth season. The pay for men at front desks exceeded £50. Back-desk newcomers got £35: rather less, it was true, than could be commanded by good shorthand typists, something of a rarity in Houston. Further snags were implicit in this comparison. Whereas a shorthand typist—and Hallé players —could be sure of work and pay all the year round (overwork and underpay, in the case of the latter), the orchestral players of Houston and certain other American cities earned on a seasonal basis only. Long before he took over, Barbirolli knew that to make ends meet during the dead season some of the Houston players supplemented their earnings by selling shoes, insurance and the like; one man had a milk round. On weighing up the problem at close quarters he said how unfortunate it was that highly trained musical artists should be put to such shifts. More work for the players was the only solution. At his instigation schedules were planned between his first and

N

second seasons for concerts in hitherto untapped suburban areas. Thus the players' situation mended somewhat.

Rehearsal in the Music Hall was at the rate of two-and-a-half hours for every concert. As usual he interleaved general rehearsals with sectional ones. As much as ever was heard about the importance of playing with the 'point'. He often discoursed on the difference between a true pianissimo and the sound of a sore throat. The loved, almost statutory Barbirolli scores took their turns, several of them recurring, in a seasonal procession that was to spread over six and a half years: among symphonies the Haydns and the Mozarts, the Beethovens and the Schuberts, the Brahmses (including No. 3, which he had tended to fight shy of) and the Bruckners, Mahler's No. 9 and (more than once) the 'Resurrection'; Nielsen's No. 5, the Tchaikovskys and the Dvořáks. For the rest he predictably did a lot of Vaughan Williams and Elgar, a certain amount of Walton, *La Mer* (of which he never surfeited) the suite from Debussy's *Pelléas* and the full *Daphnis et Chlöe* ballet score. He celebrated Verdi's birth centenary with a painstaking, resplendent *Requiem* (he brought in solo singers from Glyndebourne and the New York Metropolitan Opera) and that of Wagner with an all-Wagner night which offered as well as the *Siegfried Idyll* his *Götterdämmerung* 'tonepoem'. Apart from the Nielsen and Mahler nights little came up that marked off Houston in the 1960s from New York around 1940 or even Glasgow in the 1930s. He made rather a point, however, of Shostakovitch's 'cello concerto and Symphony No. 5, Bartok's third piano concerto and Hindemith's *Symphonic Metamorphoses* on a Theme by Weber.

He and Lady Barbirolli—who was at his side season after season, often with oboe for concerto work but peeling off occasionally for chamber music on platforms outside Houston as well as in it—got on in good-neighbour fashion with Houstonians of all walks and persuasions. Houston had rather the idea that international conductors were remote, cloud-capped creatures who, when they appeared among humdrum humans, descended and condescended from on high. It was remembered that on his Monday and Tuesday concert days, Stokowski was incommunicado, all telephone calls barred. Even the Symphony management could not get through to him. Barbirolli, on the other hand, was accessible at all times except when on the rostrum, to anybody and everybody with serious business. He and Evelyn went to theatres and other people's concerts; whether they sat in stalls or in boxes was all the same to them. They shopped in the fish market. They shopped in stores. They carried parcels to their motor-car. Houston loved them for this. A note was made about it in one of the Symphony programmes. Barbirolli might not have been a 'Sir' at all; which made the fact that he was one all the more piquant. His decisive contacts were, of course, with his players. If he had not been agreeable in their sight he and Evelyn could not have become ex-officio Houstonians as quickly as they did. After his first season he said to the writer:

The orchestra is splendidly good. Of course, their years with Stokowski certainly gave them a sense of sound. Some people say I like sound too much. I don't believe that. I don't believe you can make sound too beautiful. Technically I am the opposite of Stokowski in some ways. As you know, I insist on everybody bowing alike. My first words to the orchestra were: 'In my insistence on bowing I am not criticising your previous chief.' Everybody has his own theory and practice in these matters. Myself I learned music in terms of bowing and fingering. Unless other people do that I think they are doing it all wrong. Already we've got the Hallé sound. Evelyn comes to the first rehearsal of mine with a new orchestra. She goes away. She doesn't attend for a couple of days. Then the third day she says the new orchestra sounds like the Hallé. I have conducted sixteen American orchestras including the Big Four—New York, Boston, Philadelphia, Chicago. After a bit they all acquire my characteristics for good or ill. They love it. Hard to explain this sound I infect them with. An intangible thing.

'Signature sound' was a matter to which he often adverted. He cited a senior Boston critic as saying, 'It's extraordinary how this man has completely changed the sound of our orchestra [the Boston Symphony] in three days. It now sounds more like a European orchestra. He has given it a European patina, like old bronze.' He added: 'You see, you have a particular sound in your mind wherever you are. You somehow make them [i.e.,

orchestras anywhere] make that sound. Last time I was in
Berlin Herr Stresemann, the manager of the Philharmonic,
said: "Ah! The Barbirolli sound is back. It will be back again
when you conduct us next time." He liked the Barbirolli sound.
It's induced by some means, nobody knows what.' Perhaps
psychology was what did it? To an Australian interviewer he
had said: 'The secret of being a good conductor is to be a good
psychologist. I bully those who need it, encourage the shy ones,
persuade those who just need persuasion, and when I've finished
every orchestra I conduct sounds a little bit like me.'*

Houston's concert hall seated something over 3,000. It could
not be said that he jammed the place from his very début.
What could be said was that over two seasons, concert by
concert, support grew steadily until big audiences and standing
ovations, some of them prolonged, were the order of the day.
There was always a swarm of college and high school students
in seats at concessionary prices. It might have been expected
that Barbirolli's Mozart-to-Mahler spectrum would have irked
some of them. Why no Stockhausen, Messiaen, Webern, Elliott
Carter, late Stravinsky, mature Schönberg? Such questions
seem never to have been so much as bruited either publicly
or, to any significant extent, privately. It was accepted that
Barbirolli knew best; that he was giving them the right thing.
Such was the measure of his prestige. For what they received
the student concertgoers were truly—and respectfully—
thankful. Barbirolli in turn was thankful about his players.
At the end of one of his early seasons he told an exulting audience
that Houston Symphony was great, a treasure, something to be
nurtured. 'In no city in the world', he asserted, 'could an
orchestra serve me better.'

No man in his right mind uses such words without following
them up to appropriate purpose. A year later he and the
Houston Symphony were off on their first tour of the Eastern
seaboard. In three weeks they played nineteen cities, ringing
the changes on Beethoven's Symphony No. 7, Tchaikovsky's
No. 4, Dvořák's No. 4 and Vaughan Williams's No. 6, with
half a dozen programme fillers by Berlioz, Verdi, Delius,
Mendelssohn and Richard Strauss. The heady thing about the
nineteen cities was that one of them happened to be New York

* *Sydney Morning Herald*, 30th, May 1955.

and another Washington. In New York they played the new-fangled Philharmonic Hall, part of the Lincoln Centre for the Performing Arts. All gilt and glass, blue and gold, this auditorium could seat 2,600. There were only seventy empty seats on the night. Smart, warmhearted audience. Houston had sent a 'delegation' of forty. The programme bracketed the Sixth of Vaughan Williams and Beethoven's Seventh. The Vaughan Williams has an Epilogue of murmurous, meandering wraiths. Always it strikes wonder and at least a touch of awe. On occasion it assumes an almost theatrical dimension. So it was, by common consent, on the night of March 3rd, 1964. Beethoven followed Vaughan Williams without obliterating him. Even so, it was a Seventh that offered debating points. In the Trio he had the horns lift up their bells and in the last bar of all made the drums sound like guns going off. The critics were there in strength. What one of them called 'the aggressive spit and polish' of the playing made what others as well as the writer accepted as a welcome change from much that had been heard latterly on the Eastern seaboard. There were fortissimos that struck the *New York Times* as wiry and even raucous, though this, or something like it, might (suggested the *Boston Globe*) have been the desiccating effect of 'that miserable Philharmonic Hall [which] is unflattering even to a great string ensemble.' There were no other adverse notes of any moment. After their fashion the critics were nearly as cordial as the audience, who gave Barbirolli six recalls. These he shared with the orchestra, sometimes acknowledging the applause modestly from afar with waves of his handkerchief. In the end admirers invaded the platform and ringed him about, clapping and shouting with delight.

Something of the same euphoria marked the end of the Washington concert. Detained at the White House on affairs of State, President Johnson reached Constitution Hall late. They told him the last movement of the Vaughan Williams symphony was about to begin. He stayed on in his limousine and had a Texan personage or two presented to him there. Joining Mrs. Johnson and their eldest daughter in the presidential box after the interval, he listened to Beethoven's Seventh with chin studiously propped on palm. When it was over he clapped with everybody else for full five minutes to a flicker of flashbulbs. The 'delegates' had much to talk about on getting back to Houston. After taking over the orchestra in 1961, Barbirolli had misquoted Churchill to General Hirsch, saying, 'Give me the troops [i.e., musicians of the right quality] and I will finish the job.' As he stepped off the airliner Hirsch was there again, with outstretched hand and smile. Barbirolli picked up the 1961 analogy and rounded it off. 'General, mission accomplished!' he exclaimed. The Mayor was there as well. Conferring honorary citizenship upon Barbirolli and handing over a token key to the city, he thanked him for safely delivering Houston's 'cultural CARE package' to the East and said what a pleasure it was to read in the New York newspapers that their ideas of Houston would have to be remodelled. The nominal purpose of the tour had been to celebrate the orchestra's golden jubilee. It had also been a great trooping the colour for Houston.

Money entered into the picture, of course. The jubilee season ended a week later with Barbirolli's first Houston production of *The Dream of Gerontius*. The programme that night carried, on a page facing the opening stanzas of John Henry Newman's mystical text, an advertisement SOUNDS OF THE CITY, by one of Houston's legion banks. It read: 'The outstanding performance of the Houston Symphony Orchestra under Sir John Barbirolli is a milestone in the cultural development of Houston. Our appreciation of this achievement stems from the recognition of goals similar to our own. Constructive banking, like constructive cultural development, fosters further development of a dynamic city.' This had a fine, elevating ring. Just what it meant took some working out. It was evidence of the earnest fraternisation which Barbirolli had to put up with. He put up with it very well. On official occasions he spoke of Houston as 'our great city' or 'this great city of ours'. He spoke of his ambition, of the 'simple duty' he had undertaken, to provide the people of Houston with 'one of America's finest symphony orchestras'.

Again he had won wide popular following, the acclaim of a community for whom he was less an artist than a picturesque, romantic 'character'. Their warmth towards him gave comfort in a crucial hour of grief, the second most crucial hour of its sort in his life. The first hour had been when Lorenzo died.

Now the hour had struck for Louise: for Nonna, Mémé (as the family alternatively called her), Lorenzo's widow. On the eve of her ninety-first birthday she was struck down by coronary thrombosis, as her son was to be, and died quickly. Barbirolli flew to Houston and started the 1962–63 season twelve days later. His head was erect, his heart stricken. To his Houston friends he had talked often of his mother. They knew of her as 'a wonderful young lady of ninety'. That was his own phrase. The friends affectionately conspired. The outcome was a Louise Barbirolli Memorial Fund, whose material purpose is to support the endowment of Houston's orchestra in perpetuity. Its intangible purpose was to let him know that, thousands of miles from his and Evelyn's fireside, they would always be among people who constantly thought for their happiness and that they could always count upon Houston as a second home city.

In Houston everything was spick, span and ruthlessly new except for a few such things as the Music Hall. Before Barbirolli's time there ended a concert hall-cum-opera house was built with a roof that could be lifted and lowered and walls that could trundle in and out in such a way as to seat 1,800 or 3,000 or just about any-sized audience in between. In three years eight and a half million dollars had been pumped into the city by culture-bent philanthropic foundations, most of it for music and the performing arts generally. The Houston Symphony and other cultural agencies, agog about their prospective new home, long before the roof was on it, invited Barbirolli to open the place with a stately concert. He accepted with delight.

It was tempting to draw comparisons with Manchester. Not all the comparisons were in Manchester's favour. Perhaps because of Barbirolli's more frequent and longer absences (he regularly shot off to Houston as soon as the Hallé season was well begun and returned as regularly early every New Year), there had been some falling off at the Free Trade Hall and outbreaks of grumbling both private and in print. Whether because of their limitations or because it is hard for guest conductors however accomplished to win the affection and loyalty of a particular public, those who took his place on the Hallé rostrum did not consistently draw the old Hallé crowd in the old numbers. The programmes they put on were rarely 'Barbirolli programmes'. After all, they had their own prefer- ences and specialities and their own careers to promote. On nights devoted in part to 'this modern stuff' the ratio of empty seats was noticeable. There were nights when even Barbirolli himself came up against a recrudescent conservatism or back- woods outlook. For a programme that coupled Elgar's *Falstaff* and Bartok's Concerto for Orchestra he found the hall half full.

Progress of a sort was achieved in certain material matters. The 'Factory' at Hewitt Street had always been cramped and stuffy. It now became exasperating because of electric trains passing close by. The orchestra evacuated and went out to an ebony black Congregational church in the former working-class suburb of Hulme, thus taking part in a transformation that went wider and deeper than music. For much of the 1960s much of Hulme was desolation. Acre upon acre of mean streets had been pulled down. The local authority was taking its time about putting up better. Zion 'Congs', with little else, survived in a desert of flattened rubble. Nearby a mobile library, sunk almost to the hubs in cindery soil and sparse grass, served a non-existent population. Hulme was, in short, an ugly void. It must have chilled the heart of many a guest conductor who, with rehearsals on hand, set eyes on it for the first time. A few whitebeards were left who remembered Zion before the Kaiser's war, with a congregation of eight or nine hundred every Sunday morning and every Sunday night. By 1939 the congregation had shrunk to two hundred. After the demolitions an average morning congregation was twenty-five, an average evening one about fifty—and most of these were oldsters who came in by bus for old times' sake from the new estates to which they had moved.

The minister remained. 'People', he said, 'don't *believe* any more.' Pending housing redevelopment and new opportunity for spreading the Word, he turned Zion into a business. When he heard the Hallé were looking for a new rehearsal place, he spruced up the main church hall and invited them to give it a trial. The trial was a success. He let the hall for rehearsals at twenty-five pounds a date. At the same time he let off what was once the 'intermediate' Sunday school. This became the Hallé's music library. Other parts of a rambling building were a rent collector's office, overflow classrooms for a primary school and offices where union dues were paid. To hear and watch Barbirolli, black rehearsal-jacket buttoned up to the neck Toscanini fashion, endlessly burnishing *Verklärte Nacht* or *The Swan of Tuonela* or Mahler's No. 3 or Bruckner's No. 7 or the finale of *Le Baiser de la fée* at this forlorn suburban crossroads was a bizarre experience, especially when the place happened to be cluttered (as at least once happened) with blinding lamps and television cameras, one of them mounted on a 'dolly' which, with operator on board, endlessly moved in and out, focusing on Barbirolli. A time came at any rehearsal when the music had to end. Those who had made beauty and those who had drunk it in went out into a void. Contrast with the beauty they had heard made the rubble twice more melancholy than before.

There had been another change of roof: the Barbirollis' own. They now lived in a ripe Victorian house in a street with handsome and vestigial lamp standards in Salford, a borough which so blends into Manchester that nobody but a chartered surveyor can be sure where one starts and the other ends. Because of bygone sootfall, Walton Lodge, New Hall Road, looked as though, like Zion 'Congs', it had been carved out of ebony. A snug, roomy, inconvenient sort of house. Like others adjoining, it so belonged to the past that on first sight one seemed to have turned a corner into 1880 or, at latest, 1908.

There was much to see inside that proclaimed John and Evelyn. More than most people they were to be judged by the things they lived amongst: by the 1740 display cabinet with Sèvres plaques showing rustic youths and maidens and a minute porcelain 'cellist, lace cuffed and tiewigged, playing from music on a music stand, the whole domed under glass; by the splendid families of Georgian glass and Lowestoft ware, the latter dominated by a buxom teapot with gilt knob on lid; by vintage playbills which Evelyn had bought at sixpence a time before the war from trays outside a dealer's shop in a passageway off St. Martin's Lane—Weber conducting *Oberon* at Covent Garden in 1826, the first London performances of *Così fan tutte*, *Fidelio* and *Il Barbiere*, an 1827 concert bill (Covent Garden again), with miscellany of artists, among them 'the celebrated Master Liszt'; by the Nelson snuff box, with Nelson's portrait on lid, a reminder of Barbirolli's Nelson cult. He had a cult for Napoleon, too. In his study on the ground floor, no bigger than a box room, hung a photograph of himself as an infant 'with a forelock', he would venture, 'rather like Napoleon's, don't you think?' There were other relics on the study walls. Four of the scholarship and prize certificates that came to him as a boy, for example. One of them bore the date June 13th, 1913. He was thirteen years old at the time. From that day forth 13 was his lucky number. Superstitions he took seriously, or pretended to: 'You'll not catch me starting anything on a Friday', he used to say. 'That's the Italian side of me.'

More photographs. One of Barbirolli kneeling in academic gown before the Queen Mother (Chancellor) at a London University degree ceremony. Another of Barbirolli conducting Horowitz and orchestra in a crammed Queen's Hall. Date: March 1926. A third of Barbirolli conducting a shirt-sleeved Fritz Kreisler in some concerto at a recording session. Autograph letters, too. One was signed by Gioacchino Rossini, Paris, September 1865. Another bore Franz Liszt's name. Neither said anything of great interest. The study had a display cabinet of its own. The oddments in it ranged from cricket (a Lord's Taverners' shield inscribed to Sir John Barbirolli, President, 1958) to Sibelius (an intact, sealed cigar left by the composer and given to Barbirolli by the composer's family.) There was an upright piano which seemed to make itself as small as it could. It was in a walnut case, an old-fashioned Blüthner from Leipzig. He played a couple of chords on it and said to a visitor: 'You can't get these nowadays unless you're very lucky.' In the corner stood a gramophone. For the visitor's benefit he put on *Jazz Sebastian Bach*, an assortment of Bach's keyboard works sung by a French group, Les Swingles, with string band and jazz-type rhythm section. He said how good the Swingles were and scrutinised the visitor almost anxiously in hope that his face would light up sympathetically.

Among shelved scores were ten editions, mostly different ones, of Bach's St. Matthew Passion music and standard critical works on how to prepare it for performance. These had been his tools. Other scores lay casually about. They bore his bowing and other marks. He had used the flyleaves of some for jottings also about surgery, in which his hobby-interest remained ever alert. There was a copy of Mahler's No. 6. This he had bowed while on tour with the Houston orchestra in 1964. The flyleaf carried four memoranda. One said it was time he gave serious thought to getting some 5-string double-bass fiddles. The other three read: 'Periosteum.—Tough, adherent covering of a rib' 'Pericardium.—Thin covering over the heart.' 'Fascia.— Tough tissue over the muscles.' Mahler's No. 7 he finished bowing at Streatham in August 1960. The flyleaf reminded him to look up cures, if there were any, for disseminated sclerosis and tubular meningitis.

Part of Walton Lodge was made over to the office. Threads ran from that office over land and sea to more than thirty countries and seventy or more orchestras, these including the most famous ones in the world. He had conducted them all. The office was run by his secretary, the calm, splendid Brenda Bracewell. With so many promoters abroad and at home bidding and at times queuing for his services, the apparently simple job of ensuring that one assignment did not clash with the next and that there were means and time enough for getting from one to another became burdensome and exceedingly complex. On top of this there were programmes to plan and negotiate and, in many cases, band parts to check and ship. It is doubtful whether a more complicated and nicely poised one-man business existed anywhere in the land. Here are random, day-to-day citations from a Hallé office précis of his engagements for a sequence of fifteen months during the mid-1960s:

Travel to Rome (Santa Cecilia Orchestra), four rehearsals, two concerts. . . . To San Remo (San Remo Orchestra), rehearsal, rehearsal, concert. To Venice (La Fenice), rehearsal, rehearsal, rehearsal, concert. Return to Manchester. . . . To Harrogate, rehearsal and concert. . . . To King's Lynn. . . . To Buxton Festival. . . . Fly to Budapest (Philharmonie Orchestra), rehearsal, rehearsal and concert; rehearsal, rehearsal and concert. . . . London. Rehearsal with New Philharmonia Orchestra, rehearsal with ditto. Fly to Montevideo with New Phil. Concerts Montevideo. Night journey to Buenos Aires. . . . To São Paulo. . . . To Rio, concert,

concert (recurring). . . . Fly with New Philharmonia to
Milan. . . . Fly to Manchester. . . . Travel to Birmingham,
York, Wolverhampton. . . . Salisbury, Winchester, Portsmouth [all] with Hallé. . . . Fly to Houston, October 18.
Fly back November 27. . . . *Messiah*, Belle Vue. . . . Fly to
Belgrade (Belgrade Philharmonic Society), rehearsal, rehearsal, rehearsal, concert. . . . To Berlin (Berlin Philharmonic Orchestra), rehearsal (recurring), concert, concert,
recording sessions, concert. . . . Manchester. . . . Houston. . . .
Miami Beach. . . . Staten Island. . . . Montclair. . . . Knox-
ville. . . . Clemson. . . . Columbus. . . . To London for recording sessions. To Manchester overnight: rehearsal and concert
with past and present students of Royal Manchester College
of Music. . . . Overnight to London: rehearsal and concert
with First Orchestra, Royal Academy of Music. . . . Croydon,
Guildford. . . . Margate. . . . Play 'cello in Haydn quartet
and Franck piano quintet, Westminster Abbey, with King's
Lynn Ensemble. . . . Fly to Genoa: rehearsals (3) and
concert. . . . Zürich (Tonhalle Orchestra). . . . Venice (La
Fenice). . . . Bexhill. . . . Buxton. . . . Open-air concert with
Hallé, Ken Wood. . . . To Taormina for students' conducting
course (seven days) with Taormina Orchestra. . . . Manchester. . . . Bedworth, Bridlington, Barry. . . . Fly to
Houston. . . .

The fifteen months from which the foregoing items are taken
included fifty-one days that were marked 'free days'. The 'free'
days were nominal as to probably ninety per cent of them,
most of them taken up by score-reading, marking of master
copies, replying to letters and dealing with administrative
matters. The same months included 133 days of travel or, if
added together, four solid months of airliners, railway trains,
motor-cars and the occasional ship: a perpetual criss-crossing
of continents which took its own toll of stamina. As the decade
went on he became more footloose, more of a darter-about.
His parishes were now hemispheres. Towards the end of 1966
he resigned from the chief-conductorship of the Houston
orchestra; early in 1968 from that of the Hallé itself. Henceforth
he was Conductor Emeritus of the one and Conductor Laureate
of the other. He would still go to Houston every year, but for a

limited number of concerts. So far as the Hallé was concerned
he would still take a number of mid-week and Sunday concerts,
though fewer than before. The old treadmill (not that he
ever called it that) of concerts with the Hallé in innumerable
other towns at home was over for good.

What these withdrawals meant was that he was going to be
more busy, if anything, not less. To his Houston people he
explained that he was going to conduct more recordings and
take up more overseas assignments. To the Hallé Society he
explained that his allotted span being nearly run (he was now
in his sixty-ninth year), he intended to return somewhat to
his old love, opera. Pressing invitations were constantly coming
in from great opera houses. He was going to give himself the
pleasure of accepting some of them.

Was there no hidden determinant?

The summer before his death he talked with this writer
during a Hallé rehearsal-break in London. Setting me down
in a chair, he put his hands on my shoulders and, without
preamble, said: 'There's something I want to tell you as a
friend. I started a new career in my sixties. Why? Because I
needed money. I had to earn thousands, because thousands had
gone.'

He told of a reversal of fortunes which had come about not
through unwise speculation or anything resembling it but
through circumstances which he could not have been expected
to foresee and through agencies which had seemed utterly
dependable. The details were given in confidence and cannot
be narrated here. All that need be said is that the reverse was
one that gave much distress, not on pecuniary grounds alone,
to the Barbirollis and much concern to their intimates.* To
conclude that the comings and goings and general accelerando
of the last years were dictated by pecuniary pressure would be
mistaken, however. The imperious Barbirolli drive came from
deep inside, was part of his marrow, had always been there and
would continue there until death peremptorily felled him.

* A summary of his will was made public on December 18th 1970.
According to this he left £36,307 gross and a net estate valued at nil. He was
understood to have made provision for Lady Barbirolli during his lifetime.

CHAPTER TWENTY-TWO

MOTO PERPETUO——

AFTER an interlude with another recording company he returned to the old label, H.M.V., and associated ones under the aegis of E.M.I. He went out on recording missions, some of them linked with public concerts, to Berlin, Vienna, Rome, Paris, a little greyer, a little thinner, sleeping minimally at night and making up for this by strategically timed catnaps during the day. Given a sofa or a comfortable chair, he could fall asleep precipitately during rehearsal breaks and waken up refreshed after half an hour or less without so much as knuckling an eye. He stayed in small hotels or *pensions* and cultivated unpretentious restaurants which he knew to have good kitchens.

He shrank more than ever from ostentation, from 'stylish' living. This is how he put it in 1964, some allusion having been made to social occasions, parties and like pleasures: 'I go out occasionally if I have to, but I can't pretend to like it a great deal. I'm a very shy person, in fact—*not* an unfriendly person. The idea of going to a smart restaurant gives me the willies. It's one of the things I've loved up here [Manchester]. They haven't demanded anything like that of me.'

His friends were as concerned as ever about the little he ate whether out or at home. He preferred, on the whole, to attend to that little himself. When abroad he would seek out approved 'delicatessens' and charcuteries and return to his bedroom-bathroom suite with small parcels, boasting how he had bought salami or Parma ham at threepence a helping cheaper than in showy shops. Of over-eating, even of average eating habits, he was apt to be mildly censorious. More than once during a nerve-testing rehearsal sequence with some Italian orchestra, a player would say marvellingly, 'But, Maestro, you are never tired! How do you keep so wide-awake?' He would reply, 'Because I eat no lunch. You, on the other hand, not only eat lunch. You eat too much of it, all of you. That's why you are tired in the afternoon.' When afternoon sessions nearer home struck him as inattentive he was known to exclaim: 'Soup, roast, pudding! Soup, roast, pudding! That's why you're making these mistakes.'

Since his days with Gaisberg recording methods had been not so much reformed as liberated. Electronic tape was in. The day of the long-play disc and stereophonic sound was reaching high noon. He adapted himself absorbedly to the new tricks and techniques. Recording the four Brahms symphonies and the shorter Brahms orchestral pieces with the Vienna Philharmonic Orchestra and much Mahler with the Berlin Philharmonic and the New Philharmonia of London, he was found to be uncommonly quick; and nobody was more surprised at his quickness than himself. Often he begged for more recording sessions than he turned out to need. With the New Philharmonia at Watford he completed Mahler's No. 5 and No. 6 in a total of four sessions fewer than had been scheduled. Ultrasensitive to the atmosphere of a session, he knew when his players were really caught up and fired by the music. Often it was as though he were on a public rostrum with a 'live' audience behind him. In short, he brought to the recording floor an acute sense of performance and always aimed at long, definitive takes. The alternative way (which can produce equally good results) is to record a symphony in bits. You play the bits, or some of them, time after time, pick out the bits that are best and string them smoothly together so that they sound as if the whole score had been played straight through. This way did not appeal to Barbirolli at all. In Vienna he did several Brahms symphonic movements virtually complete in one run.

He was never insatiable for playbacks. Usually one playback sufficed. If what he heard had flaws here and there he would re-record corresponding snippets in the routine way and have them substituted. But he was never jumpily fastidious; never, as some have been known to, tinkered obsessively. Before passing a take he liked to have a supporting opinion. He would say to Ronald Kinloch Anderson,* who directed most of his

* Senior Recording Producer, International Artists' Department, E.M.I. Ltd.

recordings during the 1960s: 'You think it's all right. I think it's all right. Fine. Let it go.'

The public concerts that preceded or followed his recording sessions or punctuated them often brought new prestige. Sometimes they encountered blank misunderstanding. His following with the Berlin Philharmonic public remained cordial, almost hero-worshipping through season after season. On outstanding Mahler nights he was acknowledged by sober judges to have given Berlin concert-goers a renewed and perhaps completer possession of music that was supposed to be particularly their own. Sometimes he tried his hand at 'importations'. These did not always prosper. With l'Orchestre nationale de Paris he did Nielsen's No. 5. Paris did not know what to make of it. An unlucky occasion. He put it behind him quickly. With the Vienna Philharmonic he did *La Mer*, a score they had not set eyes or thoughts on for years. The rehearsals were a tussle. The performance was not much better, judging from his comments later.

'They did their best', he said. 'I had a hell of a time to get them to play as well as they did. They still just don't *know* this piece.'

Although pleased with their work on the recording floor, he sometimes spoke of the Vienna Philharmonic with a surprise that verged on scorn; he was quoted as saying that they were living on their reputation, not renewing it.

In 1966, having conducted his way along a chain of Italian cities, the last of which was Florence, he arrived with Evelyn one sweltering August day in Rome. As well as rehearsing and conducting a number of concerts during the same period with the Santa Cecilia Orchestra, he was to record *Madama Butterfly* at the Teatro dell'Opera with Renata Scotto, Carlo Bergonzi, Ronaldo Panerai, Anna di Stasio and others. The first thing he saw outside the railway station was a poster announcing open-air performances of *Butterfly* at the Baths of Caracalla. They were to run concurrently with his *Butterfly* recording sessions on alternate nights. The same orchestra, that of the Opera, would be playing in both. 'My God!' he exploded, 'I'm to interest them in *that*!' As usually happened for recordings during the summer recess, a platform had been built out from the stage over a considerable part of the stalls. Barbirolli had a look right away at the proposed lay-out of his forces. He would be out on the platform, the orchestra disposed in a wide semi-circle before him. His solo singers would be on the stage, the orchestra between him and them. The chorus would be somewhere behind the soloists.

The lay-out would not do, he said. He asked that the gap between the orchestra and the cast be much narrowed. This reflected a foible of his. When conducting solo singers he always wanted them so near that he could 'read' their faces, watching the words come out syllable by syllable. At home, when recording with, for example, the admired Janet Baker in song cycles and other forms for solo voice and orchestra, he had a small platform placed for her in mid-orchestra, directly facing him. Such arrangements involved the engineers in ticklish balance arrangements so that the singer should not overspill into the orchestra's microphone and the orchestra into hers. It was only rarely that niceties of this kind were conceded. Barbirolli was a special case, however. It was worth while going to some trouble to make him feel happy. The lay-out for *Butterfly* was 'concertina'ed' accordingly. He would have liked the singers even closer in. The technicians had done as much as they could, however. He was not always an easy man to satisfy.

On the morning of the first session he stood at a pass door from the wings. One minute to go. He paused, listening grimly to chatter, shouting, instruments being tuned up. The noise was no greater than usual when an Italian pit orchestra is about to start a rehearsal. 'I'm not going on', he told an aide, 'until there is absolute quiet. Where's the *ispettore* [orchestral manager]? Get hold of the *ispettore* and tell him what I say.' Somebody ran the *ispettore* to ground. The *ispettore* moved among the players' desks, gesticulating, pleading and rebuking. 'If there's not silence there'll be no Maestro.' This was the effect of what he said.

The din subsided. Barbirolli came on. Or rather, he made his entry. Climbing to the orchestral platform, he did not take his place at once but, pacing slowly, walked away from the orchestra and made a wide circuit before mounting the rostrum. The players watched and were humbled. Silence prevailed. Such a silence in such a situation had never been known in that theatre before. From the rostrum he greeted them in Italian, saying how pleased he was to be there and what a good job they were going to make of *Madama Butterfly*. The orchestra applauded obstreperously.

Time pressed because of imminent staff holidays. In the ordinary way *Butterfly* would have been spread over fourteen three-hour sessions. Barbirolli got it out of the way in ten sessions of four hours each. On top of this he put in piano rehearsals with the singers. From the start he treated *Butterfly* as a great work. He did not say it was great in so many words but made it clear that that was what he thought from the finesse and reverence he brought to every page. He brought patience, too. Butterfly's entry music, most of it offstage with women's chorus, lasts a matter of minutes. To get the right musical textures and the illusion of distance and of voices coming always nearer, he worked at it for three hours. Elsewhere he attended to the words as scrupulously as the notes; no drama coach could have been more concerned with refinements of characterisation. In the scene where Goro the marriage broker shows Pinkerton round the house which has been leased for 'nine hundred and ninety-nine years', he did much verbal pointing and sharpening. Discussing these minutiae with de Palma, who sang the part, he agreed that Goro was a ruffian but held that he was an elegant ruffian and must be made to sound just that.

He nursed the singing magnetically, mouthing the words while 'beating' the music. On pianissimos he would let his jaw drop and lift his eyebrows adjuringly. Kinloch Anderson had a telling phrase for all this: 'He breathes the words into the singers' mouths.' The sun blazed implacably, day after day, until the last session. This had been reserved for the Flower Duet (Butterfly and Susuki, act two). The session was timed to end at 5 p.m. sharp, when Barbirolli was to leave for an airflight to London. No sooner had the session begun than the weather broke. Thunder crashed, rain drummed on the roof of the theatre. Recording was out of the question. He put the orchestra through a token rehearsal against the noise. The storm drew off at four o'clock. He completed the Flower Duet to everybody's satisfaction at one minute to five and caught his plane.

Recording grand opera is one thing, performing it publicly another. Notwithstanding the invitations he had been receiving from the great opera houses, it was a longish time before he made his bow to a new public in any one of them. He returned to Rome in the spring of 1969 to conduct an *Aida* revival by which the management set great store. Attending some of the *Butterfly* rehearsals, the artistic director of the Teatro dell'Opera had been impressed by the beauty of tone which Barbirolli got from the tough, hardbitten pit orchestra and also by the discipline he imposed on the players without leaving sore feelings in his wake. Immediately after the last *Butterfly* session, indeed, the players had given him a supper to show their admiration. The management knew he would be welcome inside the house and were pretty sure the Roman public would be pleased. He had not conducted opera publicly for fourteen years, that is to say, since the 1954–55 season at Covent Garden, when his renewed connection petered out with a handful of *Bohèmes*. His spokesman, Crickmore, had as good as said that the Covent Garden musical directorship could have been his for the asking. Soon after these last *Bohèmes*, however, Rafael Kubelik was appointed to the post; and the chance was not to return, a fact which saddened a substantial pro-Barbirolli party among English opera-goers.

For *Aida* he had a fortnight of rehearsals. At the first one, for orchestra only, history repeated itself. Again he stood at the pass door. The time had come for the rehearsal to start. Again the players were talking, laughing, cross-talking and tuning-up to the top of their bent. He sent in a message: No rehearsal until the noise stopped. Instantly a silence fell as of the tomb. Again he walked to the rostrum with studied slowness. Instead of taking up the baton he began talking about *Aida* and went on for a long time. The upshot of his talk was that *Aida* was 'un opera inesplorata'. An aggressive thought, all things considered. For all his Italian look and his fluent Venetian dialect, Barbirolli was given to talking about something called cricket, quoted Churchill often and with zest and was obviously English to the marrow. In the land of Giuseppe Verdi, where *Aida* was mother's milk for all and bread and butter for many, an Englishman was coolly telling them they hadn't yet got to the bottom of a score everybody knew so well that nobody gave it a second thought. It sounded uncommonly like cheek. But it was reverent cheek. They rose to it.

In rehearsal he whittled and honed and polished away as ever at pianissimos. 'Softer. . . . Softer still', he bade the Radames at one point. 'If you don't sing this softly', he said, 'you'll not be heard out in front.' Rome is still musing over this paradox. What did it mean? Nobody could be sure. Certainly it worked in the Nile Scene and in much of the last act. These were agreed by old hands to have subtleties of strand and colour which, in Rome, at any rate, nobody had suspected to be there. Before the Nile Scene particularly he genuflected. 'Quel terzo atto!' he said. 'Chè bellezza, chè miracolo, chè poesia!' He was nearing seventy. Act three held more wonder for him than when he was twenty. Somebody in the orchestra called him The Wizard. The nickname caught on. 'A Roma', he would boast to friends elsewhere in Italy, 'l'orchestra mi chiama Il Mago'; and he would chuckle himself into a spluttering cough over it.

From London members of the Barbirolli 'clan' and from Manchester twenty of his 'supporters' flew in for the opening night which, like the ones that followed, lifted Barbirolli to the skies. The public of the Teatro dell'Opera took him to its bosom so impetuously and warmly that he almost forgave their intrusive (and predictable) clapping and cheers on certain vocal climaxes. It was Gwyneth Jones's night as well as his. Miss Jones was one of the young native singers whose talents, nursed at Covent Garden, had latterly given something like international standing and lustre to the old house and, more importantly, its resident company. She had worked with Barbirolli before. During the previous summer she had sung Desdemona 'opposite' the Otello of James McCracken and Dietrich Fischer-Dieskau's Iago in his recording of Verdi's opera. This he conducted in the assembly room of one of those London suburban town halls which, complete with town clerks, treasurers, sewage departments and (in some cases) police mortuaries, proved such a boon to hard-pressed recording managers during the boom-phase of stereo-recording.

No more solemn charge than *Otello* had come his way. His father and grandfather, as we know, had played in the pit at

the first production of *Otello* in Milan eighty years earlier.
Thus he early conceived for the score a double reverence:
that of an impassioned Verdian, that also of a son and grandson.
He was destined never to conduct *Otello* in the theatre. Three
months before Walthamstow he had done two concert performances of it with a different set of principals in Manchester.
At the end of each performance there was an ovation that
shook the Free Trade Hall to its girders.

E.M.I. had mooted the recording two years ahead. It had
never been out of his head in the interim. He had known every
stave of it for thirty or forty years from performances which he
had attended and from casual reading of the score. It did not
follow from this that he knew *Otello* in the absolute sense or
anything approaching it. For over a year he took the score on
his travels. It was with him in Vienna when he was working
on the Brahms symphonies. He regularly took it to bed with
him, poring into the small hours and again on early waking,
over phrasing tactics, shades and piquancies of characterisation
and countless verbal pointings. All the time his mind's ear was
devouring the details of Verdi's instrumentation and assessing
them against microphone 'play' and control-room techniques.
While in Berlin for concerts with the Philharmonic he ran into
his Iago, Fischer-Dieskau. Together they put Iago's words and
music under the microscope. He said how delighted he was to
find a singer whose first point and last were the composer's
directions—pianissimos included. At Walthamstow he went to
the piano and rehearsed the children's chorus in the Garden
Scene, act two. The piano part hereabouts is not a demanding
one. The children were impressed just the same. Before the
recordings proper began he had a full rehearsal, a pre-polishing
of especially important or problematical bits, with the orchestra,
on this occasion the New Philharmonia of London, with which
he had become much identified both in the concert hall and on
recording-floors.* The trumpets which, group by group,

* In August 1965 he had taken over the last 'leg' of the New Philharmonia's tour of South America and the Caribbean, the first part of the
tour having been attended to by other conductors. He visited São Paulo,
Rio de Janeiro (where he had an audience of 15,000 in a stadium), Port of
Spain and Kingston, conducting seven out of a total of twenty-seven
concerts. He and the orchestra rounded off by flying to New York and

scream triumphantly from different points backstage to mark the Venetian ambassador's arrival in the third act had a half-day to themselves. He posted one group at the back of the hall, another group in the lobby, a third in a corridor. Each group had its sub-conductor who followed Barbirolli's cues and beat on closed-circuit television. For the broodings and uphill charge of muted double-basses when Otello enters Desdemona's bedchamber he had thought of calling a sectional rehearsal. None was needed. The double-basses of the New Philharmonia gave him the right tone and homogeneity from the start. Also they were in tune. He beamed, and had reason to.

Thus to the end: the end, that is to say, of the heartrending fourth act. He told his friends in Rome later that after Gwyneth Jones had sung the Willow Song and Ave Maria, case-hardened technicians were in tears. It was not the singing alone that had moved them. The genius of Verdi had counted for as much. Also that of Boito. He held that among operas *Otello* was the perfect drama. Nothing would be cut from it. Nothing could be added.

There were foreign assignments of high moment outside his recording missions. After rehearsals which spread over a fortnight, he and Pierre Boulez, the brilliant and (as conductors go) young French composer-conductor, at this writing chief-conductor-elect of the B.B.C. Symphony Orchestra, flew with that orchestra early in January 1967 to Prague, first stop on a Central European and Soviet tour which was to take them as far as Leningrad. The going was hard: twelve concerts and two days of travel (Warsaw to Moscow and Moscow to Leningrad) in fourteen days through bitter weather, 20° C. below zero being the top temperature. Some of the double-basses cracked with cold half-way through the tour and had to be taken to an orchestral workshop in Moscow for repair. All the trains were

performing in a gigantic marquee at the Long Island Festival. His programmes included, as to symphonies, Haydn's No. 88, Beethoven's Nos. 5 and 7, Brahms's No. 1 and Tchaikovsky's No. 5; also two *Bachianas Brasilieras* (Villa-Lobos), two *Gymnopédies* (Satie), the *Young Person's Guide* (Britten), the Brahms–Haydn variations, the *Walk to the Paradise Garden*, the *Firebird* suite, the Dvořák 'cello concerto and Mozart's fourth horn concerto (with Alan Civil).

warm and comfortable, which was as well; the party had to stay aboard one of them for twenty-three hours.

Barbirolli conducted twice in Moscow and once each in Prague, Warsaw and Leningrad. Boulez did the same. They took with them distinctive cargoes. Debussy was one of the few composers on whom their allegiances overlapped. To Boulez, because he was a Frenchman, the programme planners had allocated *La Mer* and *Images*, both of which but more particularly *La Mer*, had been Barbirolli 'country' for thirty years and more. For the rest Boulez did Weber (Variations Op. 30 and *Six Pieces* Op. 6), Schönberg (*Five Orchestral Pieces*), Stravinsky's *Song of the Nightingale* tonepoem, Bartok's second piano concerto, excerpts from *Wozzeck* and the *Altenberg* Lieder of Alban Berg (with Heather Harper), and the original version (only nine minutes long) of his *Éclat*, a glitter and crepitation of patterns as far away as could be imagined from traditional forms and, perhaps, from the aesthetic that inspired those forms.

Against this repertory—almost, it might be said, in reply to it—Barbirolli affirmed the *Eroica* Symphony, Haydn's No. 83, Sibelius's No. 2, Mahler's No. 4 as well as a Mahler song group with orchestral accompaniment (Heather Harper being the singer in these and the Mahler symphony) and oddments of a matching sort. For the end concert of the tour (Leningrad) he reserved Tchaikovsky's B flat minor piano concerto (soloist: John Ogdon) and his adored E flat symphony of Elgar. Twice (Prague and Moscow) he did the Elgar 'cello concerto with a highly gifted young English soloist, Jacqueline Du Pré.

As a double-decker scheme that played off idiom against idiom and, up to a point, epoch against epoch, the tour as a whole and even isolated pairs of concerts within it, had both originality and piquancy. Reading through newspaper critiques that piled up copiously in city after city, one comes again and again upon contrasts drawn and preferences either hinted at or set aside in favour of the general conclusion: 'Different temperaments, different techniques—both good!' In Boulez a cold intellectual brilliance and analytical detachment were diagnosed; in Barbirolli a fund of impulse and Romantic warmth that harmonised with what one Polish writer called

his actor's head and profile. Did he take the finale of the
Eroica too slowly? Did he fondle loved phrases elsewhere to a
degree that imperilled symphonic cohesion? Writers here and
there conveyed as much; which is what writers had been
conveying, in an incidental way, off and on, since the early
1920s.

In certain cities Barbirolli found himself among old friends.
He had been on the Central European trail before. Smetana
Hall, Prague, exploded joyously at the sight of him. He had
been there in 1960. Smetana Hall had exploded similarly then.
He had been there as far back as the summer of 1958 with the
Hallé. It was then that Prague's cult for him had taken root.
On that occasion he did two symphonies, Bruckner's No. 4
and Vaughan Williams's No. 8. At the end of his second
concert that year the clamorous audience would not leave.
They swarmed to the front of the platform, clapping and
bravoing. Some handed up posies of wild flowers. After ten
minutes of this he went back to the rostrum and played an
'extra', *l'Après-midi d'un faune*. He took more bows, then retreated
to his dressing-room and began to change. The clamour continued. He dressed again and, returning, gave them the *España*
of Chabrier. After further bows he signalled the orchestra off.
If he had not done so they might still have been there until
two in the morning. After nine years Prague's affection for him
was undimmed. One of the Czech newspapers stated the case
in a headline that even an untutored English eye could understand: TRIUMF JOHNA BARBIROLLIHO.

Well disposed audiences are not always well behaved. His
second Moscow concert, in the Tchaikovsky Hall, got off to an
unhappy start. He had chosen as his opening piece something
Russian, easy to digest and solemn, the overture to *Ivan the
Terrible*, alias *The Maid of Pskov*. He was hoping for a suitably
solemn mood in the hall. He did not get it. When the time
came for him to start people were still trooping in and sorting
out their seats talkatively. He stood in the wings with Freda
Grove, the B.B.C. concerts organiser. 'I'm not going on until
they're quiet,' he said. An announcer's voice, to which little
attention was paid, signalled Sir John Barbirolli on to the
platform. Nobody could have shut the announcer's mouth.

His announcement had been pre-recorded and went over according to timetable.

After five minutes Barbirolli fancied the noise was subsiding. He went on and found that if anything it was getting worse. People were walking about, standing about, chatting, disputing. He turned and stared daggers at them. He rapped the rostrum rail with his baton. He said, 'Will you be quiet, please!' All to no purpose. Pale with anger, he stepped down and walked off. In the wings he grasped Miss Grove's arm, his way with anybody when he had a serious point to emphasise, and said, 'I will teach them manners'. A hundred or so latecomers had still to get to their seats. Gradually the hall lapsed into a slightly apprehensive silence. His withdrawal had sunk in. When he did make his entry, thirteen minutes after time, the audience applauded penitently. Their ovation after Beethoven's Seventh, at the end, went on for ten minutes.

The following summer, that of 1967, was tangled, perturbed and, in some ways, beyond compare. The order of going in his engagement book was: Three days with the Hallé in Bordeaux, where he was to conduct festival concerts towards the end of May. Then straight to Berlin for six concerts with the Philharmonic Orchestra, Beethoven's 'Choral' Symphony being his main business there. From Berlin he and Evelyn were to fly direct to Tel Aviv, where he was to do eight performances of the Verdi Requiem for the Israel Philharmonic, four others following in Haifa and Jerusalem, in celebration of that orchestra's launching thirty years earlier by Arturo Toscanini.

The Israel Philharmonic meant much to him. Since 1960 he had conducted them at yearly or two-yearly intervals. Had he lived he would have reappeared with them in 1972. As Barbirolli saw and felt them, these were something more than professional assignments. Just what his feelings were he once tried to put into words—and failed. There were certain things in life, he said, that had made a tremendous impression on him. On such occasions a man was transported: 'Your feelings go so deep that you do not talk about them. An experience of this kind came to me when I saw the Sea of Galilee for the first time. I tried to write to my family about it. I couldn't. Not a word was written. That was the most extraordinary experience I ever had, so extremely personal that I cannot even bear to think about it.' This was said in a context that had to do with religious belief and emotion, matters on which he was never glib.

He and Evelyn set off for Tel Aviv by way of France and Germany on May 23rd. The previous day Egypt had closed the Strait of Tiran to Israeli shipping. The Middle East was on a time fuse. Throughout their time in Bordeaux and during their first days in Berlin the scent of war grew stronger, the imminence of it more evident. While rehearsing in Berlin he received a cable from Tel Aviv suggesting that the Verdi Requiem be dropped and that 'in view of the circumstances' he should do twelve performances of Beethoven's 'Choral' Symphony instead. Was that agreeable? Certainly, he replied. Thus, for a liturgical text a secular one was substituted, that of Schiller, who, while mindful of the Deity, preaches in Beethoven's finale the brotherhood of man: 'Alle Menschen werden Brüder'.

Three days later the Six Days War began. It looked for a while as if hostilities would overlap his concerts. There was no talk or thought of cancelling these. At the same time it would not have been proper in such a situation to take his continued cooperation for granted. At the suggestion of Israeli interests in this country he was contacted in Berlin by the Hallé office and asked whether, so far as he was concerned, the concerts were still on.

'But of course', was the effect of his reply.

The original plan had been that they should fly out from Berlin on June 11th. Not until that day did the Middle East cease-fire become effective and the war end. Meantime civilian flights to Tel Aviv had been suspended. Barbirolli stayed on in Berlin for two days to conduct an extra performance of the 'Choral' Symphony, he and his soloists and the choir and the orchestra giving their services in aid of the Red Cross and a Middle East aid fund. To say that an ovation followed the last bar would be pallid understatement. What happened was a demonstration. Undoubtedly Barbirolli was the immediate object of it. Never before had he heard such heartfelt clamour. According to a writer in the 1967–68 issue of HALLÉ (magazine), it went on for thirty-five minutes.

Next day the Barbirollis were on the first civilian flight to Israel out of Berlin. He conducted his first Tel Aviv concert on June 15th, as originally arranged. At each of his twelve concerts he coupled the 'Choral' Symphony with Mozart's No. 40. Every night the hall was packed, his audiences aggregating 30,000, and at the end the audience stood and cheered and surged up to the platform. In conversation afterwards Barbirolli did not conceal the thrill it had given him to be there in Israel's 'hour of trial and triumph'. Beethoven's 'Choral' Symphony, he added, was just the right expression of it.

Before leaving for further concerts in Germany, he and Evelyn glimpsed the Old City sector of Jerusalem, now occupied by Israeli forces. White flags hung from many windows; there were bombed and shelled buildings and, on either side of the track, minefields behind barbed wire. After passing through army check-points they had a glimpse of Bethlehem, too. The Church of the Nativity was given over to row upon row of tanks. They had seen nothing like this since the Hallé's battlefront concerts around Christmas 1944. The scale here was tiny by comparison, and in other ways the likeness was far from absolute. Israel in arms and lightly scarred by war had an eeriness of its own.

In Israel he is not forgotten. His name is perpetuated by a memorial that will not readily be expunged. Less than a year before the Six Days War he and the Hallé Orchestra gave a concert in Manchester for the Jewish National Fund: 'On Hearing the First Cuckoo', Beethoven's first piano concerto (with Ashkenazy) and Brahms's Fourth Symphony. In gratitude Israel dedicated to him three square miles of land scheduled for resettlement in Netua, Upper Galilee and near the Lebanese border. Before his last visit to Israel he received an official parchment recording that the estate had been named Nachla Barbirolli in his honour.* With the parchment came details of redevelopment plans that were afoot; how access roads were to be built, old natural forests restored, new

* He was in good company. Hitherto dedications through the Jewish National Fund had been of plantations. Thus there are the Balfour Forest, the King George V Forest, the Queen Elizabeth Coronation Forest, the Winston Churchill Forest, the Toscanini Forest, etc.

forests planted. This time he found words. In accepting the parchment he expressed his profound admiration for Israel's achievements and for the practical idealism and the endless, enduring effort of her people.

It had been hoped that after his concerts in 1967 he would visit Nachla Barbirolli for an inauguration ceremony. The turmoil of the times ruled this out. No later opportunity occurred. The rest was silence; a silence resonant with sweet remembered sounds and acclamation.

The time had come for his last foreign tours with the Hallé. In twenty-five years there had been many such apart from those touched upon already in these pages. There is nothing for it but another backward glance.

In the summer of 1957 he took the orchestra to Ravello, southern Italy, and conducted four festival concerts up a mountainside in the garden of the Villa Rufolo. That he should have got there at all was a near miracle. At a recording session a month or so earlier he had missed his footing and fallen ten feet from the platform, landing on his back. The outcome had been a fractured vertebra, damaged left shoulder joint, bruises, cancelled concerts and, for a while, difficulty in walking. The recent illness and major operation had reduced his weight to eight stone, a providential thing; a heavier man, he was told, would probably have been killed outright.* Again: uncanny recuperation. By the time he reached Ravello the worst of the hobble was gone.

Ravello is an ancient township of clustering red roofs poised on a tall hill overlooking the Campanian coast and round a corner from the Bay of Naples. The garden of the Villa Rufolo, where the concerts were held, hung above the town itself. It lay between ravines and precipices and had an orchestral platform at one end sustained by metal scaffolding more or less artfully concealed by greenery. From this eyrie the players,

---

* There had been another mishap that nearly cost his life. In September 1948 he returned by road from a West Country tour to open the Hallé's season in the North. He had a front seat. There was a head-on collision. His sun-glasses were smashed, his face and leg muscles cut and torn, and he suffered great pain. Only a few concerts were cancelled, however. At the Hallé's opening concert of the season he conducted from a chair.

when they let their eyes and minds stray, saw a sea of improbable blue one thousand feet below and, closer in, vineyards, terraced lemon trees and welter upon welter of flowers. An unlikelier place for symphonic music could not have been imagined. A polyglot audience of a thousand, divided up at different levels by low walls and screens of verdure into several small audiences that were cosily secluded from each other, turned up late in the afternoon when fierceness had gone from the sun and attended to time-honoured Barbirolli assortments: *l'Après-midi*, *La Mer*, splendid hewings from Wagner (with solo soprano) and so forth. There had been a little trouble about rehearsals. To avoid the broiling heat of the day, Barbirolli had them start at 6 a.m. Even so, by seven o'clock on the first morning the sun had so smitten one wing of the orchestra that varnish was beginning to melt on fiddles, and harp strings and timpani skins were in a poor way. After that Barbirolli saw to it that the entire orchestra should be in the shade at rehearsal all the time. Rehearsals went on until 9 a.m. The players were free from then until 5 p.m. They loved that.

Acoustically the Rufulo garden was described alternatively and according to temperament as quite good, surprisingly good and not at all bad. Barbirolli brought out the Barbirolli *pianissimo* more than once. Everybody said how audible it was and how breathtaking, for who, during a Barbirolli *pianissimo*, ventured to breathe? On the first night far-off and not so far-off church bells made a nuisance of themselves; so did the honkings of traffic on bendy mountain roads. A word with the church authorities and the bus company had mitigating effects. There was much bird song as well. About this nothing could be done.

The Ravello concerts were part of a festival devised for culture-haunted tourists. Few locals could have readily afforded to buy tickets, still less the sort of clothes that culture-haunted tourists wear. To put things right, Barbirolli staged for the locals' benefit a supplementary concert of Johann Strauss waltzes and so forth one night when the main concert was over. The venue was at the top of the church steps. Nobody had to pay. The music started at 10 p.m. and went on for over an hour. A supposedly impromptu affair had been judiciously leaked in advance. Result: a great crowd and delight on every face in it. At the end: flowers for Barbirolli and drinks all round.

A year later they made for Germany, Austria, Poland and Czechoslovakia. Something has been said of the ovation they got in Prague. In its way the first concert of this tour, at Hagen, Westphalia, was equally a milestone, for Hagen was the town where the author of their corporate being, Charles Hallé (baptised Carl) was born in 1819. The Hagen occasion was almost as much against the odds as Ravello had been. On the day of the concert an unexploded bomb, a relic of Hitler's war, was turned up by workmen on a site near the concert hall. It was touch and go whether or not the concert would have to be cancelled. A bomb disposal unit went to work. They defused the bomb and cleared it soon before the concert was due to begin. Concurrently the orchestra were having difficulties of their own. They reached Hagen an hour late after six or seven hours on the road. A van containing the heavy musical instruments was held up on the Belgo-German frontier and arrived an hour later still. Barbirolli had reckoned on two and a half hours of rehearsal. He had time for only half an hour. This was, however, enough in all conscience for such Hallé 'regulars' as the *Fennimore and Gerda* intermezzo, the *Enigma* variations and Beethoven's Seventh. The audience liked the Elgar piece so much that they applauded in the middle of it. After the concluding ovation Barbirolli gave a little speech about what Carl Halle (the name in its original form was not accented) had done musically not only for Manchester but also for Britain. He gave this speech twice, first to the audience, then in the bandroom to members of the Hagen Orchestra, who had been waiting there for him to come off. Flowers: smiles: acclamations. Cordiality and comradeship abounded.

They were in Germany again eight years later. This trip (five concerts in ten days) left one especially gleaming memory. On their way from Düsseldorf to Hamburg they paused at Hanover. In the Grosser Kuppelsaal, a great circular hall, white-domed and a-glitter with chandeliers, he rounded off with Tchaikovsky's Fourth and brought over 3,000 to their feet tumultuously. The tumult lasted for twenty minutes. It was as much Barbirolli worship as Tchaikovsky worship.

Another great travelling year was 1961. First they played Basle, Berne, Zürich; then off for 6,000 miles of air 'hops', twelve concerts and aggregate audiences of 24,000 in Mediterranean countries. They travelled as far wide of beaten tourist tracks as Istanbul and Dubrovnik. In Cyprus he conducted on an August evening in the castle courtyard at Kyrenia, went fishing afterwards with a Cypriot fisherman called Angelo, conducted locals in folk songs at a stylish tavern and tried his foot at a folk dance or two. After an interim of turbulence Cyprus had changed from Crown Colony status to Independent Republic just a year earlier. Barbirolli and the Hallé were helping to celebrate the Republic's first anniversary. A former Governor was reported as saying that their concerts in Kyrenia and Episkopi had done more for good Anglo-Cypriot relations than could have been contrived with a million pounds of Whitehall money. . . .

In the Roman amphitheatre with seats for 4,000 at the foot of the Acropolis they gave three concerts, Manchester's contribution to the Athens Festival. The concerts were attended by half the Greek royal family, the prime minister and many others from on high. He conducted Gina Bachauer in the second Brahms piano concerto and Isaac Stern in the violin concerto of Beethoven, performances of grandeur. The acoustics of the Odeon of Herod, as the amphitheatre is called, were designed not so much for symphonic music as for the spoken word. To one listener the *Fennimore and Gerda* intermezzo sounded like 'sweet nothings uttered in Wembley Stadium'.* The Greek audiences took everything joyously, were greedy for encores and got them.

The tour ended in Turin, where he did Vaughan Williams's No. 8. Turin enjoyed it to the extent of applauding between movements. Barbirolli did not bridle. He said, as he had said before, that to say one must never applaud between the movements of a symphony was snobbery.

That he could not take the Hallé to the United States still piqued him. Private and public subsidisers were interested in other territories, however, among them Central and South America. On a Sunday in June 1968, little more than a fortnight after the Hallé's home season had ended, he and the orchestra, most of them in a chartered plane with instruments, others by scheduled service, flew from Manchester Airport or

* Brian Magee, *The Guardian*, 29th August 1961.

Heathrow via Miami to México City. There were one hundred and ten in the party. During six weeks they were to cover 20,000 miles, playing eleven cities in eight countries.* There would be as many free days as working days, abundant sight-seeing and cocktail parties at every turning. Some of the latter turned out to be remarkably lavish and rather in the nature of stand-up banquets. The Hallé's most ambitious peacetime tour had taken two years to plan. The estimated cost of it was £120,000. Towards this the British Council had given £30,000, there were grants from interested industrial and commercial combines, and it was expected to recoup much at box offices.

Barbirolli took with him six symphonies: Schubert's No. 9, Berlioz's *Fantastic*, Tchaikovsky's No. 4, Dvořák's No. 7, Elgar's No. 2 and Britten's *Sinfonia da Requiem*; also *The Swan of Tuonela* (Sibelius), a *Rosenkavalier* suite, the *Symphonic Metamorphoses* of Hindemith, overtures by Wagner (*Mastersingers*), Verdi (*The Force of Destiny*), Rawsthorne (*Street Corner*), Rossini (*Silken Ladder, Thieving Magpie, Siege of Corinth*) and Berlioz (*Corsair, Roman Carnival*); and the usual parcel of Johann Strauss sweet-meats. There were two piano concertos, Beethoven's No. 4 and Rawsthorne's No. 2, with Denis Matthews as pianist, one violin concerto, that of Walton, and a second piece for violin and chamber orchestra, Vaughan Williams's *The Lark Ascending*, the soloist in these two being Martin Milner, the Hallé's leader since Laurance Turner's retirement from that position in 1958.

The tour opened with four concerts in Mexico: three in México City, where the hall had a glass ceiling and resplendent tiers of boxes and balconies, and one in Puebla, a motorcoach ride away, where they played in—or under—a sort of vast inverted saucer made of timber. It was Puebla that gave them their first taste of Latin-American concertgoers' casual and leisurely ways. Late arrivals drifted in throughout the *Master-singers* overture and hunted loquaciously for their seats. Barbi-rolli conducted in repressed fury. At the end of the overture he turned round and shouted in Italian, 'Shut up and sit down!' Not much heed was paid. Incursion and disturbance continued

---

* The countries were: Mexico, Venezuela, Trinidad, Jamaica, Peru, Chile, Argentina, Brazil. The cities were: México City, Puebla, Caracas, Port of Spain, Kingston, Lima, Santiago, Buenos Aires, Porto Alegre, São Paulo and Rio de Janeiro.

With Dietrich Fischer-Dieskau (Iago) during playback of Verdi's
Otello which he conducted for H.M.V.-Angel, 1968.

Photo: Erich Auerba

At recording session, Musikvereinsaal, Vienna, while conducting
Vienna Philharmonic Orchestra in Brahms orchestral cycle, 1967.

during much of the *Sinfonia da Requiem*: Leningrad over again
but more so. It was not until after the interval, when he turned
to the *Fantastic*, that calm prevailed. In México City there were
difficulties of another kind. The place is more than 6000 feet
above sea level. At rehearsal wind instruments kept going awry.
to Barbirolli's exasperation.

'It's the altitude, Sir John', somebody ventured.

When this explanation was offered a second time he exclaimed:
'Altitude, altitude! Don't give me that again. It doesn't affect
me. Why should it affect you?'

His irritability may have had a physical source. At his third
concert and the preceding rehearsal he was obviously in poor
shape; on the rostrum he lacked drive and concentration. Of
the Walton violin concerto, which came before Tchaikovsky's
No. 4, a seasoned player commented long afterwards: 'I was
thankful we managed to get through it.' Another occasion of a
like kind was the one-night stand at Porto Alegre, Brazil.
Barbirolli arrived there 'in need of lots of rest' through overwork, as a British Council observer put it, to find the centre of
the town sealed off by military police against a threatened
student demonstration. The concert was to have begun at 9 p.m.
The orchestra were in their places betimes. Then the audience
began to trickle in. Half an hour later they were still trickling.
The woodwind amused themselves by playing free and sotto-
voce versions of South American national anthems which the
orchestra had got up especially for the tour. It was 9.45 p.m.
before the audience had settled in and Barbirolli reached the
rostrum. It was clear from his gait and gestures that he was not
himself. According to the entourage he had been prescribed
sedatives against overstrain. Apparently the treatment had not
worked as intended; he seemed to be under sedation still when
he picked up the baton. Especially in the Britten *Sinfonia* some
of his tempi were conspicuously slow. After the Britten came
Schubert's No. 9, the 'Great' C major. Parts of this were as
sluggish as the Britten. In the eyes of South American audiences, however, he could do no wrong. This concert, like the
ill-starred night in México City, ended in rowdy enthusiasm
and two encores—the *Radetzky March* and *Tales from the Vienna
Woods*. It usually happened that, however fatigued he might be
to start with, the physical act of conducting restored him to

o

alertness. This time no. His hosts had arranged parties before
and after in his honour. He cut them with apologies and went
early to bed. Next day he was bright and composed. He looked
as if he had shed ten years.

Then Caracas, Venezuela. Two concerts had been fixed for
the Aula Magna of the Central University, which held 2,600.
For the first concert (Verdi, Britten, Berlioz) the place was
two-thirds full. For the second (Rawsthorne overture, Sibelius's
Swan, Beethoven's fourth piano concerto and Tchaikovsky's
No. 4) it was three-quarters full. Both audiences were of the
elegant sort, the womenfolk befurred and gemmed. Everybody
was there who was anybody in Caracas. Police in soldierly
uniforms patrolled the precincts with automatic weapons.
At the first rehearsal tempers frayed. Could it be that Barbirolli's
ears were beginning to fail him? That morning things were
played and things were said that he did not catch. Misunderstandings resulted. In trying to sort the misunderstandings out
people made them worse. A youngster at a rear desk muttered
something disobliging about Barbirolli. He was put in his place
by his neighbour, an older and wiser man.

'People aren't coming to these concerts', said the neighbour,
'to hear *your* beautiful playing. You wouldn't be here, none of
us would be here, but for that deaf old so-and-so (as you call
him) up there with the stick.'

The youngster took his neighbour's point and was sorry for
what he had said.

That first Caracas concert is remembered for two other
things: a notoriously tricky rhythmical passage in Britten's
'Dies Irae' movement where everybody got across everybody
else, producing two or three bars of chaos; and Barbirolli's
breakneck acceleration at the end of the Ball scene in the
Fantastic Symphony which set the house in a roar.

The second Caracas concert, too, had its moments. This was
on June 12th. The orchestra took their places for a nine o'clock
start. Barbirolli was expected on the platform any moment.
Two young men scrambled up on to the platform instead and
started haranguing. They were science students with grievances
to air about a tight educational budget, limited research
facilities and a canteen that closed on Sundays. The audience,
bewildered at first, began to clap ironically. There were booings

and catcalls from the 'unreserved' balcony. The catcalls were
understood to be from students who dissented from the dissi-
dents. A column of students five or six deep came marching in
through a side door. As they marched they sang the Venezuelan
national anthem. The elegant audience stood up as a mark of
respect. The marchers took up positions along the front of the
platform and in the side aisles. Barbirolli put their number at
five hundred. As the harangues continued he began to feel
nervous about security. He said: 'There are violins on that
platform worth £30,000. It only takes one person to get wild....'
He signalled his players off: and off they came. The harangues
ended. The students marched off the way they had come.
Again they sang the national anthem. Again the elegant
audience stood up respectfully. Then Barbirolli came on,
radiant with relief. He spoke a couple of jocular sentences in
Italian and was roundly cheered.

The concert began forty minutes late. The first half of the
programme got a relatively tepid hearing, not because of tepid
playing but because the audience were still wondering what
might happen next. After the interval all was well. Tchaikovsky's
No. 4 had them on their feet and raving for more. He gave them
Pomp and Circumstance March No. 1. Adoring dins. It was
midnight and time for bed. A little girl who should have been
there already was led on to the platform. She kissed Barbirolli,
Barbirolli kissed her back. Collective ecstasy.... After the
concert Hallé officials hunted high and low for a plaque bearing
the City of Manchester coat-of-arms, one of a series of plaques
which, suitably inscribed, were presented with the Lord Mayor
of Manchester's compliments to alcaldes, prefectos and other
heads of local government along the itinerary. The plaque
couldn't be found; it had been stolen or mislaid. Barbirolli
gave the president of the municipal council an inscribed history
of the Hallé Orchestra as consolation. All ended beamingly and
convivially.

The symphony that meant most to him on this tour was
Elgar's No. 2. Not that he played it as often as the Tchaikovsky
or the Schubert or the Britten. Such a work is not for all
audiences or for every occasion. In Kingston, Jamaica, his
performance of it ended at eleven o'clock. As the final *pianissimo*
died away a public clock began chiming the hour all too

audibly and just off key. That made him wince. In Santiago (Chile) the audience applauded between the Scherzo and the finale. That he did not mind. He repeated what he had said when the Turiners similarly broke in upon Vaughan Williams's No. 8: that in certain symphonies there were certain places (and this was one of them) where applause, far from being intrusive (as the snobs contended) should be welcome. In general, Central and South America had not heard a note of Elgar's No. 2 before. 'But how they take to it!' he exclaimed. 'They know it is not only English music but *great* music.'

Here and there, as has been conveyed, the Hallé came upon less than full houses. There were those who argued that people had stayed away because the programmes were too 'modern'. Others said they stayed away because the programmes weren't 'modern' enough. Sometimes dear seats or overmuch cultural competition or other snags of a practical sort were brought up. In Rio de Janeiro there were noticeable gaps in stalls and boxes. The Hallé had been preceded there by the English Chamber Orchestra, for whose concerts droves of people had got into the theatre without paying. To avoid a repetition of this the promoters had set up ticket-sales points outside the theatre and 'patrolled' the entries. 'Perhaps we were too successful', reflected an organiser ruefully. One thing stayed constant, however. Whether a house was packed to the roof or slightly underpopulated, Barbirolli always got a thundering ovation and always had to play at least one 'encore'.

The tour reached its peak in Buenos Aires. There were three chockablock nights at the Teatro Colón, 'one of the most beautiful opera-houses in the world. It gives one a great uplift in such a theatre to see an audience of four thousand, nearly all in evening dress, standing up and cheering.' These were Barbirolli's words on his homecoming. They denote especially the first of his three Colón nights. He did Verdi, Britten, Berlioz. Never, by most accounts, did Hallé sound have greater fire or as much in it of velvet and steel. Seven days before, amid the old gilt and plush of the theatre at Lima, he had exclaimed in mid-rehearsal, on a morning of toil and frustration: 'A rehearsal is something to enjoy. I'm not enjoying this rehearsal one bit. If I don't enjoy rehearsals any more it's time for me to give the whole thing up.' But now appetite and joy were back

uncorroded. Years fell from him. The house went off its head.
The Hallé had encountered many a delirious house before,
especially in Germany, but nothing to touch this; that first
Colón night outraved, out-thundered everything.

The night that followed was a gala night and suitably
starched. The President of the República Argentiná, Lieut.-
General Juan Carlos Onganiá, entered the presidential box
with most of his cabinet. He was applauded decorously. When
Barbirolli came on the audience 'gave some idea what applause
could really be'. The phrase is from a player. More than one
foreigner felt the contrast was pointed. Then came the
Argentinian national anthem. It opens *maestoso*, proceeds to a
melancholy middle section and ends *vivace*. Barbirolli's 'romantic
treatment' of all this 'brought titters from the upper galleries'.*
Titters were not the general response, however. This performance and that of 'the Queen' which followed straight upon it
had the audience explosive with joy. Something of the kind
happened all along the route. Strangers would come up to him
with thanks for letting them hear how their national anthems
should *really* sound. Of the Colón occasion the British Council
representative reported home: 'The importance of the impact
of this manifestation of British cultural life can hardly be
exaggerated. . . . The President and most of his ministers were
witness of, and appeared to share in, the enthusiastic reception
given by a notable audience which filled the Colón to overflowing. The importance of this at a time when admittedly
relations have been somewhat strained for some time can
readily be imagined. It was indeed impressive to see the
Argentine President and the British Ambassador standing
together for a most rousing rendering of God Save the Queen
which followed the Argentine national anthem.'

Another note from Argentina to the British Council dwelt
upon the two packed concerts in São Paulo and upon 'the
superb display of British musicianship which . . . should do
much here to shake the sense of musical superiority felt and
sometimes shown by many Germans and descendants of
Germans in the local population'. Elsewhere the point was
made that although originally the British Council had been

* Michael Mainwaring, *Buenos Aires Herald/Manchester Evening News*,
July 8th 1968.

twitted somewhat for sending a provincial orchestra abroad, the Hallé 'sold' splendidly on Barbirolli's name and, when it did arrive, 'dispelled the illusion that London is the only source of good classical music from Britain'.

CHAPTER TWENTY-THREE

——E MORTAL

His seventieth birthday neared. He worked no less insatiably for that. At one time he had toyed with the idea of making seventy the end of the road. His talk now was on different lines. Seventy, he held (or jocularly quoted others as holding), was the age at which a born conductor was really beginning to fathom music and had some glimmering of what to do with it. Whether, in working insatiably, he knew what he was taking out of himself is questionable. At another suburban town hall, the one at Watford, he recorded Mahler's Symphony No. 5 with the New Philharmonia Orchestra. One day he successfully got a movement on tape before the mid-afternoon break. After the break he started on the finale. Thus far the day had been productive and strenuous. He persisted with the finale for half an hour or more without getting anywhere. True cohesion had gone, as happens with the best of orchestras when its players are tired. He was tired himself and didn't know it but looked it. He rapped the orchestra to a halt and said to Kinloch Anderson, 'We'll have to do this tomorrow morning. It's not good enough.' Anderson agreed. 'They're fagged', he said. 'Yes, yes, I realise that', said Barbirolli. 'You know, they haven't got my staying power.'

Age nibbled in petty ways. He sat down at the piano with a woman colleague and friend to play in one of the Erik Satie duets, *Morceaux en forme de poire*, another of his 'party pieces.' Rheumatism had stolen a march on his tendons, pulling them together. A thought struck him which he described later: 'I told myself, "Here is something I shall never be able to do again. I shall never be able to stretch an octave." That was a terrible thought.' The stretch and agility of his hands had been exceptional. When he played the 'cello and often when conducting, his thumbs used to bend back like ram's horns. Providentially, the trouble was limited to his right hand, that is to say, his bow hand. He could still play the 'cello.

In rehearsal his unquenchable pursuit of nuance gave rise to increasing wonder, which delighted him. He crowed about it. Coming back from another Italian jaunt, this time to Milan, he said how amazed the Italians were when he told them his age. 'They ask me', he went on, 'whether I *never* get tired. I say: "Never when I'm making music." ' He would vaunt his engagement diaries: 'I haven't a free day for two years ahead!' Then a rider: 'I can't have much time left. I'm making the most of it.' During the last years irascibility showed publicly now and then. More than once in mid-performance he rapped out the rhythm with his stick on the desk, a method not supposed to be used outside rehearsal and even then only when things are going slackly or awry. There was a Manchester performance of the 'Resurrection' symphony in which, as well as desk rapping, he turned so many pages too quickly during the opening movement that he seemed to have lost his way momentarily. Such incidents pained a few of his admirers, embarrassed more.

Because of his multiple commitments elsewhere, his work with the Hallé in Manchester continued to dwindle, falling during the 1960s, so far as the Manchester concerts were concerned, to less than half the total, then to less than a third, finally to a mere handful. For 1970–71, the season he did not live to see, he was listed for only four programmes, each made up in large part of Barbirolli favourites which now make melancholy reading.* Season after season the Hallé called in a posse of guest and assistant conductors of diverse professional outlook and varying eminence. As things stood the Society had no choice in the matter. Between October and May the Free Trade Hall would hear ten or a dozen supplementary batons, each of whom injected or tried to inject his own musicianship into an orchestra which had been trained and moulded in a quite

---

* Chausson's *Poème de l'amour*, the 'Tallis' Fantasia and *Wasps* overture of Vaughan Williams, the *Young Person's Guide* (Britten), the Fauré Requiem, the Bartok Concerto for Orchestra, Ravel's *Daphnis et Chloë* suites (linked), the *Irmelin* prelude (Delius), the *Eroica* Symphony and Mahler's No. 7.

different image. As early as 1963 it had been put to Barbirolli
that his long and regular absences from Manchester and the
rostrum miscellanies that replaced him could not be good for
the orchestra's quality. He replied: 'People are rather inconsist-
ent. If I'm there all the time it's dictatorship. If I'm away,
that's wrong, too.'* At rehearsal he taught and drilled as
insistently as ever, but, since his players saw a good deal less
of him than in the palmy 1950s, the old *rapport* became intermittent. When *rapport* came back the old magnificence, the
sense of unique occasion, came back with it; few happenings on
English concert platforms held and penetrated audiences as,
for example, his Brahms second and fourth symphonies did,
or his *Fantastic*, or his Tchaikovskys, or his Vaughan Williams
No. 6, or a whole range of late-Romantics up to Nielsen.

He was made a Companion of Honour amid rejoicing that
spread beyond musical circles and was true as a bell. In
October 1969 he went to the Palace and received the insignia
from the Queen. After the formality they talked about his
forthcoming concerts in America; also about the 'cello, for the
Prince of Wales had been taking lessons on that instrument.
Soon after this he and Evelyn were on their way to Houston,
where he was to conduct three programmes, repeating each of
them twice, the first lot in November-December, the second in
mid-February.

Thus it fell out that he celebrated his seventieth birthday,
2nd December, far from home, or, at any rate, in his home
from home, as Houstonians claimed it to be. On his birthday
night he merged his own anniversary with that of a greater,
Hector Berlioz. As 1969 was Berlioz's death-centenary year,
he made over the night to the *Fantastic* and *Harold in Italy*.
Something over a fortnight later he was back in the Free Trade
Hall with a programme which had in it much of the marrow of
his career: Elgar's Introduction and Allegro, Vaughan
Williams's Sixth and Beethoven's Seventh: a sort of delayed
birthday present to himself. There was a tinselled Christmas
tree with affectionate messages of greeting. And who, remembering it, will forget his first Belle Vue *Messiah* for three years, the
one which was also to be his last? As tradition dictated, this

* Quoted in *HALLÉ* (magazine), Season 1963-64.

o*

was a Sunday afternoon occasion. Everybody wanted to be there. Nearly everybody, it seemed, *was* there. People brought babies, toddlers, vocal scores and, to the 'popular' parts of the house, quantities of sweets in crackly paper. The traffic jam afterwards was a mile long. The cockles of a multitude of hearts were warmed, Barbirolli's among them.

So into 1970: of which he was to know seven months. They were months as packed as any except for times when he suffered certain physical buffets. These, although they presaged the end, he endured with something like impatience, reluctant (whatever the doctors might say) to spend a day more in recuperation than his restless spirit decreed. In mid-April he conducted concerts in Munich, then took a night off for *La Bohème* at the City opera-house. While signing autographs after the performance he collapsed and was taken to hospital. 'Temporary exhaustion' was diagnosed. He left hospital next morning and rested for a day or two at the house of friends. His mind was full of Dublin. Our Lady's Choral Society of that city were preparing their silver jubilee, and he would have charge of the jubilee concerts. There were to be two of these. In the vast National Stadium he was to conduct *The Dream of Gerontius* and the Verdi *Requiem*.

Two miles out on the South Circular, the National Stadium is not much of a concert hall. It isn't one at all, indeed. Boxing matches are staged to admiration there, and 'pop' singers cram the place to the roof; but the peculiar acoustics fragment complexer ensembles in a way that makes serious musicians blush for their city. For serious music on a biggish scale, however, the National Stadium was the best that could be found. There had long been talk, and the talk was still being heard, of a State-sponsored concert hall in Dublin to salute the memory of John F. Kennedy. The project seemed to be evaporating for want of an agreed site and (it was alleged) for want of zeal and drive among the politicians. The problem of where to perform was aggravated by that of where to rehearse. Barbirolli was to take choir rehearsals in one church hall, orchestral rehearsals in another and the soloists somewhere else. It seemed 'monstrous' to one Dublin commentator that 'this very distinguished elderly musician should have to traipse round this city from venue to venue'; that 'one of the greatest conductors in the world . . . should try to rehearse *The Dream of Gerontius* under conditions which no trade union leader would tolerate for the lowest of his manual workers.'*

Barbirolli knew full well what he was taking on. What buoyed him against inconvenience and shabbiness, crampings and makeshifts was a sovereign talisman, joy: the joy an innate and seasoned music-maker takes in the music he is making. *Gerontius* and the Verdi *Requiem* were worlds which, once he entered upon them, robbed his immediate environment of relevance, almost of substance. The sway Newman's poem and Elgar's music had over him were the theme of many a rehearsal anecdote. He used to work over the Demons' Chorus with pertinacity and mime; pretend to be a Demon himself, crooked, crawling and venomous.

'Don't be so bloody polite', he told one lot of Demons. 'Let's have a bit of snarl. I want nasal tone on *Ha! Ha!* Show your teeth a bit. . . . That's it!' When they came to a quasi-lullaby metre in the chorus 'Praise to the Holiest', he told women singers in Montgomeryshire to sing it as though they were rocking a baby. Their first attempt displeased him. 'If you rocked a baby like that,' he said, 'you'd give it stomach-ache.' Everybody laughed at this and, at the next try gave him the lilt he wanted.

Devotion to the music was not the only factor in 1970. With it went devotion to Our Lady's Choral Society. A dozen years earlier he had brought them to the Free Trade Hall and, at the end of their *Gerontius*, had made a speech saying how good it was to hear 'this Roman Catholic work sung from the hearts and throats of ardent Roman Catholics.'—a notion that caused muttering among Manchester's aesthetes, of whom some were sceptics and others felt that singers' religious beliefs could not determine the artistic quality of their singing. His greatest adventure with the Society had been in 1958, when he journeyed with them to Perugia for the Umbrian music festival. On the stage of the handsome town theatre he had two hundred and thirty voices. His orchestra was that of the Maggio Musicale, Florence. First he did *Gerontius*, then *Messiah*. He thought this *Messiah* his best to that date. The audience behaved as though it was the best *Messiah* that had been conducted by anybody.

* Fanny Feehan, *Hibernia*, 15th May 1970.

Their applause was frenzy and thunder. They had the *Hallelujah* Chorus twice and clamoured for it a third time, but there was no time for that; the performance did not end until one in the morning. When the recalls and standing ovation were over, Barbirolli and his singers were cheered through the streets to their hotels.

From Perugia to Castelgandolfo, the Pope's summer residence. In the oval Hall of the Swiss Guards adjoining the Papal apartments, he conducted Part I of *Gerontius* while Pope Pius XII listened not from the elevated throne he customarily used for audiences but from a chair nearer to the singers and below the level of their platform. The Pontiff had been given a copy of the vocal score bound in white leather and gold and followed the performance bar by bar, word by word, sometimes nodding his head, sometimes tapping a red-sandalled foot to the rhythm. The singers were in sensitive, fervent voice. After the performance Barbirolli was presented to the Pope, who gave him a Papal medal and, speaking in Italian, warmly praised the performance. Of Newman's poem and Elgar's music he said: 'This, my son, is a sublime masterpiece.' For all his eighty-three years, the Pope's step and gestures that morning were alert; he was gracious and fluent of smile and speech. A week later he suffered a stroke. While briefly recovering he heard something from the Toscanini recording of Beethoven's Symphony No. 1. On the following day he had a second stroke and died.

'So', said Barbirolli, 'the last "live" music that His Holiness heard was the choir singing "Go forth upon thy journey, Christian soul." And in ten days he was dead. Sometimes I ponder what it must have meant to Elgar if he could have known about this, because, you know, Elgar was a Catholic.'*

We have strayed from Dublin, May 1970.

He arrived for rehearsals a fortnight before the concerts, which were spaced three days apart, and, as it happened, a fortnight after his collapse in Munich. His doctors had advised him to cancel Dublin. As usual, he paid no heed. Before his first session with the choral society, in a crowded room with

---

* But, it seems, a lapsed one in the end. See *Portrait of Elgar* by Michael Kennedy, Oxford University Press, 1968.

billiard tables up a stair in Aungier Street, it was conveyed
to the singers, who included many who had not sung for him
before, that the moment he walked in everybody was to stand
up—otherwise he'd be sure to walk out. This instruction was
followed to the letter. There were so many singers and so
many of them were taller than he, that, as he made his
way to the rostrum, he was lost to view by most in the rear
ranks.

Carmel Hall was a noisy place. Traffic noises from Aungier
Street amounted to continuous din. As the evening went on a
persistent bumpety-bump sounded from a floor above. Barbirolli
did not mind at all. His ears were unbeatable professional ears.
Nothing reached them they didn't mean to hear. What he did
mind, what he seemed ready to be tetchy about, was when
the singers didn't watch him. 'All eyes on me, please', he bade.
'I'm not much to look at, I know, but make the best of it.'
This was said while he was working on a page where he wanted
'a sound like John McCormack used to make. . . . My late
father gave him his first engagement, and, bless his heart, he
never forgot it.' The heartfelt touch was shrewdly placed. The
most adulated Irish tenor of this or any other century, whose
spell once rivalled that of Caruso, died in Dublin in 1945, the
year Our Lady's Choral Society was founded; his great singing
days long by. Yet in Dublin his name had lost none of its
magic.

At each of eight rehearsals Barbirolli kept the singers on their
feet for two hours at a stretch. Sometimes he thought of things
outside music, strictly considered. How a choir should stand
up and sit down on cue, for example. He pointed out that there
were innumerable wrong ways of doing this. One night he
spent ten minutes teaching them the right way. Another thing
he told them went deeper. In Manchester it would have had
a contentious ring. 'This work', he said of *Gerontius*, 'can only
be sung by Catholics. You are Catholics. It can only be conducted
by a Catholic. I am a Catholic.' . . . He ended with two
full rehearsals for principals, choir and the Radio-Telefeis
Eirann Symphony Orchestra. Nothing like his method had
been seen in Dublin before. On points of tone quality and
phrasing he refused to compromise. He knew just what his
forces could give and never put down his baton until they had

given it. 'What thoroughness!' Irish professionals exclaimed. 'Who', it was asked, 'heard of a conductor before who could drive singers and players to wilting point and leave them happy?'

Gerontius and the *Requiem* came and went, drawing full houses and leaving a wake of jubilation. What kind of performances were they? While rating *Gerontius* as a profoundly satisfying one, the critic Charles Acton* voiced the shame so many felt at welcoming Barbirolli 'in that musically impossible place, where hardly anyone can hear a balanced performance'. Acton testified as to the excellence of the violas. He happened to be seated near them. The violins he could barely hear at all. From where he sat the Verdi *Requiem*, three nights later, was similarly fragmented—'and ninety per cent of the audience must have received an even more unbalanced performance than I did'. It is probable that Barbirolli was the only one among thousands who had a clear idea what was going on on either night. What he heard satisfied him. After *Gerontius* he said of Our Lady's Choral Society that it was of international class. The National Stadium, he agreed, left a lot to be desired. But, he told his Dublin friends, it had an acoustic potential. He was sure it could be made into a marvellous concert hall; that was to say, a place where (a) the hearing would be good in all parts whatever the seat prices and (b) young people could have their ices and their 'cokes'—'even if the Masters of the past would not have approved'. He did not make a point, as many other notables were doing in most walks of life, of wooing the young just because they were young; when he did speak up for them it was usually to take their side (not that they really needed such partisanship) against 'respectable' concertgoing manners. In Sydney he had said: 'I like young audiences because they are not too stuffy and polite to clap and stamp their feet and make a noise as if they actually *enjoy* music.' Stuffiness and politeness still raised their heads in the concert hall, but their hour of social esteem was ended.

At a silver-jubilee Mass in the Pro-Cathedral he was accommodated with a special prie-dieu. From this he heard the choir sing Mozart in C. Then: speechmaking, presided over and

* The passages quoted are from his 'critiques' in the *Irish Times* of 14th and 18th May 1970.

apostolically blessed by the Choral Society's founder, Dr. McQuaid, Archbishop of Dublin. Barbirolli said it was eighteen years since he first became associated with Our Lady's Choral Society, 'which has enshrined itself in my heart'. He had eleven weeks to live. During those weeks he unwittingly said many goodbyes. The Dublin goodbye had a poignancy of its own because of the nature of his links there. The celebrant of Mass in the Pro-Cathedral had been the Very Reverend Andrew Griffith, director of the Choral Society and old friend. Father Griffith, who had been with him on the Italian journey in 1958, was an amateur musician and the priest of a double-barrelled parish, Tallaght-Bohernabreena, 7000 souls, a satellite community some eight miles from the centre of Dublin. After the Stadium concerts he saw John and Evelyn off at Dublin Airport. He said to Barbirolli: 'Will you please come to Dublin next season, or as soon as you can make it, and do Mahler's *Resurrection* Symphony? Will you give me a firm promise on that, John?'

Barbirolli paused. His eyes went moist. Then he said: 'I'm afraid, old boy, that this is the last time you'll see me. However. . . .' He left a sentence in mid-air. But one thing was clear. He knew he was a dying man.

Father Griffith will reappear briefly at the end of our story.

The shades were drawing in, the sands running out; and there was much work to do. From Dublin, with little pause, he made for London. There he put in four recording sessions with the Hallé, the main business being Sibelius's Symphony No. 6. He had done all the other Sibeliuses. Now the set was complete. Another adieu had been said. As usual he had paved the way technically by getting up No. 6 and including it in recent concerts. The sessions went smoothly. He looked frail, had noticeably aged but was capable of spryness.

He was due one week later (May 29th) to conduct the New Philharmonia Orchestra at Croydon. Programme: his Elizabethan Suite, the *Rococo Variations* for solo 'cello and orchestra (Tchaikovsky), the *Firebird* suite and Dvořák's Symphony No. 7 in D minor. The preceding day was given over to rehearsals at the Bishopsgate Institute, City of London, not so much (as to its main room) a true rehearsal spot as a symptom of how rare such places are in and around London and the sort of makeshifts conductors have to put up with.*

Barbirolli had not been given the whole day. The morning session was Otto Klemperer's for the fourth and fifth symphonies of Beethoven. Klemperer was in his eighty-fifth year, a living reminder (as others were or had been, including Beecham, Monteux, Bruno Walter, Ansermet, Stokowski, Boult) of the notion that conductors find their best form after seventy. Barbirolli was to take over the orchestra following the lunch break. No lunch for him, of course. The soloist in the *Rococo Variations* was Norman Jones, the New Philharmonia's principal 'cellist. He had Jones in at 1.45 p.m. for a special forty-five minute session before the rehearsal proper began. To begin with they worked upstairs in the conductor's room, Jones playing selected passages of the solo part at Barbirolli's direction and taking in his ideas of phrasing and approach. It was all very amicable and engrossing. Barbirolli permitted himself the view that no conductor can 'really' conduct the *Rococo* set who has not himself played the 'cello—and played it to some purpose. After half an hour or so they went down to the Institute floor, where a pianist awaited with piano and piano transcription of the piece. Here the second phase of the preliminary rehearsal started, with Barbirolli giving the beat and pulling up to discourse technically at frequent intervals. There was nothing in the world like a 'cello and a fellow 'cellist for prompting him to hold forth. This second phase continued until the last moment; that is to say, while the members of the orchestra were drifting in from lunch, taking their places and inevitably causing minor disturbances—to which Barbirolli was as impervious as he had been to the dins in Carmel Hall. The piano rehearsal over, a full rehearsal began, continuing for three quarters of an hour. At the end of it Barbirolli said 'Fine!'—and would Jones be so good as to meet him in the upstairs room during the mid-afternoon break for a talk over the cadenza?

* 'When they [an orchestra] play at Bishopsgate you just can't hear a thing. The place is swimming in sound. If you're rehearsing a new piece you can just about sort out one note from another, but in a piece that everyone knows, when you're concerned with interpretation, a rehearsal there is absolutely useless.'—Daniel Barenboim, conductor, quoted by Stephen Fay, *Sunday Times*, 24th January 1971.

For Barbirolli no lunch break was to be followed by no tea break. The arrangement was agreeable enough to Norman Jones, who had no other rehearsal duties apart from the Variations. Barbirolli and the orchestra turned to the Dvořák and Jones made off for a meal.

When he got back halfway through the session the orchestra were packing their instruments. They looked glum. No sign of Barbirolli. What had happened? It seemed that after a movement or two of the Dvořák he had gone upstairs to the conductor's room. Then he had come back. There was a short stair down to orchestral level. When halfway down a faintness came over him. He sat down on a step and after a second or so fell back unconscious. An ambulance had taken him to hospital.

Those who knew of his previous collapse got the impression of a steadfast enemy. The enemy was stalking him. There had been ambushes. The enemy had clubbed him. He was to club him again.

The hospital they took him to was St. Bartholomew's, Smithfield. There he stayed for a week and submitted to multiple examinations and checks. While undergoing these he addressed himself exuberantly to coming tasks.

As far back as 1964 Japanese promoters had been pressing him to go out and conduct concerts with one or other of Tokyo's three symphony orchestras. Always he had replied: 'Yes, with pleasure—as soon as I can fit you in.' Not until now, six years later, was the way clear. He would be flying out at the end of July: but not alone. The New Philharmonia had been booked as well; he was to conduct them in a series of programmes at the much canvassed Expo 70, Osaka. Programme-planning, score-study, administrative detail and what not ate up hours and days.

Next after Expo 70 there would be the Edinburgh Festival. He and the Hallé were to open this in August, and one of their tasks would be Beethoven's Ninth Symphony. Already the Edinburgh chorus were being prepared by their chorus master, Arthur Oldham. Preparation in such cases can be worse than useless if the chorus master does not brief himself on the prospective conductor's tempi and trends. Oldham, learning that

Barbirolli was still in London, asked if he might come up for a consultation. By all means, said Barbirolli. Characteristically he devoted a whole lunchtime break between Kingsway sessions to Oldham and their joint problems. His collapse at Bishopsgate had taught him not a thing. Even now he could not be induced to put his feet up while others, many less than half his age, were unbending. One point that came up was the *Poco adagio* marking at bar 832 of the finale. In this bar the chorus and the solo quartet briefly overlap on the words 'alle Menschen'. Up to this point the chorus have been going at a spanking *allegro*. It was Barbirolli's idea that they should keep up this tempo in the overlap bar even though 832 otherwise marks a profound change of texture and mood. Oldham's view was that the *Poco adagio* should be taken as applying as much to the choir as to the soloists. The two of them could not agree. Oldham assumed that in rehearsal and performance Barbirolli would stick to his *Allegro assai* choice. They parted as cordially as usual, Barbirolli making off for Italy and conducting dates in Rome.

Here we must anticipate. Oldham went to Austria on holiday. It was there, at the beginning of August, that he read of Barbirolli's death. On returning to Edinburgh he found a letter awaiting him. It was from Barbirolli and dated July 14th. After thanking Oldham for his Edinburgh rehearsal arrangements he reverted to bar 832. He said he had been pondering over 'alle Menschen' at the *Poco adagio* where the solo quartet came in and would be glad to try it at that tempo once. And he was happy to say he was again keeping well.

We enter now upon his last fifteen days. They gave him so much to meditate and contrive and nuance and insist about that anyone glancing casually at his diary might have supposed that here was a man of thirty-five with twice the average thirty-five-year-old's energy. His spirit was high and tranquil. After Rome he came back to Kingsway Hall once more. That was where his effective career had started, Gaisberg at his elbow, in the late 1920s. Another uncovenanted farewell was imminent. Again he was with the Hallé. He had contracted with E.M.I. to do the *Appalachia* variations and the *Brigg Fair* of Delius. Both works had already been prepared in considerable degree at public

concerts or elsewhere. It was suggested that five sessions spread
over three days (July 15th to 17th) would be ample. Well,
. . . yes, hesitated Barbirolli. But please couldn't he have one
extra go with the *Appalachia* choir on the morning of the middle
day, bringing the total of sessions to six? It would mean turning that day, so far as he was concerned, into a three-session
one. But what harm would that do?

Suvi Raj Grubb, his recording manager on this run, gave him
his head. On the morning of the 16th, accordingly, starting
at 11 a.m., he cleaned up several choral bits that had been
nagging him and went over them with a polishing cloth, so
to speak.

'You see how right I was to call an extra rehearsal', he said
self-vindicatingly to Suvi Grubb as, with a few of the Hallé
players, they went round the corner at lunchtime for a snack
at the Hercules Pillars public-house in Great Queen Street.
This is a cosy and vestigial street with a small shop or two. Its
pavement had often been trodden by young Barbirolli on his
way to the Royal Opera pit or that of Drury Lane, 'cello slung
on his back, from wherever in Bloomsbury the Barbirollis
happened to be living. From the threshold of the pub one
could see or nearly see the tall-windowed flat over the Drury
Lane shop which had once been a Barbirolli tenancy. He used
to point it out with a certain rich pride, talking of Antonio and
Lorenzo and Nonna and his sister and brother when the three
of them were little. At the Hercules Pillars he was known fairly
well. They used to mix him what is remembered as the John
Barbirolli Special. It was compounded of Campari bitters, dry
martini, sweet martini, lemon and ice. He used to take this with
a smoked salmon sandwich. This day he took a small whisky
instead and talked and talked. About Beethoven's 'Choral'
Symphony, for example.

He cited a brassy, thunderous point in the opening movement
immediately before the recapitulation of the first subject and
ra-ta-tatted the rhythm on the edge of the table. 'At that point',
he said, 'all hell must break loose.' Suvi Grubb brought up
the Beethoven violin concerto, speaking with affection of
Barbirolli's recording of it (1936) with Fritz Kreisler on
endless 78r. discs. Ah yes, the fiddle concerto. Barbirolli's eyes
shone. For him one of the great moments was where the

second subject of the first movement is restated in the minor mode. He sang, or rather growled and croaked, both the minor and major versions and rum-tee-tee, rum-tee-teed an accompanying staccato figuration on violas and 'cellos. 'That, my dear boy', he concluded, 'is *genius*.'

(He did not always keep his melodic croakings and growlings for informal occasions. In the early 1950s when in the thick of *Turandot* or *Aida* at Covent Garden his voice was often heard *unisono* during orchestral interludes by people in the front rows of stalls immediately behind his rostrum. There were times in studios when his performances got on to recording tape. Invariably he refused at first to believe that anything of the kind had happened or could conceivably have happened. Christopher Bishop, another E.M.I. recording manager, once good-humouredly played back a tape to confute him. When it came to the point where his intrusive growlings were all too evident, he turned and 'shushed' some innocent third party. Then: 'Yes, it's me. No getting away from it. But I'm only human after all.')

The last word at the Hercules that lunchtime was about cricket. From Beethoven he modulated to Frank Woolley, the Kent all-rounder. Another case of genius, he said. He moved a beer tankard to a strategical point, said they were to imagine that was the wicket and demonstrated Woolley's cover drive, —'exquisite poetry', he said. By this time a knot of fellow customers had gathered round. 'Frank Woolley,' he pronounced, 'was one of the greatest cricketers I ever saw.' One of the listeners leaned over and said, 'I absolutely agree, sir!' 'My dear chap, of course you do!' returned Barbirolli. 'Any reasonable person would. . . . Yes, Frank Woolley was one of the greatest. They don't make 'em like that any more. I don't expect to see such cricket played again in my lifetime.'

At the Kingsway session that afternoon his spirits continued high. With this player and that he crosstalked drily and drolly on technical points with such quickness and expertness that lay listeners on the outer rim hadn't much idea what was going on except that everybody was having a jolly time. There were the usual touches of croak-singing and growl-singing.

'You're in good voice today', teased Grubb.

'Who, me?' asked Barbirolli feigning astonishment.

'Yes, you. You'll hear it on tape. The time for me to worry will be when you stop singing.' There was a lot of laughter at that.

During the break between the afternoon session and the one scheduled for 7 p.m. he was persuaded to have two sandwiches instead of one. Again they were in the 'Pillars'. Again he talked exuberantly. But shadow suddenly fell. No sooner was he back at Kingsway and making his way to the rostrum than he paused in a bemused way and muttered that he felt 'queer'. But not to worry. He'd be all right in a jiffy. Grubb led him to a chair. He rested momentarily, then said he was right as rain, and hadn't they better be getting on with *Appalachia*? No, said Grubb, weighing the risks; there was only one safe thing to do, namely, cancel that session and start again tomorrow. Barbirolli put on an incredulous stare and did a lot of exclaiming. But Grubb had his way. Next morning Barbirolli returned to Kingsway with Evelyn, easy and bright, master not only of the current situation but (such was the impression he conveyed) of anything and everything that might imaginably crop up. His first words to Grubb were: 'I hope you're looking after yourself'—a gay dismissal of the previous night's alarum.

'Look who's talking!' put in Evelyn.

So it went on until the day's end: by which time *Appalachia* had been rounded off and *Brigg Fair* disposed of with a blandness and a freshness that astonishes Grubb still.

There were to be no more Kingsway sessions.

He was down for another festival before Edinburgh, the one at King's Lynn, East Anglia, an old and picturesque seaport three miles from the mouth of the Great Ouse. Ruth Lady Fermoy has a house near Lynn: and Lady Fermoy is a musician. Nineteen years earlier she had founded a music festival which took root and is rooted still. Later she founded the King's Lynn chamber music ensemble. In this she played piano and the Barbirollis (who had long been friends) oboe and 'cello. The first violin was always the Hallé's reigning leader and the viola the Hallé's first viola. To some of the festivals Barbirolli brought his orchestra. At others he simply played in chamber music. Sometimes he did both. In one capacity or the other he had put in fourteen King's Lynn festivals and was become one of the borough's ex-officio citizens. Here, as in Houston, the townsfolk loved to see him stroll with his cane and his wide-brimmed black hat of the sort Verdi wore. To those who remembered those ornaments of the human species, he had rather the look of an Edwardian actor-manager, withal a miniature one. Naturally he had been made an honorary freeman of the town. So: fourteen festivals were behind him. Now he was ready for his fifteenth and, if he had known it, for another adieu.

On Friday, 24th July the market place was a-flutter with bunting, the inside of the corn exchange massed with flowers, the town hall fringed with plants: all this and much more for the festival's opening day. In the afternoon he worked on an Elgar programme: the Introduction and Allegro, the *Sea Pictures* (with Kerstein Meyer) and the A flat Symphony. The rehearsal was in St. Nicholas Chapel, where the concert would be. He seemed sprightly enough; went with a microscope and tweezers over music which by this time he and many of his players had in their bloodstream.

Halfway through the thing happened again. He collapsed and, in falling, struck his head. Devoted, anguished, and brave of face, Evelyn said to somebody that since John was seventy and insisted on working long hours seven days a week, this sort of thing wasn't really surprising, not that it happened often thank heavens. On coming to he was persuaded to rest; to do just nothing for a whole hour. He had a phrase of his own for the visitation: 'I just had a turn'. Long before he took the rostrum that night news of his collapse and recovery was all over the town. There was the usual ovation, but a new note could be read into it, that of affectionate concern. He was much moved. He had conducted with sinew, even electrifyingly, but now the music was over he looked tired and strained, or so some fancied. The following morning it was put out that Sir John was himself again; in fine form. That night he reappeared on the rostrum in St. Nicholas Chapel. From their pews and imported chairs a crammed audience figuratively hugged him. His programme, giving every piece its full style, this being no common occasion, was: Overture: *The Hebrides* (*Fingal's Cave*), Mendelssohn; suite from the ballet *Ma mère l'oye*, Ravel;

Fantasy-Overture *Romeo and Juliet*, Tchaikovsky; Symphony No. 7 in A major, Beethoven.

Beethoven brought a standing ovation as long and heartfelt as the previous night's. He was not to know another. Nor was he to conduct another public concert. The one at St. Nicholas Chapel, King's Lynn, on the night of Saturday, July 25th 1970 brought full close. That the orchestra concerned should have been the Hallé fulfilled, up to a point, a thought he had expressed years earlier. Somebody having speculated that he might elect to give all or most of his time henceforth to the Houston orchestra, 'No,' he said, 'I have been with the Hallé since 1943, and shall probably die with them'. If he had known this was to be the end with the Hallé—if, for example, this concert had marked his retirement—the programme would have been different. At the beginning of his twenty-first season he had conducted what he called Programme of My Choice. It was made up of the intermezzo from *Fennimore and Gerda*, the Fantasia on a Theme by Tallis of Vaughan Williams, *La Mer* and Elgar's Symphony No. 2, pieces which, as this narrative has shown, were by this time part of his very fibre. He explained: 'I didn't call it Programme of My Choice because I've never been allowed to choose a programme before—I choose 'em all, good or bad. The thought at the back of my mind was this. There has to be a last programme for everybody some day, and in my case that's what I would wish the programme to be. These are the pieces I'd like to conduct if I knew I wouldn't be conducting any more.'

The nearest he came to that dream was the Elgar item. It cannot be pretended, however, that the A flat Symphony had become as much a part of him as the Second.

He and Evelyn left Lady Fermoy's house on the Sunday morning. His last talk with her had been about what he would be playing at the King's Lynn Festival of 1971. Back to London, where they now had a pied-à-terre, something which, especially before Nonna's death, they had long refused to consider. The place was a mews flat off Baker Street. The following morning rehearsals for Japan started at Bishopsgate. In Osaka 'art' posters were out with John's beaky profile on them and the Programmes he was contributing to Expo 70. He and Evelyn were to fly out on the following Friday, two days ahead of the orchestra so that he could accustom himself to humidity. A pleasant tension was in the air of the rehearsal corridors. Everybody was bent on showing the flag to good purpose; also on having a good time. The schedule at Bishopsgate took in eighteen hours of rehearsal, spread over morning and afternoon sessions on three days, Monday to Wednesday. Thursday and Friday were to be free. Works in hand were: the *Eroica* Symphony, Britten's *Sinfonia da Requiem* (originally written for Japan, it will be remembered, but given its première by Barbirolli at Carnegie in 1941), and three Mahlers—the First Symphony, the *Kindertotenlieder* and the *Lieder einer fahrenden Gesellen*, the last two with Janet Baker.

This was the first time the New Philharmonia players had seen him since his collapse in May. Some had wondered whether they would ever see him again. What of Japan? Would he be fit? Would he be alive? Such questions had been at the back of their minds for weeks. When he took his place in front of them on the Monday morning, murmurs of greeting and congratulation rose from the entire floor. Somebody called out: 'See it doesn't happen again!' in a tone of affectionate, jollying admonition. There could be no mistaking either their regard or the pleasure it gave him.

Then to business; not business as usual but rather more than usual. At these last four rehearsal session (six had been schemed, but he did not live to conduct the last two) he was more intent and detailed and demanding than for a long time. There are players who, looking back, say he was crotchety, pernickety. These are not words of condemnation. They were words that had been used for years of Barbirolli's rehearsal ways. His human warmth and integrity and passionate musicianship were balancing qualities that put him 'in the clear' with every orchestra he dealt with. There were musical phrases which he beeswaxed for ten minutes on end without getting them quite to his liking. When passages had been repeated more than a routine number of times, players here and there began counting further repetitions under their breath, as players have done in such a situation from time immemorial. They counted just loud enough to be heard by their neighbours. Barbirolli knew what was going on. He was acquainted with players' defensive responses and devices as no English conductor before him had ever been. He went on with his beeswaxing unperturbed. He had given phrases replayed well over thirty times; not a record, for there were those at Bishopsgate that day who remembered another perfectionist who ran up forty-five.

Then the *pianos* and *pianissimos*. Out came the old Barbirolli battlecry: 'With the point, with the point! Mark it, mark it! . . . Have you marked it? . . . Just a moment.' And, leaving the rostrum, he would trot across the floor, peering at sample desks here and there to make sure that his instruction had been pencilled in.

Out on the perimeter some player was handling his instrument in a way which Barbirolli judged to conflict with the composer's intentions. He pulled the player up and put him right. He said: 'You're a long way off, I know. But getting old's a funny thing. Although I can hardly see the music, I can see you people at the back perfectly well!'

His spectacles hung from his neck by a chain. He whipped them on to verify rehearsal numbers occasionally but did not make much other use of them.

In Mahler he spent a fair amount of time over string *portamenti*. Most conductors, especially Anglo-Saxons, keep these short and, as compared with Barbirolli, prim. His preference was for richness, not to say opulence. 'Don't be ashamed of these glides and slides', he seemed to be saying. 'They aren't *immoral*, you know! *Schmalz*, you say? Listen again. You haven't an idea what Mahler means.'

On the second afternoon he worked his players to the last minute, that is to say, until City clocks were striking 5 p.m. The orchestra had a concert that night at Tooting at 7 p.m., a long way off, and had rather hoped to be let off earlier. Before dismissing them he spoke of the following day's stint and said it would be Mahler again. He struck most of the players as very much the master of his faculties and fresh enough for another hour or two of grindstone or even a full-dress concert. The spell of music-making was still upon him. Presently a chauffeur in uniform came to say his car was waiting. He said 'Goodbye' to the few who remained in the hall and vestibule, among them the Institute caretaker. He had bidden the caretaker 'Goodnight' many times in the past. This time he

shook the caretaker by the hand. That he had not done
before.

The final attack occurred early next morning.

From the mews flat he was taken by ambulance, Evelyn at
his side, to the nearest hospital, the Middlesex. They carried
him into the casualty department. The time was 6.15 a.m. It
was all over. A coronary thrombosis had killed him.*

In a sense he had come home to die. By 'home' is meant the
square mile or two of his origins. Southampton Row, where he
was born, and other sites (if not the houses themselves) where
the Barbirollis lived when he was boy, youth and young man
lay ten or fifteen minutes walk to the east. The mews flat
was not more than a quarter of a mile from the Royal Academy
of Music where he had first played in the Beethoven string
quartets and those of Debussy and Ravel.

Of his Osaka engagement he had said that Japan was about
the only country he had not yet conducted in. 'After that', he
croaked, 'it will have to be the moon.' Los Angeles and Chicago,
Helsinki and Oslo were expecting him that summer. After that
he was to have taken the old roads to West Germany and
Switzerland with the Hallé. Such itineraries were typical, as
the reader knows, of what had been going on with little
interruption for decades. That so incurable a wanderer should
have passed his last days near his springboard acres was much
against the odds, a wheeling to full circle that would have
pleased him hugely.

He had been given much and spared not a little. Latterly
he had pictured himself under protracted clinical treatments, a
crock in a wheeled chair, a rug about his knees, condemned to
undetermined spells of idleness. The picture was not a pretty
one. Fortunately it did not come true. All the time people were
counselling him, doctors the loudest, to shed much, or at least
some, or at any rate a little, of his professional load lest it crush
him. To make people happy rather than in expectation of
warding off danger, he would concede a concert or two here,
an occasional foreign trip there: and go on working in other
ways, at his desk or from his armchair, as concentratedly as

* Subordinate causes were certified as myocardial degeneration and
generalised arteriosclerosis.

ever. Idleness was the one hell he dreaded. He meant to go on working until he dropped. That, in effect, is what he did.

There was another wheel that came full circle.

Both his marriages had been non-canonical. Since he was a 'cradle Catholic' it was natural that there should be speculation about his religious position. Occasionally when showing friends architectural showpieces on the Continent, he would take them into some mediaeval or baroque church. As likely as not the friends or one among them would be agnostic. They noted how he genuflected before the high altar; and how on one such occasion he broke briefly away to kneel and offer up a prayer in a sidechapel dedicated to a saint (identity not noted) for whom he evidently had a cult. In his middle sixties he was asked whether he remained a son of the Church, and answered: 'Oh yes, yes . . . My activities don't allow me to be as regular in my duties as I might be or practise as assiduously as I could, but I am at heart a religious person. I get great strength and comfort from that and always have done; and I think I'm very fortunate.' To those versed in doctrine this may seem well-intentioned rather than positive. However, it was privately stated on high authority soon after his death that he died 'a Catholic in good standing' and that he was not in dispute with the Church in any way.

He was cremated, and the cremation was followed by a private Requiem Mass. Then came a memorial service of ecumenical tone in Westminster Cathedral. We were given lines to read from *The Pilgrim's Progress*:

> 'I am going to my Father's. . . . My Sword I give to him that shall succeed me in my Pilgrimage. . . . My Marks and Scars I carry with me. . . .' So he passed over, and all the Trumpets sounded for him on the other side.

He had asked for recorded music to be played, and this was done: a Mahler song; 'Nimrod' from the *Enigma* variations; and a Benedetto Marcello concerto with Evelyn's oboe sounding slenderly through strings. The recordings chosen were ones that he had made. Here and there among those who listened were men with fiddle cases and the like. Some had played for him in what they were listening to. Before the service Bach was heard from the organ, after it Handel. At the core of all this lay the Low Mass of Requiem, said by the priest who was his friend, Andrew Griffith. Father Griffith also put up two prayers. One was in thanks for the power and beauty of music and its deepening of mortal insights. The other was in gratitude for the joy John Barbirolli had given through the untiring exercise of his talents both as a musician and as a friend. . . .

Note the last thought. When a man is perpetually in the public eye, the talent for friendship, if he happens to be endowed with it, wins responsive friendship among legion strangers; among people who feel warmed and are content to adore from afar; people he will never meet or meet transiently at the ARTISTS ENTRANCE with programme in one hand and proffered biro in the other. These backdoor thresholds to concert halls and theatres separate anonymity, unimportance, insuccess and worthy obscurity from the mysterious Elect, those with inner treasures that shine supernally from their very trouser cuffs and astrakhan collars. It would never do to let the non-elect troop, even if they have anything of the sort in mind (which is doubtful) across these thresholds, breaching intangible divides. If that happened 'Top Talent' would be swamped and might stop being talent of any degree.

Some of the uncredentialled won through to Barbirolli, nevertheless. There was a woman who lived fifteen hundred feet up a Welsh mountain. Whenever he and the Hallé were going to be on the air she would walk down her mountain to the nearest friend who owned a radio set, for she hadn't one of her own. She did this in all weathers, six miles there and six miles back, from 1947 on. At last, having saved up a bit of money, she gave herself a treat: motor coach trip to Sheffield and Manchester: four Hallé concerts in one week. Four times she saw Sir John. By chance some official exchanged a word with her. He diagnosed a case of rare devotion. After the concert she was shown into Barbirolli's room. They talked of music, he in terms and ideas as homely as hers. She came away radiant. After another concert, again in a Northern city, there was a young man who would not leave his door. He had something to tell Sir John which he had been wanting to tell for a long time. Nobody but Sir John would do. The door was opened to him. What he had to tell took four sentences. A few years earlier he had been a helpless, hopeless epileptic, fond of music but unable to go to concerts. Throughout those years he never missed, if he could help it, Sir John and the Hallé on the air. He concluded: 'You cured me with those concerts. I have come to thank you.'

Then the letters, as many as fifty a day . . . admiring, niggling, technical in a gossiping way, cranky, grateful. He replied personally to as many as he could. Unavoidably many had to be replied to by his secretariat or the Hallé's. Towards the end more than one old friend or close acquaintance felt a bit out in the cold in consequence but on reflection understood: and now, looking back, they think of that shock of black hair forty years ago and the grey droop and tousle it became. And of lineaments ravaged by time: of things, too, that time hardly touched: the quick Latin eye, for instance; and the croaking drawl, no word wasted; and the sly smile and the knowing smile and the festive smile that could thaw a heart fresh out of a deep freeze. These things are gone. The thought is hard to take.

APPENDIX ONE

STUDENT REPERTORY

Concerted and chamber works in which Giovanni Barbirolli took part as solo or ensemble 'cellist at official concerts of the Royal Academy of Music while a student there:

Cavatina for 'Cello and Orchestra, César Cui; the *Kol Nidrei* Variations for 'Cello and Orchestra, Max Bruch; Tchaikovsky's *Rococo* Variations for 'Cello and Orchestra; 'Cello Sonata in C, Marcello; Trio in D minor, Mendelssohn; Requiem for Three 'Cellos, Popper (he took part in three performances of this); String Quartets Op. 18 No. 1 and Op. 135, Beethoven; String Quartet No. 2, Borodin; Variations in D Op. 7 for String Quartet, Taneiev; Trio in D minor, Arensky; Variations for 'Cello, Boëllmann; Quartet in E flat, (Sir) A. C. Mackenzie; Old Scotch Melodies set for Strings, A. C. Mackenzie; Phantasy Quartet, Frederick Corder; Pianoforte Quartet in G minor, Brahms; Piano Quintet, César Franck.

APPENDIX TWO

SACHA GUITRY AND CHALIAPIN

Mr. Bicknell's reminiscence dates back to the late 1920s. He says: 'Sacha Guitry and Yvonne Guitry, his wife, were playing a West End theatre. I went to one of their performances and, as they had never recorded, sent up my card and was shown in. We talked business and came to a provisional agreement about recording. He then asked me whether I knew Chaliapin, who was singing in London that season. I didn't really know Chaliapin, although I had met him. I knew, however, that Gaisberg was his dearest friend outside Russia. Guitry made it clear that he wanted to meet Chaliapin. He said: "Everybody knows he is a great singer. What they do *not* realise is that he is also the world's greatest actor. Once I thought Lucien Guitry [his father] was the world's greatest actor. Now that Lucien Guitry is dead I know that Chaliapin is the greatest. I would tell any colleague who wants to know how to move on the stage to go and see the Clock Scene in *Boris Godounov*. To see him walk across the stage and pat the children on the head, changing from parental affection to lonely tragedy.... How effortless it looks! Yet only the supreme actor can do that." '

At the Queen's Hall the Guitrys and Chaliapin were brought together and recorded a charade about their meeting without having recognised each other and how the truth mutually dawned on them. A 10-inch, 78-rev. record was made but never published, because the charade was judged not to come off. Under the arrangement with Bicknell, however, Sacha and Yvonne Guitry produced a dialogue album for H.M.V.'s French company.

APPENDIX THREE

PHILIP GODLEE

There are entertaining accounts of Godlee's versatility and other qualities in a symposium which came out after his death, *Philip Godlee by His Friends* edited by Charles Rigby, Dolphin Press, Manchester, 1954.

In and about Alderley Edge at one time he ran light entertainment of a sort now half-forgotten, a 'pierrot troupe', The Whatnots, producing their shows and taking part in patter acts as the 'corner man'. He put on an amateur production of *Trial by Jury* (Gilbert and Sullivan) in which he wore a false nose as counsel for the defence. Reference is made in the main narrative to his leading amateur string quartets and other chamber groups in classics. When rehearsing his chamber orchestra he addressed his players as 'dogsbodies' when they played ill and said the least they could do if incapable of playing the right notes was to play the wrong ones *piano*. Many stories are told of his Club Carriage. This was an unreserved compartment on the early train by which he and business cronies travelled up to Manchester daily from Alderley Edge. At stops along the line they kept 'outsiders' at bay with corporate tricks of one sort or another, including a sneezing chorus which Godlee led: 'Hish, hash, hosh; hisher, hasher, hosher!' When Godlee returned from his honeymoon in 1924 the Club laid a red carpet for him on the station platform and made a triumphal arch of Union Jacks. One of the company played 'See, the conquering hero' on the cornet, Godlee retaliating with a tune on his violin.

No incident in his public life illustrated more strikingly his pleasantly sardonic streak than the address he gave to the governors of the Royal Manchester Institution on Music and the City (February 7th 1949). To ram home the civic advertising potential of the reconstituted Hallé Orchestra he quoted at length, tongue in cheek, the preposterous Cholmondeley ('Chum') Frink's harangue to the Zenith Boosters' Club in Sinclair Lewis's *Babbit*. Although not a great one for classical music and what he called 'all that junk—I'd rather listen to a good jazz band any time than to some piece by Beethoven that hasn't any more tune to it than a bunch of fighting cats, and you couldn't whistle it to save your life'—Chum, it will be remembered, came out strongly in favour of a Zenith Symphony Orchestra 'with high-grade musickers and a swell conductor who'd shoot out on the road hollering, "This is what little old Zenith can put up in the way of culture." ' ... Any guy so myopic as to crab this orchestral proposition was passing up the chance to impress the glorious name of Zenith on some big New York millionaire 'that might—that might establish a factory here'.

Godlee followed up Sinclair Lewis with pearls from the Music Master in *Le Bourgeois gentilhomme* who demonstrated irrefutably that wars and other ills of the body politic arose simply because not enough people took the trouble to learn music, a sure means towards harmonious brotherhood and universal peace. Since Molière's purpose in this scene is to make game of M. Jourdain for swallowing such rubbish— and much more in the same vein from the Dancing Master— one is tempted to conclude that Godlee was trying the same trick on his Royal Institution audience, although his concluding phrase about 'this happy vision of Utopia and string quartets in the Kremlin' probably made his ironical intention clear to any whom it may have eluded at first blush.

If he could be something of an intellectual *farceur*, this trait and profounder ones that went to make up Philip Godlee were placed to the last particle at the service of the Hallé Orchestra, whose revival and growth he promoted with rare dash, wit and resource.

APPENDIX FOUR

THE RECORDING FLOOR

Sir John Barbirolli had a long and distinguished career as recording artist. Before the Second World War he established an enviable reputation as an accompanying conductor, working with the world's leading singers and instrumentalists. During his sojourn in America, as conductor of the New York Philharmonic-Symphony Orchestra, he made records for R.C.A. and subsequently C.B.S. When he returned to give new life to the Hallé Orchestra, he resumed his association with The Gramophone Company (E.M.I.). There was one break of seven years during which he recorded for Pye. Thereafter he returned to The Gramophone Company, for whom he continued to record until his death. Most of his output for the Company was with the Hallé Orchestra, and the repertoire, mainly symphonic, was a wide one ranging from Mozart to Vaughan Williams. Among the most valuable items from this period were recordings of the last three symphonies of Tchaikovsky, the 7th and 8th of Dvořák, both the Elgar symphonies, Nielsen's 4th Symphony and the first recording of Vaughan Williams's 8th Symphony, dedicated to 'Glorious John'.

Listed below is the main bulk of Sir John's recordings made for E.M.I. in the LP and stereo era. This discography is not complete down to the last detail and excludes a number of unpublished recordings which were not approved for issue. Among late recordings yet to be issued are Tchaikovsky's 'Francesca da Rimini' (with the New Philharmonia Orchestra), a Grieg selection and some Sibelius, including certain of the 'Scènes Historiques' (with the Hallé).

DOUGLAS PUDNEY

Note.—Asterisks denote 'mono only' recordings. These are no longer generally available in the U.K. All ASD prefixes, SAN and TWO denote stereo recordings all of which were available in the U.K. at the time of going to press.

		Recorded	
Brahms: Symphony No. 3	The Hallé Orchestra	May '52	BLP 1015*
Tchaikovsky: 'Swan Lake' suite *Bizet:* L'Arlésienne	The Hallé Orchestra	Dec. '50	BLP 1004*
Haydn: Symphony No. 83 (La Poule) *Haydn:* Symphony No. 96	The Hallé Orchestra	Dec. '49 April '52	ALP 1038*
Rubbra: Symphony No. 5	The Hallé Orchestra	Dec. '50	BLP 1021*
Vaughan Williams: Sinfonia Antartica	The Hallé Orchestra/Margaret Ritchie and a section of the Hallé Choir	Sept. '53	ALP 1102*
Sibelius: Symphony No. 2	The Hallé Orchestra	Dec. '52	ALP 1122*
Schubert: Symphony No. 9 in C major	The Hallé Orchestra	Dec. '53	ALP 1178*
Rimsky-Korsakov: Capriccio Espagnol *Debussy:* Prelude à l'après-midi d'un faune *Chabrier:* 'España'	The Hallé Orchestra	Dec. '53 Dec. '53 Jan. '54	BLP 1058*
Saint-Saëns: Carnival of the Animals arr. Landauer: Strauss Fantasy	The Hallé Orchestra/Rawicz and Landauer	Feb. '54 Feb. '54	ALP 1224*
Elgar: 'Cockaigne' Overture arr. Barbirolli: An Elizabethan Suite	The Hallé Orchestra	Jan. '54 Jan. '54	BLP 1065*
Ibert: Divertissement *Fauré:* 'Pelléas et Mélisande' Suite	The Hallé Orchestra	Jan. '54 Jan. '54	ALP 1244*
Elgar: Symphony No. 2	The Hallé Orchestra	June '54	ALP 1242*
Vaughan Williams: Tuba Concerto *Vaughan Williams:* Oboe Concerto	London Symphony Orchestra/ Philip Catelinet London Symphony Orchestra/ Evelyn Rothwell	June '54 July '55	BLP 1078*
Villa-Lobos: Bachianas Brasileiras, No. 4 *Sibelius:* The Swan of Tuonela *R. Strauss:* 'Die Liebe der Danae' symphonic fragments	The Hallé Orchestra	Jan. '55 Jan. '55 Jan. '55	ALP 1335*
Elgar: Introduction and Allegro for Strings *Vaughan Williams:* Five Variants of Dives and Lazarus	The Hallé Orchestra	Sept. '53 Dec. '53	BLP 1049*
Vaughan Williams: Symphony No. 5	The Philharmonia Orchestra	May '62	ALP 1957* ASD 508

		Recorded	
⎧ *Elgar:* Introduction and Allegro for Strings	Strings of the Sinfonia of London	May '62	ALP 1970* ASD 521
⎪ *Elgar:* Serenade in E minor		May '62	
⎨ *Vaughan Williams:* Fantasia on a Theme by Thomas Tallis		May '62	
⎩ Fantasia on 'Greensleeves'		May '62	
⎧ *Tchaikovsky:* Piano Concerto No. 1	The Philharmonia Orchestra/ John Ogdon	Dec. '62	ALP 1991* ASD 542
⎨ *Franck:* Variations Symphoniques		Dec. '62	
Elgar: Symphony No. 1	The Philharmonia Orchestra	Aug. '62	ALP 1989 ASD 540
⎧ *Elgar:* 'Enigma' Variations	The Philharmonia Orchestra	Aug. '62	ALP 1998 ASD 548
⎩ *Elgar:* 'Cockaigne' Overture			
Mahler: Symphony No. 9	Berlin Philharmonic Orchestra	Jan. '64	ALP 2047/8 ASD 596/7
⎧ *Elgar:* Symphony No. 2	The Hallé Orchestra	April '64	ALP 2061 ASD 610
⎨ *Elgar:* 'Falstaff' symphonic study		June '64	ALP 2062 ASD 611
Schubert: Symphony No. 9 in C major	The Hallé Orchestra	June '64	*ALP/ASD 2251
⎧ *Tchaikovsky:* Serenade for strings	Strings of the London Symphony Orchestra	Sept. '64	*ALP 209 ASD 646
⎨ *Arensky:* Variations on a Theme by Tchaikovsky		Sept. '64	*ALP 209 ASD 646
Elgar: The Dream of Gerontius	The Hallé Orchestra/Hallé Choir/Sheffield Philharmonic Chorus; Ambrosian Singers; Janet Baker; Richard Lewis; Kim Borg	Dec. '64	ALP 2101/ ASD 648/
⎧ *Elgar:* Cello Concerto	London Symphony Orchestra/ Jaqueline du Pré	Aug. '65	*ALP 210 ASD 655
⎨ *Elgar:* Sea Pictures	London Symphony Orchestra/ Janet Baker		
⎧ *Sibelius:* 'Finlandia'	The Hallé Orchestra	Jan. '66	*ALP/ASD 2272
⎪ 'Karelia' Suite			
⎨ 'Pohjola's Daughter'			
⎪ Valse Triste			
⎩ Lemminkainen's Return			
Purcell: 'Dido and Aeneas'	English Chamber Orchestra/ Victoria de Los Angeles: Heather Harper; Peter Glossop; Robert Tear; The Ambrosian Singers	Aug. '65	*AN/SAN 169
⎧ *Elgar:* Pomp and Circumstance Marches 1-5	The Philharmonia and New Philharmonia Orchestra	Aug. '62 and July '66	*ALP/AS 2292
⎨ Elegy			
⎪ Sospiri			
⎩ 'Froissart' Overture		July '66	

		Recorded	

Ireland: A London Overture
Bax: 'Tintagel'
Delius: The Walk to the
   Paradise Garden
Delius: Prelude to 'Irmelin'
   A Song of summer
	London Symphony Orchestra	Dec. '65
		Dec. '65
		July '66
		
		July '66
		July '66
			*ALP/ASD
			2305

Sibelius: Symphony No. 2 The Swan of Tuonela	The Hallé Orchestra	July '66 Jan. '66	*ALP/ASD 2308
Puccini: 'Madama Butterfly'	Orchestra and Chorus of the Opera House, Rome/Renata Scotto; Carlo Bergonzi; Rolando Panerai	Aug. '66	SAN 184/6
Sibelius: Symphony No. 5 Symphony No. 7	The Hallé Orchestra	July '66 July '66	ASD 2326
Brahms: Piano Concerto No. 1	New Philharmonia Orchestra/ Daniel Barenboim	Aug. '67	ASD 2353
Beethoven: Symphony No. 3 (Eroica)	B.B.C. Symphony Orchestra	May '67	ASD 2348
Vaughan Williams: A London Symphony	The Hallé Orchestra	July '67	ASD 2360
Sibelius: Symphony No. 1 'Pelleas et Melisande' excerpts	The Hallé Orchestra	Dec. '66 Sept. '67	ASD 2366
Mahler: Symphony No. 6 *R. Strauss:* Metamorphosen	New Philharmonia Orchestra	Aug. '67 Aug. '67	ASD 2376/7
Brahms: Piano Concerto No. 2	New Philharmonia Orchestra/ Daniel Barenboim	Aug. '67	ASD 2413
Brahms: Symphony No. 1	Vienna Philharmonic Orchestra	Dec. '67	ASD 2401
Brahms: Symphony No. 2 Tragic Overture	Vienna Philharmonic Orchestra	Dec. '66 Dec. '67	ASD 2421

Brahms: Symphony No. 3
   Variations on St. Antoni
   Chorale
	Vienna Philharmonic
	Orchestra
		Dec. '67
		Dec. '67
			ASD 2432

Brahms: Symphony No. 4 Academic Festival Overture	Vienna Philharmonic Orchestra	Dec. '67 Dec. '66	ASD 2433
Ravel: Schéhérazade *Berlioz:* Les Nuits d'été	New Philharmonia Orchestra/ Janet Baker	Dec. '67 Aug. '67	ASD 2444
Schoenberg: Pelleas und Melisande	New Philharmonia Orchestra	Sept. '67	ASD 2459
Haydn: Cello Concerto in D *Monn:* Cello Concerto in G minor	London Symphony Orchestra/ Jaqueline du Pré	Dec. '67 Sept. '68	ASD 2466

Recorded

Delius: In a Summer Garden	The Hallé Orchestra;	Aug. '68	ASD 247
Hassan. Intermezzo and Serenade	Robert Tear	Aug. '68	
A Song before Sunrise		Aug. '68	
La Calinda		Aug. '68	
On Hearing the First Cuckoo		Aug. '68	
Summer Night on the River		Aug. '68	
Late Swallows		Aug. '68	
Debussy: La Mer	Orchestre de Paris	Dec. '68	ASD 2442
Nocturnes		Dec. '68	
Verdi: Otello	New Philharmonia Orchestra/ Ambrosian Opera Chorus/ James McCracken; Dietrich Fischer-Dieskau; Gwyneth Jones	Nov. '68	SAN 252/
Purcell: Suite for Strings, Woodwind, Horns	The Hallé Orchestra	May '69	ASD 2496
Corelli: Oboe Concerto in F	New Philharmonia Orchestra/ Evelyn Rothwell	Nov. '68	
Bach: Sheep may safely graze	The Hallé Orchestra	May '69	
Marcello: Concerto in C minor	The Hallé Orchestra/Evelyn Rothwell	Sept. '69	
arr. Barbirolli: Elizabethan Suite	B.B.C. Symphony Orchestra	May '67	
Mahler: Symphony No. 5	New Philharmonia Orchestra/	July '69	ASD 2518/
Five Ruckert Songs	Janet Baker	July '69	
Sibelius: Symphony No. 4	The Hallé Orchestra	May '69	ASD 2494
Rakastava		Aug. '69	
Romance in C		May '69	
Verdi: Requiem Mass	New Philharmonia Orchestra and Chorus/Montserrat Caballé/Fiorenza Cossotto/ Jon Vickers/Ruggero Raimondi	Aug. '69	SAN 267/
R. Strauss: Ein Heldenleben	London Symphony Orchestra/ John Georgiardis—solo violin	Sept. '69	ASD 261
Sibelius: Symphony No. 3	The Hallé Orchestra	May '69	ASD 264
Symphony No. 6		May '70	
Delius: Appalachia	The Hallé Orchestra/	July '70	ASD 263
Brigg Fair	Ambrosian Singers	July '70	
J. Strauss: Der Radetzky March	The Hallé Orchestra	Dec. '66	TWO 18c
The Blue Danube—waltz		Dec. '66	
Thunder and Lightning polka		Dec. '66	
Champagne Polka		Dec. '66	
Perpetuum Mobile		Dec. '66	
Gypsy Baron overture		Dec. '66	
R. Strauss: Der Rosenkavalier—Suite		Dec. '66	
Lehar: Gold and Silver—waltz		Dec. '66	
Grieg: Peer Gynt—Incidental Music	The Hallé Orchestra/ Sheila Armstrong; Ambrosian Singers	Jan '68 Aug. 68	TWO 269

INDEX